Teaching and Learning for Social Justice and Equity in Higher Education

C. Casey Ozaki · Laura Parson
Editors

Teaching and Learning for Social Justice and Equity in Higher Education

Content Areas

palgrave
macmillan

Editors
C. Casey Ozaki
Education, Health, & Behavior
Studies
University of North Dakota
Grand Forks, ND, USA

Laura Parson
North Dakota State University
Fargo, ND, USA

ISBN 978-3-030-69946-8   ISBN 978-3-030-69947-5   (eBook)
https://doi.org/10.1007/978-3-030-69947-5

This Palgrave Macmillan imprint is published by the registered company Springer Nature Switzerland AG
The registered company address is: Gewerbestrasse 11, 6330 Cham, Switzerland

CONTENTS

NOTES ON CONTRIBUTORS

Jessica A. Adams (she/her/hers) was born and raised in Alaska where she spent her childhood outdoors, cultivating a love of biology. Married to a military man, she has spent over 20 years teaching diverse populations across the country. With each move, Jess enjoys learning about local flora and fauna, as well as experiencing regional instructional strategies and educational pedagogies. Currently, a teaching faculty member at the University of Rhode Island (URI), Jess teaches large introductory biology classes with a focus on social justice issues, their role in her course design, and works to expand her student's cultural humility. This aim for inclusive pedagogy has led to a deeper connection with her students. Jess holds an M.S. in secondary education from Texas A&M, an M.S. in biological sciences from the University of Nebraska, and is a Ph.D. candidate at URI in biological sciences focusing on Science Education and Society.

Carolina Alvarado (she/her) holds a bachelor's degree in Engineering Physics and a doctorate in Physics Education from Tecnologico de Monterrey. She is currently an Assistant Professor in the Department of Science Education at California State University, Chico. Her work focuses on supporting K-12 teachers to implement culturally responsive scientific practices to empower students. Her approach to teaching physics relies on exploring how to implement scientific practices while recognizing and challenging structural barriers in science and science education. Dr. Alvarado has previously served in the American Association of Physics Teachers (AAPT) as the chair of the Committee on International

Physics Education, the chair of the Committee on Diversity, and as the first female elected to serve as President of the AAPT Mexico Chapter.

Frim Ampaw (she/her/hers) is a Professor in the Department of Educational Leadership at Central Michigan University, where her area of focus is higher education administration. She is particularly focused on understanding the experiences of students from low socioeconomic backgrounds and underrepresented minorities in transitioning to college, during college as well as in the labor market. Dr. Ampaw is a quantitative methodologist and has conducted extensive research on women and minorities in STEM education in understanding their selection and persistence within the major. In her current appointment, she teaches courses in quantitative research, higher education policy, and finance.

Sonya L. Armstrong (she/her) is Associate Professor and Director of the Doctoral Program in Developmental Education at Texas State University. She served as a practitioner in first-year and developmental education contexts at community colleges and universities, including teaching developmental reading, basic writing, and learning strategies courses, as well as directing a college reading and learning program.

Cynthia A. Brewer (she/her) is an Adjunct Professor of Integrated Reading and Writing at Austin Community College and a K-12 Reading/Dyslexia Specialist at Round Rock ISD. She holds a Master's of Education in Reading Education and is currently an advanced doctoral student in Developmental Education at Texas State University.

Mariko L. Carson (she/her) is a Lecturer within the Academic Writing Program at the University of Maryland College Park and an Associate Adjunct Professor in the Written Communication department at the University of Maryland Global Campus. She holds a Doctor of Education in Reading and has taught college composition and reading courses for over 9 years at both the 2- and 4-year collegiate levels. Mariko also serves as a reviewer for the Journal of College Reading and Learning.

Kathy Carter (she/her/hers), Ph.D. is a Professor Emerita in the Department of Teaching, Language, and Sociocultural Studies at the University of Arizona. Her scholarly inquiry in the areas of teaching, learning, and narrative methods spans over a 25-year period. She has been a visiting scholar and invited speaker in Australia, Sweden, Switzerland, Norway, England, and Canada. In addition, she has served as Division K (Teaching and Teacher Education) Vice-President of the American Educational Research Association, a research-based organization with a membership of over 25,000 scholars in over 85 countries. Her AERA Vice-Presidential address, "The Place of Story in Teaching and Teacher Education" is often credited with providing impetus to challenge the longstanding dominant research paradigm that privileged the voices of academics and marginalized the voices of teachers. Her present work, both in research and teaching, focuses on preparing teachers to teach toward goals of equity and social justice.

Julie Chiki (she/her) is the Director of Student Success and Retention in the Russ College of Engineering and Technology at Ohio University, where she teaches learning community and engineering overview classes. She is pursuing a Ph.D. in Higher Education from Ohio University, and holds a master's degree in College Student Personnel from Ohio University and a bachelor's degree in journalism from Northwestern University. Her research interests include advising as teaching, academic momentum, and working with college students.

Virginia Clinton-Lisell (she/her/hers) is an Assistant Professor in Educational Foundations and Research at the University of North Dakota. She holds a master's degree in Teaching English to Speakers of Other Languages from New York University and a doctorate in Educational Psychology from the University of Minnesota. Dr. Clinton-Lisell's research focuses on the psychology of language, open educational resources, and student attitudes toward active learning.

Geraldine L. Cochran (she/her/hers) is an Assistant Professor of Professional Practice in the Department of Physics and Astronomy and the Office of STEM Education at Rutgers University. At Rutgers, Cochran teaches the introductory physics courses for engineering students and conducts equity-focused research in STEM education. Cochran earned her B.S. degree in physics and her B.S. degree in mathematics from Chicago State University (CSU) in Chicago, IL. She also earned her M.A.T. with a specialization in secondary school physics from CSU. She earned her Ph.D. in curriculum and instruction with a cognate in physics and her Ed.S. in science education with a specialization in teacher preparation from Florida International University. Cochran is passionate about teaching physics and supporting efforts to broaden participation in STEM fields. Cochran's research focuses on creating, quantifying, and visualizing inclusive environments and using an intersectional approach to broadening participation in physics.

Abigail R. Daane (she/her/hers) Formerly teaching at both the high school level as a Knowles Science Teaching Fellow and at the university level, Dr. Daane now teaches at South Seattle College. She has been teaching for over 20 years in various subjects: dance, drama, leadership, teaching methods, nature of science, earth/life/physical science, biology, chemistry, math, astronomy, and physics. Dr. Daane strives to increase equity in STEM, leading and learning through physics education research. Her work focuses on designing curricula to increase awareness about issues of equity and inclusion in STEM at the college level using the Underrepresentation Curriculum (underrep.com). She also works with national societies, universities, and laboratories to provide K-16 professional development on equity-focused science teaching. Dr. Daane uses her experience in multi-level teaching to create classroom environments that focus on valuing student voice, encouraging growth through curiosity and connection, and pushing on systemic barriers.

Antonio Duran (he/him) is an Assistant Professor in the Administration of Higher Education program at Auburn University. His research interrogates how historical and contemporary legacies of oppression influence college student development, experiences, and success. In particular, he is passionate about using intersectional frameworks to understand and challenge how systems of power and oppression manifest in higher education settings.

Howard L. Dooley Jr. (he/him/his) is the project manager of the Rhode Island Technology Enhanced Science and Computing Program, RITES+C, which is a Practitioner/Researcher Partnership established in 2008 and hosted by the Computer Science and Statistics Department at the University of RI. The Partnership's mission is to create, support, and maintain equity of access and achievement in computer science courses and disciplinary computational opportunities for all K-12 public school teachers and students in Rhode Island. Howard has a life-long love for the sciences and the nature of science. He has been a member of the RI educational community for 40+ years, with the continuing focus of engaging all members of our society in a deeper understanding of the sciences and technology.

Staci Gilpin (she/her/hers) is an Assistant Professor in the School of Education at the College of St. Scholastica and a doctoral student in Educational Foundations and Research at the University of North Dakota. She holds a master's degree in Special Education from the University of Wisconsin-Superior. Before moving into higher education, she worked in K-12 schools for two decades as a teacher, instructional coach, and administrator. Staci is an advocate for quality online instruction as an avenue to provide access to higher education for students who are from underrepresented groups, geographically limited, and for those that require more flexible learning environments. She has facilitated over thirty online courses and designed several more. Staci specializes in creating community in online courses, using collaboration online, and inclusive teaching practices. Her research focuses on online student engagement, the role of values, and fostering persistence.

Caitlin A. Hamstra is the international student coordinator at O'Gorman High School in Sioux Falls, South Dakota. She earned her Ph.D. at Central Michigan University in Educational Leadership with a focus on Higher Education. Her research interests include international graduate teaching assistants, international student experiences, and curriculum, instruction, and assessment in the second language classroom.

Dawn X. Henderson (she/her) is the co-Director for the Collective Health and Education Equity Research (CHEER) Collaborative in North Carolina. She has served as a faculty member at Winston-Salem State University, North Carolina A&T State University, and instructor at Saint Augustine's College, North Carolina State University, and the University of North Carolina at Chapel Hill. She is the Program Director/Research Scholar in the Center for Truth, Racial Healing & Transformation at Duke University. Her teaching in higher education focuses on increasing community engaged learning and improving students' social justice orientation. She holds a Ph.D. in psychology from North Carolina State University and a master's in Curriculum and Instruction. She has published and presented on the benefits of experiential and service-learning to underrepresented students.

Anne M. Hornak (she/her/hers) is a Professor in higher education at Central Michigan University. She teaches courses in gender, ethics, and social justice. She earned her Ph.D. at Michigan State University in Higher Education Administration and has spent her career thus far in academia. Anne's research focus is community college student affairs and leadership, ethical decision-making, and intercultural development.

Amy Gratch Hoyle (she/her/hers) is Professor and Dean of the School of Education and Human Services at Neumann University. Her research interests include higher education faculty and PK-12 teachers teaching and advocating for social justice; courageous conversations about race in higher education and PK-12 classrooms; and antiracist education in online teaching environments.

Simone Hyater-Adams (she/her) is a physicist, artist, educator, and researcher with a passion for creating more opportunities for Black STEM students. After receiving her B.S. in Physics from Hampton University, she pursued graduate studies at the ATLAS Institute at the University of Colorado Boulder (CU Boulder) where she was a National Science Foundation Graduate Research Fellow. In her graduate research, she used her personal experiences from pursuing physics to guide her interdisciplinary research examining the connections between performance art and identity for Black Physicists. This work was awarded the Harry Lustig Award from the American Physical Society's Four Corners Section. Currently, Simone is an Education and Diversity Programs Manager at American Physical Society working with their National Mentoring Community. In addition to this work, Simone also develops and facilitates equity workshops with goals to cultivate more inclusive and equitable STEM learning and working environments.

Romeo Jackson (They/Them) currently serves as the LGBTQ & Gender Program Coordinator at the University of Nevada, Las Vegas and Ph.D. student at Colorado State University in the Higher Education Leadership. Their research, writing, and practice explores Race/ism, anti-Blackness, and Settler Colonialism within a Higher Education Context with an emphasis on the experiences of Queer and Trans Students of Color.

Erin Lord Kunz (she/her/hers) is an Associate Professor of English, Chair of the English, Communications, and Performing Arts Department, and interim director of institutional accreditation and academic and co-curricular assessment at Mayville State University. Her research interests are ecological literacy in composition and social justice pedagogies.

Elizabeth M. Legerski (she/her/hers) is an Associate Professor of Sociology at the University of North Dakota. Her research interests include gender, family, social inequality, and health and social policy. Her work explores the way family characteristics, employment opportunities, social policies, and religious values shape the lives of low-income, working-class, and other marginalized families. She is also interested in the scholarship of teaching, including the use of open education resources and technologies to reduce education inequalities. Her work has been published in journals such as *Social Forces*, *Gender & Society*, *Sex Roles*, *GLBT Family Studies*, *Health Sociology Review*, *Journal of Interpersonal Violence*, *Sociology Compass*, and *Frontiers in Education*.

Catherine Ma (she/her/hers) is an Associate Professor of Psychology at Kingsborough Community College. Being an immigrant, first-generation college graduate, and mother of three, she earned her doctorate in Social-Personality Psychology from the Graduate Center of the City University of New York (CUNY). She has presented and written extensively on the maternal experiences of breastfeeding, mothering challenges in medicine, critiquing the current breastfeeding paradigm, racial bias in youth sports, the impact of Asian American Studies in academia, imposter syndrome, and teaching racism in the classroom. Her current research focuses on how to counter negative stereotypes of immigrants among community college students by participating in a psychology of immigration course. Dr. Ma is an active board member of the Asian American/Asian Research Institute of CUNY. She dedicates her time to mentoring students of color and established the Yuet Chun & Tai Yee Ma Memorial Endowed Scholarship Fund to honor the legacy of her grandparents.

C. Casey Ozaki (she/her/hers) is a Professor and Chair for the Department of Education, Health, and Behavior Studies at the University of North Dakota. She has an M.Ed. in Student Affairs from the University of Southern California and a Ph.D. in Higher Education from Michigan State University. Her research bisects both the student affairs and teaching and learning areas of college campus with a shared focus on diverse students, their outcomes, and factors that influence those outcomes. As part of this focus, she has explored the role of student affairs professionals at community colleges—the institutions that serve the most diverse and high-risk college students. Dr. Ozaki also researches assessment of learning across creative arts and a range of disciplines and professional fields. Her recent focus has been on the integration of diversity, inclusion, and equity as a critical perspective and framework in college teaching and learning. Dr. Ozaki recently served UND as a Faculty Fellow for Inclusive Excellence where her role is to provide education and consultation for faculty and departments on the development and integration of inclusive and equitable practices in their teaching, curriculum, programs, and overall relationships with students.

Laura Parson (she/her/hers) is an Assistant Professor of Educational and Organizational Leadership at North Dakota State University. Her Ph.D. is in Teaching & Learning, Higher Education from the University of North Dakota. She has an M.Ed. in Adult Education from Westminster College with a certification in Teaching English as a Second Language (TESOL). In her research, she seeks to identify where and how institutional disjunctures occur in higher education for women and members of minoritized groups. She is a qualitative methodologist, with a focus on ethnographic and discourse methods of inquiry. Her research questions seek to understand how policy, procedures, discourses, and institutional environments inform student experiences, and how the institution coordinates those factors through translocal practices. To accomplish that, she asks how decolonizing pedagogical and curriculum approaches can create a more inclusive and equitable higher education space. She received the 2019 NASPA Ruth Strang award for research concerning women in higher education and was the first recipient of the Gloria Nathanson Research Fund for International Research.

Ebony Nicole Perez (she/her/hers) is a graduate of the University of Pittsburgh School of Social Work. She currently serves as an Assistant Professor of Social Work and Department Chair at Saint Leo University. She is a Racial Scholar and Qualitative Researcher who is dedicated to research that focuses on empowering marginalized communities. Her research agenda seeks to understand the nuances and complexities of the role of social work educators in preparing future practitioners for antiracist praxis. Her secondary research strand focuses on the participation and achievement of Students of Color in higher education. Furthermore, Dr.

Perez's research and scholarship aims to advance inclusive and transformative policies and practices. Dr. Perez has over 15 years of experience in Social Work practice and has held various roles including Behavioral Specialist, Research Associate, Inpatient Psychiatric Social Worker, and Pediatric ICU Social Worker. She received her Ph.D. in Curriculum and Instruction: Higher Education Administration and a graduate certificate in Diversity in Education from the University of South Florida (USF). In addition to scholarship and research, Dr. Perez has served on community boards and is currently serving as a member of the Council on Social Work Education (CSWE) Council on Racial, Ethnic, and Cultural Diversity. Dr. Perez is also committed to Faculty Development with a focus on peer mentoring and supporting the success of Black Women and Women of Color Scholars in the Academy.

Henrietta Williams Pichon   (she/her/hers) is the Interim Dean in the College of Education at New Mexico State University. She earned a B.A. in English and an M.Ed. in secondary English education from Louisiana Tech University. She earned a Ph.D. in education administration (higher education) from the University of New Orleans. Her research and teaching interests have always included access, development, and persistence of historically underrepresented groups in higher education to include students, faculty, and staff. Recent titles of work include: "A Community Ecological Model of Socio-academic Integration: Understanding the Experiences of Minoritized Students in Higher Education," "Parental Attachment of Students as They Move through Tinto's Rites of Passage: Separation, Transition, and Incorporation," "Moving beyond Unresolved Fear to Socio-academic Integration: Helping Students Cope within a Community College-State University Campus-Sharing Environment," and *"Descubrimento Mi Lugar*: Understanding Sense of Belonging and Community of Black STEMH Students Enrolled at a Hispanic Serving Institution." She belongs to several professional associations: AABHE, AERA, ASHE, and NASPA. She has also held faculty positions at Rowan University and Northwestern State University, as well as worked on retention initiatives at the University of New Orleans.

Chanda Prescod-Weinstein (she/they) is an Assistant Professor of physics and core faculty in women's and gender studies at the University of New Hampshire. She holds an AB in Physics and Astronomy and Astrophysics from Harvard College, an M.Sc. in Astronomy and Astrophysics from the University of California at Santa Cruz, and a Ph.D. in Physics from the University of Waterloo and Perimeter Institute in Canada. Prescod-Weinstein's research areas include particle cosmology and Black feminist science, technology, and society studies. Her service to the community has included co-founding the American Astronomical Society Committee for Sexual-orientation and Gender Minorities in Astronomy, chairing the National Society of Black Physicists Cosmology and Gravitation Committee; and engaging in extensive science and society outreach through social media as well as public speaking. Prescod-Weinstein is the author of *The Disordered Cosmos: A Journey into Dark Matter, Spacetime, and Dreams Deferred* (Bold Type Books, 2020).

Bri Rhodes (she/her/hers) is a doctoral student in the University of North Dakota's Education Foundation and Research Department. She also serves as the Director of International Student Advising at Mount Holyoke College. Her research interests include emotional labor and caring work as relates to identity and positionality. Her work focuses on the expectations individuals face to perform emotional labor and caring work, often based on gender or racial identity, created disproportionate burdens and thus forming a barrier not faced by the more privileged. Additional interests are education as a tool of liberation, increasing access to higher education for underrepresented groups, and decolonizing the classroom. Her work has been published in Frontiers in Education.

Grace Sallar (she/her) is the Assistant Dean for Student Services at the Russ College of Engineering and Technology, Ohio University. She is currently a Ph.D. student in Civil Engineering at Ohio University, where she also received her master's and bachelor's degrees in the same major. Her research interests include the improvement of teaching practices for engineering and technology classes, maximization of the academic experience for students, and underrepresented students' success in higher education.

Ariel L. Steele (she/her/hers) is a doctoral candidate in the Higher Education Ph.D. program at Auburn University. She has an M.S. in Biological Sciences from Auburn University and a bachelor's in biology from the University of St. Thomas. Her research interests focus on the intersections of gender and STEM education and on understanding how discourses impact the experiences of women and underrepresented groups in STEM higher education using institutional ethnography and critical discourse analysis. Specifically, her research focuses on understanding the experiences of women in STEM undergraduate and graduate programs and how discourses can contribute to or perpetuate the "chilly climate" that makes it challenging for women to persist. She is also interested in discipline-based education research in biology and how the teaching and learning environment can be used to promote equity and inclusion.

Amanda Sugimoto (she/her/hers), Ph.D., is an Assistant Professor in the Department of Curriculum and Instruction at Portland State University. In teacher education, she focuses on ways to prepare preservice and inservice elementary teachers to work equitably with elementary-aged students. As a teacher, she has extensive experience working with linguistically, culturally, and racially diverse students both in the United States and abroad. Her research focuses on improving the educational experiences and access of linguistically and culturally diverse students in schools, particularly in mathematics.

Annemarie Vaccaro (she/her/hers) is a Professor for the College Student Personnel Program at the University of Rhode Island. Annemarie's scholarship focuses on social justice in higher education, with a focus on minoritized college students, faculty, and staff. Annemarie also writes about praxis—where she explores how holistic and inclusive higher education is designed, delivered, and evaluated. She has authored many articles and book chapters and co-authored three books: *Centering Women of Color in Academic Counterspaces: A Critical Race Analysis of Teaching, Learning, and Classroom Dynamics* (with Melissa Camba-Kelsay); *Decisions Matter: Using a Decision Making Framework with Contemporary Student Affairs Case Studies* (with McCoy, Champagne & Siegel); and *Safe Spaces: Making Schools and Communities Welcoming to LGBT Youth* (with August & Kennedy). She earned her Ph.D. (Higher Education) and M.A. (Sociology) from the University of Denver and an M.A. from Indiana University of Pennsylvania (Student Affairs in Higher Education).

Jeanine L. Williams (she/her) is Professor and Program Director Chair of 100-Level Writing Across the Curriculum at the University of Maryland Global Campus. She holds a Ph.D. in Language, Literacy, and Culture and has over 10 years' experience teaching developmental literacy. Jeanine serves as a postsecondary literacy consultant, publishes and presents on postsecondary literacy issues, and is co-editor of the *Journal of College Reading and Learning*.

List of Figures

List of Tables

CHAPTER 1

Introduction

Laura Parson and C. Casey Ozaki

Since the first volume in this series, and, indeed, since the initial drafts for this volume, Volume II of four,[1] were written, the United States has changed. Not, perhaps, in the ways that some may think—racism has not gotten worse per se, although there has certainly been a resurgence of overt and violent racist acts since the election of Donald J. Trump to the presidency in 2016—what has changed is white America's realization and awareness of racism. We say this not to diminish the unique brutality of the murders of George Floyd and Breonna Taylor, but to emphasize how their killings are modern evidence of centuries of police brutality against

---

[1] Since the publication of Volume I, we have added a fourth volume to the series. This volume will focus on education in virtual and online settings in response to the need for a larger discussion about teaching for social justice and equity in those settings.

L. Parson (✉)
North Dakota State University, Fargo, ND, USA
e-mail: laura.parson@ndsu.edu

C. C. Ozaki
Education, Health, & Behavior Studies, University of North Dakota, Grand Forks, ND, USA
e-mail: carolyn.ozaki@UND.edu

Black persons. Indeed, now more than ever it is deeply unsafe to be a Black person in America regardless of gender, sexuality, class, and setting.

Yet, to be Black or Indigenous or Trans has always been unsafe. What is new in 2020 is a widespread awareness of racism and great momentum from across American society and, indeed, the world, to work toward change. This awareness and the associated momentum has resulted in, for some, personal learning and work toward becoming an antiracist. Others have joined Black Lives Matter protests, some protests that are still ongoing as of the writing of this chapter in September 2020. Still others in positions of power have worked to change company policies, hire more Persons of Color, create more inclusive hiring policies, and make marketing more representative. Yet, at the same time, others have worked to re-assert white superiority, doubled-down on "All Lives Matter" rhetoric, worked to reinforce racial hierarchies, and engaged in further violence against Black and Trans persons. As faculty, staff, and administrators in higher education, we will encounter students from across the spectrum of awareness in our classroom (and, perhaps, encounter colleagues from both groups as well). Institutions of higher education and the people who work there have a critical opportunity to provide opportunities for those learning about and committed to social justice and becoming antiracist to do just that by deepening their awareness of injustice and inequity and learn how to enact antiracist, inclusive, and equitable practices into their daily lives. Too, higher education provides a space to challenge antiracist beliefs and behaviors and, if not to change deeply held entrenched beliefs, to at least propose an alternative way to view the world. Through antiracist, inclusive, and feminist pedagogies, higher education practitioners can effect larger societal change by educating future decision-makers while also changing the nature of higher education itself by making it a better place—more inclusive, diverse, equitable, and empowering.

In the Teaching and Learning for Social Justice in Higher Education series, our goal is to draw on the most updated knowledge about the science of learning and effective teaching to recommend actionable approaches to improve the practices of student affairs, advising, and career services professionals in ways that promote social justice. In Volume I, the chapters focused on theory of teaching and learning and, through a critical lens and informed by other theories of higher education and adult learning, provided an application of how that theory can be reconceptualized and reconstructed to promote equity and diversity. In Volume II, authors apply critical, feminist, decolonial, and antiracist pedagogies to promote social justice in specific content areas. In each chapter, authors discuss and demonstrate how to teach through a social justice lens in their own fields from STEM fields to psychology to educational leadership. In doing so, each chapter presents both context critical for understanding how their field of study has reinforced racist, gendered, or colonizing systems and structures and provides actionable ways to address, counter, and change those beliefs through teaching and learning decisions. Each chapter provides specific classroom examples and artifacts, both lesson plans or a sample syllabus.

Chapter 2, Courageous Conversations about Race in an Online Education Course, provides recommendations for fostering courageous conversations about race in online settings, using the example of an online social work class. In this chapter, the author provides recommendations that support the development of dispositions that promote reflection and action—important components of social justice education.

Chapter 3, Promoting a Social Orientation Among Students of Color in Psychology, authors discuss how to help students of color develop a value orientation toward social justice in an introductory psychology course. They provide examples of how syllabus design can inform classroom settings that foster a safe space for discussions about social inequity.

Chapter 4, Ecological Writing Processes to Promote Environmental and Social Consciousnesses, provides a deep exploration of how ecological writing processes can be used to promote environmental and social conscious. In this chapter, the author incorporates indigenous and feminist ways of knowing to see how writing assignments can be a part of social (in)justice awareness. Through that lens, this author provides examples of how to develop writing assignments that foster both environmental awareness and acts as a medium to process a new awareness of societal inequity.

Chapter 5, Incorporating culturally responsive education in STEM Gateway Courses, presents a model of culturally relevant education in STEM gateway courses, a model based on problem-based learning (PBL).

Extending the usefulness of the PBL model, the authors in Chapter 6, Teaching Social Justice Through Project-Based Learning in Engineering, discusses applications of PBL in engineering courses. The authors apply principles from bell hooks' *Teaching to Transgress* to create PBL activities where students are presented with real-world problems that reflect the lived experiences of women and persons of color.

Chapter 7, Social Justice and Physics Education, continues to discuss inequity in STEM education by exploring the history of Physics. By deconstructing this history and uncovering how knowledge that is presented as fact can be both biased and incorrect, the authors provide examples of how to incorporate a history of a field of study into the classroom.

Continuing discussion of the nature of knowledge, Chapter 8, Promoting Equity in Introductory Biology Classrooms, presents an approach to teaching biology through a feminist lens. In Chapter 8, the author provides suggestions for evidence-based practices to improve learning through a critical feminist lens.

Chapters 9 and 10 share a focus on the development of cultural competence. In Chapter 9, Teaching Race and Racism in Social Work Education, the authors discuss how to foster cultural competence in a social work classroom. Like Chapter 2, the importance of critical conversations is a key element for helping students to develop cultural competence. Chapter 10, Teaching and Learning for LGBTQ Justice: An Examination of a Professional Learning Series for Faculty Development in Health and Helping Fields, provides an example of a faculty development workshop designed to help faculty develop competence in teaching and working with their LGBTQ peers.

Like Chapters 4, 11 also provides recommendations for writing activities that promote social justice. In this chapter, Problematize, Theorize, Politicize, and Contextualize: A Social Justice Framework for Postsecondary Integrated Reading and Writing Instruction, the authors view literacy as emancipatory through which instructors can create writing activities that prompt students to critically explore their own experiences as a lens to view inequitable systems and structures.

Chapter 12, What is my educational experience? The Use of Autoethnography as an Instructional Tool in an Online Introduction to Educational Leadership Course, uses the example of an autoethnography assignment as a way to prompt students to explore their own experiences in education, positive and negative, and seek out literature and research that helps them understand how to make education more equitable.

Chapter 13, Narratives of Bystanding and Upstanding: Applying a Bystander Framework in Higher Education, explores student narratives of bystanding and upstanding as a lens to help teacher education students understand how to be better upstanders in their own classrooms.

Chapter 14, Incorporating Antiracist Education Using Aspects of Asian American Studies to Teach about Race and Discrimination, discusses antiracist pedagogical practices in classroom through the lens of teaching a psychology course. In this chapter, the author discusses how to create inclusive and safe classroom spaces that foster an open dialogue about races, and provides sample activities that use current events as a prompt for a deeper exploration of race and racism in the United States.

Chapter 15, Open Educational Resources as Tools to Foster Equity, explores Open Educational Resources (OER) and how they can be used to promote social justice through access and de-centering course readings.

Finally, Chapter 16, The Role of Power and Oppression in the Classroom: Actualizing the Potential of Intersectionality in Teaching and Learning, advocates for the use of intersectionality as a viable theoretical and practical approach for addressing social justice in the classroom.

Our hope, across the series, is to create a comprehensive volume that can help higher education practitioners apply the critical science of teaching and learning in higher education to promote social justice through creating more equitable spaces and emancipating access to content, learning environments, and empowerment. This is an unprecedented time and an opportunity to be a part of structural change, and we hope that this volume and series can be a part of working toward structural change through making higher education more equitable and more inclusive for Persons of Color but also to foster a new generation of antiracist graduates who can work for structural and systemic change after graduation.

CHAPTER 2

Courageous Conversations About Race in an Online Education Course

Amy Gratch Hoyle

Key Terms and Definitions

Asynchronous Discussion	Asynchronous discussions are online discussions that participants can participate in at any time as opposed to synchronous discussions which take place in real time.
Courageous Conversations	Courageous conversations are conversations that encourage and sustain interracial dialogue about race and have the potential to lead to action and progress.
Racism	"In the United States and Canada, racism refers to white racial and cultural prejudice and discrimination, supported by institutional power and authority, used

A. G. Hoyle (✉)
Neumann University, Aston, PA, USA
e-mail: HOYLEA@neumann.edu

© The Author(s), under exclusive license to Springer Nature Switzerland AG 2021
C. C. Ozaki and L. Parson (eds.), *Teaching and Learning for Social Justice and Equity in Higher Education*,
https://doi.org/10.1007/978-3-030-69947-5_2

to the advantage of whites and the disadvantage of people of Color. Racism encompasses economic, political, social, and institutional actions and beliefs that perpetuate an unequal distribution of privileges, resources, and power between whites and people of Color" (Sensoy & DiAngelo, 2012).

White Supremacy   "The academic term used to capture the all-encompassing dimensions of white privilege, dominance, and assumed superiority in society. These dimensions include: ideology, institutional, social, cultural, historical, political, and interpersonal" (Sensoy & DiAngelo, 2012).

In response to incidents on campus and throughout the nation, the President of Cabrini University, a small private non-profit institution of higher education, stated that issues around diversity generally and race specifically must be addressed in our community and in our nation (D. Taylor, personal correspondence, October 2016). Addressing such issues requires community members to engage in challenging conversations about race. As Cornel West (1993) articulated, race is an issue in American life that needs critical examination, and this examination must compel us to take action for racial justice. Talking about race and racism is critical to understanding our worlds and can provide a cognitive framework for taking socially responsible action.

Within higher education, schools have a moral imperative to prepare socially responsible critical democratic citizens; discussions about race are necessary "dismantle racism" (Bolgatz, 2005a, p. 5). Specifically, Tatum (1992) argued that universities must create a forum for discussions about race in order to create successful multiracial campuses. Miller and Donner (2000) explain that "dialogues about race and racism offer individuals an opportunity to explore who they are in relation to others while also affording them the opportunity to ponder the meanings of their own and others' social identity and group membership" (p. 34). In this chapter, we refer to these forums when they are held in the classroom as "courageous conversations." Understanding of self and others can be a basis for taking action for more socially just communities. Yet, creating such a forum for discussions about race on a college campus poses a number of challenges. For instance, faculty members are often reluctant to have these conversations fearing they are unprepared and may sound racist themselves. In addition, faculty are reluctant because conversations about race can be divisive (Bolgatz, 2005b; Singleton, 2015; Wormell, 2016). Much of the literature and research on the challenges of facilitating discussions about race in the college classroom has been focused on and even assumes a face-to-face environment, but, as online coursework and programs continue to proliferate and become commonplace for even the most traditional of institutions, there is an equal imperative to develop antiracist curriculum and conversations in remote learning settings as well. Facilitating conversations about race in online courses can both change and increase the challenges experienced in traditional face-to-face settings.

This chapter builds on the results of a qualitative study that explored the experiences of students participating in conversations about race and racism in a fully online section of a graduate Sociocultural Foundations of Education course. The course was required for all students completing a Master of Education degree at Cabrini University. In this course, students engaged in discussions about race, racial identity development, white privilege, racism, and racial injustice. I analyzed a single asynchronous threaded discussion in the course; findings revealed ways in which the discussion was and was not productive and provided greater understanding for how to engage students in courageous conversations in asynchronous online discussions. Building on those findings, I recommend several key strategies for promoting productive and constructive courageous conversations about race in online courses and discuss informed pedagogical strategies that interrupt student resistance to these conversations. First, I provide an overview of literature about courageous conversations and online discussions. Second, I describe the findings from the study and the adjustments I made to the Social Foundations course based on the initial research findings. Those changes yielded more constructive conversations about race, privilege, and racism that led to the concrete recommendations for practice I make to conclude this chapter.

COURAGEOUS CONVERSATIONS ABOUT RACE

Reflecting what is found in the literature (see Bolgatz, 2005b; Singleton, 2015; Tatum, 1992), conversations about race and racism in the higher education classroom are challenging when the course is taught in the traditional face-to-face modality. Research suggests that teachers may avoid conversations about race fearing it will stir things up that they are unprepared to handle. Further, teachers report that they are concerned about saying or doing the wrong thing (Wormell, 2016) and may believe that examining race will actually create or reinforce racism (Bolgatz, 2005a). Indeed, these difficult conversations can be divisive and may result in students opting out of participating or engaging in class (Zuniga et al., 2007).

Strategies for addressing the challenges of facilitating and promoting conversations about race in the traditional, face-to-face classroom setting have been the focus of previous studies (see Bolgatz, 2005a, b; Tatum, 1997; Wormell, 2016). Similarly, there is an abundance of literature that examines and provides guidance for overcoming difficulties teaching online classes generally and in asynchronous online discussions specifically (see Gao et al., 2009, 2013; Gunawardena et al., 2016). There has been little research, however, that examines the challenges of and providing strategies to enhance conversations about race in online courses. Given the increase in the number of online courses and programs in higher education and the overwhelming need to confront racial injustice, it is essential to understand both the uniqueness of the online environment and the practices that help respond to facilitating learning about a deeply challenging topic, race and racism, in a distance setting.

One such pedagogical method is the "courageous conversation." According to Singleton and Hays (2008), "courageous conversation is a strategy for breaking down racial tensions and raising racism as a topic of discussion that allows those who possess knowledge on particular topics to have the opportunity to share it, and those who do not have the knowledge to learn and grow from the experience" (p. 18). Singleton (2015) argues that courageous conversation "engages those who won't talk; sustains the conversation when it gets uncomfortable or diverted; [and] deepens the conversation to the point where authentic understanding and meaningful actions occur" (p. 26). They provide the opportunity for people to "work together to create solutions for problems about which we are afraid to talk" (Ferlazzo, 2017). At their best, courageous conversations lead to action and progress. According to Meyer (2006), controversial discussions such as these may be essential to foster learning and the construction of knowledge. Meyer suggests, "If one's educational purpose is to create learning, perhaps sensible controversy in any setting [online or face-to-face] is needed to encourage new ways of thinking" (p. 184).

The literature suggests a wide range of reasons to support having dialogues about race and racism in schools. According to Miller and Donner (2000), "dialogues about race and racism offer individuals an opportunity to explore who they are in relation to others while also affording them the opportunity to ponder the meanings of their own and others' social identity and group membership" (Miller & Donner, 2000, p. 34). Further, Zuniga et al. (2007) suggested that participation in intergroup dialogue "can increase students' understanding of themselves and others, their comprehension of the roots and operations of structural discrimination and cultural hegemony, and their commitment to take concerted action to create more socially just lives and communities" (pp. 89–90). Not only are there positive outcomes for discussing race and racism, there are negative consequences when it is not addressed. When teachers fail to talk about race, the curriculum is impacted and the "hidden curriculum teaches a powerful message that race and racism are not worthy of students' attention" (Bolgatz, 2005b, p. 34).

However, conversations about race, especially interracial dialogues, are uncomfortable and can even be dangerous (Singleton & Hays, 2008). According to Wormell (2016), instructors often avoid such conversations in schools, afraid of stirring up divisive emotions and opinions that they are not prepared to handle. They may also be afraid of losing friends, saying or doing something wrong, or appearing racist and also fear that examining race explicitly might reinforce racism (Bolgatz, 2005b). Therefore, preparing and supporting instructors with strategies for facilitating difficult conversations is critical.

Strategies for Courageous Conversations

The literature includes a range of principles and strategies to promote conversations about race and racism. Bolgatz (2005b) suggested that overall "putting the issue of race on the table is not a matter of charisma. Rather it is about taking risks, being open to hearing what students think, and maintaining an atmosphere of respect" (p. 34). Wormell (2016) integrates these same ideas in a list of principles to be reviewed and agreed on by the class in order to have candid discussions about racism with students and colleagues:

- "Assume that the other person is doing the best she can;
- Forgive yourself & others for making mistakes;
- Suppress hidden agendas and the urge to preach or politicize;
- Remain nonaccusatory;
- Seek first to understand, then to be understood;
- If you disagree with someone, paraphrase that person's point before responding;
- Avoid language that blames;
- Don't ask anyone to speak for a whole race;
- Acknowledge that candid conversation makes us all vulnerable;
- Avoid associating the quality of a colleague's teaching with comments offered in conversation about racism" (p. 21).

Wormell's principles support the creation of the atmosphere of respect suggested by Bolgatz. Further, Singleton and Hays (2008) recommend guidelines to help create safe spaces to explore race and racism and thus offer opportunities for learning—the Four Agreements of Courageous Conversation. These guidelines set the expectations for students that they must stay engaged, expect to experience discomfort, speak their truth, and expect a lack of closure (Singleton & Hays, 2008). Maintaining these agreements is not easy to do and requires commitment and practice in traditional classroom settings.

In addition to the importance of maintaining an atmosphere of respect, students need a historical perspective in order to better understand the experiences of people different from themselves. Zeichner et al. (1998) explained that students must "examine their own and others' multiple and interrelated identities…(and) understand their own identities as complex multidimensional people in a multicultural society" (p. 168) and then reexamine their beliefs about others. In order to do this, it is critical that students receive "accurate information about the histories, contributions, and current status of various racial, ethnic, and cultural groups" (Zeichner et al., 1998, p. 168). These recommendations are consistent with deKoven's (2011) work which stressed that as members of the dominant culture, white students often lack awareness of how the past has shaped the present for Persons of Color. According to deKoven, conversations about race are stifled when students "overtly or inadvertently use their own lives as a guide by which to measure the lives of persons of color" (p. 156). A historical perspective can help students to not judge the experiences of others based on their own experiences and background. Facilitating courageous conversations in an online learning environment brings additional challenges.

ONLINE LEARNING AND ASYNCHRONOUS DISCUSSIONS

The Distance Education Enrollment Report 2017 indicates that in 2015, over six million students in higher education took at least one distance education course. The number of distance education students increased 3.9% over two years leading up to the 2017 study; approximately 29.7% of students are now taking distance education courses (OLC, 2017). Given the increase in the number of students taking online courses in higher education, a better understanding is needed of the type of interactions needed in order to have discussions about controversial topics and the methods that foster student engagement in such interactions.

Research suggests that discussions about controversial topics, while challenging in any course context, are perhaps more challenging in the online environment (Meyer, 2006). For example, Meyer (2006) compared student reactions to conversations about controversial topics such as race, politics, and gender in a hybrid course between face-to-face and online discussions. While students in Meyer's study were less comfortable discussing controversial concepts than noncontroversial concepts, most of the students in the study preferred the face-to-face over online discussions of controversial topics. Further, students worried about hurting another's feelings, although face-to-face discussions generated the most disagreements. Regardless of this, Meyer concluded that the face-to-face discussions appeared to provide a setting more conducive to the discussion of controversial topics.

However, with such a dramatic increase in online learning, there is an increased need to learn how to engage students in courageous conversations in online environments. Research has identified strategies that strengthen online discussions. First, asynchronous online discussions support interaction among students and can help build community in online courses (Gao et al., 2013). Because asynchronous discussion "free learners from time and space constraints, providing ample opportunity for communication" (p. 469). Second, an instructor should actively guide and orchestrate the discourse in an online discussion in order to create a sense of teaching presence (Shea et al., 2006). Shea et al. (2006) suggest that the aspects of online courses that promote teaching presence are instructional design and "directed facilitation" of discourse. While both are important to creating a sense of learning and community, students in their study identified directed facilitation as more important (Shea et al., 2006). Directed facilitation includes whether the instructor is seen as drawing in participants, creating an accepting climate for learning, keeping students on track, and diagnosing misperceptions. In addition, Shea et al. (2006) reported that students disclosed a better sense of learning and community when the instructor was seen as identifying areas of agreement and disagreement, helping students resolve areas of disagreement, reinforcing student contributions, injecting their own knowledge, and confirming student understanding. These teacher behaviors can enhance a student's sense of teacher presence in online courses and create a greater sense of learning and community.

Despite arguments in favor of asynchronous online discussions, others argue that they might not be the best approach to support teaching and learning conversational content (Thomas, 2002). Gunawardena et al. (2016) found that sharing and comparing information was more common in asynchronous online discussions, but that those experiences did not reach deeper levels of engagement that are essential to the construction of knowledge. Further, Gao et al. (2013) indicated a variety of constraints to online discussions that used threaded forums that included a lack of focused conversations and difficulty fostering in-depth and interactive discussion. Specifically, Gao et al. (2009) created a useful theoretical framework for analyzing the productivity of online discussions. Based on this framework, Gao et al. (2013) proposed the Productive Online Discussion Model (see Table 2.1) which suggested that in a productive online discussion, "it is essential for participants to embrace the following four dispositions: (1) discuss to comprehend, (2) discuss to critique, (3) discuss to construct knowledge and (4) discuss to share" (Gao et al., 2013). The Productive Online Discussion Model provides a framework of dispositions based on the premise that they are necessary in courageous conversations which demand both cognitive and affective engagement by participants.

Table 2.1 Productive Online Discussion Model (Gao et al., 2013)

Disposition 1: Discuss to comprehend
Actively engage in such cognitive processes as interpretation, elaboration, making connections to prior knowledge
Learner Actions
(a) Interpreting or elaborating the ideas by making connection to the learning materials
(b) Interpreting or elaborating the ideas by making connection to personal experience
(c) Interpreting or elaborating the ideas by making connection to other ideas, sources, or references
Disposition 2: Discuss to critique
Carefully examine other views and be sensitive and analytical to conflicting views
Learner Actions
(a) Building upon other students' posts by adding new insights or ideas
(b) Challenging the ideas found in the learning materials
(c) Challenging the ideas in other posts
Disposition 3: Discuss to construct knowledge
Actively negotiate meanings, and be ready to reconsider, refine, and sometimes revise their thinking
Learner Actions
(a) Comparing and contrasting views from the texts or other students' posts
(b) Facilitating thinking and discussions by raising questions
(c) Refining and revising one's own views based on the texts or other students' posts
Disposition 4: Discuss to share
Actively encourage and support other students' thinking and share improved understanding based on previous discussions
Learner Actions
(a) Showing support and appreciation
(b) Synthesizing discussion contents
(c) Coming up with ideas or questions that invite further discussion

---

While all four dispositions are necessary for a productive online discussion, discussing to critique and discussing to construct knowledge are most vital for conversations about race and racial inequality. The overarching goal of courageous conversations, to promote, strengthen, and maintain interracial dialogue in order to address persistent disparities, requires students to participate in critique and knowledge construction, rethinking their taken-for-granted assumptions about race and racial justice, and encouraging one another to consider new information from multiple perspectives.

In order to create a deeper understanding of content in the Sociocultural Foundations of Education course examined in this study, the students and instructor must engage in discussions about race and racism even though such discussions are often challenging for students. The study presented in this chapter was designed to explore limitations to and supports for these conversations in an online environment, specifically in asynchronous online discussions. Two research questions were posed at the outset of the study:

1. What dispositions, necessary for productive online discussions, are reflected in online conversations about race in the course?
2. What pedagogical strategies can be used to promote productive courageous conversations in the online environment?

METHODOLOGY

The qualitative study was based on analysis of one online threaded asynchronous discussion in a section of a Sociocultural Foundations of Education course. Participants interacted within online discussions in the course, and the researcher collected data from these discussions following the implementation of the course. A professor/researcher stance (Lytle & Cochran-Smith, 1992; Cochran-Smith & Lytle, 2009) situated the researcher as instructor in the course. Institutional Review Board (IRB) approval was obtained prior to the beginning of the course.

All students earning a Master's of Education degree at the institution of higher education in this study, regardless of their program of study, are required to take the course, Sociocultural Foundations of Education. The course description is broad but suggests that students in the course will examine inequities in education as they relate to larger society:

> In light of the fact that the system of schooling should be based on principles of equitable access and that every individual has a right to educational opportunities which are just, fair and democratic, students will examine key contemporary issues, policies, and debates in education as they relate to larger society. (Course Description)

The course description and learning outcomes are in the course syllabus and are presented to students at the start of the course. Two of the course objectives directly support the need for students to study issues around race and racism:

1. Students will understand the full significance of diversity in a democratic society and how that bears on equality of educational opportunity and school governance.
2. Students will explain how education can serve the Common Good and promote equality and social justice in a democratic society using knowledge of sociological, historical, political and theoretical foundations of education.

The study of race and racism is more directly connected to additional course teaching goals, developed by course instructors but not written in the syllabus and conveyed only indirectly to students. These deeper goals include:

1. Engage students, most of whom are practicing PK-12 teachers, in courageous conversations about race in order to address persistent racial disparities;
2. Promote self-reflection and the development of empathy and self-awareness;
3. Promote a deeper level of learning (i.e., the co-construction of knowledge); and
4. Inspire teachers to take action in their classrooms and schools as antiracist educators and agents for change in regard to promoting racial equality in schools and society.

In order to achieve these goals and effect change in the behavior and attitudes of teachers, there was a focus on both affective and cognitive approaches to learning throughout the course. While there is a great deal of information that students must learn related to racism in society and schools such as the historical roots and contemporary manifestations of racism and discrimination, it is equally important that students engage in discussions at a more personal and emotional level than is often thought to be needed in academic learning situations. It is through a combination of learning the historical roots and having these deeper conversations that students come to understand themselves and others in the world. In the course, cognitive and affective approaches to learning are integrated and are grounded in learning as an active process in which the students and teacher actively construct knowledge in a community of practice. The construction of knowledge means that the learners and teacher "create deeper understanding of course content and new knowledge through interacting with members of the learning community" (Lai, 2015, p. 564). Because this affective work is rarely part of classroom activities and discussions, students in my classes have typically not been comfortable with this.

Procedure

During the second week of this 8-week online course, students read and watched videos before participating in a discussion about privilege. The required readings for the module included McIntosh (1989), Tatum (1992), Fiarman (2016), and the first chapter in Howard (2016). Before responding to the initial prompt, students should have read about white privilege, resistance to talking about racism, unconscious bias, and the need to examine all of these things in order to teach for racial justice. The focus of the online discussion was privilege. Students were required to respond to this initial prompt early in the week through a discussion board post and then respond to other students' responses throughout the week:

> As the readings and video in this module make clear, each of us benefits from some unearned privileges as a result of our group identity. Consider how privilege has impacted your experiences, especially your educational experiences. How have you benefited? And, in what ways do you see the effects of privilege playing out in our classrooms and schools?

Analysis did not focus on the number of posts because the course requirement states students must post at least three times during the discussion and most students posted only three times. Content analysis was used to systematically evaluate the discussion posts and interpret and code the textual materials. Through this analysis, themes were identified. Interpretation of themes was used to determine whether the discussion was a productive online discussion based on Gao et al.'s (2009) Productive Online Discussion Model.

Nineteen students, in a variety of graduate programs in education—post-baccalaureate secondary certification, post-baccalaureate PK-4 certification, special education certification, and Master of Education—were enrolled in the course. Ten students previously took at least two fully online courses, three had taken hybrid courses in which approximately

50% of the course was offered online, and six students identified this as their first online course. One student participant identifying as Hispanic, three as Black, and the remaining fifteen as white/non-Hispanic. Consistent with work by Meyer (2006), race appeared to be a factor in student responses to discussions about race in this online learning environment, however, I did not explore participant racial identity in this study. Pseudonyms are used throughout this chapter.

While every thread in multiple discussions has been analyzed for the main study, findings and analysis discussed in this chapter are based on a single thread of the online discussion about how privilege impacted each student's experiences. Selection of this thread was based on the high number of students who participated and on the fact that this thread reflects the findings in the overall study in terms of productivity dispositions. All dispositions exhibited in the online discussions generally are exhibited in this thread specifically, which included the initial post and eleven replies, including two from the instructor.

FINDINGS

As research suggests (Meyer, 2006), students are often resistant to talking about race and racism. Rachel, one of the students in the course, expressed such resistance in her initial post in this discussion when she talked about white privilege.

> *After reading the articles and watching the videos for this week's discussion, I do have to admit I got mad. Before even beginning looking over anything, I think it sad that racism is even a topic of conversation. Being a White female a part of a middle-class family, I did not have to worry about money for college, and I was able to get a great education at my public high school. If you were to just read that sentence, you probably already 'judged' and thought I lived a great childhood. After reading the articles, I almost felt bad for being White and truthfully no one should ever feel bad about their race.... I believe that it is not about race, it is about how you present yourself. Socioeconomic plays more of a factor in situations than race. My fiancé, who is black, had the same privileges I did. He went to the same high school, went to a private college and ended up owning his own business. Race has nothing to do with what we were presented with and how we have benefited in life.*
> (Rachel)

I responded to Rachel's post before other students did and suggested that focusing on one Black person's story is not always helpful when examining issues such as structural racism and dominance. I also suggested a couple of short articles about intersectionality. In retrospect, I wish I had simply asked some probing questions in order to engage the student in reflection and critique.

Fortunately, Douglas, another student in the class replied with a number of questions. Douglas's post involved an effort to "discuss to critique" Rachel's post reflecting Gao et al.'s (2013) Disposition 2. He challenged Rachel's ideas, writing:

> 'My fiancé, who is black, had the same privileges as I did… Race has nothing to do with what we were presented with and how we benefited in life.' I have a lot of questions about your post. What does the word 'privilege' mean to you? Do you feel that you and your fiancé had exactly the same experiences growing up? Do you feel that you have had the same opportunities? Do you feel that you have had the same access to opportunity? Have you ever been followed around by a store's loss prevention staff? Have you ever been pulled over for DWB? (Douglas)

Rachel responded to Douglas saying, "Privilege to me is some sort of advantage that someone has over someone else. I do feel that we had the same access to opportunity… I have not been followed around by a store's loss prevention staff or been pulled over for DWB, as he never has ever either." While Douglas attempted to discuss to critique, Rachel stifled further conversation, avoiding critical reflection and dialogue entirely.

Theresa challenges Rachel's position, reflecting Disposition 2, but does so less directly than Douglas. Theresa writes,

> When I was growing up, I felt very similarly to your response. I watched many people around me have more 'advantages' than I did, and when I finally heard of the term White privilege my sophomore year of college, I felt attacked. Me? Privileged? These people who used this term had no idea what I went through in life to get where I was. There were people of color around me who had 'easier' lives than I did, or so I assumed. But what I've come to realize is that privilege is not necessarily what a person has gone through, but rather what a person has not had to go through. (Theresa)

Again, this post could lead to rich conversation about privilege and racism. Instead, Rachel replies by saying, "Thanks," and no one else engages in this line of the discussion. The dispositions for productive online discussion were largely absent in this exchange.

Attempting to make the discussion more productive, I responded again to Rachel saying that white privilege is not the idea that what a white person accomplishes is unearned or that all white people have it easy. I suggested instead that white privilege is the built-in advantage that white people have separate from effort. I asked her to consider whether or not there have been advantages built into her experiences simply because she is white. Neither Rachel nor any other student responded to my post so there was no development along this line of discussion which was an opportunity to "discuss to comprehend" by making connections to personal experience in order to interpret and elaborate on ideas presented in Rachel's post (Disposition 1).

Reflecting Disposition 1 to some degree, some students connected ideas in the readings to personal experiences and feelings, making connections to prior knowledge, discussing to comprehend, and engaging in both cognitive and affective learning. The students do not, however, interpret or elaborate on ideas and do not make connections to texts or ideas beyond those ideas based on their personal experiences. Both Douglas and Theresa engage in Disposition 2, discussing to critique, when they challenge the ideas in Rachel's post. The discussion falls far short of being productive, however, given such efforts to critique are met with silence when neither Rachel nor any other student reflects on the questions raised by Douglas and Theresa. As indicated, some students make connections to personal experience, but this seems to be done to reinforce one's position and not to interpret or elaborate. And while Douglas and Theresa challenge the ideas in the initial post, there is no discussion beyond the initial critique. Without further discussion, there is no opportunity for construction of knowledge (Disposition 3) in that students do not engage in negotiating meanings or in reconsidering and revising their thinking. While the course is based on the premise that in order to promote racial justice we need to engage in courageous conversations about race and racism, the asynchronous online discussion format in this example was not working. As this discussion indicates, change was needed and with changes to course design and teacher presence, students engaged more productively in discussions about race and privilege later in the course. The increased productivity indicates that the changes made and described below support courageous conversations about race in online courses generally and in asynchronous online discussions specifically.

Reflection: Rachel's post potentially opened the door to many important conversations about race and privilege. I or one of the other students could have encouraged Rachel to reflect on her ideas and consider why others might challenge this perspective. In addition, I could invite other students to respond based on their understanding of course texts, their own feelings around the topics, and their own lived experiences. Rachel indicated that the topic of privilege brings up negative emotions for her, so it might have been helpful for Rachel or me to ask if any other students experienced these or other feelings. It would also be beneficial to deconstruct Rachel's narrative and consider why the story of one Black person may not reflect the structural racism that impacts people of color daily. This post, however, was one of nineteen initial posts in an asynchronous online discussion and none of these things happened. As a result, the discussion that followed was much less productive, much less courageous than it might have been.

IMPLICATIONS: FACILITATING COURAGEOUS CONVERSATIONS IN ONLINE COURSES

This discussion thread illustrated the problems of fully online threaded discussions as described by Gao et al. (2009). It also revealed some ways instructors might better engage students in the construction of knowledge related to race, racism, and racial justice in online settings. In the thread described above, students did not participate in ongoing discussion with one another, but simply posted a single reply directly to Rachel's post. Based on the analysis presented here and a wider analysis of threaded discussions in the course, adjustments were made in future iterations of the course. The adjustments described below are ones that promoted more meaningful and transformative courageous conversations in future offerings of this online course and are strategies that can enhance the construction of knowledge in other online courses.

Revising the Discussion Format and Focus

Having students participate in small group rather than whole class asynchronous discussions can encourage more interaction among participants.

When students in this course participated in small group discussions they were more likely to respond to another student's ideas in an ongoing discussion. In addition, in asynchronous discussions the discussion prompt requires careful attention. A prompt that asks a more direct question about how a specific idea in the text makes students feel will promote a more engaged discussion in which students are willing to be more vulnerable and in which affective learning takes place. A prompt that encourages students to find material in the text to challenge such feelings promotes deeper reflection.

Adjusting the Overall Course

In addition to revisiting the asynchronous online discussion prompt and the grouping of students in the discussion, adjustments to the overall course were made in order to foster courageous conversations. First, I added new key topics to the curriculum and new texts. For instance, because students need to understand race and racism from a historical perspective in order to understand and accept how privilege plays out in their own lives (Zuniga et al., 2007), the curriculum was revised to include reading about and discussing the history of race, race relations, and racism. I added Sensoy and DiAngelo's (2012) book, *Is Everyone Really Equal?*, which introduces readers to key concepts in social justice education including, prejudice and discrimination, oppression and power, privilege, racism, and white supremacy. Taking time to study these concepts provided students with deeper understanding as well as language needed for conversations about race and racism. In order to foster courageous conversations, therefore, it is important to consider curricular changes, allowing time for students to examine their own and other racial identities, the history of race, racism, and white supremacy in the United States, and other social justice concepts.

Engaging the Affective Domain

As mentioned, this work requires both cognitive and affective learning experiences, and revisions to the course design have taken both aspects of the learning experience into account. While some student participants mentioned feelings about ideas presented in the course, they did little to investigate the feelings or to critically examine their own lived experiences. Personal experiences and feelings were accepted at face value and not scrutinized to understand how these formed identities and taken-for-granted assumptions. In order to support affective learning it is valuable to help students deconstruct their personal narratives.

Engaging in more learning experiences that are both cognitive and affective requires devoting additional time to creating "safe spaces" for conversation in the class (Kay, 2018). In order to maintain a "safe" space and an atmosphere of respect throughout conversations about race and racism, it is critical that time is set aside to establish agreements at the start of the online course just as it is in the face-to-face course. In the face-to-face setting, an entire class session had always been devoted to developing agreements or principles that would guide the courageous conversations throughout the course. The online course is only eight weeks long, so time had not devoted to establishing the agreements or guidelines. The results of this study made clear that taking this time at the start of the course was essential. While Singleton and Hays' (2008) Four Agreements were the basis for our discussion of agreements and guidelines, each class was encouraged to include in their guidelines whatever they decided was needed to create and maintain a space in which they could hold courageous conversations. While establishing our agreements, I provided examples from various sources including Singleton and Hays' (2008) agreements, Wormell's (2016) principles, and others. The discussion needed to establish the agreements provided an excellent opportunity to practice listening to one another and respecting multiple perspectives. In addition to establishing and committing to our agreements, I reminded students frequently that a strong opinion is not the same as informed knowledge and that putting effort into protecting rather than expanding our current worldview prevents our intellectual and emotional growth. The class agreements were revisited throughout the course and were especially important when conversations get heated on one hand, or stall on the other.

Reinforcing Agreements

Conversations during online synchronous sessions provide opportunities for reinforcing the agreements made as well as for developing the dispositions (Gao et al., 2013; see Table 2) needed for productive online discussions. I made adjustments to reinforce those agreements and develop dispositions. During synchronous sessions, I will post responses to comments that model dispositions for productive online discussions.

My comments, for instance, were designed to prompt reflection and dialogue about uncomfortable or even contentious topics. Singleton and Hays (2008) provided several reflective questions that prompt both critical reflection and thoughtful dialogue: "(a) Can you tell me what you mean when you say...? (b) Is it possible for you to say more about...? (c) Have your thoughts been shaped by others or is this your own personal perspective? (d) Why do you think others might want to challenge your perspective?" (p. 21). These questions promoted reflection as well as ongoing discussion when used in instances where there was pervasive silence following a student's comment or when a student's comment seems to reflect a racist ideology. Further, during synchronous class meetings, students had opportunities to work in small groups in breakout rooms. This provided another opportunity to reinforce class agreements, created a safe space, and encouraged the construction of knowledge. I was able to visit these virtual breakout rooms and facilitate conversations, reinforcing what was needed to create a safe space and a conversation that included negotiation of meaning.

Maintaining Teacher Presence

In conjunction with curricular and pedagogical adjustments, the study reinforced the need for teacher presence in online courses. As indicated by Shea et al. (2006), teacher presence must be promoted in online courses in order to generate a sense of connectedness among learners and to engage learners in more critical reflection. Through a combination of independent writing, asynchronous discussions, and synchronous online sessions, I am able to engage with students as they process knowledge in a variety of ways. Throughout the study of white supremacy, students wrote reflective journal entries which I read and respond to but did not grade. After reading about white supremacy, students began participating in small group asynchronous online discussions. The goal of the discussion for each group was to identify misconceptions about white supremacy and explain how it is manifested in institutions. We then hold an online synchronous session with the entire class in which each group presented their conclusions and students talked about the aspects of the small group discussion and the study of white supremacy that were challenging and/or made them uncomfortable. Based on this discussion, we reviewed misconceptions about racism and began to define antiracist education. In addition, throughout the exploration of white supremacy, students engaged with authors of various texts, their peers, and the instructor. Being exposed to multiple perspectives in a variety of formats provided opportunities for knowledge construction and refining and revising one's worldviews.

One of the issues that seems to stifle online asynchronous discussions was some students' lack of clarity about the audience. As mentioned above, using small group asynchronous discussions was also beneficial to address that concern. In small groups, students began talking with one another rather than simply writing to and for the instructor. Typically, a student's first post is written to the person who has created the prompt, most often the instructor. In the revised course, students worked in groups of three or four; this structure encouraged them to write to and for each other. I would then join the conversation, asking questions and adding information; however, the conversation in this instance was more natural and fluid.

Teacher presence in these asynchronous discussions must be intentional. First, I encouraged students to focus on areas of agreement and disagreement (between the students, between the students and the texts, etc.). Second, I asked questions to encourage students to help students resolve disagreements and look for consensus or at least understanding of one another's views. Third, I reinforced student contributions to the discussion and added my knowledge while also confirming student understanding. Teacher presence is essential in online courses and small group asynchronous discussions can provide more opportunities for teachers to engage with learners in constructive ways.

Course Assignments: Privilege

Assignment 1: Privilege and Cultural Identity Development (Journal Entry)

Students complete this journal writing assignment after completing the McIntosh (1989), Tatum (1992), and DiAngelo (2018) readings as well as the Introduction and Chapter 1 in Howard (2016) and after a synchronous discussion about categories of oppression and agent and target groups. This assignment is shared with only the instructor who provides feedback, asking questions to encourage students to engage in critical reflection. Through some questions I am able to bring relevant ideas from the texts to the student's attention. This assignment is required but not graded.

In this week's journal entry you will reflect on your own cultural identity development and how privilege has played out in your life. There are many categories of oppression including racism, classism, sexism, heterosexism and ableism. We have discussed agent and target groups in each of these categories. Identify a category in which you are a member of the agent group and reflect on the unearned privileges you have been given as a result of this group membership.

Assignment 2: Racial Privilege (Asynchronous Online Discussion)

After receiving feedback on Assignment 1, we engage in a synchronous discussion about unearned privileges generally and racial privilege specifically. Students discuss the following prompt online in small groups. The instructor engages in the small group conversations with the goal of encouraging groups to ask questions, engage with the texts, and challenge one another's taken-for-granted beliefs.

The texts explored in this unit suggest that each of us benefits from some unearned privileges as a result of cultural group identity. In what ways do you see the effects of racial privilege played out in classrooms and schools? Have you witnessed the effect of racial privilege in your own educational experience (as a member of either the agent or target group)?

CONCLUSION

Deliberate and consistent teacher presence and intentional course design are essential when developing and implementing online courses, especially courses that seek to engage students in cognitive and affective learning. When the educational outcomes include participation in courageous conversations about race in order to address persistent racial disparities, attention to teacher presence and course design is even more vital.

Based on findings from the initial study described in this chapter, a number of adjustments have been made to this course and are resulting in more productive conversations about race. Focus has been placed on more frequent and varied approaches to teacher presence, a shift in course curriculum to emphasize key concepts in social justice education, and a change in pedagogical approaches to teaching. It is important that I continue to study the course generally, focusing on the dynamics and content of online discussions, to ensure that the changes made in the course continue to generate more productive and courageous conversations.

The research also needs to be extended to include attention to the influence of race and gender. In a face-to-face class setting, interracial dialogue is necessary for courageous conversation (Singleton, 2015). In generating such conversation face-to-face, when and how the instructor engages with students, teacher presence, is a key factor, suggesting teacher presence is also a key factor in online spaces. Future research must include attention to the intergroup aspects of online discussion. For example, the race as well as the gender identities of students need to be included in the analysis in order to understand who participates, how and when they participate, in what ways they participate, as well as how participation by students of different genders and races influences the dispositions of students and the outcomes of the discussion.

It is critical that we engage in discussions about race and racism as an important step in the move to action for racial justice. While challenging, with thought given to course design and teacher presence, it is possible to create a forum for these discussions in online courses. While such dialogues do not guarantee action, through the construction of knowledge around race and racism in the United States students gain the capacity to become engaged citizens in the fight against racism. As with other antiracist education, an approach to education that emphasizes courageous conversations about race focuses on the inequitable distribution of power. Sensoy and DiAngelo (2012) explained that antiracist education, "centers the analysis on social, cultural, and institutional power that so profoundly shape the meaning and outcome of racial difference... Antiracist education seeks to interrupt these [power] relations by educating people to identify, name, and challenge the norms, patterns, traditions, ideologies, structures, and institutions that keep racism in place" (p. 119). With thoughtful course design and intentional teacher presence in online courses, students exhibit dispositions—discussing to comprehend, critique, construct knowledge, and share—which are critical to courageous conversations about race and the action for social justice generated as a result of these conversations.

REFERENCES

Bolgatz, J. (2005a). *Talking race in the classroom.* Teachers College Press.

Bolgatz, J. (2005b). Teachers initiating conversations about race and racism in a high school class. *Multicultural Perspectives, 7*(3), 28–35. https://doi.org/10.1207/s15327892mcp0703_6.

Cochran-Smith, M., & Lytle, S. L. (2009). *Inquiry as stance: Practitioner research for the next generation.* Practitioner's Inquiry. Teachers College Press.

D. Taylor (personal correspondence, October 2016).

deKoven, A. (2011). Engaging White college students in productive conversations about race and racism: Avoiding dominant-culture projection and condescension-judgment default. *Multicultural Perspectives, 13*(3), 155–159. https://doi.org/10.1080/10509674.2011.594394.

DiAngelo, R. (2018). *White fragility: Why it's so hard for White people to talk about racism.* Beacon Press.

Ferlazzo, L. (2017, September 24). Response: 'Courageous conversations' are needed to discuss race in schools. *Education Week: Teacher Blog.* Retrieved from http://blogs.edweek.org/teachers/classroom_qa_with_larry_ferlazzo/2017/09/response_courageous_conversations_are_needed_to_discuss_race_in_schools.html.

Fiarman, S. E. (2016). Unconscious bias: When good intentions aren't enough. *Educational Leadership, 74*(3), 10–15.

Gao, F., Wang, C. X., & Sun, Y. (2009). A new model of productive online discussion and its implications for research and instruction. *Journal of Educational Technology Development and Exchange, 2*(1), 65–78.

Gao, F., Zhang, T., & Franklin, T. (2013). Designing asynchronous online discussion environments: Recent progress and possible future directions. *British Journal of Educational Technology, 44*(3), 469–483. https://doi.org/10.1111/j.1467-8535.2012.01330.x.

Gunawardena, C. N., Flor, N. V., Gomez, D., & Sanchez, D. (2016). Analyzing social construction of knowledge online by employing interaction analysis, learning analytics, and social network analysis. *The Quarterly Review of Distance Education, 17*(3), 35–60.

Howard, G. R. (2016). *We can't teach what we don't know: White teachers, multiracial schools* (3rd ed.). Teachers College Press.

Kay, M. R. (2018). *Not light, but fire: How to lead meaningful race conversations in the classroom.* Stenhouse Publishers.

Lai, K. (2015). Knowledge construction in online learning communities: A case study of a doctoral course. *Studies in Higher Education, 40*(4), 561–579. https://doi.org/10.1080/03075079.2013.831402.

Lytle, S., & Cochran-Smith, M. (1992). Teacher researcher as a way of knowing. *Harvard Educational Review, 62*(4), 447–475.

McIntosh, P. (1989, July/August). White privilege: Unpacking the invisible knapsack. *Peace and Freedom Magazine*, pp. 10–12.

Meyer, K. A. (2006). When topics are controversial: Is it better to discuss them face-to-face or online? *Innovations in Higher Education, 31,* 175–186. https://doi.org/10.1007/s10755-006-9019-3.

Miller, J., & Donner, S. (2000). More than just talk: The use of racial dialogue to combat racism. *Social Work with Groups, 23*(1), 31–53. https://doi.org/10.1300/J009v23n01_03.

OLC. (2017). *New study: Over six million students now enrolled in distance education.* Online Learning Consortium. Retrieved from https://onlinelearningconsortium.org/news_item/new-study-six-million-students-now-enrolled-distance-education/.

Sensoy, O., & DiAngelo, R. (2012). *Is everyone really equal?: An introduction to key concepts in social justice education.* Teachers College Press.

Shea, P., Li, C. S., & Pickett, A. (2006). A study of teaching presence and student sense of learning community in fully online and web-enhanced college courses. *Internet and Higher Education, 9,* 175–190.

Singleton, G. E. (2015). *Courageous conversations about race: A field guide for achieving equity in schools.* Corwin.

Singleton, G. E., & Hays, C. (2008). Beginning courageous conversations about race. *Pollock* (M ed., pp. 18–23). Getting real about race in school: Everyday antiracism.

Tatum, B. D. (1992). Talking about race, learning about racism: The application of racial identity development theory in the classroom. *Harvard Educational Review, 62*(1), 1–25. https://dx.doi.org/10.17763/haer.62.1.146k5v980r703023.

Tatum, B. D. (1997). *"Why are all the Black kids sitting together in the cafeteria?": And other conversations About race.* Basic Books.

Thomas, M. J. W. (2002). Learning within incoherent structures: The space of online discussion forums. *Journal of Computer Assisted Learning, 18,* 351–366. https://doi.org/10.1046/j.0266-4909.2002.03800.x.

West, C. (1993). *Race matters.* Vintage.

Wormell, R. (2016). Let's talk about racism in schools. *Educational Leadership, 74*(3), 16–22.

Zeichner, K. M., Grant, C., Gay, G., Gillette, M., Valli, L., & Maria Villegas, M. (1998). A research informed vision of good practice in multicultural teacher education: Design principles. *Theory into Practice, 27*(2), 163–171.

Zuniga, X., Nagda, B. A., Chesler, M., & Cytron-Walker, A. (2007). *Intergroup dialogue in higher education: Meaningful learning about social justice.* San Francisco: Josey-Bass.

Recommended Readings

Bolgatz, J. (2005). *Talking race in the classroom*. New York: Teachers College Press.

DiAngelo, R. (2018). *White fragility: Why it's so hard for White people to talk about racism*. Boston: Beacon Press.

Howard, G. R. (2016). *We can't teach what we don't know: White teachers, multiracial schools* (3rd ed.). New York: Teachers College Press.

Kaplowitz, D. R., Griffin, S. R., & Seyka, S. (2019). *Race dialogues: A facilitator's guide to tackling the elephant in the classroom*. New York: Teachers College Press.

Kay, M. R. (2018). *Not light, but fire: How to lead meaningful race conversations in the classroom*. Portsmouth, New Hampshire: Stenhouse Publishers.

Pollock, M. (Ed.). (2008). *Everyday antiracism: Getting real about race in school*. New York: The New Press.

Sensoy, O., & DiAngelo, R. (2012). *Is everyone really equal?: An introduction to key concepts in social justice education*. New York: Teachers College Press.

Singleton, G. E. (2015). *Courageous conversations about race: A field guide for achieving equity in schools*. Thousand Oaks, CA: Corwin.

CHAPTER 3

Promoting a Social Justice Orientation Among Students of Color in Psychology

Dawn X. Henderson

KEY TERMS AND DEFINITIONS

Underrepresented students	Students from groups in the United States that are underrepresented in the psychology workforce and doctoral pipeline. Groups include Black (comprise about 13.4% of the population), Latinx (about 18.3% of the population), and Native American (about 1.3% of the population; U.S. Census Bureau, 2019).
Students of Color	Students who either self-identify or become identified as Black, Latinx, Hispanic, Asian, and Native American and mixed race.

D. X. Henderson (✉)
Duke University, Durham, NC, USA
e-mail: dawn.henderson@duke.edu

© The Author(s), under exclusive license to Springer Nature Switzerland AG 2021
C. C. Ozaki and L. Parson (eds.), *Teaching and Learning for Social Justice and Equity in Higher Education,*
https://doi.org/10.1007/978-3-030-69947-5_3

33

Close to forty years ago, Dr. Kenneth Clark, the first Black president of the American Psychological Association (APA), and Dr. Mamie Clark used their role as psychologists to study the adverse effects of racial segregation on Black children and to advance civil rights legislation in the United States (Benjamin & Crouse, 2002; Leong et al., 2017). Together, they challenged segregation policies and advocated for equality in education (Clark & Clark, 1939, 1950). Direct experiences with racism and observing racial injustice likely shaped their values, beliefs toward social justice, and motivation to devote their careers to improving mental health for Black children. The Clarks' lived experiences growing up during a time of legal racial segregation likely influenced their decision to work to transform the system of public education and to advocate for change. Hypothetically, there may have been educators in each of the Clark's lives who saw their potential and who sought the need to prepare the Clarks to become research advocates. To prepare students to become advocates, change agents, and to be the next Drs. Mamie and Kenneth Clark entails promoting values for equity, well-being for all humanity, and justice in the classroom.

This chapter began with Dr. Mamie and Kenneth Clark because they persisted through an education system that marginalized their identities and they used their intellectual power to advocate for transformation. According to the National Center for Education Statistics (2019), psychology is the third most popular major among Black and Latinx students and the fourth most popular major among individuals who self-identify as Asian. Like the Clarks, Students of Color may pursue psychology because it offers theories that explain many societal issues, and they see the major as preparing them to address such challenges (APA, 2013; Burnes & Singh, 2010). One can look into the mental health system in the United States and see that Black, Latinx, Asian, and Native Americans remain underserved (National Council for Behavioral Health, 2019). Students who come from these communities or observe these health inequalities often see the discipline of psychology as a pathway to promote well-being (Thrift & Sugarman, 2019; Vasquez, 2012).

The need to address social inequalities may be why psychology remains a popular major among Black, Latinx, and Asian American students. As such, the discipline of psychology can be a powerful medium for social justice education. This chapter provides a brief overview of how individuals develop a value orientation and discusses how specific learning experiences can increase a student's value orientation toward social justice.

I will cite literature from the scholarship of teaching and learning (SoTL) across disciplines to explicate the link between a value orientation toward social justice and motivations and behaviors. Next, I reflect on my work teaching undergraduate psychology to students at Historically Black Colleges and Universities (HBCUs) and teaching majority first-generation college students to highlight core elements of teaching and learning social justice education. Building on literature and my experiences, I provide recommendations to improve pedagogy, syllabus and assignment design in the learning environment to promote social justice in psychology and other disciplines. Lastly, I share assessment practices and findings to inform those interested in improving social justice teaching and education.

A Value Orientation Toward Social Justice

A value orientation describes the values and beliefs individuals rely on to shape their orientation toward the world and related motivations (Betancourt et al., 1992; McClintock & Allison, 1989; Messick & McClintock, 1968). A value orientation stems from formal learning, informal learning, and membership in different cultural groups (Cox et al., 1991; McClintock & Allison, 1989; Murphy & Ackermann, 2014). For example, Black and Latinx communities have a strong value orientation toward education, where parents often convey the message that getting an education is about freedom and equality (Franklin, 2002; Valencia, 2002). Adult models and messages from adults and peers can convey what is right versus wrong, norms, and build a value orientation (Betancourt et al., 1992; Lee et al., 2010). Consider how children who grew up in a home where they received constant messages about the importance of going to college may retain this belief in adulthood and have different values toward education versus someone who does not grow up in that environment. A value orientation will inform how individuals make decisions, their behaviors, and whether they value collective well-being over individual well-being (McClintock & Allison, 1989; Murphy & Ackermann, 2014). Seeing and experiencing injustice in the world, accompanied by interactions and messages that project injustice is wrong can begin to shape a value orientation toward social justice.

A value orientation toward social justice may stem from a combination of messages conveyed from others, expectations, and observations of group advantages and disadvantages (Van Zomeran et al., 2008).

Direct experiences, such as observing injustice in one's neighborhood and community against people who share similar social identities, can also impact one's value orientation. Also, messages conveyed from family members and membership in particular religious organizations and groups can influence an orientation that seeks to stand against injustice. Thomas et al. (2012) demonstrate that through engagement in advocacy and collective action, marginalized groups exercise agency while aligning a value orientation with specific behaviors. Drs. Mamie and Kenneth Clark's experiences with racial discrimination and marginalization and their membership in the Black community influenced their values. These collective experiences and interactions more likely shaped their desire to advocate against racial segregation in public schools.

One can argue that a value orientation toward social justice may already be relatively high among Students of Color. A previous study found that undergraduate students in psychology who self-identified as Black and Latinx were more likely to have a high-value orientation toward social justice (Henderson et al., 2019). Several other studies have found that many Students of Color enter courses and majors with a high value for equity and a strong desire to engage in social action or social justice behavior (Gibbs & Griffin, 2013; Garibay, 2015; Henderson et al., 2019; Henderson & Wright, 2015; McGee & Bentley, 2017). Other scholars note that "working for social change" is a common motivator for choosing a major and career interests among Black and Latinx students (Gibbs & Griffin, 2013; Garibay, 2015; McGee & Bentley, 2017). Torres-Harding and colleagues (2014) further demonstrate that Black students are more likely to express creating equality and combatting injustice as the impetus to their career aspirations. The sense of activism that emerges across Students of Color may be connected to personal experience with injustice or just an increased awareness of how injustice plays out in society (Thomas et al., 2012; Van Zomeren et al., 2008).

At its core, a value orientation toward social justice manifests in beliefs that value collective well-being over individual well-being and through behaviors where people are advocating against inequity or working to change social inequalities in neighborhoods and communities (Hardiman et al., 2007; Leong et al., 2017). Theoretically, students can begin to shift their values toward social justice if they experience injustice directly or begin learning about and witnessing injustice in their social world (Einfeld & Collins, 2008; Lee et al., 2010). For many Black, Latinx, Asian, and Native American students, experiences and observations of racism, racial marginalization, and injustice will shape their orientation toward the world and related motivations (Betancourt et al., 1992; McClintock & Allison, 1989; Messick & McClintock, 1968). Higher education institutions offer pathways for students to gain formal and informal learning, knowledge, and skills that prepare them to pursue goals (Cox et al., 1991; McClintock & Allison, 1989; Murphy & Ackermann, 2014). The need to address injustice and the need to stand against racism motivates student persistence in higher education, choice of major, and career interest (Gibbs & Griffin, 2013; Soria & Stebleton, 2013).

Linking Social Justice Education to Student Outcomes

Postsecondary education is ostensibly guided by a belief that individuals need education beyond what they have learned in K-12 institutions; students need to build competencies in order to gain the knowledge and skills needed to meet the demands of an everchanging and transforming workforce. Numerous higher education institutions infuse social justice principles into their mission and curricular standards (Stearns, 2009). Indeed, social justice education potentially increases student competence in addressing injustice and advocating for equity. According to Shaull in Friere's Pedagogy of the Oppressed:

> Education either functions as an instrument that is used to facilitate the integration of the young generation into the logic of the present system and bring about conformity to it, or it becomes "the practice of freedom," the means by which men and women deal critically and creatively with reality and discover how to participate in the transformation of their world. (p. 34)

Transforming our social world, bending the arc toward social and racial justice encompasses both formal and informal learning. Formal learning often occurs in classrooms through approved curriculum driven by standards and competencies students must achieve to transition from one level to the next. Informal learning can happen beyond the classroom through social interactions students have with peers, faculty, and other adults in their lives. Education allows students to connect new learning with previous learning (Ambrose et al., 2010). Both formal and informal learning experiences in undergraduate courses can increase student attitudes, beliefs toward social justice, and social justice behaviors (Ginwright & Cammarota, 2015; Henderson et al., 2019; Henderson & Wright, 2015; McAuliff et al., 2013; Mitchell & Soria, 2016; Schlehofer & Phillips, 2013).

Social justice education entails the practice of critical reflection in the learning process. Both students and educators learn to reflect critically on privilege and learn how to use dialogue a process for perspective-taking and to learn about and value diverse perspectives and realities (McAuliff et al., 2013). Critical reflection allows students to increase self-awareness while also improving their interpersonal skills (Einfeld & Collins, 2008; Mitchell, 2007, 2014). Increased empathy and valuing diverse perspectives and experiences can occur through formal and informal learning experiences. For example, immersing students in diverse communities to learn more about social inequalities from community members can lead to positive shifts in students' social justice attitudes (Ginwright & Cammarota, 2015; McAuliff et al., 2013; Mitchell & Soria, 2016). The combination of formal and informal learning that arises from interpersonal interactions with diverse people and localities can lead to a higher awareness of social inequalities and a stronger desire to address injustice (Ginwright & Cammarota, 2015; McAuliff et al., 2013; Mitchell & Soria, 2016; Schlehofer & Phillips, 2013).

Linking social justice education to the social sciences, and psychology specifically, can have several benefits to how students see themselves in the world. For example, Cattaneo et al. (2019) found that infusing social justice principles into an undergraduate psychology course transformed student thinking from placing blame on individuals to developing a more critical analysis of systemic influences on success and failure. Specifically, focusing on community engagement has been related to increased social awareness and advocacy. Students who begin to feel they can make a difference in their social world and experience alignment between their values and learning show increased motivation for learning (Gibbs & Griffin, 2013; Soria & Stebleton, 2013). For example, Henderson et al. (2019) demonstrated that undergraduate students who had a high degree of community engagement in their psychology course and perceived others participating in advocacy were more likely to demonstrate favorable social justice attitudes and behaviors. Other studies suggest that students who volunteer in their local communities and have service-related learning are more likely to possess favorable beliefs toward empowering others and exhibit behaviors related to increased social advocacy (Mitchell & Soria, 2016). Volunteering and working with members in a diverse community, working with others to solve problems can give students a sense of purpose and promote a more favorable orientation toward social justice.

RECOMMENDATIONS FOR SOCIAL JUSTICE EDUCATION: A MODEL IN PSYCHOLOGY

If education is perceived as a pathway to freedom and equality in communities of color in the United States (Franklin, 2002; Valencia, 2002), then social justice education in psychology links education to the actual ability to advocate against and address injustice (Henderson et al., 2019; Henderson & Wright, 2015). Psychology is a discipline that many undergraduate students pursue to prepare them for medical professions, as educators, mental health, and social service providers. For some, the undergraduate psychology degree is an introduction to research and the foundation to graduate and doctoral training in social and behavioral science research. The need to improve the learning environment for racially diverse students while also addressing a history of exclusion in higher education necessitates infusing social justice into the core elements of the psychology classroom and learning environment. These core elements include pedagogy, syllabus and assignment design and includes practices that reinforce application (Howell & Tuitt, 2003; Luke et al., 2013; O'Brien et al., 2008; Simons et al., 2012). In the examples that follow, course mapping aims to connect course objectives with assignments and student competencies.

Pedagogy that Promotes Pro-social Justice Value Orientation

Pedagogy in the higher education classroom may be inclusive of the instructor and the student. Watkins and Mortimore (1999) define pedagogy as "any conscious activity by one person designed to enhance learning in another" (p. 3). The authors do not place the sole responsibility of learning on the instructor but instead take an inclusive stance that suggests the instructor and student both serve as conveyers of learning. Thus, it is vital to consider how educators are practitioners of social justice education and models for the behaviors they seek in students. Educators who seek to espouse social justice education in their courses must recognize that students are co-learners and co-arbiters in the learning environment. Students learn from explicit messages and expectations from the instructor and also learn by observing adults and peers (Howell & Tuitt, 2003; Luke et al., 2013; O'Brien et al., 2008; Simons et al., 2012).

Pedagogy in the undergraduate psychology course repositions Students of Color and centers their voices, realities, and perspectives as valuable. Scholarship and voices from individuals who share the racial and cultural identities of students remain invisible in psychology and other disciplines; therefore, the educator must present knowledge differently. For example, learning with peers accompanied by opportunities to learn autonomously can provide benefits. When there exist opportunities for both autonomous and group learning, Students of Color report a higher degree of trust, belonging, and a positive sense of community (Henderson et al., 2019; Hunn, 2014).

Reflection. First, it is important for instructors to reflect critically on values, beliefs, and how they inform pedagogical decision (Ambrose et al., 2010; Funge, 2011). Reflective practice requires instructors to think critically about their sociocultural history, behavior, and adjust practices accordingly (Funge, 2011 Jay & Johnson, 2002). Through reflective practice, individuals should question their values and assumptions and begin to display more open-mindedness and social responsibility (Jay & Johnson,2002). As a result, the highly reflective educator will recognize where they make errors in judgment. They will become critical of the content in their courses and challenge content that reinforces privileging knowledge of one group (i.e., white men) while excluding knowledge of other groups. Through reflective practice, educators can begin to model how they challenge injustice and provide students with opportunities to do the same (Adams et al., 2016). Increased self-awareness will allow the educator to position themselves in the learning environment differently and position knowledge differently.

Recommended Pedagogical Practices. I offer three recommendations for educators to practice in their pedagogy:

- Create opportunities for students to lead topics they deem relevant and shift the facilitation of learning back into student's hands, which promotes a more inclusive pedagogy (Howell & Tuitt, 2003).
- Use dialogue as a way for students to initiate ideas for debate and to facilitate group discussion (Nagda et al., 1999). Allowing students

to identify topics and share divergent ideas and perspectives position them as critical agents in the learning process (Friere, 1993).

- If teaching face-to-face, disrupt the traditional classroom structure by creating opportunities for students to be at the front of the classroom. Alternately, an instructor could change their position in the classroom to create a visual dynamic that reinforces equal status. If teaching online, instructors could provide students with the opportunity to lead the introduction and course objectives.

Recommendations for Syllabus Design

The syllabus is a document that communicates teaching philosophies and competencies related to a discipline or field (O'Brien et al., 2008), often the primary conveyor of curriculum standards and competencies, and it acts as a mapping structure between knowledge and practice (Luke et al., 2013). Integrating the universal themes of diversity, racism, and oppression, and advocacy are essential in syllabus design. For example, Hong and Hodge (2009) found in their analysis of 31 social work syllabi for courses that focused on social justice had themes that focus on oppression, social change, and diversity. Similarly, Pieterse et al.'s (2009) analysis of 54 syllabi from counseling and counseling psychology programs found that 40% addressed content related to multicultural issues such as racial and ethnic groups, racism, and LGBTQ topics. Educators can integrate themes into learning objectives, description of assignments, and also through course readings. In addition to a thematic focus on social justice topics, Gallor (2017) asserted that introducing perspectives, research, and literature from groups who have been traditionally marginalized and ignored in psychology and education should be integrated into the syllabus. Whether the syllabus is a traditional text design or visual graphic, it is the primary roadmap for linking social justice competencies to student learning in the course.

Learning outcomes expressed in the syllabus should also explicitly communicate student responsibility to themselves and their broader community (Gallor, 2017). One way to explicate learning objectives in the syllabus is to map social justice themes to learning outcomes. Table 3.1 provides an example of an exercise mapping social justice learning objectives to the psychology knowledge base, specifically undergraduate psychology (American Psychological Association, 2013). The second column outlines the theme of diversity, systems analysis, and

Table 3.1 An example of mapping social justice topical themes to learning objectives

Psychology learning objective	Social justice theme	Social justice learning objective
Students should demonstrate fundamental knowledge and comprehension of the major concepts, theoretical perspectives, historical trends, and empirical findings to discuss how psychological principles apply to behavioral problems	Diversity Systems analysis Multi-methodologies	Students should demonstrate fundamental knowledge of (1) diverse theoretical perspectives in psychology; (2) the sociocultural ecological factors that shape behavioral problems; and (3) how multi-methodologies advance psychological theories and empirical, findings

Note Learning Goal 1: Knowledge base in psychology. American Psychological Association (2013)

multi-methodologies into the learning objective. The language in the third column articulates what the students should demonstrate at the end of the course. Many universities provide syllabus templates or require instructors to include institutional policies while granting instructors a degree of autonomy in syllabus design. The expectations communicated in the syllabus, the representation of diverse perspectives in the readings, and clear learning objectives that demonstrate the link between social justice themes reinforce a value orientation toward social justice.

Recommendations for Assignment Design

Assignment descriptions and criteria can be included in the syllabus; assignments allow students to practice and apply knowledge to real-world tasks and challenges. Course mapping also allows students to make connections between learning objectives and assignments. Table 3.2 provides an example of how I link assignments in an undergraduate psychology class to skills and learning objectives. Each assignment description informs students how they will increase knowledge about their social identities and also delves into how their identities influence their values and vice versa (Mitchell & Soria, 2016). Educators should consider structuring assignments in the course to sequence students from self-awareness to practice and application. Second, assignments should provide opportunities for students to practice and apply knowledge to real-world tasks

Table 3.2   An example of mapping learning objectives to course assignments

Learning objective	Course assignments	Description	Skills
(1) Understand diverse theoretical perspectives in psychology	Course readings	Course readings include the integration of scholars who are women, indigenous schools of color, and international	Critical thinking Information literacy Diversity awareness
(2) Explore the sociocultural and ecological factors that shape behavioral problems	"I am my community" assignment	An interview with individuals who have social identities different from own; an analysis of how sociocultural experiences influence their values and beliefs	Systems-level analysis
	Community engagement (service requirement and paper)	Required 20-hours of community engagement; a reflection paper that includes an analysis of how different sociocultural factors influenced self-perception and the context	Civic engagement
(3) Demonstrate how multi-methodologies advance psychological theories and empirical findings	Issue brief	Research an issue to identify a problem in a local community, identify how different socio-ecological systems influence the issue, and develop a call to action. The issue brief will require interviews with key informants and gathering data to identify the problem and justify the call to action	Advocacy Critical thinking Quantitative reasoning

and challenges. Through real-world assignments scaffolded from self-awareness to application to practice helps students develop an awareness of the discipline from diverse perspectives and develop a self-awareness when they reflect on these perspectives. In Table 3.2, the "I am my community" assignment asks students to reflect on their identities, influencers of that identity, and then to interview two individuals who have different identities from themselves. Finally, students were asked to reflect on similarities they shared with others and recognize differences in a written synthesis.

While assignments may include opportunities for students to improve writing and critical thinking, it is essential to provide students with real-world applications. Traditionally, undergraduate psychology courses rarely address student values nor include community-engaged learning experiences (Homa et al., 2013; Stoloff et al., 2010). A previous content analysis of undergraduate psychology curriculum programs found that courses that stressed social justice and community engagement accounted for less than 14% of undergraduate programs (Stoloff et al., 2010). There are several ways to use assignments in ways that allow students to gain practical knowledge and skills. One example found in the literature immerses students in local and diverse communities to solve problems or provide services (Simons et al., 2012; Wurdinger & Carlson, 2010; Zimmerman et al., 2013). Community-engaged learning may be less common in psychology, yet community-engaged learning can help students examine assumptions, biases, and prejudices.

Assignments directed toward increased self-awareness and one's responsibility to a broader community can allow students to model social justice behaviors (Ginwright & Cammarota, 2015; Henderson et al., 2019; McAuliff et al., 2013; Mitchell & Soria, 2016). When students see themselves as resources to their communities by offering services, time, and knowledge and simultaneously learn from interactions with community members, they increase knowledge of group processes, diversity, and other dimensions of human behavior (Gallor, 2017; Ginwright & Cammarota, 2015; McAuliff et al., 2013; Schlehofer & Phillips, 2013). Community-engaged learning is an essential feature of social justice education because it immerses students in settings where they must make associations between learning content in class to practical and real-world challenges (Hardiman et al., 2007; McCabe & Rubinson, 2008; Schlehofer & Phillips, 2013).

Recommendation for Assessment Design

Assessment in the higher education classroom is a type of action research that informs teaching and new instructional approaches (Walvoord, 2004). Hutchings (2000) encourages educators to think of assessment as a way to gain insight into what is working in the learning environment and what is not. Additionally, assessments should be designed to understand student competency and evaluate changes in belief systems (Burnes & Singh, 2010). A multi-method approach in assessment design will assess student learning and provide feedback that can be used for course improvements. It includes more traditional forms of assessments like multiple-choice exams, quizzes, questionnaires, and assessment in the form of student essays and open-ended measures; this variety of methods may be highly useful when students have diverse learning needs and knowledge acquisition abilities (Nummedal et al., 2002).

For example, I explored ways students can practice autonomous and group learning through a collaborative exam. Specifically, I designed group exams that required students to collaboratively identify factors contributing to a social dilemma and to identify a psychology theory that could be used to solve the dilemma. In exams that include multiple-choice and open-ended responses, I ask students to reach a consensus about their response to a multiple-choice question and to provide the rationale for their response. Though there was some student resistance to this exam format, student exam grades increased by five points.

In Fig. 3.1, I share a multi-method approach. I began to assess my teaching and student learning from approaches that would provide a more in-depth analysis of the impact of completing a psychology course. I designed the model from two papers previously published on infusing social justice education into the undergraduate psychology course (Henderson et al., 2019; Henderson & Wright, 2015). Using validated quantitative measures and assessing artifacts collected from student learning is a way to communicate to students that the instructor values all of the ways a student learns and acquires knowledge. Integrating qualitative data, such as student essays and other course artifacts, can improve how instructors evaluate learning. Quantitatively, the Social Justice Scale (SJS; Torres-Harding et al., 2012) and Doolittle and Faul (2013) Civic Engagement Behavior Scale provide some ways to assess a student's values, beliefs, and behaviors over time. I have found that assessment design is a way to gather evidence of learning and improve pedagogy,

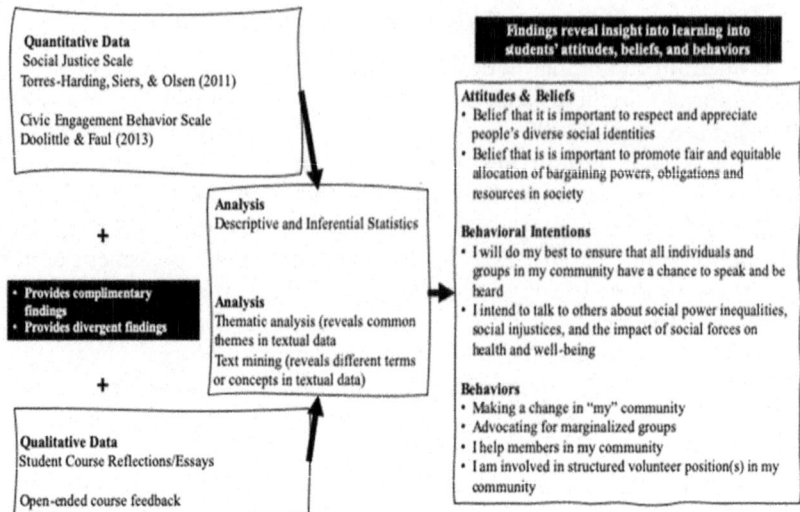

Fig. 3.1 Using a multi-method approach to assess social justice attitudes, beliefs, and behaviors

syllabus, and assignment design. A multi-method approach to monitoring change in student learning over time helps advance research on social justice education and learning (Hutchings, 2000).

CONCLUSION

Formal and informal learning in higher education can begin to shape one's value orientation toward social justice and social justice behaviors. While this chapter focused on psychology courses, emerging literature in STEM education also suggests that Students of Color are more successful in courses that connect learning to local community issues and challenges (Hernandez et al., 2013). Promoting a value orientation toward social justice may require a significant paradigm shift in higher education, and when systems are resistant to change, research becomes a critical tool for empowerment. Learning that values reflective practice, engagement in diverse communities to develop solutions to societal problems, a critical analysis of social systems may be particularly valuable to Students of Color (Gibbs & Griffin, 2013; Garibay, 2015; McGee & Bentley, 2017;

Soria & Stebleton, 2013). Transforming higher education, teaching, and learning requires a willingness to disrupt traditional modes of education and learning if we seek to change the under-representation of Students of Color to representation and increase their ability to become the next Drs. Mamie and Kenneth Clarks of the world.

References

Adams, M., Bell, L. A., Goodman, D. J., & Joshi, K. Y. (2016). *Teaching for diversity and social justice.* London, UK: Routledge.

Ambrose, S. A., Bridges, M. W., DiPietro, M., Lovett, M. C., & Norman, M. K. (2010). *How learning works: Seven research-based principles for smart teaching.* Wiley.

American Psychological Association. (2013). *APA guidelines for the undergraduate psychology major.* https://www.apa.org/ed/precollege/about/undergraduate-major.

Benjamin, L. T., Jr., & Crouse, E. M. (2002). The American Psychological Association's response to Brown v. Board of Education: The case of Kenneth B. Clark. *American Psychologist, 57*(1), 38–50. https://doi.org/10.1037/108 12-013.

Betancourt, H., Hardin, C., & Manzi, J. (1992). Beliefs, value orientation, and culture in attribution processes and helping behavior. *Journal of Cross-Cultural Psychology, 23,* 179–195. https://doi.org/10.1177/002202219223 2004.

Burnes, T. R., & Singh, A. A. (2010). Integrating social justice training into the practicum experience for psychology trainees: Starting earlier. *Training and Education in Professional Psychology, 4,* 153–162. https://doi.org/10.1037/a0019385.

Cattaneo, L. B., Shor, R., Calton, J. M., Gebhard, K. T., Buchwach, S. Y., Elshabassi, N., & Hargrove, S. (2019). Social problems are social: Empirical evidence and reflections on integrating community psychology into traditional curriculum. *Global Journal of Community Psychology Practice, 10*(1), 1–29.

Clark, K. B., & Clark, M. K. (1939). The development of consciousness of self and the emergence of racial identification in Negro preschool children. *The Journal of Social Psychology, 10,* 591–599.

Clark, K. B., & Clark, M. P. (1950). Emotional factors in racial identification and preference in Negro children. *Journal of Negro Education, 19,* 341–350. https://doi.org/10.2307/2966491.

Cox, T. H., Lobel, S. A., & McLeod, P. L. (1991). Effects of ethnic group cultural differences on cooperative and competitive behavior on a group task.

Academy of Management Journal, 34, 827–847. https://www.jstor.org/stable/256391.

Doolittle, A., & Faul, A. C. (2013). Civic engagement scale: A validation study. *Sage Open, 3,* 1–7. https://doi.org/10.1177/2158244013495542.

Einfeld, A., & Collins, D. (2008). The relationships between service-learning, social justice, multicultural competence, and civic engagement. *Journal of College Student Development, 49,* 95–109. https://muse.jhu.edu/article/233953.

Franklin, V. P. (2002). Introduction: Cultural capital and African American education. *Journal of African American History, 87,* 175–181. https://doi.org/10.1086/JAAHv87n2p175.

Friere, P. (1993). *Pedagogy of the oppressed.* New York, NY: Continuum International Publishing Group.

Funge, S. P. (2011). Promoting the social justice orientation of students: The role of the educator. *Journal of Social Work Education, 47,* 73–90. https://doi.org/10.5175/JSWE.2011.200900035.

Gallor, S. (2017). A social justice approach to undergraduate psychology education: Building cultural diversity, inclusion, and sensitivity into teaching, research, and service. *Psi Chi Journal of Psychological Research, 22*(4), 254–257. https://doi.org/10.24839/2325-7342.JN22.4.254.

Garibay, J. C. (2015). STEM students' social agency and views on working for social change: Are STEM disciplines developing socially and civically responsible students? *Journal of Research in Science Teaching, 52,* 610–632. https://doi.org/10.1002/tea.21203.

Gibbs, K. D., & Griffin, K. A. (2013). What do I want to be with my PhD? The roles of personal values and structural dynamics in shaping the career interests of recent biomedical science PhD graduates. *CBE-Life Sciences Education, 12,* 711–723. https://doi.org/10.1187/cbe.13-02-0021.

Ginwright, S. A., & Cammarota, J. (2015). Teaching social justice research to undergraduate students in Puerto Rico: Using personal experiences to inform research. *Equity & Excellence in Education, 48,* 162–177. https://doi.org/10.1080/10665684.2014.959331.

Hardiman, R., Jackson, B., & Griffin, P. (2007). Conceptual foundations for social justice education. In M. Adams, L. A. Bell, & P. Griffin (Eds.), *Teaching for diversity and social justice* (pp. 35–66). New York, NY: Routledge/Taylor & Francis Group.

Henderson, D. X., Majors, A. T., & Wright, M. (2019). "I am a change agent": A mixed methods analysis of students' value orientation towards social justice in an undergraduate community psychology course. *Scholarship of Teaching and Learning in Psychology,* 1–13. http://dx.doi.org/10.1037/stl0000171.

Henderson, D. X., & Wright, M. (2015). Getting students to "go out and make a change": Promoting dimensions of global citizenship and social justice in an undergraduate course. *Journal of Contemporary Issues in Higher Education, 1,* 14–29.

Hernandez, P. R., Schultz, P. W., Estrada, M., Woodcock, A., & Chance, R. C. (2013). Sustaining optimal motivation: A longitudinal analysis of interventions to broaden participation of underrepresented students in STEM. *Journal of Educational Psychology, 105*(1), 89. https://doi.org/10.1037/a0029691. https://doi.org/10.1037/a0029691.

Homa, N., Hackathorn, J., Brown, C. M., Garczynski, A., Solomon, E. D., Tennial, R., ... Gurung, R. A. R. (2013). An analysis of learning objectives and content coverage in Introductory Psychology syllabi. *Teaching of Psychology, 40,* 169–174. https://doi.org/10.1177/0098628313487456.

Hutchings, P. (2000). *Opening lines: Approaches to the Scholarship of Teaching and Learning.* Carnegie Publications, the Carnegie Foundation for the Advancement of Teaching.

Hong, P. Y. P., & Hodge, D. R. (2009). Understanding social justice in social work: A content analysis of course syllabi. *Families in Society, 90,* 212–219. https://doi.org/10.1606/1044-3894.3874.

Howell, A., & Tuitt, F. (2003). *Race and higher education: Rethinking pedagogy in diverse college classrooms.* Cambridge, MA: Harvard Educational Review.

Hunn, V. (2014). African American students, retention, and team-based learning: A review of the literature and recommendations for retention at predominately White institutions. *Journal of Black Studies, 45,* 301–314. http://www.jstor.org/stable/24572850.

Jay, J. K., & Johnson, K. L. (2002). Capturing complexity: A typology of reflective practice for teacher education. *Teaching and teacher education, 18*(1), 73–85. https://doi.org/10.1016/S0742-051X(01)00051-8.

Lee, C. T., Beckert, T. E., & Goodrich, T. R. (2010). The relationship between individualistic, collectivistic, and transitional cultural value orientations and adolescents' autonomy and identity status. *Journal of Youth and Adolescence, 39,* 882–893. https://doi.org/10.1007/s10964-009-9430-z.

Leong, F. T. L., Pickren, W. E., & Vasquez, M. J. T. (2017). APA efforts in promoting human rights and social justice. *American Psychologist, 72,* 778–790. https://doi.org/10.1037/amp0000220.

Luke, A., Woods, A., & Weir, K. (Eds.). (2013). *Curriculum, syllabus design, and equity: A primer and model.* New York, NY: Routledge.

McAuliff, K. E., Williams, S. M., & Ferrari, J. R. (2013). Social justice and the university community: Does campus involvement make a difference? *Journal of Prevention & Intervention in the Community, 41,* 244–254. https://doi-org.libproxy.lib.unc.edu/10.1080/10852352.2013.818486.

McCabe, P. C., & Rubinson, F. (2008). Committing to social justice: The behavioral intention of School Psychology and Education trainees to advocate for lesbian, gay, bisexual, and transgendered youth. *School Psychology Review, 37*, 469–486.

McClintock, C. G., & Allison, S. T. (1989). Social value orientation and helping behavior. *Journal of Applied Social Psychology, 19*, 353–362. https://doi.org/10.1111/j.1559-1816.1989.tb00060.x.

McGee, E., & Bentley, L. (2017). The equity ethic: Black and Latinx college students reengineering their STEM careers toward justice. *American Journal of Education, 124*, 1–36. https://www.journals.uchicago.edu/doi/abs/10.1086/693954.

Messick, D. M., & McClintock, C. G. (1968). Motivational bases of choice in experimental games. *Journal of Experimental Social Psychology, 4*, 1–25. https://doi.org/10.1016/0022-1031(68)90046-2.

Mitchell, T. D. (2007). Critical service-learning as social justice education: A case study of the citizen scholars program. *Equity & Excellence in Education, 40*, 101–112. https://doi.org/10.1080/10665680701228797.

Mitchell, T. D. (2014). How service-learning enacts social justice sensemaking. *Journal of Critical Thought and Praxis, 2*(2), 1–28. https://doi.org/10.31274/jctp-180810-22.

Mitchell, T. D., & Soria, K. M. (2016). Seeking social justice: Undergraduates' engagement in social change and social justice at American research universities. *Civic engagement and community service at research universities* (pp. 241–255). London, UK: Palgrave Macmillan.

Murphy, R. O., & Ackermann, K. A. (2014). Social value orientation: Theoretical and measurement issues in the study of social preferences. *Personality and Social Psychology Review, 18*, 13–41. https://doi.org/10.1177/1088868315501745.

Nagda, B. A., Spearmon, M. L., Holley, L. C., Harding, S., Moïse-Swanson, D., Balassone, M. L., et al. (1999). Intergroup dialogues: An innovative approach to teaching about diversity and justice in social work programs. *Journal of Social Work Education, 35*, 433–449. https://doi.org/10.1080/10437797.1999.10778980.

National Center for Education Statistics. (2019). Undergraduate and graduate degree fields. Status and trends in the education of racial and ethnic groups. Retrieve from https://nces.ed.gov/programs/raceindicators/indicator_REF.asp.

National Council for Behavioral Health. (2019). *Stigma regarding mental illness among people of color*. https://www.thenationalcouncil.org/BH365/2019/07/08/stigma-regarding-mental-illness-among-people-of-color/.

Nummedal, S. G., Benson, J. R., & Chew, S. I. (2002). Disciplinary styles in the scholarship of teaching and learning: A view from psychology. In M. T. Huber & S. R. Moreale (Eds.), *Disciplinary styles in the Scholarship of teaching and learning: Exploring common ground* (pp. 163–180). American Association for Higher Education.

O'Brien, J. G., Millis, B. J., & Cohen, M. C. (2008). *The course syllabus: A learning-centered approach* (2nd ed.). San Francisco, CA: Jossey-Bass.

Pieterse, A. L., Evans, S. A., Risner-Butner, A., Collins, N. M., & Mason, L. B. (2009). Multicultural competence and social justice training in counseling psychology and counselor education: A review and analysis of a sample of multicultural course syllabi. *The Counseling Psychologist, 37*, 93–115. https://doi.org/10.1177/0011000008319986.

Schlehofer, M. M., & Phillips, S. M. (2013). Teaching experientially in the undergraduate community psychology classroom. *Journal of Prevention and Intervention in the Community, 41*, 55–60. https://doi.org/10.1080/10852352.2013.757978.

Simons, L., Fehr, L., Blank, N., Connell, H., Georganas, D., Fernandez, D., & Peterson, V. (2012). Lessons learned from experiential learning: What do students learn from a practicum/internship? *International Journal of Teaching and Learning in Higher Education, 24*, 325–334. https://eric.ed.gov/?id=EJ1000685.

Soria, K. M., & Stebleton, M. (2013). Major decisions: Motivations for selecting a major, satisfaction, and belonging. *NACADA Journal, 33*, 29–43. https://doi.org/10.12930/NACADA-13-018.

Stearns, P. N. (2009). *Educating global citizens in college and universities: Challenges and opportunities.* New York, NY: Taylor & Francis.

Stoloff, M., McCarthy, M., Keller, L., Varfolomeeva, V., Lynch, J., Makara, K., ... Smiley, W. (2010). The undergraduate psychology major: An examination of structure and sequence. *Teaching of Psychology, 37*, 4–15. https://doi.org/10.1080/00986280903426274.

Thomas, E. F., Mavor, K. I., & McGarty, C. (2012). Social identities facilitate and encapsulate action-relevant constructs: A test of the social identity model of collective action. *Group Processes & Intergroup Relations, 15*, 75–88. https://doi.org/10.1177/1368430211413619.

Thrift, E., & Sugarman, J. (2019). What is social justice? Implications for psychology. *Journal of Theoretical and Philosophical Psychology, 39*, 1–17. https://doi.org/10.1037/teo0000097.

Torres-Harding, S. R., Siers, B., & Olson, B. D. (2012). Development and psychometric evaluation of the social justice scale (SJS). *American Journal of Community Psychology, 50*, 77–88. https://doi.org/10.1007/s10464-011-9478-2.

Torres-Harding, S. R., Steele, C., Schulz, E., Taha, F., & Pico, C. (2014). Student perceptions of social justice and social justice activities. *Education, Citizenship, and Social Justice, 9*, 55–66. https://doi.org/10.1177/1746197914520655.

U.S. Census Bureau. (2019). *Quick facts: United States.* https://www.census.gov/quickfacts/fact/table/US/PST045219.

Valencia, R. R. (2002). Mexican Americans don't value education! On the basis of myth, mythmaking, and debunking. *Journal of Latinos and Education, 1,* 81–103. https://doi.org/10.1207/S1532771XJE0102_2.

Van Zomeran, M., Postmes, T., & Spears, R. (2008). Toward an integrative social identity model of collective action: A quantitative research synthesis of three socio-psychological perspectives. *Psychological Bulletin, 134,* 504–535. https://doi.org/10.1037/0033-2909.134.4.504.

Vasquez, M. J. T. (2012). Psychology and social justice: Why we do what we do. *American Psychologist, 67*(5), 337–346. https://doi.org/10.1037/a0029232.

Walvoord, B. A. (2004). *Assessment clear and simple: A practical guide for institutions, departments, and general education.* San Francisco, CA: Jossey-Bass and Wiley.

Watkins, C., & Mortimore, P. (1999). Pedagogy: What do we know? In P. Mortimore (Ed.), *Understanding pedagogy: And its impact on learning* (pp. 1–7). Thousand Oaks, CA: Sage.

Wurdinger, S. D., & Carlson, J. A. (2010). *Teaching for experiential learning: Five approaches that work.* Lanham, MD: Rowman & Littlefield.

Zimmerman, L., Kamal, Z., & Hannah, K. (2013). Pedagogy of the logic model: Teaching undergraduates to work together to change their communities. *Journal of Prevention and Intervention in the Community, 41,* 121–127. https://doi.org/10.1080/10852352.2013.757990.

Recommended Readings

Christensen, L. (2017). *Reading, writing, and rising up: Teaching about social justice and the power of the written word.* Milwaukee, WI: Rethinking Schools.

Love, B. L. (2020). *We want to do more than survive: Abolitionist freedom and the pursuit of educational freedom.* Boston, MA: Beacon Press.

Watson, D., Hagopian, J., & Au, W. (2018). *Teaching for Black lives.* Milwaukee, WI: Rethinking Schools.

CHAPTER 4

Ecological Writing Processes to Promote Environmental and Social Consciousnesses

Erin Lord Kunz

Key definitions:

Ecocomposition, or ecological composition, was defined by Sidney Dobrin and Christian Weisser in 2002 as

> the study of the relationships between environments (and by that we mean natural, constructed, and even imagined places) and discourse (speaking, writing, and thinking). Ecocomposition draws from disciplines that study discourse (primarily composition, but also including literary studies, communication, cultural studies, linguistics, and philosophy) and merges their perspectives with work in disciplines that examine the environment (these include ecology, environmental studies, sociobiology, and other "hard" sciences). As a result, ecocomposition attempts to provide a holistic, encompassing framework for studies of the relationship between discourse and environment. (p. 572)

E. L. Kunz (✉)
Mayville State University, Mayville, ND, USA
e-mail: erin.kunz@mayvillestate.edu

C. C. Ozaki and L. Parson (eds.), *Teaching and Learning for Social Justice and Equity in Higher Education*,
https://doi.org/10.1007/978-3-030-69947-5_4

According to David Orr (2004), education is foundationally environmental. Instructors cannot teach and learn apart from the environments they are situated in, and therefore instructors must be able to understand these environments and see their educations as inextricably connected to the environment. The climate crisis of the twenty-first century further necessitates that educational structures teach students how to be environmental citizens so that students are able to respond to a changing natural world by utilizing the skills learned in the classroom. Instructors expect students to be literate in reading, mathematics, and history; additionally, they must insist that students are ecologically literate and able to live well in their respective ecological systems.

Ecological literacy does not only mean that students are aware of the natural ecosystem; it means that they are aware of their social ecosystems as well as how the environment is connected to race, class, and gender. By helping students understand the environment they are situated in, instructors are helping them understand how their environments are equitable to all people or how they or not, how their environments promote justice or how they fail to do so. It therefore follows that instructors cannot promote justice and equity among their students without infusing their various disciplines with ecological literacy.

This chapter will discuss how environmental and social consciousnesses can be implemented in an ecological composition, or ecocomposition, curriculum. Ecocomposition was defined by Sidney Dobrin and Christian Weisser in 2002 as, "the study of the relationships between environments (and by that we mean natural, constructed, and even imagined places) and discourse (speaking, writing, and thinking)" (p. 572). Creating a curriculum that examines this relationship between environment and discourse enhances a student's ability to understand how their work in a composition classroom is connected to the environment. I posit that a socially-minded ecocomposition curriculum can push students to see how social inequities manifest in various environments and how their writing, or discourse, can respond to social inequities in a more just manner. In this chapter I will outline how to establish an ecocomposition curriculum during each phase of the writing process: reading, invention, drafting and revising, and editing. By focusing on these aspects of the writing process in relation to ecocomposition, I hope to show how writing curriculums can promote more environmentally and socially just communities.

Ecological Reading in Process Pedagogy

Reading, or prewriting, is often considered the start of the writing process (Murray, 1972). This section will discuss how an ecocomposition program can utilize local contexts, Indigenous knowledge, and feminist critiques to support student reading and prewriting. Establishing these concepts can help support students to become critical readers, and by extension, more environmentally and socially aware citizens.

Reading for Local Contexts

Understanding both place, where one is literally situated, and space, how one moves through the world, helps instructors to understand students and helps students to understand their surroundings. According to Reynolds (2004), places cut across the diversity of a student body given that the individuals that make up a class share at least one place in common—the shared space of the composition classroom. Cultural identities influence how individuals move through and perceive these communal spaces, making shared places a useful experience in which to engage students and illuminate social issues in our world.

Often scholarship is employed without concern for the region in which it is happening, and this can result in institutions of higher education drastically underserving the communities in which they are situated (Owens, 2001). In order to allow the work of the university to influence what happens outside of the academy, there need to be opportunities to focus on the community. Students should be able to reflect on their lived experiences or the act of being in their places. According to Owens (2001), "throughout the curriculum we need to create opportunities for students to examine their immediate communities, since without heightened local awareness one cannot develop an understanding of sustainability" (p. 104). The goals of a sustainable curriculum cannot be achieved without engagement with local sustainability issues (Orr, 2004). To accomplish this engagement, the university curriculum often engages the local community through student service-learning projects that task students with the assignment of reaching out to a politician, nonprofit, or business in the community and composing for that particular writing situation. While these assignments may serve as examples of public writing for students, they are not designed to offer a nuanced understanding of place. Reynolds (2004) critiques modern service-learning practices as being too altruistic without enough critique of the ideologies that perpetuate social injustices in the first place. By having students read places, or research their local surroundings (their neighborhoods, jobs, dorms, commutes, etc.), students and instructors get better acquainted with the lived experiences of a place. By incorporating process-based practices, like peer review, students then read about each other's places, grow awareness of what it means to live in their local community, and see how what they are learning at the university is connected to how the community functions. This process helps them to be educated as whole persons (Orr, 2004).

Owens (2001) argues that if students do write for community projects, be that nonprofit or for-profit, the dialogue needs to be bi-directional. Often, written service-learning programs only work to serve the economic needs of the community and forgo the cultural analysis that was previously a part of the class reading and research practices (Owens, 2001). A sustainable ecocomposition program is framed through social-epistemology: a "method of discovering and even creating knowledge, frequently within socially defined discourse communities" (Berlin, 1987, p. 183). Through that lens reading and writing for places in the community will necessarily come with social, economic, political, and environmental critiques of entities in the community. As a result, if community sponsors are open to having students write for their concerns and demands, they also need to be open to dialoguing about academic critiques of place and space in order to create more just practices as a natural consequence of working with thoughtful university students. In other words, students should not practice critiquing social spaces in the classroom and then abandon these ideals the minute they begin composing for "real life" writing situations. There should be an ongoing conversation of how the local environment influences how the students— and the larger community—live, and how university work also influences the practices of the community.

Indigenous Knowledge

A crucial component for a writer to be successful in the process of writing is to understand the context in which they are writing. An ecocomposition program takes this rhetorical focus a step further by incorporating a social-epistemic framework, ecological design intelligence, and a land ethic (Berlin, 1996; Orr, 2004; Leopold, 1966). In other words, rhetorical context does not end with a sophist dedication to argumentation but to understanding context in order to create the most communicative, ethical message possible. As discussed in the last section, dialogue should be established in order to attain mutually beneficial communications between the university and the community.

Within an ecocomposition program, this means that students creating written projects must attend to local contexts and Indigenous knowledges. Many locations across the United States have rich Indigenous traditions that are often marginalized and should be recovered as a core piece of the context of those places. Examining the local traditions in these areas necessarily means exploring the Indigenous cultures, communities, knowledges, and historical trauma. According to Davey et al. (2006), Western educational systems have systematically ignored Indigenous knowledges and identities, reinforcing colonizing patterns of willful ignorance of local history, violence, and colonialism.

Snively and Corsiglia (2001) write that the way to resist Western hegemony is to recognize Traditional Ecological Knowledge (TEK), a knowledge that incorporates the historical knowledge of a place and its people who are impacted by relativist understandings of an area. Much of the ecological crisis has been caused by ignoring TEK and uncritically embracing Western modern science (WMS), a science that is sustained by economic growth and white capitalist patriarchy (Snively & Corsiglia, 2001; hooks, 1984). TEK resists capitalistic interpretations of progress and provides a basic understanding of sustainable living in a place, an understanding that synthesizes hundreds and even thousands of years of stories and lessons about living in a particular location.

Because ecocomposition focuses on making education a sustainable contribution to the betterment of our environment, it follows that local Indigenous knowledges should be examined within the curriculum so that diverse groups in a place are not further marginalized by silence and ignorance (Orr, 2004). A question that takes into consideration these concerns within an ecocomposition program might be as follows: how can students understand the writing process as an awareness of local, Indigenous knowledges as they write for local and global concerns in an ecologically responsible way? Composition students should feel confident that they understand local and Indigenous needs as they write and that their words convey multicultural awareness, inclusiveness, and a commitment to Indigenous needs. It is the responsibility of an ecocomposition program to give students the tools and exposure to Indigenous knowledges so that by the time they leave the classroom, they have a basic awareness of the history of their community so they can communicate in a way that is both non-offensive and ethically committed. If instructors are not educating students to respond to the needs of their local environments, they are failing them and ceasing to make the university relevant (Orr, 2004).

The concrete inclusion of Indigenous knowledges means reading and analysis of Indigenous concerns. On a macro level, this could mean exposing students to basic Indigenous histories, such as those illustrated in documentaries like *The Canary Effect*, and then having students reflect and respond in writing to how American history is constructed and who has the power to construct that history. Then, when students have to think/write about these matters in their personal and professional lives, they will have the appropriate exposure to Indigenous concerns so they can communicate responsibly in various rhetorical situations. Students can then move to the local level, and, after receiving basic information about local Indigenous tribes and reservations, respond in culturally-aware prose to the issues important to Indigenous communities. Finally, by incorporating TEK into an ecocomposition curriculum, students are naturally exposed to perspectives that illustrate how knowledge and education can be useful outside of sole economic gain but also in order to be ecologically responsible.

Feminist Critiques

Cooper (1986) posits that ecological writing is a web of social activity that cannot only be described but should be analyzed and even amended. In an ecocomposition program with a social-epistemic framework, reading assignments should be interpreted and grappled with. Students should not be passive, but instead see how writing comprises a variety of constructed knowledges that are socially situated and available for critique (Cooper, 1986). This type of critical reading establishes that the process of writing begins with close reading and that one's responses to arguments and ideas are bound up in an ongoing conversation.

Feminist ecological critiques, like Indigenous critiques, are crucial in order to analyze how power is distributed within writing systems and environmental systems. Ecocomposition draws from many disciplines and methodologies in order to study the relationship between discourse and environment, which is similar to the goal of ecological feminism (Dobrin & Weisser, 2002; Warren & Cheney, 1991). Warren and Cheney (1991) concentrate on the intersection between ecology and feminism, which focuses on environmental systems of domination. The authors advocate for a worldview that gives voice to disadvantaged populations and resists destructive socioeconomics. Similarly, Schneiderman (2011) explains that the agenda of feminists to overcome oppression for disadvantaged populations intertwines with environmental injustice. Oftentimes places of serious environmental degradation are places where people are marginalized in other ways and are disenfranchised from political processes. Gender, race, class, and environment overlap and must be examined in relationship to each other (Schneiderman, 2011, p. 126). In other words, the goals of feminism to critique dominant systems of power pairs with the ecological goal of understanding how systems function. Ecocomposition furthers this examination within the framework of power distribution in written systems, in which writers who lack the education, writing skills, or social capital to enter a dominant discourse (such as academia) continue to see their concerns marginalized or not taken seriously.

The inclusion of ecological feminism in an ecocomposition program is not simply a thematic choice but a perspective that situates readers in a way that makes them aware of power dynamics in writing and illuminates how rhetoric is used to promote justice or injustice. By examining places, students will necessarily investigate who has access to resources, who has the power to determine resources, and how these power dynamics can be altered (Reynolds, 2004). Rhetorical awareness is key in educating composition students, and an ecocomposition program can incorporate rhetorical ecological feminist agency as a key component in the curriculum (Ryan, 2012). Rhetorical ecological feminist agency "values experiential knowledge alongside disciplinary knowledge and recognizes that place and situation constitute knowledge" (Ryan, 2012, p. 80). Like Indigenous knowledge, rhetorical ecological feminist agency sees intrinsic worth in relativist, local knowledges that resist the homogeneity of WMS. Students and faculty have experiential knowledge of their places, and this knowledge should be valued alongside disciplinary knowledge.

By focusing on gender within an ecocomposition program, students become exposed to a variety of viewpoints and start critiquing social norms—the universal "he" as a pronoun, for example. While these written critiques seem small, they help students become more epistemically responsible (Ryan, 2012). Ryan uses the term "epistemic responsibility" to describe the responsibility to examine what one knows and identify where that knowledge comes from. Epistemic responsibility illustrates a continuance of Berlin's (1996) social-epistemic composition pedagogy; writers must understand the context and the constructed nature of their knowledge and apply that knowledge ethically. When reading Indigenous and feminist texts, students should be made aware of the way discourse functions in society and their responsibility to produce, alter, or resist discourse in a way that resonates with an understanding of ecological design intelligence (Orr, 2004). From the perspective of an ecocomposition program, students should know how their knowledge about places and environment is constructed and be able to apply their experiential knowledges in their personal and professional lives in a way that is environmentally ethical. Ecofeminism pairs with these goals by providing students with a way to critique gender issues in the process of writing their projects.

To summarize the needs of reading within an ecocomposition writing process, there are several features that need to be present. First, instructors should include texts that will promote active conversation about ecological concerns, not just from the perspective of environmental themes, but also that promote a social-epistemic awareness that is holistic and interdisciplinary. Along with this curricular design, students should have the opportunity to use their own experiences and knowledge to examine their local places in order to share their understandings with other students and to come to better awareness of what makes a place sustainable or not. Finally, students should be given the opportunity to develop the tools needed to analyze, critique, and resist discourse as appropriate to their lived experiences, identities, and cultures. This means explicitly including an emphasis on both Indigenous knowledges and feminist critiques in order to continue to promote a holistic understanding of discourse and socially conscious reading skills. By establishing ecological reading practices as part of the writing process, students can begin to understand their writing projects as being part of the social web of written discourse (Cooper, 1986).

Ecological Invention in Process Pedagogy

This section will create a bridge between reading in the writing process and invention in the writing process. Linking invention to ecocomposition, I will discuss the need for kinesthetic movement and the outdoor environment when exploring ideas and creating arguments for papers. Though the writing process is recursive and does not need to be completed in the linear order described here, I maintain that it is helpful for students to at least articulate a writing process so they can meld components of it to their needs and experiences.

Kinesthetic Movement and Outdoor Environments

The importance of kinesthetic movement in writing is related to good reading/analysis, invention, and wellness in general. Reynolds (2004) explores different ways of moving through spaces with the image of the "flaneur," who "embodies the spatial practices of walking as writing, writing as walking; his main focus is to absorb and render the city through writing" (p. 70). This concept is useful in thinking about how composition students can learn descriptive techniques and understand writing as a movement. When students become part of the conversation through reading and writing, they often think of metaphorically moving through texts and ideas and arriving at conclusions. Reynolds (2004) shows how it is also possible to literally move through places in order to arrive at conclusions. By actually going to places that are included in written arguments, moving between texts and physical places, students begin to examine the intersection between discourse and environment by using one to further understand the other (Dobrin & Weisser, 2002). A place could potentially inform a paper topic, while a text about a place could further inform the socio-historical features of that place. Students then must negotiate between the two in order to see how discourse is shaped by geography and in what ways geography can better inform discourse.

Many university instructors are beginning to insist on assignments that have students investigating outdoor environments in order to draw a closer connection between discourse and nature (Reynolds, 2004; Lucksinger, 2014). Alongside including kinesthetic movement in the curriculum, an ecocomposition program should predictably include opportunities for students to get outside of the four walls of the classroom. Moving outside and through communities helps students understand that their writing is not only meant for the privileged space of the university but that writing can also be a way to engage in issues of justice and equity in their communities. Nabhan (1994) argues that formal education can stifle the development of ecological knowledge, and therefore socio-cultural knowledge, when students do not get the opportunity to actually investigate their surroundings.

This engagement with the outdoors can be—and some would argue should be—an enjoyable experience (Sobel, 1997). Enjoyment is an important feature of ecological education and the lack of it a serious concern for ecological educators. Sobel (1997) argues that part of the ecological crisis is caused by too much indoor time in school, combined with apocalyptic rhetoric about the environment, which results in "ecophobia." Students need time to explore their local surroundings in order to grow an affinity for them, and, in turn, so they want to protect the places in which they live. The list of the problems attached to the current ecological crisis can be overwhelming, but we have no choice other than to look to the future, try to reverse the damage, and try to reestablish a human connection with nature (Owens, 2001). Gruenewald (2003) advocates for decolonization, ceasing to exploit the environment, and reinhabitation, or reconnecting with the environment. The structure of the classroom on Indigenous lands is inherently colonial, and the current capitalist, merit-based structure of schooling is inherently patriarchal. By allowing the class the freedom of the outdoors, instructors can cease to contribute to ecophobia and in a radical way teach resistance to the typical failures of education. Through ecocomposition, instructors disrupt what Orr (2004) describes as the business of education, which prepares students for the global economy without concern for environmental ethics.

By reconnecting with movement and the outdoors, ecological education becomes incorporated into the curriculum and gives students a tangible way to think about the writing process, to think about invention. Instead of assigning vague brainstorming activities, or worse—not addressing invention at all—students will have the opportunity to test ideas about their written arguments, geographical autobiographies, place-descriptions, etc., by actually moving among those places. If an ecocomposition program is truly committed to socially just and equitable education, it follows that students should be literally moving through their communities to learn about the social features of said communities.

Ecological Drafting and Revising in Process Pedagogy

Allowing students to draft freely, with guidance and little pressure of assessment, helps them to develop ideas without fear of making mistakes. Drafting avoids stifling student creativity by giving them the opportunity to work and think through the writing process (Murray, 1972). Within an ecocomposition program, drafting and revision would follow many of the usual standards of composition programs, given that drafting inherently captures the holistic and social nature of writing. Multiple drafts, peer reviews, and student-instructor conferences are all useful strategies that are foundational to the process movement.

One benefit of having students submit multiple drafts before the final assessment is to give them an opportunity to rework their ideas and retrace their steps. If students are writing about a specific location, going there on repeated occasions and revisiting their drafts helps to illuminate how perspectives can change, and how a place can be impacted by other people, political decisions, economics, etc. As students negotiate the space between discourse and environment, they will have multiple opportunities to reflect on how their discourse is representing the environment and how reoccurring visits to a place shape the way one articulates that place. Not only does this type of drafting typically produce more thoughtful papers, but it also reinforces the idea that education is a holistic process that links the student to their own writing needs and the needs of the community at large.

Another crucial component to revision is feedback from one's peers. A guided peer review process is an opportunity to address student writing from an ecological perspective. While the readings, assignment prompts, and guidance during invention will establish an ecological framework for a class, it is possible that students complete these assignments without critically addressing the social-epistemic features of their work. Using drafting and revision to intervene at the right moments helps students to see their work from this critical light. By having peers assess one another's work from the perspective of social-epistemic ecocomposition, students will have to consider the intersection between discourse and environment. A main goal of the revision process should be to have students grapple with how place functions within a story, narrative, or prose (Lucksinger, 2014). Examples of questions that can guide students in peer review are as follows:

- In what ways does this paper address ecological concerns?
- How is the environment addressed in this paper, and from what perspective (conservationist, economic, Indigenous, etc.)?
- Who gets to control how spaces function in the prose? What stakeholders are interested in the space?

- Would you articulate spaces differently than what is in the paper? Why or why not?
- How is the prose organized, and how does the organization impact how the reader interprets the space?
- Where can the writer elaborate more, with either sensory description or sources? Do any of the descriptions require more thorough research?
- How is this place limited by the way it is discussed? Or, how is this place accessible according to the perspective people have of it? What type of rhetoric is used to describe it?
- What, ultimately, is the argument of this piece? What are the ecological ramifications of such an argument?
- What was your understanding of this place before reading this paper? How has that understanding changed? Will your behavior change as a result of this new understanding?

The responses to these questions contribute to the writing process in two main ways: first, the writer receives feedback on his or her work and can revise accordingly, and two, the reader has to reflect on the writer's perspective of the intersection between discourse and environment. By seeing one perspective of this intersection, and offering feedback that can shape the discourse, students can see the social-epistemic nature of writing and how multiple stakeholders are involved in creating knowledges.

Another key strategy in the revision process is instructor-student conferences. These individualized sessions help students revise from their point of understanding and within their unique paper. This is a crucial component of an ecocomposition program because it offers the most localized type of education possible. Just as one does when visiting a new place, when writing in a new and difficult genre, one can also look for familiar signs to make one's way (Reynolds, 2004). With a helpful travel guide, a writer can still follow their course but with the tools and knowledge of someone who has tread the same path before. This is the function of a travel guide and a writing instructor. Students determine their arguments and their writing goals, but instructors can help them shape those arguments and goals by pointing out familiar signs in order to help them make their way through organization, elaboration, revising, and brainstorming. Travel guides have the social capital to help travelers make sense of a place, and instructors have the genre knowledge to help writers make sense of discourse.

The instructor-student conference also functions as a way to engage in the writing process while developing more ethical relationships in higher education (Murray, 1972). Often conferences are when instructors really get to learn about the student's interests, goals, and desires, but also the things that may be impeding their education such as family issues, financial concerns, or roommate problems. While some may take the position that these issues, positive or negative, are not the professor's concern, an ecological approach to writing understands all of these concerns as pieces of the web that affect the whole; one change reverberates through and changes the makeup of the web (Cooper, 1986). Empathizing with students through their writing and education process is not simply a moral choice made by a nice instructor; it is the core of what it means to teach whole persons, within communities, in a holistic way, from an ecological perspective. By modeling what it looks like to be sincerely concerned about various components of a student's life, rather than just a narrow vision of meritocratic academic success, students are also educated about how their schooling, choices, and behavior affects other people, the community, and the environment.

Ecological Editing in Process Pedagogy

Teaching editing, or grammar, is the final piece in the process of an ecocomposition program. When I use the term editing, I am referring to surface-level errors, mechanical or grammatical, that are noticeable or distracting but do not impede in understanding the student's message. For students, editing is often seen as their Achilles' heel, the thing that will prevent them from being taken seriously or turning in a good paper. It is a reality that students, stakeholders outside of academia, and even professors within academia put great emphasis on thorough editing.

According to Murray (1972), editing instruction should come at the end of the writing process in order to give students the opportunity to try out ideas without the fear of mechanical errors. Hartwell (1985) argues that grammar instruction does not help, and can actually inhibit, the development of writing skills. Therefore composition programs have often taken the foundational approach, based on these findings, to embrace drafting and save editing instruction for the end of the process.

Within the framework of a social-epistemic ecocomposition program, the goal of editing instruction would be to help students understand the expectations of local discourses and ecologies. In other words, grammar instruction is not taught as objective knowledge, but as the subjective privileging of particular ways of speaking and writing that are connected to class, gender, race, and geography. The teaching comes in at particular moments in the classroom that are appropriate for the particular concern, rather than as a warning to the class that creates a dynamic of fear about lower-order writing issues.

An example of how to teach a grammatical issue is based on need and geography. A common geographical, grammatical inconsistency I see in North Dakotan vernacular is to say "I seen" rather than the standard "I saw." Rather than lecturing on past tense verbs before students have even begun writing, pointing out the inconsistency in context can be more helpful (Hartwell, 1985). Discussing how the reader then interprets the writing when there is an inconsistency like this (are they seen as less educated? do people take their ideas less seriously? are they seen as less professional?) helps writers see how editing issues are connected to social context and are not simply an objective issue. It may even be appropriate to suggest times when you could purposefully say "I seen" instead of "I saw," maybe in creative writing or with a sense of irony, if it is appropriate in a given rhetorical context. It is also useful to analyze local speeches and prose pieces to see in what ways speakers and writers purposefully include local vernacular, whether that is slang, grammatical errors, local sayings, or local stories.

Establishing this form of editing instruction not only provides a basic education in grammar; it provides an understanding of the social, constructed nature of discourse and how discourse is linked to sociological issues. These seemingly lower-order writing concerns can then lead to higher-order writing conversations, such as writing with the universal masculine pronoun, or the basis for political correctness, or the argument for teaching local vernaculars. By showing how editing issues are related to the privileging of certain discourses, students may actually care about editing issues even more than they did previously, without the need for overt editing instruction. Finally, this type of editing instruction further promotes equitable relationships between instructor and student, establishing that the goal of education is not to mark every mistake a student makes but to help them grow in a holistic, purposeful understanding of the writing process.

An Ecological, Recursive Process

Though composition programs do their best to define the goals and outcomes of writing education and to provide pedagogical strategies to accomplish these outcomes, the reality is that each semester and class is going to be markedly different from the other, given the uniqueness of the individual needs and diversity across the student body. Rather than seeing this diversity and change as problematic, and trying to create objective measures to assess a subjective process like writing, an ecocomposition program embraces the fact that localized education is necessary within the context of a community. The dynamic between the instructor and class will always be changing, and this is a metaphor for ecological systems inside and outside the classroom.

This articulation of a writing process in an ecocomposition program attempts to offer students and faculty tangible strategies to teach writing that do not refute that writing is recursive and fluid. By articulating invention and linking it to kinesthetic movement and the outdoors, students have a way of thinking about brainstorming; they have something they can actually do to begin to invent. By thinking about reading and editing within the framework of social-epistemic rhetoric, with Indigenous and feminist critiques in mind, students have a goal at these points in the process; they know what to look for and what to do. Analysis of readings and the shaping of a writing project cease to be mysterious because they have been instructed in actionable ways about how to begin writing and how to revise writing within a socially responsible context. By simply maintaining that this process is changeable and flexible (you can edit while you draft and you can reread while you edit!), composition instructors can be helpful travel guides through the writing process without taking over a student's journey.

Conclusion

College composition can be, and should be, tailored to help students develop a social-epistemic framework, or the ability to understand the origins of their knowledge and how their discourse shapes the world (Berlin, 1987). In the twenty-first century, it is crucial that instructors understand how their academic projects and the university system can contribute to or detract from ecological and social justice based on the assignments they teach and the way they structure their classrooms. An ecological writing process not only helps prepare students for academic writing demands but also critiques the world they are situated in to make positive environmental and social change.

APPENDIX A

Writing Assignment 1: Geographical Autobiography

In this course, we've been discussing concepts such as environmental writing, the flaneur, sense of place, place-based education, critical pedagogy, reinhabitation, and land ethics. For this paper, I'd like you to investigate these concepts from a personal perspective. In what ways can you absorb your environment? How has place influenced the way you understand yourself? How can you understand the way your geographical background has influenced your perspective on the world?

You will write a 5–7 page geographical autobiography in which you detail your background, childhood, and memories from the vantage point of geography. Questions you might ask yourself are as follows:

- Where have I lived and traveled, and how have those places impacted how I see the world?
- How have the social, religious, economic, political, racial, environmental, and—especially—geographical aspects of your upbringing influenced you?
- How might your understanding of self be different if you were born in another part of the world, to another family, with a different religion and/or economic class?
- What are some of your best memories of your personal geographies? What are some of the worst memories of your personal geographies?
- How do landscapes, environment, and ecologies mirror your personality or identity? For example, does growing up on an isolated prairie make you more introverted? Does growing up in a bustling city make you more extroverted?

You will be graded according to the following questions:

- Does the author write a geographical autobiography that focuses on a hybrid of her personal story and the geography from which that story emerges?
- Does the author write the geographical autobiography with thoughtful details, smooth transitions, and rhetorically appealing organization?
- Is the writing and project organization professional in structure and free of grammatical/mechanical error? Is intellectual property appropriately accounted for through documentation standards?

Writing Assignment 2: Community Engagement Project

This writing project involves extensive research in which you will actively engage in your community. You will choose an issue, organization, or place in the city that is important to you and you will engage with that choice over the course of the semester. You could, for example, choose to research recycling options in the city or services for domestic abuse victims. If you are actively involved in a church or nonprofit, you could decide to make that organization your focus of study. Perhaps you're drawn to particular places in the city—a park, a basketball court, or a derelict neighborhood; you could concentrate your efforts there. Whatever seems most compelling to you is a good place to start your work. You will be engaging with it all semester, so it should be something important to you.

Before you begin working with your issue, organization, or place, be sure that you have permission to begin this project with the stakeholders connected to your focus of study, and that they have a full understanding of what the project entails. You will begin the project by researching your focus of study, using both primary and secondary sources:

- What is the issue, organization, or place you are researching? What is its history, and who currently interacts with it?
- How has your focus of study impacted the city? Who has it impacted?
- Walk around your organization or place, or to the different locations your issue most impacts in the city. What do you see? How is it situated in the city? What are the current conditions?
- Talk to people associated with your focus of study. What have been their experiences? What positives and negatives do they see? (Be

sure to record responses accurately and be transparent with any participants about how you're using the information they give you.)

Next, you will begin writing an investigative proposal for your focus of study, detailing its history, impacts, goals, and needs within the city. This part of the project will be entirely unique to each student depending on their focus of study. Be thorough, using both primary and secondary sources, and write a detailed account of your issue, organization, or place. This part of the project should be between 4 and 6 pages.

Now consider the goals and needs of your focus of study, paying attention to how they might impact the community:

- How does your focus of study serve the community well? What positive impacts do they have? How might they continue the practices that seem beneficial to the city?
- Are the goals and needs of your focus of study beneficial to everyone in the community? If not, why? Who does your focus of study serve? Does it harm anyone?
- How could the issue, organization, or place you are studying be more inclusive for diverse sets of people? What language might they use to improve inclusion?
- How could the issue, organization, or place you're studying be more sustainable in the environment it is situated? What language might they use to improve sustainability?
- What concluding remarks or insights can you offer your focus of study?

This part of the proposal should follow a typical proposal format. Be sure to provide a thorough discussion of what you discovered during the investigation phase and why it is relevant today. Consider your language, vocabulary, and tone when writing recommendations and be sure to remain respectful to all potential stakeholders of your project. This section should be 2–4 pages.

You will be graded according to the following questions:

- Does the project choose a suitable focus of study that is thoroughly researched?

- Does the writer use both primary and secondary sources, detailed descriptions, and personal encounters to write the investigative proposal?
- Do the recommendations focus on all members of the community, considering the needs of different ethnic, gender, and socioeconomic identities?
- Do the recommendations refer to issues of sustainability, understanding how the focus of study operates within the local context of the community?
- Is the writer sensitive to language and tone, making an effort to be simultaneously clear, direct, and thoughtful?
- Is the writing and project organization professional in structure and free of grammatical/mechanical error? Is intellectual property appropriately accounted for through documentation standards?

References

Berlin, J. (1987). *Rhetoric and reality: Writing instruction in American colleges, 1900–1985.* Southern Illinois University Press.

Berlin, J. (1996). *Rhetorics, poetics, and cultures: Refiguring college English studies.* Urbana, IL: NCTE.

Cooper, M. M. (1986). The ecology of writing. *College English, 48*(4), 364–375.

Davey, R., Shanks, J., Stewart, D. A., Thunder Woman, Y. (Producers), Davey, R., & Thunder Woman, Y. (Directors). (2006). *The canary effect* [Motion Picture]. Available https://www.youtube.com/watch?v=lD7x6jryoSA.

Dobrin, S. I., & Weisser, C. R. (2002). Breaking ground in ecocomposition: Exploring relationships between discourse and environment. *College English, 64*(5), 566–589.

Gruenewald, D. (2003). Foundations of place: A multidisciplinary framework for place-conscious education. *American Education Research Journal, 40*(9).

Hartwell, P. (1985, February). Grammar, grammars, and the teaching of grammar. *College English, 47*(2), 105–127. http://www.jstor.org/stable/376 562?origin=JSTOR-pdf.

hooks, b. (1984). *Feminist theory: From margin to center.* Boston, MA: South End Press.

Leopold, A. (1966). *A sand county almanac.* New York, NY: Oxford University Press.

Lucksinger, A. S. (2014). Ecopedagogy: Cultivating environmental consciousness through sense of place in literature. *Ecopedagogy, 14*(2), 335–369.

Murray, M. (1972). Teach writing as a process not product. In V. Villanueva & K. L. Arola (Eds.), *Cross-talk in comp theory: A reader* (3rd ed., pp. 3–6). NCTE.

Nabhan, G. P. (1994). Children in touch, creatures in story. In G. P. Nabhan & S. Trimble (Eds.), *The geography of childhood: Why children need wild places* (pp. 79–107). Beacon Press.

Orr, D. (2004). *Earth in mind: On education, environment, and the human prospect*. Island Press.

Owens, D. (2001). *Composition and sustainability*. National Council of Teachers of English.

Reynolds, N. (2004). *Geographies of writing: Inhabiting places and encountering difference*. Southern Illinois University Press.

Ryan, K. J. (2012). Thinking ecologically: Rhetorical ecological feminist agency and writing program administration. *Journal of the Council of Writing Program Administrators, 36*(1), 74–94.

Schneiderman, J. (2011). The common interests of earth science, feminism, and environmental justice. *NWSA Journal, 9*(2), 124–127.

Snively, G., & Corsiglia, J. (2001). Discovering indigenous science: Implications for science education. *Science Education, 85*, 6–34.

Sobel, D. (1997). Sense of place education for the elementary years. In *Coming home: Developing a sense of place in our communities and schools. Proceedings of the 1997 forum*. http://files.eric.ed.gov/fulltext/ED421312.pdf.

Warren, K. J., & Cheney, J. (1991). Ecological feminism and ecosystem ecology. *Hypatia, 6*(1), 179–197.

Suggestions for Further Reading

Coe, R. M. (1975). Eco-logic for the composition classroom. *College Composition and Communication, 26*(3). Retrieved from Dobrin, S. I., & Weisser, C. R. (2002b). *Natural discourse*. State University of New York Press.

Duncan, D. J. (2001). Spirit-fried no-name river brown trout: A recipe. In *My story as told by water* (pp. 273–282). Sierra Club Books.

Edbauer, J. (2005). Unframing models of public distribution: From rhetorical situation to rhetorical ecologies. *Rhetoric Society Quarterly, 35*, 4.

Ede, L. (2004). *Situating composition: Composition studies and the politics of location*. Southern Illinois University Press.

Garrard, G. (2007). Ecocritcism and education for sustainability. *Pedagogy, 7*(3), 619–654.

Glotfelty, C., & Fromm, H. (1996). Introduction: Literary studies in an age of environmental crisis. In *The ecocriticism reader: Landmarks in literary ecology*. The University of Georgia Press.

Gruenewald, D. (2006). Resistance, reinhabitation, and regime change. *Journal of Research in Rural Education, 21*(9).

Reiff, M. J., Bawarshi, A., Ballif, M., & Weisser, C. (Eds.). (2015). *Ecologies of writing programs*. Parlor Press.

Ryden, K. C. (1993). *Mapping the invisible landscape: Folklore, writing, and the sense of place*. University of Iowa Press.

Shepley, N. (2013). Rhetorical-ecological links in composition history. *Enculturation: A Journal of Rhetoric, Writing, and Culture*. http://enculturation.net/rhetorical-ecological-links.

Weisser, C. R. & Dobrin, S. I. (2001). *Ecocomposition: Theoretical and pedagogical approaches*. State University of New York Press.

CHAPTER 5

Incorporating Culturally Relevant Education (CRE) in STEM Gateway Courses

Caitlin A. Hamstra, Frim Ampaw, and Anne M. Hornak

KEY TERMS AND DEFINITIONS

Critical pedagogy	This is an approach to teaching that embodies the tenets of critical theory and criticality. Critical pedagogy is underscored by the idea of addressing issues of domination in knowledge construction, with the idea of challenging that domination.
Culturally relevant education	This approach to teaching and learning encompasses critical pedagogy, culturally relevant pedagogy,

C. A. Hamstra
O'Gorman High School, Sioux Falls, SD, USA

F. Ampaw (✉) · A. M. Hornak
Central Michigan University, Mount Pleasant, MI, USA
e-mail: ampaw1fd@cmich.edu

	and culturally responsive teaching. This is about naming power differentials and working to deconstruct those power imbalances in the classroom.
Culturally relevant pedagogy	This type of pedagogy is grounding the learning experience in the relevant identities and cultures students bring to the classroom. The approach is reframing a culturally neutral curriculum to culturally relevant.
Culturally responsive teaching	This approach to teaching and learning is about creating classroom spaces that are ground in the learners' lived experiences. Creating these opportunities includes taking into account the cultural frames that students have experienced and creating a curriculum and activities that are inclusive of those cultures.
STEM gateway courses	These courses are typically defined as first- and second-year courses that are pre-requisites for higher-level coursework. They tend to be high enrollment and foundational to continuing in STEM fields.

Numerous national reports have indicated pedagogical shortcomings regarding undergraduate courses in the Science, Technology, Engineering, and Mathematics (STEM) fields (American Association of Physics Teachers, 1996; Steen, 1987). These reports found that course sizes are often too large, taught by graduate teaching assistants, lacking in active engagement during sessions, and deficient in the use of a culturally inclusive curriculum. To improve undergraduate STEM education, the National Science Foundation created the Center for the Integration of Research, Teaching, and Learning, which provides guidelines for STEM undergraduate education. However, the focus in addressing these STEM education problems has been on active engagement, learning communities, and broadening the participation of diverse individuals, with minimal attention paid to the inclusion of a culturally responsive curriculum (National Science Foundation Center for the Integration of Research, Teaching, and Learning, 1996).

In this chapter, we will synthesize the literature related to culturally relevant education (CRE) and discuss how this applies to the teaching of STEM gateway courses. We will then develop a framework for use in the design of culturally responsive teaching with STEM education. Finally, the chapter will conclude with specific recommendations for the design and implementation of CRE in STEM gateway courses. Within the recommendations, we include a questionnaire for faculty to use as a template for assembling ongoing teams or research groups.

Culturally Relevant Education

CRE encompasses critical pedagogy (Freire, 2005), culturally relevant pedagogy (Ladson-Billings, 1995), and culturally responsive teaching (Gay, 2002, 2010). Critical pedagogy centers on creating learning spaces for awakening to occur. This happens by deconstructing the norms of power in the classroom and the privileged positions with which learners arrive (e.g., race, class, gender, sexual orientation, religion, nationality, and language) (Darder, 2003). Culturally relevant pedagogy focuses on "...empower[ing] students intellectually, socially, emotionally, and politically by using cultural [grounding] to impart knowledge, skills, and attitudes" (Ladson-Billings, 1994, pp. 17–18). This particular pedagogy focuses on the curriculum and the structure of a course and whether these decisions are centered around instructor knowledge and preference or reflective of the various identities within the classroom. Culturally responsive teaching centers the practices of affirmation, validation, personalization, and rapport building as central tenets in the learning process (Hammond, 2015). Teaching aspects here focus on how an instructor frames the instruction and assessment of learning within a course. Together, these three components make up the framework for CRE, which Kotluk and Kocakaya (2018) define as "a pedagogy aimed at educating students in terms of intellectual, social, emotional, critical and democratic competence, considering the cultural values and references that affect the knowledge, skills, and attitudes of students" (p. 100).

Calls to reform STEM courses for improved and more equitable outcomes are plentiful, particularly for gateway courses. We propose that

CRE is a pedagogical approach critical to address the inequities and changes needed for effective reform.

STEM GATEWAY COURSES

Typically, gateway courses are foundational, high-enrollment, and high-risk classes that students usually take in the first two years of their college careers (Koch & Rodier, 2014). These classes are considered high risk because students tend to withdraw or fail the courses at a higher rate than other courses at the same level. Additionally, for STEM majors, these courses serve as access points to advancing within the field. STEM gateway courses tend to be more high-risk than entry-level courses in other fields because they require students to earn higher than a passing grade in order to major in that field. As a result, these courses have been identified as a barrier to secondary admission into many STEM-related fields (Cohen & Kelly, 2018; Gasiewski et al., 2012).

Furthermore, gateway STEM courses often go beyond the pre-requisites for STEM majors, serving as required general education courses for other majors. Due to the foundational nature of these courses, the curriculum is often dense and focused on introducing students to the essential principles of the field. In turn, faculty members who teach these courses sacrifice pedagogy in order to ensure coverage of the material. Because of these factors, gateway courses, in general, have been cited as barriers for at-risk students, which often includes underprepared students, students with minoritized identities, female students, and first-generation students (Weddle-West & Bingham, 2010).

The low success rates in these courses have been ascribed to a lack of engaging pedagogy and the competitive environment created by instructors who grade on a curve (Handelsman et al., 2004; Seymour & Hewitt, 1997). Because the focus tends to be on delivering content, the conventional method for teaching has depended on lecture and faculty transmission. Faculty often come to class, lecture for the majority of the session, and then assess using forced-choice tests and exams. However, success in STEM gateway courses should be about scientific thinking abilities and their capability to apply content knowledge (Conley, 2005). A more student-centered approach to STEM education would mean providing students with the opportunity to reflect on their learning, ask questions for both clarity and understanding, and actively engage in the co-construction of knowledge (Borrego et al., 2010). In recognition of these concerns, the US Department of Education and higher education institutions, hoping to increase participation and diversify the STEM workforce, have focused on improving STEM gateway courses (Lewis et al., 2009).

Reforms related to STEM gateway courses in the last twenty-five years have primarily focused on active learning, student engagement, and delivery method. Fairweather (2008) posited three objectives in the efforts to improve student learning in STEM courses: improving teaching, student learning, and student learning productivity. This quest has led to the proliferation of active learning classrooms and flipped classrooms. The literature written about these reforms shows some limited success in improving outcomes for all students, but without promising results for students with underrepresented identities (Triesman, 1985). Another major reform is the idea of using small cooperative groups that will study together both inside and outside the classroom (Fairweather, 2008). This idea has shown limited success for students with underrepresented minorities. This is partly due to the lack of intentionality regarding the choices in the leadership and formation of the groups. There have been reforms at the national, disciplinary, institutional, and even department level that have made an incremental change in student success, but no major shifts. This further reinforces the need for a paradigm shift to more criticality in design, implementation, and assessment.

Gateway courses have come under significant pressure for reform, and STEM gateway courses have become significant barriers for students who wish to continue in the field (Seymour & Hewitt, 1997). A more student-centered approach would improve the success rates of higher-risk students. The success of these students is critical, as a multicultural workforce is essential for engagement in a global world, and, in turn, it is critical to have diverse STEM-educated professionals.

THE NEED FOR CRITICAL PEDAGOGY

To improve the success rates of students with underrepresented identities, critical pedagogy must be implemented in STEM gateway classes. Critical pedagogy is the application of critical theory in the classroom. Its major tenet is the understanding that knowledge, and the construction of knowledge, are not, and cannot be, politically neutral (Freire, 2005). By default, education is "structured around historical and contemporary legacies of inequality" (Kincheloe & McLaren, 2011, p. 300). Therefore, the task of engaging in critical pedagogy is to actively identify ways that systems of power simultaneously privilege certain learners and oppress others (Freire, 2005). Thus, the major thrust of critical pedagogy is to design classroom spaces that are challenging to our society. Teaching from a critical pedagogy perspective involves using critical reflections and critical actions to create opportunities for students to deconstruct the idea of normal, which is constructed around privilege and power (Darder, 2003).

The inclusion of critical pedagogy in classrooms is essential for improving student engagement, achievement, and persistence (Milner, 2007). This is increasingly important because college and university classrooms today are more diverse than they were 20 years ago, which includes social identity diversity as well as international students studying in the United States (NCES, 2019; Opens Doors, 2018). The increase in diversity and variety of cultural differences requires faculty to rethink how they are teaching and facilitating learning in their classrooms. This is especially true in STEM gateway courses. As a result, faculty need to implement culturally relevant education, which involves recognizing how student's cultural backgrounds and lived experiences impact how they engage within the classroom (Ladson-Billings, 1994, 2009).

THE NEED FOR CULTURALLY RELEVANT PEDAGOGY

Not only must STEM pedagogy be critical, but it should also be culturally relevant. The major tenets of culturally relevant pedagogy (CRP) are academic success, cultural competence, and sociopolitical consciousness (Ladson-Billings, 1994). Academic success is measured by intellectual growth that results from classroom instruction. Cultural competence focuses on students learning about their own culture while also learning about, appreciating, and celebrating other cultures. Sociopolitical consciousness is the application of what is being learned in a traditional classroom to real-world problems and issues. Bridging these across the curriculum and classroom is the hallmark of CRP. When students are connected socially and academically, they tend to be more successful (Kendricks & Arment, 2011). Thus, the need for CRP in STEM gateway courses is critical and highly recommended to ensure the retention of diverse students. Though, how CRP is practiced differs across disciplines and faculty members.

CRP is anchored in the idea that classrooms should be learning spaces where students are seen as subjects rather than objects (Ladson-Billings,

1994). The practice is designed to interrupt the notion of equity as sameness since students are culturally different and bring their unique experiences to learning. Instead, CRP engages across differences, and effective faculty offer counter-narratives to our understanding of historical representations, which in turn legitimize students' real-life experiences as part of the curriculum. Finally, teaching is centered on the idea that if students do not see themselves reflected in what is taught, they have no catalyst to learn. Therefore, by its very nature, the practice must be differentiated on a class-by-class basis.

The Need for Culturally Responsive Teaching

An integral part of CRP is culturally responsive teaching, which is about creating inclusive classroom spaces by intentionally designing opportunities that explore learning from the student's lived cultures (Gay, 2018). CRP's goals are to deconstruct power and privilege in the classroom to increase capacity for all to learn (Freire, 2005). Furthermore, culturally responsive teaching advocates for students to be introduced to relevant problems and for students to be included as co-constructors of their knowledge-building (Brown et al., 2018). This requires the inclusion of student cultures within both the instruction and curriculum development and thus is accomplished in diverse ways within the classroom. Following, we introduce a framework of culturally relevant education in a STEM gateway course.

Framework of Culturally Relevant Education in a STEM Gateway Course

Aronson and Laughter (2016) synthesized Gay's (2010) discussion of culturally responsive teaching and Ladson-Billings (1995) culturally relevant pedagogy to define culturally relevant education (CRE). CRE is described as a "collection of pedagogies of opposition" (p. 140) that uses social justice tenets to address the pluralistic nature of our society (Aronson et al., 2016). CRE is seen as encompassing the two frameworks with CRT focusing on the competence and practice and CRP focusing on the attitude and disposition. Aronson and Laughter then defined CRE as involving instructors who connect academic skills with cultural references, require critical reflection, support student cultural competence development, and "unmask and unmake oppressive systems" through critical discourse (p. 167; Fig. 5.1). CRE is a comprehensive approach that engages students intellectually, socially, emotionally, and politically by grounding learning in their cultural understandings of the world. This approach is used to impart knowledge, skills, and attitudes (Ladson-Billings, 1994, 2009) and has proven successful for Students of Color whose voices are often lost in classrooms (Milner, 2007).

CRE centers students in the classroom and engages them by connecting the course learning outcomes to lived experiences and the real world. This requires instructors to provide space for students to connect their cultural references to the material. Instructors must recognize that despite their own identities they form a part of an oppressive education system that has engaged all students in the dominant culture. Culturally relevant education seeks to unmask this and provide ways for students to

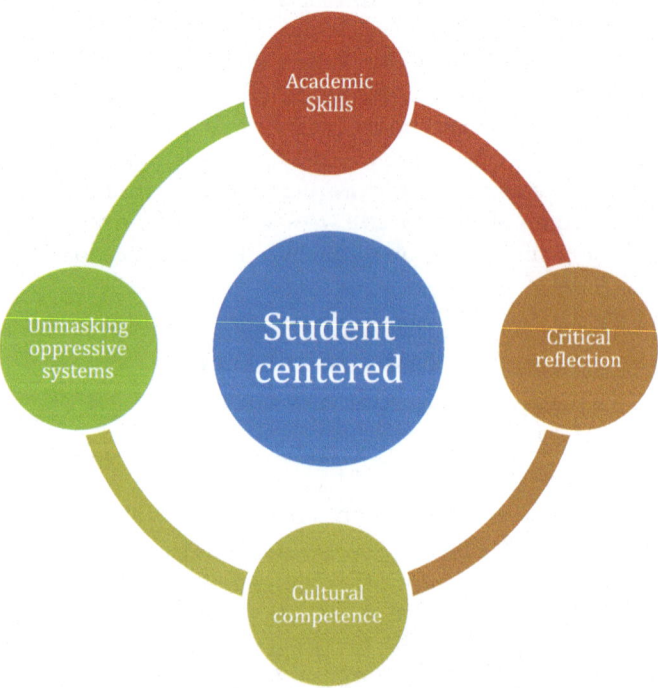

Fig. 5.1   Tenets of culturally relevant education

build cultural competence in whatever course is being taught. This can and should be done even in foundational STEM courses.

Implementing a CRE framework in STEM gateway classrooms takes a multifaceted approach. To implement a culturally relevant education framework, faculty consider who the learners in their classrooms are— where they are coming from and what their cultural backgrounds are (Han et al., 2014). Faculty must also develop meaningful relationships with students, getting to know them as individuals, and what their goals are (Han et al., 2014). A crucial part of developing relationships with students is to understand their cultural and discourse backgrounds (Mitchell, 2010) and how closely connected students are with their cultural backgrounds. Using this knowledge, faculty can then understand how students learn and implement appropriate strategies into their teaching methodology. As they get to know their students and their backgrounds, they can design curricula and lessons to respond to their cultural backgrounds and needs, rather than those of the majority culture. These practices show students that they belong in these fields, thus encouraging them to continue with STEM majors.

Helping students develop critical consciousness is another crucial aspect of CRE (Han et al., 2014). To do this, faculty purposefully design courses to change the way students understand their power and to upend their assumptions about cultural narratives, which increases their cultural responsiveness (Han et al., 2014). While helping students develop critical consciousness, faculty must also critically reflect on their own beliefs and experiences. This can occur through journaling, book clubs, or any other formalized reflection experience (Darder, 2003; Han et al., 2014). This practice enables faculty to understand their own beliefs, assumptions, and actions and how they relate to their own culturally relevant practice. Finally, faculty must learn to be flexible in their teaching and develop their ability to improvise in the classroom (Mitchell, 2010). Flexibility and supportive relationships with students help build meaningful relationships, creates safe learning environments (Han et al., 2014), connect with traditional cultural values (Mitchell, 2010), and are adaptable and supportive of the wide variety of cultures and backgrounds of the globalizing world. When faculty understand each student's cultural background and implement pedagogies that values those cultures, faculty are displaying each student's inherent value and worth (Mitchell, 2010). Understanding the cultural background of each student will help faculty have meaningful relationships with their students and will subsequently help them better support their students in their STEM gateway courses.

Challenges. Implementing CRE comes with several challenges. First, CRE can be difficult for practitioners to define. Han et al. (2014) reflected that while they were dedicated to implementing CRP, they had experienced a difficult time defining it; each author had a different definition and version of how it should be implemented in the classroom. Second, the CRE literature is dominated by implementation in P-12 education with a dearth of literature regarding the implementation of culturally relevant pedagogy in higher education (Han et al., 2014). Although some of the lessons learned through P-12 education can be applied to higher education, they are often vastly different educational landscapes, and higher education students are less ethnically diverse than P-12 education in the US (Han et al., 2014). As a result, the practices of P-12 CRP education do not always fit practices of higher education. Fourth, culturally responsive educators are often isolated and implementing CRP in their classes across the curricula without sharing with colleagues across campus (Han et al., 2014). Furthermore, the authors explained that for culturally responsive pedagogy to have an impact on students, it could not be isolated to one or two courses. Instead, it needs to be part of an institution's explicit instructional plans (Han et al., 2014). Therefore, institutions need to provide space and time for faculty to share and promote their culturally responsive practices in order to integrate them across the curriculum.

Practical Examples of Culturally Relevant Education in a STEM Classroom

In the next section, we will discuss some of the popular practices in STEM reforms and offer ways in which instructors can incorporate culturally relevant education into their instruction. We will discuss how this is done in the traditional classroom environment as well as within labs, which are crucial aspects of STEM pedagogy. In these examples, and at the heart of culturally relevant education, it is clear that education must be student-centered, and the lives and experiences of the students must be incorporated into the classroom.

Active Learning

Active learning has been one of the most endorsed pedagogical changes in the STEM classroom. Felder and Brent (2009) defined active learning to consist:

> of short course-related individual or small-group activities that all students in a class are called upon to do, alternating with instructor-led intervals in which student responses are processed, and new information is presented. (p. 2)

Active learning has been implemented in various ways, from the use of clickers in large lecture classrooms to redesigning entire classrooms to ensure students are sitting together and engaging with each other. Active learning techniques are effective ways to move from the passive nature of lecturing to engaging students in the learning process. However, instructors who do not engage students from a culturally responsive pedagogy framework may end up creating more tension within students as students with marginalized and underrepresented identities. Felder and Brent (2009) offered a basic format for engaging in the process: (1) Form groups, select a recorder, (2) pose a challenging question and allow time for completion, (3) Stop the activity and ask for volunteers to respond. They also offer variations of this structure, which include the think-pair-share or thinking-aloud pair problem-solving.

To reframe these activities from a culturally responsive pedagogy requires faculty to be intentional about who is in the classroom. When students form their own teams, the social dynamics become enhanced and often students who are on the margins are left out. Random assignment of groups with changing formats not based on where students are situated will reduce these dynamics. For example, instructors cannot use random assignment based on counting off a number all the time, since students tend to always sit in the same space. Variations in the ways small groups or pairs are created will serve the advantage of students getting to know people, as well as reducing identity-based dynamics in the classroom. Similarly, instructors need to be cognizant of who records/reporters during the activity are and rotate that role as needed.

Cooperative Teams

Most gateway STEM courses include lecture and laboratory components with the lab assignments usually completed within a team. Additionally, classes that are not lab-based (e.g., math), often have students working in collaborative groups. Therefore, cooperative teams and tasks already play an established and important role in STEM gateway courses. However, in CRE, the goals, tasks, and assignments for cooperative learning must honor, engage, and be constructed around the cultures and backgrounds of the students in the class.

Students of Color with close ties to their traditional cultures often benefit from cooperative tasks because they tend to approach tasks in more "inductive, interactive, and communal" ways (Gay, 2018, p. 121). While this is not the case for all Students of Color, awareness of cultural patterns in student approaches to tasks is essential for CRE (Gay, 2018). For example, African American and Latinx cultures tend to value highly contextual problems, and Latinx and Asian American cultures are more inclined to group learning contexts (Gay, 2018). To implement cooperative tasks in culturally responsive ways, faculty should be aware of the traditional cultural backgrounds of their students. Additionally, they must also understand their learners on an individual level, including how closely affiliated they are to those cultures, as some students may have different individual preferences or not have close ties with their cultural backgrounds.

When designing cooperative tasks in a culturally relevant classroom, faculty should design tasks and create groups purposefully (Appendix A). First, faculty should create a safe learning space, helping students build trust with each other by frequently working in pairs and groups (Bondy et al., 2007; Ukpokodu, 2011). When students work together frequently, they get to know each other and learn to trust and respect each other, which is critical for students to feel safe in their learning groups. Second, faculty should create heterogeneous groups based on ability, race, gender, and language background (Ukpokodu, 2011). When groups have students from various backgrounds, with various strengths, and different preferred task performance approaches, they are more culturally responsive. Third, faculty should establish democratic values and behaviors for the class, as well as establishing rules, expectations, and participation roles for all activities (Bondy et al., 2007; Ukpokodu, 2011). Without these established norms, cooperative tasks can increase tension among students and decrease learning.

Clear rules and guidelines are critical for cooperative tasks. Faculty can develop culturally responsive rules after they get to know their students; however, students can also work together to create their own rules and guidelines for group activities. Faculty can act as facilitators in these discussions, encouraging students to think critically about ways to engage all students from all backgrounds. After rules have been established in the class, they should be written down, disseminated, and reviewed regularly, and following the rules should be an expectation of the course. As students gain comfort in their roles and work in groups, they can change their roles based on their strengths and learning needs. Finally, learning tasks should be complex, require each group member to contribute meaningfully to the goal of the task, and connect with each student's life experiences (Ukpokodu, 2011). Creating complex tasks in which all students are actively engaged in the learning process establishes a requirement that all students work together to achieve the course goals, and it also demonstrates the faculty member's high expectations for students. To connect with their student's lives, faculty can use the language, examples, and metaphors with which students are familiar (Bondy et al., 2007; Ukpokodu, 2011). Group work is not necessarily cooperative and culturally responsive; however, with purposeful planning and support, group work can become a collaborative task in a culturally relevant classroom.

Inquiry-Based Learning

In P-12 schools across the nation, the Next Generation Science Standards have been implemented, which urged science teachers to focus on inquiry as a process of teaching sciences. However, this push has not made its way fully into the college classroom, especially in the foundational gateway courses. Culturally relevant teaching requires a second look at the STEM curriculum with the understanding that most of what is considered fundamental is rooted in the dominant culture. STEM gateway courses are usually made up of facts and formulas applied to various problem sets. Instructors typically do not provide the why or the applicability of the work.

The shift to a more student-centered approach to teaching and learning is anchored in the idea of problem-based learning. The concept revolves around getting students engaged and active in their learning. There are many ways to implement problem-based learning in STEM gateway courses, and no one way is better than another. Instead, the success of PBL in this context is more about understanding who students are and creating classroom spaces that consider their social identities. Studies by West and Herman (2015) and Adair et al. (2001) showed that at-risk and underrepresented students have greater rates of success in active and problem-based learning classrooms. The studies show evidence of increased levels of academic confidence, retention in courses, and persistence to graduation.

One way to accomplish these goals is the use of the Cognitive Apprenticeship model (Collins et al., 1991). Apprenticeship requires learners to see the steps and processes that lead to the final product. While STEM gateway courses typically focus on the principles without revealing the goal, cognitive apprenticeship requires scaffolding the course in steps that engages the student in the exploration, discussion, and evaluation of carefully selected phenomenon in socially and culturally relevant ways (Brown et al., 2018). Cognitive apprenticeship in STEM classrooms requires instructors to ask: "What are they doing, why are they doing it, and how will success in what they are doing help them find a solution to the problem?" (Collins et al., 1991, p. 11). This approach allows students to be cognizant of their learning and provides an opportunity to frame the work in their own experiences.

Training of Graduate Teaching Assistants/New Instructors

Preparing and training new faculty and graduate teaching assistants (TAs) to be culturally responsive teachers is critical for the success of students in STEM gateway courses as it will help reduce the gaps in diverse student representation in the STEM fields. TAs and new faculty are often the instructors for gateway courses and usually come into the role with limited experience teaching. TAs may also be teaching recitation sessions and leading lab courses. Limited experience usually challenges the teaching skills of these instructors and most of them have a limited understanding or ways to implement CRE within their courses. To address the limited experiences, institutions often have training sessions for both TAs and new instructors and culturally responsive teaching should be integrated into those training programs.

Not only should new faculty and TAs be trained in CRE, new faculty and TA training courses themselves must also be culturally responsive, particularly as the number of international students studying STEM fields continues to increase (Open Doors, 2018). Facilitators of new faculty orientation and TA training must understand the backgrounds of the new faculty and TAs in order to be culturally responsive and to meet their needs. Appropriate TA training programs are critical for TA success, as they increase self-efficacy, self-confidence, and teaching effectiveness (Boman, 2013; Dimitrov et al., 2013; Young & Bippus, 2008). However, it is challenging for faculty with little training in CRE themselves to implement it in the coursework training of doctoral students (Han et al., 2014) and recently graduated faculty.

When specifically addressing training sessions, faculty and teaching assistants should participate in CRE workshops, which help them understand what it is, how to implement it, and "how to teach with culturally relevant lens" (Smith et al., 2018). Additionally, one area that higher education can draw from is the education that faculty in P-12 provide for pre-service teachers on CRE. For example, Smith et al. (2018) engaged pre-service teachers in workshops that helped them develop creative and new ways to implement culturally relevant strategies into their classrooms. The workshop challenged pre-service teachers to think critically about a subject and a text. The authors reported that after the workshop, the pre-service teachers had developed new ways to engage their future students to think critically about important topics that were not presented in the workshop. Therefore, specifically designed workshops helped instructors teach through a culturally responsive lens.

In training programs, TAs first need to be introduced to the idea of CRE, read current publications on the topic, and engage in discussions about the topic (Barnes, 2006). These opportunities provide the foundation for TAs as they begin to think about their teaching practice and how to incorporate CRE into it (Smith et al., 2018). Programs should also provide opportunities for TAs to reflect on their own intersectionality and privilege, how that has had an impact on their educational experiences, and how it connects to CRE in their own practice (Darder, 2003; Han et al., 2014). Training programs should also give TAs the opportunity to practice CRE in their teaching prior to entering the classroom. Micro-teaching lessons, which are mini-lessons that pre-service teachers and TAs plan and implement as a part of their pre-service teaching training, are an opportunity for TAs to think about and implement how they would use CRE in a lesson (Barnes, 2006; Gorsuch et al., 2013). Micro-teaching opportunities are, by definition, short but they should be responsive to student needs and be culturally responsive.

CRE training should not end with the completion of TA training; it should be an ongoing process as TAs transition from emerging to expert teachers. TAs should have follow-up sessions with experienced faculty and other TAs to discuss and reflect on their teaching experiences and how they are implementing CRE. These follow-up sessions provide valuable touch-points for faculty to ensure TAs use CRE, TAs have opportunities to ask questions and discuss issues they may have, and TAs have time to reflect on their use of CRE. The follow-up sessions can be incorporated into existing meetings about curriculum and assessment, as CRE is a critical piece to creating equitable STEM gateway courses.

CONCLUSION

The success of all students in STEM gateway courses is important; however, the gaps in diverse student representation in STEM fields make culturally relevant education a priority. Teaching reforms within STEM gateway courses have shown some limited success but we argue in this chapter that culturally relevant education needs to be incorporated to reach all students and diversify the pipeline. We provide a framework for STEM instructors to be prepared and to use critical pedagogy, culturally responsive teaching, and culturally relevant education in STEM gateway courses, which is critical as these courses serve as a crucial pipeline to diversifying the STEM workforce.

APPENDIX A

Teaching Artifact

This artifact provides an example to assist faculty to create permanent teams for lab work or research projects that incorporates the principles of culturally relevant education. We provide a sample questionnaire for students to complete during the first class and considerations to set up the team.

Sample questionnaire

Academic Experience and Career Goals

1. What is your anticipated major and career goals upon graduation?

2. Of the past courses you have taken in your major which was your favorite, and why?
3. Of the past courses you have taken outside of your major which was your favorite, and why?

Research Interests (These are sample questions for a research project, can be adjusted to meet learning goals of an assignment)

1. What are some questions or problems that you would like to explore in this class? For example, "Why was Covid-19 more deadly for men than women?" or "How was the spread of Covid-19 mitigated by widespread testing in South Korea?"
2. What are some problems in your community/communities that you would like to investigate in this class? For example, "How does the increase of lead in water affect children?"
3. Why are you interested in these topics?

How I work…circle the statement(s) that best describe preferences for organizing your work

1. I prefer to work independently and then come together with teammates.
2. I prefer to work issues out collaboratively throughout the whole process.
3. I prefer my self-reliance and pulling my weight prior to the team meeting.
4. I prefer to work from the collective, share resources, and co-create materials for the group.
5. I prefer to learn independently.
6. I prefer to learn through group dialogue and interaction.
7. I am competitive in how I approach my learning.
8. I am collaborative in how I approach my learning.
9. I am more technical and analytical in my approach to problem-solving.
10. I am more relational in my approach to problem-solving.

Other
Your group will work closely together with every class for the entire semester. Therefore, it is important that I am made aware of all potentially relevant information/issues before I organize these groups. In the space below feel free to write anything that you feel I should know before assigning you to a group. This question is optional.

General Considerations as you create groups from the response

- Teams of 3–5 members ideal

    - Aim for even distribution of ability levels and learning styles
    - Ensure diverse groupings
    - Maximize potential for positive interactions
    - Have all students create group guidelines for the class and have each group create their own standards for clear expectations and positive interactions, which they share with the instructor.

- Require team members to reflect on their participation throughout the semester

    - Provide opportunities for students to give feedback on the group collective for each major group assignment
    - Require a mid-semester and final peer evaluation of the group including a self-evaluation
    - Be prepared to address group dynamics regularly with individuals and formally with the group at mid-semester and end of the semester.

- Ongoing support

    - Create multi-modal ways for teams to communicate with one another. Some may prefer using space outside the course management system; however, this needs to be inclusive and accessible to all
    - Be prepared to coach on issues related to self-confidence. Find mechanisms to recognize group members that are not as confident and may retreat during the semester.

References

Adair, J. K., Reyes, M. A., Anderson-Rowland, M. R., & Kouris, D. A. (2001). Workshops vs. tutoring: How ASU's minority engineering program is changing the way engineering students learn. In *Proceedings—Frontiers in Education Conference, 2.*

American Association of Physics Teachers. (1996). Physics at the crossroads: Innovation and revitalization in undergraduate physics-plans for action. Executive summary. In *Proceedings of the American Association of Physics Teachers Physics at the Crossroads Conference.* College Park, MD: American Association of Physics Teachers.

Aronson, B., Amatullah, T., & Laughter, J. (2016). Culturally relevant education: Extending the conversation to religious diversity. *Multicultural Perspectives, 18*(3), 140–149.

Aronson, B., & Laughter, J. (2016b). The theory and practice of culturally relevant education: A synthesis of research across content areas. *Review of Educational Research, 86*(1), 163–206.

Barnes, C. J. (2006). Preparing preservice teachers to teach in a culturally responsive way. *The Negro Educational Review, 57*(1–2), 85–100.

Boman, J. S. (2013). Graduate student teaching development: Evaluating the effectiveness of training in relation to graduate student characteristics. *Canadian Journal of Higher Education, 43*(1), 100–114.

Bondy, E., Rozz, D. D., Gallingane, C., & Hambacher, E. (2007). Creating environments of success and resilience: Culturally responsive classroom management and more. *Urban Education, 42,* 326–348.

Borrego, M., Froyd, J. E., & Hall, T. S. (2010). Diffusion of engineering education innovations: A survey of awareness and adoption rates in US engineering departments. *Journal of Engineering Education, 99*(3), 185–207.

Brown, B. A., Boda, P., Lemmi, C., & Monroe, X. (2018). Moving culturally relevant pedagogy from theory to practice: Exploring teachers' application of culturally relevant education in science and mathematics. *Urban Education, 54*(6), 775–803. https://doi-org.cmich.idm.oclc.org/10.1177%2F0042085918794802.

Cohen, R., & Kelly, A. M. (2018). Community college chemistry coursetaking and STEM academic persistence. *Journal of Chemical Education, 96*(1), 3–11.

Collins, A., Brown, J. S., & Holum, A. (1991). Cognitive apprenticeship: Making thinking visible. *American Educator, 15*(3), 6–11.

Conley, D. T. (2005). *College knowledge: What it really takes for students to succeed and what we can do to get them ready.* San Francisco: Jossey-Bass.

Darder, A. (2003). *The critical pedagogy reader.* London, UK: Psychology Press.

Dimitrov, N., Meadows, K., Kustra, E., Ackerson, T., Prada, L., Baker, N., Boulos, G. M., Potter, M. K. (2013). *Assessing graduate teaching development programs for impact on future faculty*. Higher Education Quality Council of Ontario.

Fairweather, J. (2008). *Linking evidence and promising practices in science, technology, engineering, and mathematics (STEM) undergraduate education.* Washington, DC: Board of Science Education, National Research Council, The National Academies.

Felder, R. M., & Brent, R. (2009). Active learning: An introduction. *ASQ Higher Education Brief, 2*(4).

Freire, P. (2005). Pedagogy of the oppressed/Paulo Freire. New York and London: Continuum.

Gasiewski, J. A., Eagan, M. K., Garcia, G. A., Hurtado, S., & Chang, M. J. (2012). From gatekeeping to engagement: A multicontextual, mixed method study of student academic engagement in introductory STEM courses. *Research in Higher Education, 53*(2), 229–261.

Gay, G. (2002). Preparing for culturally responsive teaching. *Journal of Teacher Education, 53*(2), 106–116.

Gay, G. (2010). *Culturally responsive teaching: Theory, research, and practice.* Teachers College Press.

Gay, G. (2018). *Culturally responsive teaching: Theory, research, and practice.* Teachers College Press.

Gorsuch, G., Meyers, C. M., Pickering, L., & Griffee, D. T. (2013). *English communication for international teaching assistants.* Waveland Press Inc.

Hammond, Z. (2015). *Culturally responsive teaching and the brain: Promoting authentic engagement and rigor among culturally and linguistically diverse students.* Corwin.

Han, H. S., Vomvoridi-Ivanovic, E., Jacobs, J., Karanxha, Z., Lypika, A., Topdemir, C., & Feldman, A. (2014). Culturally responsive pedagogy in higher education: A collaborative self-study. *Studying Teacher Education, 10*(3), 290–321. https://doi.org/10.1080/17425964.2014.958072.

Handelsman, J., Ebert-May, D., Beichner, R., Bruns, P., Chang, A., & DeHaan, R. (2004). Policy forum: Scientific teaching. *Science, 304*(5670), 521–522.

Kendricks, K., & Arment, A. (2011). Adopting a K-12 family model with undergraduate research to enhance STEM persistence and achievement in underrepresented minority students. *Journal of College Science Teaching, 41*(2), 22–27.

Kincheloe, J. L., & McLaren, P. (2011). Rethinking critical theory and qualitative research. In k. hayes, S. R. Steinberg, & K. Tobin (Eds.), *Key works in critical pedagogy* (Vol. 32, pp. 285–326). Sense Publishers.

Koch, A. K., & Rodier, R. (2014). *Gateways to completion guidebook.* John N. Gardner Institute for Excellence in Undergraduate Education.

Kotluk, N., & Kocakaya, S. (2018). Culturally relevant/responsive education: What do teachers think in Turkey? *Journal of Ethnic and Cultural Studies, 5*(2), 98–117.

Ladson-Billings, G. (1994). What we can learn from multicultural education research. *Educational Leadership, 51*(8), 22–26.

Ladson-Billings, G. (1995). Toward a theory of culturally relevant pedagogy. *American Educational Research Journal, 32*(3), 465–491.

Ladson-Billings, G. (2009). *The dreamkeepers: Successful teachers of African American children.* Wiley.

Lewis, J. L., Menzies, H., Najera, E. I., & Page, R. N. (2009). Rethinking trends in minority participation in the sciences. *Science Education, 93*(6), 961–977.

Milner, H. R., IV. (2007). Race, culture, and researcher positionality: Working through dangers seen, unseen, and unforeseen. *Educational Researcher, 36*(7), 388–400.

Mitchell, R. (2010). Cultural aesthetics and teacher improvisation: An epistemology of providing culturally responsive service by African American Professors. *Urban Education, 45*(5), 604–629. https://doi.org/10.1177/004208590934783.

National Center for Education Statistics. (2019). *Fast facts: Degrees conferred by race and sex.* Retrieved October 24, 2019, from https://nces.ed.gov/fastfacts/display.asp?id=72.

National Science Foundation Center for the Integration of Research, Teaching, and Learning. (1996). *Shaping the future: New expectations for undergraduate education in science, mathematics, engineering, and technology.* Arlington, VA: National Science Foundation.

Open Doors. (2018). *Fast facts: International students in the US.* Retrieved October 24, 2019, from https://www.iie.org/Research-and-Insights/Open-Doors/Fact-Sheets-and-Infographics/Fast-Facts.

Smith, R., Ralston, N., & Waggoner, J. (2018). Impact of culturally responsive teaching workshop on preservice teachers: How to each Columbus from multiple perspectives. *AILACTE Journal, 15,* 61–76.

Steen, L. (1987). Mathematics education: A predictor of scientific competitiveness. *Science, 237*(4812), 251–302. http://www.jstor.org/stable/1699967.

Triesman, P. (1985). *A study of mathematics performance of black students at the University California, Berkley.* An unpublished dissertation.

Ukpokodu, O. N. (2011). How do I teach mathematics in a culturally responsive way? Identity empowering teaching practices. *Multicultural Education, 19*(3), 47–56.

Weddle-West, K., & Bingham, R. (2010). Enhancing recruitment, persistence, and graduation rates of students of color. *National for Applied Research Journal, 24*(1), 7–20.

West, M., & Herman, G. L. (2015). Mapping the spread of collaborative learning methods in gateway STEM courses via communities of practice. In *Proceedings of the 122nd American society for engineering education annual conference and exposition (ASEE 2015)* (Vol. 26, pp. 1–26).

Young, S. L., & Bippus, A. M. (2008). Assessment of graduate teaching assistant (GTA) training: A case study of a training program and its impact on GTAs. *Communication Teacher, 22*(4), 116–129.

Recommended Readings

Aronson, B., & Laughter, J. (2016). The theory and practice of culturally relevant education: A synthesis of research across content areas. *Review of Educational Research, 86*(1), 163–206.

This article provides the best synthesis and integration of what it means to connect the principles of culturally relevant education. Aronson & Laughter provide a summary of the important theoretical perspectives that undergird the framework. The authors then present the results of their literature search on empirical studies that address incorporating CRE or social justice frameworks within a classroom. They present a table with each article, reviewed, the CRE markers incorporated in the pedagogy, a description of the study, and the effect on student outcomes. The end of the article then synthesizes the literature by discussing how it was incorporated in specific content areas including Mathematics and Science. The main limitation of this article is that the discussion occurs from a K-12 perspective, but it offers important areas that can and will translate to a college course.

Gay, G. (2018). *Culturally responsive teaching: Theory, research, and practice.* Teachers College Press.

In culturally responsive teaching, Gay uses personal stories to show how culturally responsive teaching can improve the achievements of underrepresented students. The book provides clear insights from research and theory that inform teaching practice. Chapter 2 of the book is especially critical as it sets up the conceptual model for thinking through culturally responsive teaching. The rest of the chapters then provide clear practical approaches and examples that assist an instructor to implement the concepts.

CHAPTER 6

Teaching Social Justice Through Project-Based Learning in Engineering

Julie Chiki and Grace Sallar

KEY TERMS AND DEFINITIONS

Broadening participation initiatives	Programs first funded by the National Science Foundation to diversify STEM fields and improve persistence of traditionally underrepresented students through support such as scholarships, undergraduate research, and mentorship.
Project-based learning	A type of active learning that centers on an authentic and

---

J. Chiki (✉) · G. Sallar
Ohio University, Athens, OH, USA
e-mail: julie.chiki@ohio.edu

G. Sallar
e-mail: sallarg1@ohio.edu

C. C. Ozaki and L. Parson (eds.), *Teaching and Learning for Social Justice and Equity in Higher Education*,
https://doi.org/10.1007/978-3-030-69947-5_6

	complex problem and encourages students to draw on their own experiences to produce a public product through teamwork, reflection, and ongoing feedback and revisions.
S_{TEM}J	Social justice-driven STEM education; a framework that combines understanding historical systems of oppression to inform local social justice change using STEM knowledge and skills.
Transgressive teaching	A model that aims to disrupt traditional learning methods by emphasizing collaboration between instructors and students and crossing boundaries of race, gender, and class to re-engage students and draw out the perspectives traditionally missing from STEM fields.

In the last few decades, project-based learning and broadening participation initiatives have emerged as popular strategies to increase interest and engagement in the STEM fields, particularly in engineering (Hirshfield & Koretsky, 2018; Holloman et al., 2018; James & Singer, 2016; Savage et al., 2007). Project-based learning encourages teams of diverse individuals to work together and solve complex problems that require multiple viewpoints, which research shows leads to greater innovation (Díaz-García et al., 2013; Nathan & Lee, 2013), stronger financial performance (Hunt et al., 2014) and more developed environmental policies (Li et al., 2017). At the same time, broadening participation initiatives, which aim to strengthen the pipeline of low-income and underrepresented students to STEM fields through scholarships, undergraduate research, and mentorship, have brought in more students without fully attending to the needs of these students and the values they bring to the field beyond national economic competitiveness (Baber, 2015). The convergence of these trends is ripe for social justice pedagogical innovation in STEM education, because students share an increasingly diverse space where they must learn to build trust and depend on each other to accomplish technical projects. Using elements of the $S_{TEM}J$ framework (Madden et al., 2017) and the transgressive STEM teaching model (Barnes-Johnson & Johnson, 2018), built on the foundation of bell hooks' *Teaching to Transgress* (1994), we explore the use of social justice informed project-based learning initiatives that incorporate the strengths of women, students of color, LGBTQ, low-SES, and differently abled students in a first-year introductory engineering course focused on the engineering design process. These groups have been marginalized and kept out of the STEM pipeline with stereotypes about poor math and science ability (Garriott et al., 2017), a lack of mentorship and role models in educational and professional spaces (McGee, 2015), and a middle-class white man-dominated culture that creates an unwelcoming climate for underrepresented students (Litzler & Young, 2012; Tonso, 2006), which has led to a persistent gap in retention rates (Chen, 2013; Roy, 2018).

We teach a large, project-based engineering overview course that uses reflection and discussion to develop not only technical skills but also the understandings of social justice and equity in design, problem-solving, and team dynamics. This chapter includes lesson plans from our course that could be integrated into existing design- or project-based courses.

Broadening Participation Initiatives

Efforts to increase representation of minoritized students have proliferated at the national, state, and institutional levels (Baber, 2015; Holloman et al., 2018). One of the most well-known programs, the National Science Foundation's (NSF) Broadening Participation Framework for Action launched in 2008, signaled heightened interest at the national level in increasing the number of women and underrepresented minorities in STEM fields (James & Singer, 2016). By 2016, statistics collected by NSF showed that women were earning bachelor's degrees in science and engineering at equal rates as men, but were still underrepresented in the workplace (National Center for Science and Engineering Statistics [NCSES], 2019). The share of racially minoritized students earning degrees has also gradually increased, although they remain underrepresented in terms of degrees earned and educational and occupational attainment (NCSES, 2019). In 2016, underrepresented minorities made up 28% of the U.S. population (14% Hispanic/Latinx, 12% Black, 2% American Indian/Alaska Natives/Native Hawaiians/Other Pacific Islander) but earned only 22% of science and engineering bachelor's degrees and just 9% of doctorate degrees (NCSES, 2019). These same groups lagged $12,000 behind in median annual salary compared to their white counterparts (NCSES, 2019).

Although some initiatives demonstrate progress in terms of enrollment and graduation rates of women and some minoritized identities, STEM fields are still far from equitable for underrepresented minoritized students. The NSF notably does not track progress for other groups such as LGBT students, low-income students, or those with multiple, intersecting minoritized identities who are further marginalized in STEM higher education (Armstrong & Jovanovic, 2015; Moran, 2017; National Student Clearinghouse, 2015; Rozeka et al., 2018). Baber (2015) notes that the more difficult task of creating equitable environments for underrepresented students once they arrive on campus has also largely been neglected. Climate studies frequently indicate that increasing the number of underrepresented students does not automatically translate to a welcoming environment for those students, and scholars have documented a "chilly climate" for women (Litzler & Young, 2012; Tonso, 2006), students of color (Johnson, 2012; McGee, 2015), and LGBTQ students (Brinkworth, 2016; Hughes, 2017). The chilly climate can lead to experiences of alienation, harassment, lower sense of belonging, and a lack of opportunities (Cech & Waidzunas, 2011; Hirshfield & Koretsky, 2018; Stout & Wright, 2016); factors often linked to the persistent gap in retention rates (Chen, 2013; Hughes, 2018; Roy, 2018).

A myriad of strategies to improve and close outcome gaps have been proposed and implemented. Project-based learning is a pedagogical strategy aimed to increase student engagement and participation that we utilized as a medium for teaching social justice and addressing the chilly climate.

PROJECT-BASED LEARNING

Engineering education shifted toward project-based learning (PBL) in the early 2000s, driven by research from the National Academy of Engineering and new requirements from the Accreditation Board for Engineering and Technology (Savage et al., 2007). PBL is a subset of active learning, which generally refers to the increased participation of students in the learning process beyond the traditional lecture (Aydede & Matyar, 2009). PBL specifically emphasizes students' active participation in addressing a multifaceted challenge over a significant time period through research, reflection, and problem-solving concluding with publicly presenting their findings (PBLWorks, 2019). Scholars have found PBL improves outcomes such as student grades and performance (Krajcik & Blumenfeld, 2006), student engagement (Filippatou & Kaldi, 2010), problem-solving and interpersonal skills (Alacapinar, 2008), conflict management (Savage et al., 2007), and greater interest in STEM careers (LaForce et al., 2017). The project-based learning framework starts with well-defined student learning goals and contains seven key components: a challenging problem or question, sustained inquiry, authenticity, student choice, reflection, critique and revision, and a public product (Larmer, 2015).

The effect of PBL on underrepresented students is an emerging area of research with promising initial results. For example, the switch to PBL in a computer science curriculum quadrupled the enrollment of women over five years at Harvey Mudd College (Estrada et al., 2016). Instead of traditional programming assignments, the class completed a creative research project to engage students without previous programming experience. Course developers at the University of Texas at Austin (2020) found that introducing a series of hands-on projects to an Advanced Placement Computer Science Principles course led to higher year-end exam scores for women and Latinx students (Ramsey et al., 2018). The projects included "hacking" a classmate's password in a cybersecurity unit, mapping video game controller patterns to learn about data representation, and creating social media photo filters to understand digital media processing. Instructors of an NSF-funded PBL statistics course found that PBL helped first-generation, low-income, and racially underrepresented students gain confidence more quickly by answering statistical questions using real databases on topics such as adolescent health, forest ecology, and social attitudes (Dierker et al., 2012, 2018). While these are only a few examples, the results suggest that PBL should be further investigated for its impact on underrepresented students.

S*TEM*J

As we sought to increase our attention on diversity and social justice in our own project-based class, we explored frameworks to help inform our approach. We found that the S$_{TEM}$J framework (Madden et al., 2017) and the transgressive STEM teaching model (Barnes-Johnson & Johnson, 2018), built on the foundation of *Teaching to Transgress* (hooks, 1994), expanded our thinking about how social justice could be integrated into our existing course. Both models flip the traditional paradigm about reducing the "achievement gap" in STEM fields by building on student's existing knowledge of their communities to empower them to create change using STEM knowledge and skills. The S$_{TEM}$J framework uses STEM skills to help students first understand social injustice and then act to remedy those injustices (Madden et al., 2017). It begins with developing a critical consciousness through self-reflection over time and through community, which was our focus, and extends to include political efficacy and critical action.

S$_{TEM}$J also seeks to provide alternatives to the dominant, accepted approach in the STEM fields, which Madden et al. (2017) described as "emotionally-detached, rationalistic, [masculine], and white embodiment of STEM" (p. 28). Our curriculum, therefore, seeks to integrate personal and group reflection exercises to help students think through the dynamics behind their own behavior, behavior of group members, and behaviors of those in the engineering profession at large. These conversations help prompt the critical reflection necessary to start developing a critical consciousness (Freire, 2007).

We have also made adaptations to the model because our class is largely made up of white men from a variety of geographic locations and experiences, whereas S$_{TEM}$J and the transgressive STEM teaching model focus on teaching and empowering minoritized students. This population led to more conversations on valuing contributions from diverse voices;

recognizing oppression, bias, and privilege; and using privilege to create change. We made use of dialectical tensions to explore the idea that most students are likely to identify some areas of personal privilege and some areas of oppression (Todd & Abrams, 2011). We start with less sensitive topics, for example, discussing that all students in the class have the privilege to attend college and pursue a profession before introducing concepts such as white privilege, gender and heterosexual privilege, and ability privilege. We share some of our biases in a non-threatening way, such as an implicit bias test revealing our own unconscious bias toward men in science, even as female-identified instructors. In reflections, students are challenged to think about the privileges they hold and how they can use those to promote social justice.

Transgressive Teaching

The second social justice framework, transgressive teaching, aims to empower students by reinforcing the value of their own communities and perspectives and amplifying the missing voices of non-dominant cultures, which includes not only class, race, and gender, but also able-bodiedness and faith/spirituality (Barnes-Johnson & Johnson, 2018). Transgressive teaching is based on bell hooks' (1994) model, where students should "transgress" boundaries of race, gender, and class toward a position of liberation using collaboration between students and instructors to spark enthusiasm for learning. Barnes-Johnson and Johnson (2018) point out that even discussion might be deemed "transgressive" in the STEM fields, as it disrupts the traditional lecture of academe.

In our classes, instructors start this disruption on the first day by participating in activities alongside students as co-learners rather than experts at the front of the room. We have found that project-based learning furthers this idea of learning as transgressive even more, as the project relies on each student's voice and contributions to produce a successful final product. Barnes-Johnson and Johnson (2018) also highlight Kahle's (1998) equity metric, which includes benchmarks to increasing equity among students such as providing "opportunities to achieve within the context of high standards," "equitable resource allocation," "access to resources," and "facilitated participation." These standards inform the structure of our large group project, described in detail in the next section. Briefly, these include: several opportunities for formative assessment throughout a complex and challenging project, just-in-time teaching (JiTT) of technical concepts students need for each stage of the design process to provide equitable foundational knowledge, limiting all groups to the same resources to produce their designs so outside materials do not unfairly advantage some teams, and a facilitated brainstorming process that gives all initial student contributions equal weight.

Integrating Social Justice into ET 2800: Overview of Engineering and Technology

Every fall semester, we teach an engineering and technology overview class: ET 2800. The course is intended to introduce students to the fields of engineering and technology, including professional ethics and values, effective teamwork and communication skills, and the engineering design process. The course uses the $S_{TEM}J$ framework and principles of transgressive teaching to create a PBL project that provides equitable access to content knowledge and promotes equity and diversity. This section will provide an overview of the major class project and the course components built in to follow the PBL and social justice frameworks, including team development and support, reflections and peer evaluations, incorporating students' lived experiences, providing equitable access to course resources and materials, integrating social justice into design, and analyzing failure from a justice perspective.

The course is built around a series of small design projects from various engineering disciplines that all tie into a larger scenario dubbed the Engineering Exploration Project, which involves a wildfire and chemical plant explosion, creating a chasm in the only road to the plant. Students must create a disaster relief plan to rescue plant employees, which requires that they design a bridge that spans the gap in the roadway, as well as a trailer to transport the bridge. The project culminates in "Demo Day," where students demonstrate their final products and compete for various awards. The Engineering Exploration Project is designed to be a challenging problem that requires the bulk of the semester to complete, resulting in the sustained inquiry that is a hallmark of PBL. The final demonstrations are an example of another PBL component, a public product, which lends more significance to the project than a standard classroom assignment by featuring upper-class student judges and a final writeup in the weekly college e-news.

Creating and Supporting Teams

Before students begin any technical work, the first several class sessions are dedicated to forming teams and discussing team dynamics. On the first day of class, students and instructors together complete a low-stakes networking activity that gets students thinking about the skills and strengths they bring to the class (see Fig. 6.1 for detailed lesson plan and activity sheet). Through this activity, the instructors aim to acknowledge the skills each student has to offer regardless of their background or previous experience, as well as help them recognize what their peers have to offer. Instructor participation in this exercise helps foster transgressive teaching, as it disrupts student expectations of the teacher as all-knowing expert and instead places them in the position of co-learner who can benefit from students' knowledge, skills, and perspective. Beginning with an activity that highlights' students existing strengths rather than a syllabus review provides an alternative to the dominant STEM culture and sets the tone for valuing contributions from diverse voices.[1]

ET 2800 Networking Activity

---

[1] The three sample lesson plans included in this chapter come from our Fall 2019 course. It may be important to note that we use Blackboard as our course management system, which has an anonymous peer evaluation feature, and TopHat classroom software, which allows us to ask multiple choice and discussion questions during class. Twitter and Kahoot are good free alternatives if you do not have access to TopHat.

Learning Outcomes	Faulty Paradigms to Address
After this lesson, students will be able to: • Articulate the value of considering classmate's and coworker's interests, needs and concerns • Identify their network of support, including skills they have to offer and skills they can learn from classmates	• Only technical skills are required for a successful engineering career. • Engineers don't need to be sensitive to others. • Helping others is purely altruistic and reduces productivity.

Assessment/Evidence of Learning

• Completed interests/skills/abilities inventory
• Engaged class discussion
• Weekly reflection question

Lesson Plan

Networking Activity – Instructor will participate as well

- One of the most important things I want you to take from this class is a good network – one day, someone in this class might help you pass a test, help you get a job, or even be your boss. We will be doing a lot of groupwork in this class, so you will need to know each other and know what strengths everyone brings to the table.
- Individually brainstorm three things you are interested in, three skills that you can share or use to help other students, and three things others could help you (use attached worksheet)
- Use the remaining time to share your skills and interests with each other by walking around the room. Make sure to talk to people you don't know and take note of who you share similar interests with, who you might be able to help and who you may want help from.

Discussion in small groups, then share out to larger group

- What were some common interests you identified? What unique interests did you find?
- What skills does the class have to share? What skills/strengths do you need from others?
- How might being intentional about getting to know others and their skills and interests help you have a better college experience?

Reflection question for homework: What did you think of the networking activity we did in class today? What unique skills or strengths do you bring to this class? What were some other skills or strengths that you learned about from your peers?

Fig. 6.1   Getting to know your network (first week of class)

List three interests you have, three skills you possess, and three things you need help with:		
Interests:	Skills I Can Share:	Things I Need Help With:
1.	1.	1.
2.	2.	2.
3.	3.	3.

Build your network of classmates. What interests and skills do they have? How might you be able to help them?		
Who shares your interests or is interested in something you'd like to know more about? List their name and interest.	Who might you be able to share your skills with? List their name and the specific skill you can share.	Who has skills that match the areas you need help with? List their name and the specific skill you need/want.
1. Name:	1. Name:	1. Name:
Interest(s):	Skill(s):	Skill(s):
Phone number:	Phone number:	Phone number:
2. Name:	2. Name:	2. Name:
Interest(s):	Skill(s):	Skill(s):
Phone number:	Phone number:	Phone number:
3. Name:	3. Name:	3. Name:
Interest(s):	Skill(s):	Skill(s):
Phone number:	Phone number:	Phone number:

Identify at least one person in your new network who you would like to meet up with outside of class:

When forming teams for the project, the class includes several intentional elements to foster equity and peer learning. First, students complete a brief survey about their engineering experience and background to promote an even distribution of skills and interests. Each team's first task is to complete a team contract by discussing roles they might play on the team and how to encourage equal participation and responsibility. The class spends several days talking about team dynamics, starting first with general concepts of team formation (Bonebright, 2010), conflict management, and how systemic racism, oppression or bias might affect behavior on a team. As instructors, we lead discussions on why some students may not readily share their ideas and why others take a natural leadership position—these reasons might include natural introversion or extroversion, or more familiarity with concepts, but we also address systemic racism and oppression that may lead some students to believe their ideas were not as valuable or would be ignored by more dominant members of the group. We seek to help students recognize these patterns so they can identify and address challenges when they arise.

Reflections and Peer Evaluations

Throughout the course, students regularly reflect on the concepts covered in class, both individually and within their teams. Reflection is another key component of PBL because it helps students internalize their learning and think about how the content might apply in other situations (Larmer, 2015). Students complete individual reflections which are then evaluated anonymously by two of their peers through our learning management system. This helps expose students to a wider variety of perspectives and opinions that may not have been shared in class, and it also reduces the burden of grading on instructors, allowing instructors to focus on reviewing the content of evaluations. Each assignment includes a reminder that all backgrounds and opinions are valued and respected in the class, and peer evaluators are encouraged to provide both positive and constructive feedback for every reflection. This requires the evaluator to grapple with perspectives different than their own, helping to level the playing field of ideas and create a more transgressive teaching environment.

As Madden et al. (2017) highlight in the $S_{TEM}J$ framework, students need time and community to develop critical consciousness. Course assignments aim to achieve this by spacing out reflections on similar topics throughout the semester, providing the time needed to develop deeper perspectives. For example, a class session on diversity and team dynamics at the beginning of the semester is followed by a reflection on student understanding of diversity and its importance in engineering and technology. Responses from the reflections showed that the students understood the importance of diversity, however, they were surprised that perspectives of minoritized individuals were often disregarded in decision making. In a subsequent reflection on implicit bias, students could build on this first reflection to dive more deeply into the effects of implicit bias and its suppression of multiple viewpoints.

Students give and receive feedback in several other ways throughout the course, providing plenty of opportunity for critique and revision, another hallmark of PBL. This means the focus of the course is not just the final product, but continuous improvement through formative evaluation. Each team meets with an engineering success coach (graduate-level teaching assistant) at least once during the project to discuss their team dynamics and progress on the designs. These conversations focus purely on the group processes to reinforce that it is just as important to the success of the team as technical skill. Midway through the semester, teams also give and receive feedback on their designs and performance as team members. These two evaluations allow teams time to improve their designs and allows individuals an opportunity to change their behavior and contributions to the team.

Applying Concepts to Students' Lived Experiences

When teaching technical concepts, the course still aims to follow the transgressive teaching approach, which suggests that students should be able to see themselves in the curriculum and have opportunities to learn from other diverse communities (Barnes-Johnson & Johnson, 2018, p. 232). In one example, the concept of the engineering design process is introduced with a video about planning a taco party, so that students can see how they may already be using elements of what at first seems like a complicated concept (KQED Quest, 2017). In later discussions on the topic, students apply the engineering design process to problems they experience in their own daily lives. Some classroom discussions have centered around how students can ensure they are able to eat lunch in the middle of a busy class schedule or how to stretch limited meal swipes throughout the week for those who have campus meal plans. These activities make the engineering design more accessible to all students, even those who have never been exposed to engineering concepts before. When students identify real-life problems to which they could apply the design process, it also exposes others in the class to the struggles of their peers.

Leveling the Playing Field

Because the course includes students with varying levels of exposure to engineering concepts, it is important to level the playing field in terms of materials, knowledge resources, and access to spaces on campus, concepts that align with transgressive teaching and Kahle's (1998) equity metric. In the earliest iterations of the course, students were expected to do their own research as needed to inform their designs and programs, however, this often meant those with previous experience took over the project. The course now includes an introduction to bridge and trailer design, basic computer programming and manufacturing processes, as well as bringing in guest speakers who students can contact for additional support. Students participate in tours of the college's open-access machining lab to ensure all students are aware of the space and know how to access it. Finally, project materials are limited to only those available in the "ET 2800 store" to ensure that students have equal access to resources. These resources allow students without prior experience to contribute at a similar level compared to those who started with more knowledge, while still providing the PBL element of student choice so they feel ownership over the project and can use their own judgment in determining which resources to use and how to manage their team's project.

Integrating Social Justice into Design

Several of the engineering concepts in the project create an avenue for the inclusion of social justice. The disaster relief portion of the project, for example, introduces students to designing for social justice in industrial engineering and chemical engineering. This first half of the activity requires students to collect data on how long it takes them to put on a hazmat suit and other safety gear with various limitations. Students compare their initial time with no limitations, simulating an able-bodied person, with the time it takes to put on the suit with their eyes closed or without the use of an arm or leg, simulating an injury or other ability-related challenge (see Fig. 6.2 for lesson plan and project handout).

Industrial and Systems Engineering Disaster Relief Project Handout
Industrial and systems engineers make complex systems easier to manage, including disaster relief. Today's project is to plan a rescue for workers hurt as a result of a wildfire at a chemical plant. You will need the following data to complete your mission:

- Your rescue station is located 10 miles away from the chemical plant. You can travel at a maximum speed of 30 miles per hour.
- There are 30 injured workers at the site. It takes each team member 10 minutes to rescue each person, plus the time it takes to help them put on a hazmat suit. We will calculate this time in class.
- You have five people on your team and four eight-passenger vehicles.
- Each person is assumed to weigh an average of 150 lb.
- Each vehicle can carry a maximum of 1600 lbs without towing a trailer, or can carry 800 lbs and tow a trailer that has a total weight of 1000 lbs. *You can neglect the weight of the trailer for this simulation.*
- Your team should be able to carry some fire suppressants that can extinguish the fire at the plant so there are no other casualties. *Hint: Water can be very heavy, and some fire suppressants can be bad for the environment. Think about non-ozone depleting substances.*
- Assume each container filled with water weighs 100 lbs. You will need 100 containers of water in order to extinguish the fire.
- Assume each container filled with any other chemical fire suppressant weighs 50 lbs. You will need 70 containers of the chemicals in order to extinguish the fire.
- You must wear a hazmat suit before you can enter the plant and assist others.

The first part of this project is focused on collecting data. You must determine how long it takes to put on a hazmat suit before you can enter the chemical plant. We will take multiple samples during our in-class activity given the following:

Learning Outcomes	Faulty Paradigms to Address
After this lesson, students will be able to: • Articulate why statistics are not necessarily neutral data points • Identify examples of bias in engineering design	• We can design for the "average" person. • Statistics are neutral.

Assessment/Evidence of Learning
• Engaged class discussion • Explanation of statistics calculations in final paper

Lesson Plan
Review of industrial and systems engineering and its connection to disaster relief Hand out activity sheet and allow students time to read it (environmental piece is covered in a separate lesson) Ask for a volunteer from each group to wear the hazmat suit and other protective gear (recommend dust mask, safety goggles, gloves and booties; allow time for groups to record how long it takes to get dressed with no restrictions, with eyes closed and without the use of one arm. If additional students want to suit up, this will make the data more robust.) Ask each group to report out their statistics and discuss the following: • How much time should you allow for putting on protective gear at the disaster site? Why? • If students suggest using the average time – what happens if all of the people being rescued take longer than this? How else could use project the amount of time needed besides the average? • Can you think of other examples where designing for the "average" person means some people got left out? Present examples of bias in engineering design: • Gender bias in artificial intelligence (Specia, 2019) • Racial bias in facial recognition technology (Simonite, 2019) • Social class bias in transportation design (Groeger, 2016) • Reliance on male crash test dummies for safety testing (Bose et al., 2011) Closing Discussion – How do you think we can we reduce bias in engineering design? • Identify our own biases • Create diverse work teams with varied backgrounds and perspectives • Think about whose perspective is not represented • Invite people who will use your product to provide feedback

Fig. 6.2 Disaster relief activity—designing for social justice

- No physical constraints
- No vision
- Loss of the use of one arm.

Once you have collected all data, you will need to analyze your data and determine how long it will take your entire team to put on your suits. You can use this analysis to complete the rescue mission.

You will need to answer the following questions in your final paper:

- What fire suppressant did you carry with you to the site? How did you choose that suppressant, and what are the effects on the environment?
- How do you plan on transporting the chemicals to the chemical plant? How will you divide containers among the number of vehicles available?
- Given all the limitations, how long will it take for the rescue mission to be completed?
- Can all the rescues be completed in one trip, or is there a need for multiple trips?

After completing this activity, instructors lead a discussion on how engineers determine what data to use when making design choices. For example, does it make sense to take a simple average? Who gets left out in the disaster relief scenario if there isn't enough time allowed to rescue those without full use of their eyes or limbs? How can engineers plan for other unforeseen challenges that may be encountered? This conversation also illuminates the necessity of having a diversity of perspectives and experiences on the design team. The lesson also includes other examples of bias that can occur when design teams lack diversity, such as gender bias in artificial intelligence (Specia, 2019) and safety testing (Bose et al., 2011), racial bias in facial recognition technology (Simonite, 2019), and social class bias in transportation design (Groeger, 2016).

The second half of the disaster relief scenario, extinguishing the fire, covers chemical engineering and environmental justice issues. Teams research fire suppressants and consider their environmental impact, which leads to discussion on the ongoing impact of environmental damage that affects communities long after the initial disaster has passed. Some of these include the Hurricane Katrina aftermath (Burby, 2009), Deepwater

Horizon oil spill (Cope et al., 2013), Keystone Pipeline protest (Johnson, 2019), and the Bhopal gas leak (Taylor, 2014), which is covered in more depth in the next section.

Analyzing Failure from a Justice Perspective

The culmination of the semester-long project is Demo Day, when students demonstrate their final projects. Teams experience various degrees of success and failure during this demonstration, which segues to a lesson on engineering disasters (see Fig. 6.3). Students discuss various engineering disasters and the ethical breaches that contributed to those disasters, as well as how they disproportionately affected poor and marginalized communities. The conversation begins with the Union Carbide gas leak in Bhopal, India, considered to be the worst industrial disaster to date (Taylor, 2014). When students brainstorm reasons for the cause of this disaster, typical responses tend to focus on technical and communication issues. We as instructors challenge students to see the underlying bias by comparing the safety protocols to a similar plant in West Virginia only a few hours from our campus, then ask students to identify how bias has played a role in other disasters and ongoing environmental concerns.

During this lesson, instructors explain the idea of implicit biases to students and introduce Harvard's Implicit Association Tests (Project Implicit, 2011). Students are asked to take at least one test of their implicit biases and then reflect generally on their own privileges and their reactions to the role bias plays in engineering design and disasters. This activity challenges students to not only recognize oppression, bias, and privilege, but also consider how a voice of privilege could speak up on behalf of the missing voices in these scenarios and ultimately work to include those perspectives before disaster strikes.

Project Summary

The course described in this chapter represents a layered approach: teaching technical skills alongside concepts of diversity and social justice. The first layer is the complex, time-intensive assignment based on PBL principles, beginning with well-defined student learning goals and including the key components of a challenging problem or question, sustained inquiry, authenticity, student choice, reflection, critique and

Learning Outcomes	Faulty Paradigms to Address
After this lesson, students will be able to: • Articulate the concept of privilege, power and implicit bias • Examine engineering disasters for evidence of bias • Generate ideas to combat bias	• Engineering failures are always a result of technical or communication failures. • Only "racist" people have biases.

Assessment/Evidence of Learning

- Examples of engineering disasters or practices with an impact of marginalized communities
- Engaged discussion on how to address bias and oppression
- Weekly reflection question

Lesson Plan

Introductory Video: "India's Bhopal gas disaster explained," https://youtu.be/bxdm3JlN3lM
(Al Jazeera, 2014)

Discussion Question: What do you think contributed to this disaster? (most answers will likely relate to technical or communication failures)

Present excerpt from Taylor, A. (2014). Bhopal: The world's worst industrial disaster, 30 years later. *The Atlantic.* https://www.theatlantic.com/photo/2014/12/bhopal-the-worlds-worst-industrial-disaster-30-years-later/100864/:

"The company proceeded carefully, ensuring that the Bhopal plant had all the same modern technologies as its sister plant in West Virginia. The staff held rigorous training sessions for the workers, and installed a sophisticated, computerized system, just like the one in West Virginia, to alert workers to a leak. They set up loud alarm systems that could be heard for miles, distributed fact sheets about MIC to all the local hospitals, and held seminars for medical personnel on treating MIC exposure. By 1984, even as sales of Sevin tanked and the plant was operating at a loss, the company retained the full number of skilled workers and kept up its safety systems."

"At least, that would have been the responsible way to run a plant producing a highly toxic substance. But UCC didn't do any of this."

WHY NOT?

Introduction or review of privilege, power and implicit bias

Fig. 6.3 Engineering disasters and implicit bias (after an introductory lesson on engineering failures)

Discussion: What are some other examples in engineering when marginalized people have been harmed?
- Give students time to do research in pairs or small groups and share their findings with the class.
- What should we do about this?
  - Identify our own privileges and biases
  - Use your privilege to stand up for rights of those who don't have a voice
  - Think about whose perspective is not represented
  - Work with the people in the community that will be affected by your project
  - Strive to create and support diverse teams
  - Get to know people and their talents and skills that are not visible

Homework reflection: What were your thoughts on the way engineering disasters and design can disproportionately harm underprivileged groups? What are some privileges that you hold? How can you use those privileges in your work as an engineer to promote a better world?

Extra credit: To complete this assignment, take at least one implicit bias test from Harvard University's Project Implicit here: https://implicit.harvard.edu/implicit/takeatest.html and answer the following questions.
1. Why did you choose the test(s) that you took?
2. What were your results? Were you surprised by these results? Why do you think you do or don't have an implicit bias in that area?
3. Do you think this type of test is helpful for people to identify hidden biases? Why or why not?
4. What are some ways an implicit bias in the area(s) you chose could negatively impact an engineering project? Try to find an example or two from your own research. What steps could be taken to reduce bias in this area?

Fig. 6.3 (continued)

revision, and a public product. Learning outcomes for the class include understanding and applying the engineering design method to problem-solving, developing a foundational understanding of social justice and diversity concepts connected to engineering, and improving leadership, communication, and teamwork skills.

The project is based on a challenging, multi-component problem that requires sustained inquiry throughout the semester. Students learn technical aspects of the engineering design process while simultaneously reflecting on their teamwork, leadership, and communication skills within a framework of social justice. By providing access to a fixed set of materials, campus manufacturing lab, and disciplinary experts, the course gives students the ability to make their own informed choices on which resources to leverage and what role(s) they will play on the team. Reflection is incorporated throughout the course on a weekly basis, including written reflections, facilitated team discussions, and peer evaluations on product designs and individual contributions. After presenting their initial design ideas, students receive both positive and negative feedback and are allowed ample time to revise their physical work and their approach to working with their team. Finally, students all present their work in a public forum on Demo Day, displaying their work to a few hundred observers.

The second layer of social justice learning involves setting the tone of valuing diverse perspectives and creating equitable structures for the project, coupled with providing explicit instruction on social justice concepts, examples of bias in engineering design, and strategies to recognize and address oppression, bias, and privilege. In our classroom, we create a culture of transgressive teaching by participating in class activities, co-learning with our students, and using relevant examples from their lives. We build equity into our team and project structure by carefully assigning teams based on background and experience, providing foundational project knowledge and resources and introducing strategies to equitable idea generation and evaluation within teams. Instruction on social justice includes examples of bias and oppression in design and team dynamics, as well as spaced opportunities for critical self-reflection and peer feedback. We help students recognize and address bias by critiquing existing designs and prior engineering failures through a social justice lens and encourage deeper self-learning through the implicit bias test.

IMPLEMENTING SOCIAL JUSTICE EDUCATION THROUGH PBL

Shifting to PBL while incorporating social justice pedagogy can be daunting. However, the research on the benefits of the approach and our lived experience convince us that it is a worthwhile endeavor. Project-based learning keeps students engaged (Filippatou & Kaldi, 2010) and simultaneously improves problem-solving and interpersonal skills (Alacapinar, 2008). It often results in a memorable experience for both students and instructors alike (Thomas, 2000). When paired with social justice frameworks like $S_{TEM}J$ and transgressive teaching, the project provides current experiences for students to draw from in their reflections and to understand how large concepts of social justice play out on the macro-level of the engineering profession and the micro-level of their individual teams.

To create a PBL experience, we recommend starting with one small project. Our course started with three small projects that evolved into one integrated project over time. The recommendations for planning the course below are structured within Wiggins and McTighe's (2005) backward design method of (1) identifying learning outcomes, (2) determining evidence of learning, and (3) planning learning experiences:

1. Identify learning outcomes. Which course outcomes might be better achieved through a hands-on project? Building a project on just one or two outcomes to start may make the project more manageable and easier to assess.
2. Determine assessment evidence. Key PBL concepts include reflection, critique and revision, and a public product. How could you build in these elements to check for student learning and understanding? Consider multiple points of assessment to create space for further revision and feedback. How might students display their finished work beyond the classroom?
3. Plan the learning experience. What issues do your students care about? What existing resources do you have access to? Authentic projects might include partnering with a community organization, creating a product for actual use, simulating a real-world problem, or addressing students' real-world interests (Larmer, 2015).

To integrate social justice into a PBL course, one of the most obvious ways is to choose a project that focuses on social justice, perhaps a direct investigation of oppression or bias, or designing a solution to address an existing inequity. If the project is more focused on technical skills as the one described in this paper, instructors can bring in related topics for discussion: Who has the most access to the resources needed for this solution? What valuable resources or perspective might a marginalized community or person bring to the conversation? How does equity and social justice affect team dynamics and communication?

Some aspects of PBL directly overlap with basic tenets of social justice education, such as including student voices, peer feedback, and recognition for a job well done in a public product. In addition to incorporating social justice into the project, set an overall tone for the classroom beginning on day one using transgressive teaching principles. Rather than planning isolated lessons devoted to social justice topics, introduce one concept at a time to build a gradual foundation Then, refer back to that foundation and weave social justice into discussions and examples, even if they aren't the main topic of class that day. Finally, remember that incorporating social justice into a technical project is a process. Start with a few key concepts and you may be surprised how many opportunities present themselves to bring in a social justice lens.

CONCLUSION

Although we feel far from experts on the topic of incorporating diversity and social justice education into the engineering curriculum, we hope these ideas and examples spark reflection and new ways of introducing students to social justice. We find that making the concepts relevant to students' future professional identities helps the concepts take on greater importance in students' minds and allows us to engage them in meaningful conversation and reflection. We are grateful for the scholars who introduced us to the $S_{TEM}J$ framework and transgressive teaching models and hope to continue developing ideas to advance our students' understanding of social justice and ability to work toward a more equitable profession and world.

REFERENCES

Alacapinar, F. (2008). Effectiveness of project-based learning. *Eurasian Journal of Educational Research, 33,* 17–34.

Al Jazeera. (2014, November 30). *India's Bhopal gas disaster explained* [Video file]. https://youtu.be/bxdm3JlN3lM.

Armstrong, M. A., & Jovanovic, J. (2015). Starting at the crossroads: Intersectional approaches to institutionally supporting underrepresented minority women STEM faculty. *Journal of Women and Minorities in Science and Engineering, 21*(2), 141–157. https://doi.org/10.1615/JWomenMinorScienEng. 2015011275.

Aydede, M., & Matyar, F. (2009). The effect of active learning approach in science teaching on cognitive level of student achievement. *Journal of Turkish Science Education, 6*(1), 128–132. https://doi.org/10.1016/j.sbspro.2010. 03.589.

Baber, L. D. (2015). Considering the interest-convergence dilemma in STEM education. *The Review of Higher Education, 38*(2), 251–270. https://doi.org/10.1353/rhe.2015.0004.

Barnes-Johnson, J., & Johnson, J. M. (2018). *STEM21: Equity in teaching and learning to meet global challenges of standards, engagement and transformation.* Peter Lang.

Bonebright, D. A. (2010). 40 years of storming: A historical review of Tuckman's model of small group development. *Human Resource Development International, 13*(1), 111–120. https://doi.org/10.1080/13678861003589099.

Bose, D., Segui-Gomez, M., & Crandall, J. R. (2011). Vulnerability of female drivers involved in motor vehicle crashes: An analysis of US population at risk. *American Journal of Public Health, 101*(12), 2368–2373. https://doi.org/10.2105/AJPH.2011.300275.

Brinkworth, C. (2016). *From chilly climate to warm reception: Experiences and good practices for supporting LGBTQ students in STEM.* CGU Theses & Dissertations, 97. https://doi.org/10.5642/cguetd/97.

Burby, R. J. (2009). Natural disaster analysis after Hurricane Katrina: Risk assessment, economic impacts and social implications. *Journal of the American Planning Association, 75*(3), 379–380. https://doi.org/10.1080/01944360902967228.

Cech, E. A., & Waidzunas, T. J. (2011). Navigating the heteronormativity of engineering: The experiences of lesbian, gay, and bisexual students. *Engineering Studies, 3*(1), 1–24. https://doi.org/10.1080/19378629.2010.545065.

Chen, X. (2013). *STEM attrition: College students' paths into and out of STEM fields (NCES 2014-001).* Washington, DC: National Center for Education Statistics, U.S. Department of Education. https://nces.ed.gov/pubs2014/2014001rev.pdf.

Cope, M. R., Slack, T., Blanchard, T. C., & Lee, M. R. (2013). Does time heal all wounds? Community attachment, natural resource employment, and health impacts in the wake of the BP Deepwater Horizon disaster. *Social Science Research, 42*(3), 872–881. https://doi.org/10.1016/j.ssresearch.2012.12.011.

Díaz-García, C., González-Moreno, A., & Sáez-Martínez, F. J. (2013). Gender diversity within R&D teams: Its impact on radicalness of innovation. *Innovation, 15*(2), 149–160. https://doi.org/10.5172/impp.2013.15.2.149.

Dierker, L., Evia, J. R., Singer-Freeman, K., Woods, K., Zupkus, J., Arnholt, A., ... Rose, J. (2018). Project-based learning in introductory statistics: Comparing course experiences and predicting positive outcomes for students from diverse educational settings. *International Journal of Educational*

Technology and Learning, 3(2), 52–64. http://doi.org/10.20448/2003.32.52.64.

Dierker, L., Kaparakis, E., Rose, J., & Selya, A. (2012). Strength in numbers: A multidisciplinary, project-based course in introductory statistics. *Journal of Effective Teaching, 12*(2), 4–14.

Estrada, M., Burnett, M., Campbell, A. G., Campbell, P. B., Denetclaw, W. F., Gutiérrez, C. G., ... Zavala, M. (2016). Improving underrepresented minority student persistence in STEM. *CBE Life Sciences Education, 15*(3), 1–10. http://doi.org/10.1187/cbe.16-01-0038.

Freire, P. (2007). *Pedagogy of the oppressed* (3rd ed.). The Continuum International Publishing Group Inc.

Filippatou, D., & Kaldi, S. (2010). The effectiveness of project-based learning on pupils with learning difficulties regarding academic performance, group work and motivation. *International Journal of Special Education, 25,* 17–26.

Garriott, P. O., Hultgren, K. M., & Frazier, J. (2017). STEM stereotypes and high school students' math/science career goals. *Journal of Career Assessment, 25*(4), 585–600. https://doi.org/10.1177/1069072716665825.

Groeger, L. V. (2016, September 1). Discrimination by design. *ProPublica.* https://www.propublica.org/article/discrimination-by-design.

Hirshfield, L., & Koretsky, M. D. (2018). Gender and participation in an engineering problem-based learning environment. *Interdisciplinary Journal of Problem-Based Learning, 12*(1), 51–71. https://doi.org/10.7771/1541-5015.1651.

Holloman, T. K., Lee, W. C., London, J. S., Halkiyo, A. B., Jew, G., & Watford, B. A. (2018). *A historical and policy perspective on broadening participation in STEM: Insights from national reports (1974–2016).* Paper presented at 2018 CoNECD—The Collaborative Network for Engineering and Computing Diversity Conference, Crystal City, Virginia. https://peer.asee.org/29508.

hooks, B. (1994). *Teaching to transgress: Education as the practice of freedom.* Routledge.

Hughes, B. E. (2017). "Managing by not managing": How gay engineering students manage sexual orientation. *Journal of College Student Development, 58*(3), 385–401. https://doi.org/10.1353/csd.2017.0029.

Hughes, B. E. (2018). Coming out in STEM: Factors affecting retention of sexual minority STEM students. *Science Advances, 4*(3), eaao6373. http://doi.org/10.1126/sciadv.aao6373.

Hunt, V., Layton, D., & Prince, S. (2014). *Diversity matters.* http://boardagender.org/files/MyKinsey-DIVERSITY_MATTERS_2014_-_print_version_-_McKinsey_Report.pdf.

James, S. M., & Singer, S. R. (2016). From the NSF: The National Science Foundation's investments in broadening participation in science, technology, engineering, and mathematics education through research and capacity building. *CBE—Life Sciences Education, 15*(3), fe7. https://doi.org/10. 1187/cbe.16-01-0059.

Johnson, D. R. (2012). Campus racial climate perceptions and overall sense of belonging among racially diverse women in STEM majors. *Journal of College Student Development, 53*(2), 336–346. https://doi.org/10.1353/csd.2012. 0028.

Johnson, T. N. (2019). The Dakota access pipeline and the breakdown of participatory processes in environmental decision-making. *Environmental Communication, 13*(3), 335–352. https://doi.org/10.1080/17524032.2019.156 9544.

Kahle, J. B. (1998). Equitable systemic reform in science and mathematics: Assessing progress. *Journal of Women and Minorities in Science and Engineering, 4*(2&3), 91–112. https://doi.org/10.1615/JWomenMinorScie nEng.v4.i2-3.20.

Krajcik, J., & Blumenfeld, P. (2006). Project-based learning. In R. K. Sawyer (Ed.), *The Cambridge handbook of the learning sciences* (pp. 317–333). New York, NY: Cambridge University Press.

KQED Quest. (2017, April 12). The engineering design process: A taco party [Video file]. https://www.youtube.com/watch?v=MAhpfFt_mWM.

LaForce, M., Noble, E., & Blackwell, C. (2017). Problem-based learning (PBL) and student interest in STEM careers: The roles of motivation and ability beliefs. *Education Sciences, 7*(4), 92. https://doi.org/10.3390/educsci70 40092.

Larmer, J. (2015, April 21). Gold standard PBL: Essential project design elements. *Buck Institute for Education PBLWorks.* https://www.pblworks. org/blog/gold-standard-pbl-essential-project-design-elements.

Li, J., Zhao, F., Chen, S., Jiang, W., Liu, T., & Shi, S. (2017). Gender diversity on boards and firms' environmental policy. *Business Strategy and the Environment, 26*(3), 306–315. https://doi.org/10.1002/bse.1918.

Litzler, E., & Young, J. (2012). Understanding the risk of attrition in undergraduate engineering: Results from the project to assess climate in engineering. *Journal of Engineering Education, 101*(2), 319–345. https://doi.org/10. 1002/j.2168-9830.2012.tb00052.x.

Madden, P. E., Wong, C., Vera Cruz, A. C., Olle, C. D., & Barnett, M. (2017). Social justice driven STEM learning (S$_{TEM}$J): A curricular framework for teaching STEM in a social justice driven, urban, college access program. *Catalyst: A Social Justice Forum, 7*(1), 24–27. https://trace.tennessee.edu/ catalyst/vol7/iss1/4.

McGee, E. O. (2015). Robust and fragile mathematical identities: A framework for exploring racialized experiences and high achievement among black college students. *Journal for Research in Mathematics Education, 46*(5), 599–625. https://doi.org/10.5951/jresematheduc.46.5.0599.

Moran, B. (2017). Is science too straight? LGBTQ+ issues in STEM diversity. *The Brink: Pioneering Research from Boston University.* http://www.bu.edu/articles/2017/lgbt-issues-stem-diversity/.

National Center for Science and Engineering Statistics. (2019). *Women, minorities, and persons with disabilities in science and engineering: 2019 (Special Report NSF 19-304).* Arlington, VA: National Science Foundation. https://ncses.nsf.gov/pubs/nsf19304/.

Nathan, M., & Lee, N. (2013). Cultural diversity, innovation, and entrepreneurship: Firm-level evidence from London. *Economic Geography, 89*(4), 367–394. https://doi.org/10.1111/ecge.12016.

National Student Clearinghouse. (2015). *High school benchmarks.* NSC Research Center. https://nscresearchcenter.org/hsbenchmarks2015/.

PBLWorks. (2019). *What is PBL?* Buck Institute for Education. https://www.pblworks.org/what-is-pbl.

Project Implicit. (2011). *About the implicit association test.* https://implicit.harvard.edu/implicit/iatdetails.html.

Ramsey, C., Cannady, J., & DeGraff, M. (2018). Closing the gender and underrepresented minority gap in CS: UTeach computer science principles AP assessment results. *Proceedings of the 49th ACM Technical Symposium on Computer Science Education.* https://doi.org/10.1145/3159450.3162286.

Roy, J. (2018). *Engineering by the numbers.* Washington, DC: American Society for Engineering Education. https://ira.asee.org/wp-content/uploads/2019/07/2018-Engineering-by-Numbers-Engineering-Statistics-UPDATED-15-July-2019.pdf.

Rozeka, C. S., Ramirez, G., Fine, R. D., & Beilock, S. L. (2018). Reducing socioeconomic disparities in the STEM pipeline through student emotion regulation. *Proceedings of the National Academy of Sciences of the United States of America, 116*(5). https://doi.org/10.1073/pnas.1808589116.

Savage, R., Chen, K., & Vanasupa, L. (2007). Integrating project-based learning throughout the undergraduate engineering curriculum. *Journal of STEM Education, 8*(3), 15–27.

Simonite, T. (2019, July 22). The best algorithms struggle to recognize black faces equally. *Wired.* https://www.wired.com/story/best-algorithms-struggle-recognize-black-faces-equally/.

Specia, M. (2019, May 22). Siri and Alexa reinforce gender bias, U.N. finds. *The New York Times.* https://www.nytimes.com/2019/05/22/world/siri-alexa-ai-gender-bias.html.

Stout, J. G., & Wright, H. M. (2016). Lesbian, gay, bisexual, transgender, and queer students' sense of belonging in computing: An intersectional approach. *Computing in Science & Engineering, 18,* 24–30. https://doi.org/10.1109/MCSE.2016.45.

Taylor, A. (2014, December 2). Bhopal: The world's worst industrial disaster, 30 years later. *The Atlantic.* https://www.theatlantic.com/photo/2014/12/bhopal-the-worlds-worst-industrial-disaster-30-years-later/100864/.

Thomas, J. W. (2000). *A review of project based learning.* A Report prepared for The Autodesk Foundation. San Rafael, CA (online).

Todd, N. R., & Abrams, E. M. (2011). White dialectics: A new framework for theory, research, and practice with white students. *The Counseling Psychologist, 39*(3), 353–395. https://doi.org/10.1177/0011000010377665.

Tonso, K. L. (2006). Student engineers and engineer identity: Campus engineer identities as figured world. *Cultural Studies of Science Education, 1*(2), 273–307. https://doi.org/10.1007/s11422-005-9009-2.

University of Texas at Austin. (2020). *College Board–Endorsed AP CS Principles Curriculum.*

UTeach Computer Science. https://cs.uteach.utexas.edu/computer-science-principles.

Wiggins, G., & McTighe, J. (2005). *Understanding by design* (Expanded 2nd ed.). Association for Supervision and Curriculum Development.

Recommended Readings

Barnes-Johnson, J. & Johnson, J. M. (2018). *STEM21: Equity in teaching and learning to meet global challenges of standards, engagement and transformation.* Peter Lang Publishing.

Madden, P. E., Wong, C., Vera Cruz, A. C., Olle, C. D., & Barnett, M. (2017). Social justice driven STEM learning ($S_{TEM}J$): A curricular framework for teaching STEM in a social justice driven, urban, college access program. *Catalyst: A Social Justice Forum, 7*(1), 24–27. https://trace.tennessee.edu/catalyst/vol7/iss1/4.

Stoddard, E., Wobbe, K., & Bass, R. (2019). *Project-based learning in the first year: Beyond all expectations.* Stylus.

CHAPTER 7

Social Justice and Physics Education

*Geraldine L. Cochran, Simone Hyater-Adams,
Carolina Alvarado, Chanda Prescod-Weinstein,
and Abigail R. Daane*

Key Terms and Definitions

Emerging bilingual — According to Seltzer et al. (2017, p. 2), the term *emerging bilingual* includes students who are officially designated by schools as "English

G. L. Cochran (✉)
Rutgers University, New Brunswick, NJ, USA
e-mail: geraldine.cochran@physics.rutgers.edu

S. Hyater-Adams
American Physical Society, College Park, MD, USA

C. Alvarado
California State University, Chico, CA, USA

C. Prescod-Weinstein
University of New Hampshire, Durham, NH, USA

A. R. Daane
South Seattle College, Seattle, WA, USA

© The Author(s), under exclusive license to Springer Nature
Switzerland AG 2021
C. C. Ozaki and L. Parson (eds.), *Teaching and Learning
for Social Justice and Equity in Higher Education*,
https://doi.org/10.1007/978-3-030-69947-5_7

language learners ('ELLs'),'" as well as English speakers who are learning other languages (e.g., Spanish, Arabic, Mandarin). They do not use the term *ELL* because it renders the linguistic repertoires invisible.

INTRODUCTION

Within the United States, historical and current inequities and injustices in education are well-documented (Ladson-Billings, 2006, 2007), and complex issues of ethics, politics, and culture exist in classrooms (Atwater et al., 2013), including physics classrooms. However, these issues often go ignored in physics classrooms, exacerbating current injustices and inequities in the field of physics. Social justice should be an integral part of physics education. Atwater et al. (2013) assert that social justice *requires action* and that "science teacher educators must act against oppression and inequities and teach their students how to do this (p. 1298)." We begin this chapter with an examination of the history of physics and a rationale for why physics instructors must give attention to social justice in physics education.

The second section of this chapter provides a brief overview of efforts to infuse social justice and equity conversations in physics classroom, along with associated research. We also provide a detailed example of how two physicists, authors three and five, integrate equity and social justice into physics curricula. Teaching physics can be a vehicle for engaging in social justice. Previous work in physics (Rifkin, 2015), biology (Donovan, 2016, 2017), and mathematics (Gutstein, 2003) illustrates how a social justice lens can be used to understand scientific disciplines and how concepts in scientific disciplines can be used to help students understand social justice issues within particular disciplines.

However, we do not offer these examples without caution. Positionality, the power and privileges inherent in an educator's immediate respective social positions impacts their experiences (Misawa, 2010). This is particularly true when it comes to individuals with multiple, interlocking marginalized socio-demographic identities as sociocultural power and privilege shapes their experiences (Parent et al., 2013). Atwater et al. (2013) found that Black science teacher educators that infused multicultural education, equity, and social justice in their teaching faced challenges, resulting in some of them discontinuing the practice. With this in mind, authors three and five have included statements of positionality in the introduction of their lesson plans.

The authors of this chapter are all physicists engaged in social justice, committed to addressing inequities and oppression in physics and physics education through action. We have various, intersecting socio-demographic identities that motivate the work that we do and our experiences with this work. It is our hope that this chapter elucidates the need for social justice in physics education and provides examples for how one might engage in this work. The intended audience for this chapter includes physics instructors and physics teacher educators; though we hope that the included ideas and examples are useful to all teacher educators, science educators, and stakeholders in education.

Why Physicists Must Pay Attention to Social Justice in Physics

Students of physics tend to learn little history of physics as part of their formal curriculum, hearing stories about the origins of ideas and equations either as side notes in their textbooks or lectures. This minimal engagement with a whole discipline produces physics students who go on to become professional interlocutors of an official storyline that is both superficial and at odds with aligning physics as a community with social justice practices. The reason for this is tied to the very same processes that produce a need to pay particular attention to social justice in the first place: ongoing settler colonial white supremacy and its lasting effects.

In fact, the mention of settler colonial white supremacy in connection with physics immediately necessitates an explanation because the relationship is often not immediately obvious in the physics community which prides itself on being a "culture of no culture" (Traweek, 1992, p. 162). In fact, as Traweek elaborates in her ethnography of high energy (particle) physicists (1992), professional physics has a rather elaborate set of cultures with local, nationalistic features. But the belief in a culture of no culture mirrors a broader mindset in European societies and their settler colonial satellites (e.g., Canada, Australia, and the United States), which tend to hold that their culture is the supreme culture and that their tendency to uphold a mechanistic framework is therefore natural.

This mechanistic point of view is reified and valorized by the advent and incredible success of Newtonian physics in the eighteenth century. The Newtonian Physics framework is highly successful at making predictions based on a few key principles, and it is easy in hindsight to believe that the dominance of Eurocentric epistemologies is both "natural" and "scientific" and "just the way things are," as it were. In fact, we cannot come to understand the pervasive success of the mechanistic worldview that underpins modern physics without recognizing that European/settler colonial thought is underpinned by a commitment to settler colonial white supremacy that diminishes indigenous ways of perceiving and organizing knowledge about the universe (Whitt, 2009; Maile, 2015a, 2015b).

This cultural tendency is often invisible to professional physicists and even some historians of physics operating in so-called western contexts because they are typically embedded in this culture from birth (DiAngelo, 2018). In essence, the mechanistic world view is both a fascinating intellectual framework and one deeply enmeshed with white supremacy. As a result of this sometimes invisible embedding, the techno-empirical activities which have professionalized into what we call "professional physics" are enmeshed with white supremacy (Traweek, 1992; Whitt, 2009). Therefore, it is important in thinking through the idea of social justice in physics to deeply understand the origins of physics through a critical lens, rather than through the hagiography that traditionally undergirds a physics education. Rather than a march of progress produced and led by white man heroes, physics (and companion sciences like astronomy) must be understood as existing within socio-political cultures that have evolved in time but throughout the last 500 years have lived in a milieu of struggle and violence defined by colonialism and racism.

The implications for how we understand the history of physics are vast specifically because physics is traditionally placed atop the hierarchy of empirical practices, potentially with the capacity to understand the roots of the universe's very existence (Prescod-Weinstein, 2020). As a social technology, settler colonial white supremacy produces a tent of whiteness which defines people who count as "white." White people are the intended beneficiaries of settler colonial projects (Prescod-Weinstein, 2017). Core beneficiaries of this structure in the present-day are people who are solely of European descent or descendants of people who passed as such. Even of these restrictive conditions, members of any ethno-racial group can play a role in upholding the tent of whiteness, even when they are not welcome within it. Who is welcome has also shifted with time, and the outer boundaries of the tent are never static. The settler colonial tent of whiteness determines who is constructed as human, who is seen as meriting freedom of movement and thought, whose minds are worth cultivating and nourishing intellectually, and how relationships to land are determined and valued (Maile, 2015a, 2015b).

It is particularly valuable to look at examples of historical entanglement between colonialism and astronomy because the examples are myriad and somewhat mundane, which is a basic feature of how European governments operated in the eighteenth and nineteenth centuries (see Prescod-Weinstein, 2017 for a list of related readings). Although astronomy and physics initially evolved as separate disciplines, they were connected by Newton's mechanical theory of gravitation in the seventeenth century. In the eighteenth and nineteenth centuries in particular, colonized lands were instrumentalized as sites of scientific praxis. In one case, Jean-Dominique Cassini, director of the Paris Observatory, sent astronomers to the French colony French Guiana to take measurements of Mars (McClellan III, 2010). He also sent astronomers to Saint Domingue (present-day Haiti and the Dominican Republic) to engage in astronomical observations (McClellan III, 2010). NASA has since named a mission after him (NASA, 2019). His son Jacques was involved in similar expeditions involving the Caribbean island of Martinique (McClellan III & Regourd, 2000). This practice of using land access that was facilitated by colonialism to do astronomy continues today, with the extensive utilization of Native Hawaiian sacred land, Mauna a Wakea, for more than ten separate observatories (Salazar, 2014; Maile, 2015a, 2015b; Neilson & Lawler, 2019; Neilson et al., 2019).

Looking at history of physics itself, Morus connects the development of physics as a professional discipline with the specific needs of industrializing societies (Morus, 2005). In fact, in the British and American contexts, it is perhaps interesting to ask the question of how shifting energetic needs are tied to the end of the Atlantic slave trade and of slavery itself. Such a question is beyond the purview of this chapter, but represents an example of why history of physics can play a role in discourse about social justice in physics. By enriching our understanding of what physics has been to people on the losing end of power relations, we can perhaps change the balance of the equation.

SOCIAL JUSTICE IN PHYSICS CURRICULA AND RESEARCH

While the westernization of the physics discipline and physics education has created a culture that neglects its harmful and problematic
norms, values, and practices, there are currently physicists looking to
effect change by teaching about race and gender equity. Over the past
few years, physics education researchers have begun taking up the task of
creating and studying social justice and equity curriculum for the physics
classroom. The large majority of these are developed for teaching at the
high school level (Lock & Hazari, 2016; Rifkin, 2016), but this work
is also being done for teaching at the undergraduate level (Daane et al.,
2017). Many of the curricular materials developed utilize class discussion
on under-representation in physics, particularly related to race and gender.

As one example, Rifkin (2016) reported on his strategy for teaching
about the under-representation of women in physics and People of Color
in physics in his high school physics classroom. He describes his lesson
as an exploration of under-representation and has students explore the
demographic statistics of who does physics. The exploration of this data
fuels conversations about why these numbers look the way they do and
supports his inclusion of lessons focused on implicit bias and stereotype
threat in a physics classroom. Students in the class then create posters that
highlight the work of non-white physicists, which is a practice becoming
increasingly more common in introductory physics courses at the collegiate level. His article ends with advice on how to respond to skeptical
colleagues with a list of common questions and comments an instructor
might hear. He has since built on this work with other instructors to
create a full curriculum available for free online (The Underrepresentation
Curriculum, 2018). Similarly, Daane et al. (2017) report on discussions
about racial equity in an introductory undergraduate physics course at a
Predominantly White Institution (PWI). This work includes an example
unit to facilitate undergraduate students in reflecting on equity in physics.
The lessons incorporate reading and reflection with classroom discussion and always include a plan for students becoming agents of change
committed to addressing inequities going forward.

Some research focuses on the impact of discussing issues of social
justice in high school physics courses on student identity development
(Lock & Hazari, 2016; Potvin et al., 2015). Lock and Hazari (2016)
conducted case-study research on high school physics classrooms with
instructor-led discussions about the under-representation of women in

physics. This study is a part of a larger project that investigates the impact of various pedagogies on students' physics identity. The lesson includes reading materials about historical women in physics, writing an essay, and engaging in a classroom discussion bridging past to present-day experiences of women in physics. Lock and Hazari (2016) found that the discussion on present-day experiences impacted students the greatest.

Ultimately, these examples show that discussing issues of equity in the physics classroom is possible and positively impacts students (especially white women and Students of Color of all genders). While there are a few researchers focusing on best practices, this work is still new and under-studied, and it deserves more attention. Discussions that push students to question the people who do physics and why there is under-representation of any groups in physics are of value to students. However, there is much more that can be done to paint the full picture of the depth of inequity that plagues the physics field.

WHAT IS NEEDED TO MOVE FORWARD

While examples of equity-oriented physics curricula provide solid evidence of what is possible, lessons like these can be pushed further. For physics education to move toward a social justice-oriented curriculum, there are several changes that need to be made. These changes are addressed in the sections below.

Acknowledging the Nature of Physics and What Is Valued in Physics Education

Physics educators need to change what content is valued in the class-room. This may include putting less emphasis on problem-solving to make more space for teaching the context and values of physics theories. To create lessons that provide a deep understanding of the social justice and equity issues present in the physics field, much is needed. First, instructors must acknowledge their socio-demographic identities and the power that they hold over students. Power is enacted in several ways in a classroom. This includes the power that instructors and the developers of the curriculum hold over students (Delpit, 1988). This is particularly important in physics classrooms at the collegiate level where physics faculty are generally white (Ivie et al., 2014) and men (Ivie et al., 2013). Second, discussions of under-representation and diversity in physics must be expanded to include additional socio-demographic identities—moving beyond race and gender alone—and also acknowledge the impact of intersecting identities (Cochran et al., 2020). Third, instructors need support and preparation in implementing equity and social justice in classrooms supporting students of various demographic backgrounds. This is important to ensure that students are allowed the time necessary to process information that may be comfortable and to ensure no further harm is done to students from marginalized backgrounds in the process of the discussion. Indeed, Black science teacher educators found that having support helped them to overcome challenges to implementing multicultural education, equity, and social justice into their curriculum (Atwater et al., 2013). Finally, these curricular changes need to be implemented in all physics classroom nationally rather than a select few high school and introductory collegiate classes.

One way to expand and motivate equity issues in physics is to include conversations about the nature of physics, a topic that is often overlooked or implicit among the physics community. Which physicists are mentioned during instruction and which ones are acknowledged (or ignored) as important historical contributors to the field can implicitly teach what and who is, or is not, valued. The current focus on white, western, and masculine contributions to physics in the classroom has excluded people at several intersections of identity. In order to work toward correcting this, physics classes should teach about the intricate ways that settler colonial white supremacy, capitalism, and United States imperialism all contributed to create the field of physics we have today. These complex systems of oppression and their historic roots are the foundations of what we today call physics and can bolster a more thorough social justice curriculum for introductory physics.

Revisioning the Physics Classroom

Because physicists commonly are unaware of this history, and many do not value social justice and equity work, incorporating the history of physics and social justice into a curriculum may be difficult to create and execute in current physics classrooms. However, physics instructors can do so in several ways by incorporating societal context into physics topics, discussing current issues, events, and experiences of diverse physicists, and providing historical background for physics topics. Physics instructors can also include activities that highlight Physicists of Color, physicists who are gender non-conforming, non-binary, and transgender, and physi-. cists with different abilities. This may expand students' ideas about what kinds of people do physics. Discussions about Indigenous communities' engagement in physics and astronomy before "modern math and science" should also be included. For example, one might ask students to investigate what we know about the pyramids in Egypt or the contribution of Indigenous peoples to astronomy. One could take this deeper by having students reflect on why these methods are not used or acknowledged in the physics field today and connect this to the current conflict between physicists and Indigenous communities such as a discussion about the protests being held by Indigenous communities to keep telescopes off of sacred land.

By teaching the historic context of physics and having students reflect on how this history connects to the present-day, physics instructors can set the stage for reflection on inequities that are rooted deeply in the physics discipline. Instructors can go beyond the discussion of under-representation to create a deeper and more critical conversation for students helping students to understand the historical injustices and inequities that have led to the current under-representation.

Additionally, emphasizing the importance of learning both societal and historical context along with the theory and math-related content in a physics class requires integrating social justice topics into each lesson. The examples presented in this section are structured as one unit of lessons taught at one time during a physics course. However, in physics it is not uncommon to teach a quick history along with the physics theory or formula when presented in each class. This history should include information about the people credited with the discovery (and those who contributed but were not recognized for their work), details about the socio-political climate of the time, and how they contributed to the discovery. It could also include information about similar ideas contributed by nondominant cultures and People of Color. Being explicit about this information could prompt discussions around why the physics field pulls solely from western work. That context can create a space for students to understand the depth of the inequities in physics that created those we see in the field today, and deepen the discussions described in the lessons included in this chapter.

Tending to Group Dynamics and Classroom Demographics

Finally, the group dynamics of the classroom need to be considered when discussing topics about equity, social justice, power and privilege. A responsible instructor interested in facilitating conversations around these topics should seek out training to do so. Because discussing these topics can often mean discussing the lived experiences and histories of students in the classroom, instructors must learn how to facilitate the discomfort that comes with learning about power and privilege. In order to decrease the likelihood of an instructor harming students from marginalized identities who enter physics learning environments, instructors should seek guidance from others with this expertise and/or resources that have strategies for doing this.

A few things to be conscious of when teaching about equity, power and privilege in the physics classroom are: (1) many physics classrooms are overwhelmingly upper class, white, able bodied, straight men, which means those with the most power and privilege in our society are the ones taking up the most space; (2) learning about equity means that students and instructors will have to go through many moments of discomfort that will elicit emotional responses; and (3) the classroom must have a means of allowing this process to happen while causing the least amount of harm to everyone. Teaching about equity, power, and privilege in Physics is not easy: it requires self-reflection and effort to create a positive classroom experience. Not all groups will have a positive experience. However, this work is possible; it can be done. If physicists want to take seriously the idea of teaching social justice in educational spaces, and change the toxic culture of physics, physics educators must be open to this challenge.

Physics instructors and physics education researchers have already begun the work of finding ways to teach about equity and social justice in the classroom, but there is more work that can be done to advance the conversations. The issue of "underrepresentation" in physics is deeper than gaps in numbers. It has been built into the field through a history of exclusion and oppression. A curriculum that addresses this would value nontraditional information for a physics classroom, provide the full context of the core theories and formulas, teach students about the roots of the field, connect those to the inequities that exist today, and work to create a new generation of agents of change in physics.

Equity Teaching in the Physics Classroom

I, Abigail R. Daane, experience privilege in almost every facet of my identity. When I began to teach physics as a white, woman instructor, I realized that I had much to learn about cultural change. I wanted to *do* something to make the physics community more inclusive and inviting for women and People of Color. I started by working to identify my own implicit assumptions and the dominant cultural structures in the classroom that detract from student learning. This is an ongoing journey and while learning, I needed to do additional work to support my students.

When Chief Justice Roberts asked, "What unique perspective does a minority student bring to a physics class?" during the Fisher vs. UT Austin case, I found a way to explicitly discuss equity in my, then university, setting—a way of revisioning the physics classroom. The conversations felt productive and yet students pushed back: "Why are we talking about this in a physics classroom? Physics is objective—it doesn't matter who does it!" I realized that many of my students held the general views of physics as a "culture with no culture" (Traweek, 1992). The physicist's quest for objective laws and formulae supports the treatment of this subject as uninfluenced by people. Some students' ideas about physics aligned with this sentiment. If one believes that physics is objective, then there cannot be any movement toward changing the culture and practices. In this predominantly white classroom, students needed to have the opportunity to identify how humans influence physics through bias, implicit assumptions, organized power structures, etc. Students could then feel empowered to change physics and commit to action.

This lesson speaks to the call to acknowledge the nature and values of physics in the classroom by supporting students in identifying the subjectivity in physics and relating that subjectivity to systemic inequities in the field. These conversations have been productive in introductory, calculus-based classes at (1) an expensive, private institution, (2) a two-year Minority Serving Institution, as well as (3) workshops for STEM instructors of K-16 populations, and (4) high schools. By acknowledging human influence in this lesson, it opens the door to discuss the contextualizing of physics (e.g., historical & political connections) that are discussed above. This initial lesson is now a part of the Underrepresentation Curriculum (The Underrepresentation Curriculum, 2018; Rifkin, 2016; Daane et al., 2017; Eickerman & Rifkin, 2020) and can be especially productive when taught in the second half of a course that focuses on active learning and community building.

Table 7.1   Prewrite reflection questions

1. How would you define "physics?"
2. Do you think physics is subjective (i.e., based on or influenced by personal feelings, tastes, or opinions) or objective (i.e., not influenced by personal feelings or opinions)? Why?
3. Do you think racial diversity *in physics* is important? Why or why not?

Example Lesson: Physics Is Subjective

What is physics? This lesson begins with an individual reflection where students answer questions about physics content and culture (Table 7.1).

After writing their responses to the three questions, students discuss their definitions of physics in small groups of three to four students and decide on the best definition as a group. Each group leader writes their definition on the front board so that the whole class can read each one. Often, definitions involve actions such as "investigate" "study" or "experiment" and concepts such as "motion" "how things work" and "electricity."

Is Physics Subjective or Objective?

The next activity begins with a poll or clicker question where students share answers anonymously: Do you think physics is (A) subjective, (B) objective, (C) mostly subjective, or (D) mostly objective? We then ask students to move to a place in the room along a spectrum from subjective to objective based on their view about where physics falls. See Fig. 7.1 for

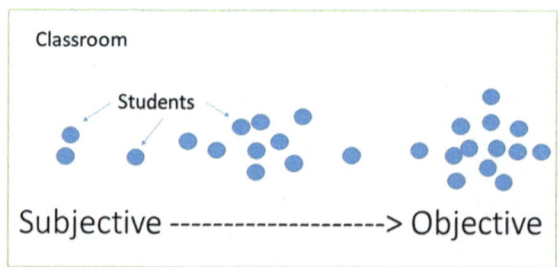

Fig. 7.1   Classroom setup

an example of a possible Classroom Setup. Once students have moved, we encourage students to find someone at another location on the spectrum and listen to be convinced to move. Students can adjust their position based on other student's ideas. Depending on where students end up, one side of the room can then talk to the other side about their perspectives in a whole class discussion. A powerful discussion question to ask those on the objective side is, "Can you see ways in which physics *is* subjective?" At this point, students often need processing time, and we ask for written responses to this question: "What are you thinking about right now and/or how are you feeling regarding our discussion?"

How Is Physics Subjective?

At this point, students are often eager to define physics, so we share the Oxford definition of science: the intellectual and practical *activity* encompassing the systematic *study* of the structure and behavior of the physical and natural world through *observation and experiment*. Through discussion, students note that humans are necessarily involved in these actions, and we ask students to think about the actions that introduce subjectivity into physics. Students then read short excerpts from Hatton & Plouffe (1997) and/or American Association for the Advancement of Science (1990) that highlight aspects of human influence including who decides what is published, taught, or funded and whose research focus and interests are pursued. We use a jigsaw method (Aronson, 1978) in which each student reads and develops expertise on one section of a reading and then shares that information with other students who have read other sections. We end class by adding to our brainstormed list about the many ways in which humans influence who does physics, what is studied, and how we use research in society.

Reflection on Lesson

We position *physics as subjective* explicitly to highlight that humans affect who, what, and how physics operates. We see this lesson as preparation for students to then consider how disparities in representation in physics (e.g., racial, ethnic, gender, etc.) hurt both the physics community and the people excluded from it. This conversation can also lead into a larger unit that includes why social justice is needed in teaching and learning physics and what we can do to improve (Daane et al., 2017; www.underrep.com).

In my classroom, these conversations are among the most important, leading to large shifts in perspective in both university (Daane & Sawtelle, 2016; Decker & Daane, 2018) and two-year college classes (Arielle Evans et al., 2019). Many students begin by taking a strong "physics is objective" stance and over time shift their ideas to recognize the ways in which subjectivity is present in the field. These conversations can have profound effects on Students of Color and women in my classrooms who might otherwise be silenced (Herrera et al., 2020; Lock & Hazari, 2016), because it acknowledges the reality of barriers and provides space to work toward changing the culture in physics. In my own experience, acknowledging subjectivity explicitly has created a powerful platform to discuss issues of social justice and motivates many more students and colleagues (of all backgrounds) to work toward cultural change.

Engaging Future Physics Teachers in Scientific Inquiry

I, Carolina Alvarado, am a Mexican, woman, physicist who currently works as an assistant professor in a recently designated Hispanic Serving Institution in rural Northern California. The work presented in this section reflects part of my journey as an educator of future K-8 teachers since my first semester working in this institution in Fall 2016. Given that physics education research has been developing collaborative curricular materials that foster the conceptual understanding of physics by engaging students in scientific practices, my teaching not only benefits from the results of research but also addresses the power dynamics in the learning environment to address practices that continue to disenfranchise People of Color and women into scientific communities.

Engaging Future Teachers in Scientific Inquiry

The course I teach targets future elementary and middle school science teachers. The class meets five hours per week and students work in groups of four, developing their own experiments for each topic. We serve 24 students with a diverse population, including emerging bilingual students, Hispanic students, and older than average students. The groups are explicitly assigned randomly for the first five weeks and change for each module of the course (a given module lasts 5 weeks). For the remainder of the course, groups are assigned by the instructor, *tending to group power dynamics* and particularly empowering People of Color and emerging bilingual students' inclusion to transform the scientific norms.

The course is designed to develop scientific practices for future K-8 teachers. Based on open inquiry, future teachers get to develop their own experiments. This writing-intensive course uses techniques that foster scientific argumentation based on initial questions, evidence, and multiple representations (Atkins Elliott et al., 2016). Throughout the course, students develop the skills to support their claims with evidence, and respond to counter-arguments. The dialog fostered in class uses responsive teaching approaches, where students explore the ideas posed by others to understand where they come from rather than just evaluating if they are correct or not (Maskiewicz & Winters, 2012). Using our class as a scientific community we create our own research conferences, poster conferences, peer-reviewed papers, clinical cases, and development of experiments. This approach *acknowledges the nature of physics and what is valued in physics education* while negotiating how we approach it.

Equity issues are addressed in the classroom dynamics as part of the scientific discipline. Topics such as the lack of diversity in STEM fields, inequitable access to science courses, and unjust practices in the classroom are embedded in our regular conversation (McGee, 2016; Tatum, 2017; Varelas, 2012). This conversation uses the student's development as future teachers to foster the conversation but also expands it to the scientific communities. I present an approach to teaching physics for future teachers that is embedded within social justice rather than disassociated. By recognizing the power dynamics as part of doing science/physics I aim to transform the classroom environment to better serve my students and thereby their future students.

Optics and How We See Each Other

As part of the course, I designed an interactive presentation showing the statistics of who becomes a STEM major and how access to science and math courses is often influenced by the zip code of those student's schools (Department of Education). Some students observed this lack of diversity in STEM for the first time while others are very familiar with it. Students then engage in reflecting on our role as individuals, as future educators, and as members of a bigger community and on how we engage in practices that perpetuate or combat the current status in STEM. This presentation allows us to go from an implicit approach used during the first few weeks (i.e., supporting each other) into naming more specific behaviors (i.e., recognizing mansplaining).

During the second unit, students explore lenses through the examination of the eye. Students construct a pinhole theater, then examine the role of having a lens in our eye, differentiating its role from the pupil's role. Each table worked on their experiments and then presented their results to the class using portable whiteboards to support their explanations. Some groups may focus on how light travel to understand the phenomenon while others rely on the description of the image observed through a lens. I use this opportunity to address representation and the interpretation of our perception.

By using an image showing the google results from searching "eyes" (see Fig. 7.2), we can explore how blue eyes are represented in an inverted ratio when compared to the ratio of blue eyes in the US population. While students are aware that blue eyes are linked to a recessive gene, their expectations align more with the portrayed representation. We then revisit the experiments students presented to understand lenses and discuss what type of generalizations or interpretations we can draw from them, differentiating the ones that focuses on understanding how light travel versus

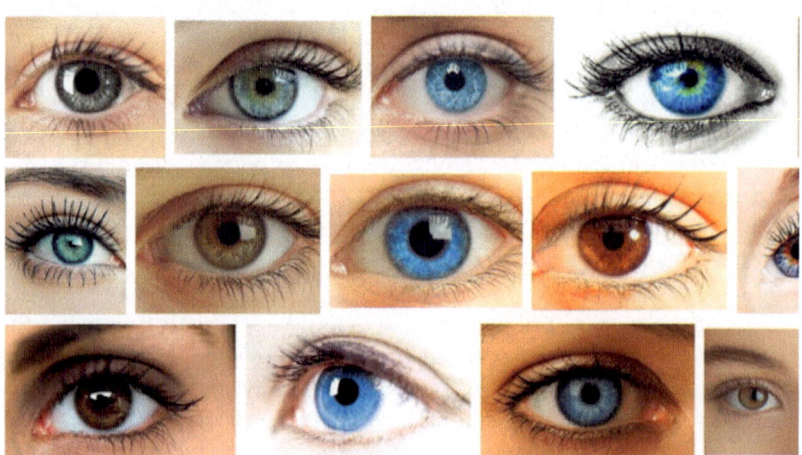

Fig. 7.2 Results of a google image search for "eye," which misrepresents the population eye color ratio

those focused on the perceived image through a lens. We use this as an example to recognize the subjectivity on how we engage in experiments.

Continuing with the practices of engaging in science by creating a claim, supporting it with evidence, and responding to someone who might differ from you, I extend this conversation of representation into addressing the controversy of supporting the Black Lives Matter (BLM) movement or All Lives Matter (ALM), as a counter-movement. This is an extra credit optional assignment where students then translate their argumentation skills developed in our science context into a social matter. This assignment was implemented in my first-semester teaching at that institution, Fall 2016, and continued in the following semester. I will discuss the analysis of the Spring and Fall 2017 responses.

All submissions came from women students, some of them identified as Latina and some as white. From the results we observed students were open to submit their assignment supporting the argument of BLM (7 students) and ALM (5 students). While the assignment required data to support the claim, multiple students arguing for ALM did not accurately identify what BLM stands for. The arguments claiming ALM often showed colorblindness, engaging in abstract liberalism, and minimization of racism (Bonilla-Silva, 2014; Jayakumar & Adamian, 2017). For example, "Some people may feel as if [B]lack lives matter would be a better choice, because of how African Americans used to be treated. But in this case, now we are in a different era." Student submissions illustrate the willingness of students to engage in conversations about inequity and also reveals the need to address color blindness in our classrooms in order to transform our current practices.

Reflection

While a physics/science course support student's development of scientific literacy skills, connecting these skills should relate to participation within the scientific community. Some of the responses showed a structured composition that resembled their use of evidence and counterarguments used in previous assignments, while others did not implement the same writing format. Integrating this conversation into the classroom is necessary to disrupt practices which will pose a challenge for both the instructor and the students. Having the opportunity to normalize conversations that address power dynamics while engaging in science is a teaching approach that I continue to choose which is sustained by the impact that it may have in the students, and particularly future K-12 teachers (Lock & Hazari, 2016). While my positionality as an immigrant (shown through a thick accent and stories that I share through the course) is not welcomed by all students, it does empower students to identify and address practices that are harmful so that we can redirect our way to engage and support new generations to do science. I engage in my teaching knowing and recognizing that I am still learning and improving my own practices, and making this process explicit with my students.

CONCLUSION

Historically, the discipline of physics and physics education has suffered from the lasting effects of settler colonial white supremacy and erased the contributions of People of Color to the discipline resulting in grave inequities and injustices in the field. In recent time, physics education researchers and physics educators have integrated social justice into physics curriculum to address these injustices and inequities. Much of this research and work has taken place in high school physics classrooms and introductory physics courses. Further, the curriculum resulting from this work has included discussion of the under-representation of particular socio-demographic groups in physics and the erasure of the contributions of People of Color to physics. To make real progress in addressing inequities and injustice in physics, social justice-focused curricular materials must be implemented in all physics courses nationally. This will require physics teacher educators to prepare prospective and future teachers to do so and faculty and administrators to be supportive of these efforts. One way to begin implementing social justice into physics curricula includes having class discussions regarding the history and subjectivity of physics. A reasonable next step is to use physics concepts to identify inequities and injustice as illustrated in the included example. Integrating social justice into physics education requires stepping outside of the confines and boundaries of what has been traditionally considered physics education and broadening the notion of what is to be counted as physics, a challenging, yet crucial endeavor.

REFERENCES

American Association for the Advancement of Science. (1990). *Science for all Americans*. Retrieved November 30, 2019, from http://www.project2061.org/publications/sfaa/online/chap1.htm.

Arielle Evans, A. A., Bretl, K. S., Ross, A., and Daane, A. R. (2019). Introductory physics students' insights for improving physics culture. In *AIP Conf. Proc., Provo, UT*, 2019.

Aronson, E. (1978). *The jigsaw classroom*. Sage.

Atwater, M. M. (2010). Multicultural science education and curriculum materials. *Science Activities, 47*(4), 103–108.

Atwater, M. M., Butler, M. B., Freeman, T. B., & Carlton Parsons, E. R. (2013). An examination of Black science teacher educators' experiences with multicultural education, equity, and social justice. *Journal of Science Teacher Education, 24*(8), 1293–1313.

Bonilla-Silva, E. (2014). *Racism without racists: Color-blind racism and the persistence of racial inequality in America*. Lanham: Rowan & Littlefield.

Cochran, G. L., Boveda, M., Prescod-Weinstein, C., & Gray, S. (2020). Intersectionality in STEM education research. In C. Johnson, M. Mohr-Schroeder, T. Moore, & L. English (Eds.), *Handbook of research on STEM education*. Routledge.

Daane, A. R., Decker, S. R., & Sawtelle, V. (2017). Teaching about racial equity in introductory physics courses. *The Physics Teacher, 55*(6), 328–333.

Daane, A. R., & Sawtelle, V. (2016). Student discourse about equity in an introductory college physics course. In *2016 PERC*, 88–91.

Decker, S. R., & Daane, A. R. (2018). Teaching about inequity: Shifts in student views about diversity in physics. In *2017 PERC Proceedings*, 108–111.

Delpit, L. (1988). The silenced dialogue: Power and pedagogy in educating other people's children. *Harvard Educational Review, 58*(3), 280–299.

Department of Education. https://www.ed.gov/stem.

DiAngelo, R. (2018). *White fragility: Why it's so hard for white people to talk about racism*. Boston: Beacon Press.

Donovan, B. M. (2016). Framing the genetics curriculum for social justice: An experimental exploration of how the biology curriculum influences beliefs about racial difference. *Science Education, 100*(3), 586–616.

Donovan, B. M. (2017). Learned inequality: Racial labels in the biology curriculum can affect the development of racial prejudice. *Journal of Research in Science Teaching, 54*(3), 379–411.

Eickerman, O., & Rifkin, M. (2020). The elephant in the (physics class) room: Discussing gender inequality in our class. *The Physics Teacher, 58*, 301. https://doi.org/10.1119/1.5145520.

Elliott, L. A., Jaxon, K., & Salter, I. (2016). *Composing science: A facilitator's guide to writing in the science classroom*. Teachers College Press.

Gutstein, E. (2003). Teaching and learning mathematics for social justice in an urban, Latino school. *Journal for Research in Mathematics education, 34*, 37–73.

Hatton, J. & Plouffe, P. B. (1997). *Science and its ways of knowing*. Addison-Wesley.

Herrera, S., Mohamed, I. A., & Daane, A. R. (2020). Physics from an underrepresented lens: What I wish others knew. *The Physics Teacher, 58*, 294.

Ivie, R., Anderson, G., & White, S. (2014). African Americans and Hispanics among physics & astronomy faculty: Results from the 2012 survey of physics & astronomy degree-granting departments. In *Focus on: A publication of the American Institute of Physics Statistical Research Center, July 2014*. Retrieved December 31, 2019, from https://www.aip.org/sites/default/files/statistics/faculty/africanhisp-fac-pa-123.pdf.

Ivie, R., White, S., Garrett, A., & Anderson, G. (2013, August 2013). Women and physics & astronomy faculty: Results from the 2010 survey of physics degree-granting departments. In *Focus on: A publication of the American Institute of Physics Statistical Research Center*. Retrieved December 31, 2019, from https://www.aip.org/sites/default/files/statistics/faculty/womenfac-pa-10.pdf.

Jayakumar, U. M., & Adamian, A. S. (2017). The fifth frame of colorblind ideology: Maintaining the comforts of colorblindness in the context of white fragility. *Sociological Perspectives, 60*(5), 912–936. https://doi.org/10.1177/0731121417721910.

Ladson-Billings, G. (2006). From the achievement gap to the education debt: Understanding achievement in US schools. *Educational Researcher, 35*(7), 3–12.

Ladson-Billings, G. (2007). Pushing past the achievement gap: An essay on the language of deficit. *The Journal of Negro Education, 76*, 316–323.

Lock, R. M., & Hazari, Z. (2016). Discussing underrepresentation as a means to facilitating female students' physics identity development. *Physical Review Physics Education Research, 12*(2), 020101.

Maile, D. (2015a, May 13). Science, time, and Mauna a Wākea: The thirty-meter telescope's capitalist-colonialist violence, part I. *The Red Nation*. https://therednation.org/2015/05/13/science-time-and-mauna-a-wakea-the-thirty-meter-telescopes-capitalist-colonialist-violence-an-essay-in-two-parts/.

Maile, D. (2015b, May 20). Science, time, and Mauna a Wākea: The thirty-meter telescope's capitalist-colonialist violence, part II. *The Red Nation*. https://therednation.org/2015/05/20/science-time-and-mauna-a-wakea-the-thirty-meter-telescopes-capitalist-colonialist-violence/.

Maskiewicz, A. C., & Winters, V. A. (2012). Understanding the co-construction of inquiry practices: A case study of a responsive teaching environment.

Journal of Research in Science Teaching, 49(4), 429–464. https://doi.org/10.1002/tea.21007.

McClellan, J. E., III. (2010). *Colonialism and science: Saint Domingue and the old regime*. University of Chicago Press.

McClellan, J. E., III, & Regourd, F. (2000). The colonial machine: French science and colonization in the Ancien regime. *Osiris, 15*, 31–50.

McGee, E. O. (2016). Devalued Black and Latino racial identities. *American Educational Research Journal, 53*(6), 1626–1662. https://doi.org/10.3102/0002831216676572.

Misawa, M. (2010). Queer race pedagogy for educators in higher education: Dealing with power dynamics and positionality of LGBTQ students of color. *The International Journal of Critical Pedagogy, 3*(1), 26.

Morus, I. R. (2005). *When physics became king*. University of Chicago Press.

NASA. (2019). *Cassini*. Last modified January 28, 2019. https://www.nasa.gov/mission_pages/cassini/main/index.html.

Neilson, H. R., Rousseau-Nepton, L., Lawler, S., & Spekkens, K. (2019). *Indigenizing the next decade of astronomy in Canada*. arXiv preprint arXiv:1910.02976.

Neilson, H. R., & Lawler, S. (2019). *Canadian astronomy on Maunakea: On respecting Indigenous rights*. arXiv preprint arXiv:1910.03665.

Parent, M. C., DeBlaere, C., & Moradi, B. (2013). Approaches to research on intersectionality: Perspectives on gender, LGBT, and racial/ethnic identities. *Sex Roles, 68*(11–12), 639–645.

Potvin, G., Hazari, Z., & Lock, R. M. (2015). Exposure to underrepresentation discussion: The impacts on women's attitudes and identities. *Physics Education Research Conference Proceedings, 2014*, 211–214. https://doi.org/10.1119/perc.2014.pr.049.

Prescod-Weinstein, C. (2017, April 25). Decolonising science reading list. *Medium*. https://medium.com/@chanda/decolonising-science-reading-list-339fb773d51f.

Rifkin, M. (2015). Physics, equity, and social justice: Why are there so few black physicists? *The Physics Teacher, 53*(7), 447–447.

Rifkin, M. (2016). Addressing underrepresentation: Physics teaching for all. *The Physics Teacher, 54*(2), 72–74.

Salazar, J. A. (2014, December 2014). *Multicultural settler colonialism and indigenous struggle in Hawai'i: The politics of astronomy on Mauna a Wākea*. Doctoral dissertation, University of Hawaii at Manoa, Honolulu.

Seltzer, K., García, O., & Ibarra Johnson, S. (2017). *The translanguaging classroom: Leveraging student bilingualism for learning*. Philadelphia, PA: Caslon.

Tatum, B. D. (2017). *Why are all the black kids sitting together in the cafeteria: And other conversations about race*. New York: Basic Books.

Traweek, S. (1992). *Beamtimes and lifetimes*. Harvard University Press.

The Underrepresentation Curriculum. (2018). Retrieved November 30, 2019, from www.underrep.com. Endnote: Classroom Setup.

Varelas, M. (Ed.). (2012). *Identity construction and science education research*. Rotterdam, The Netherlands: Sense.

Whitt, L. (2009). *Science, colonialism, and indigenous peoples: The cultural politics of law and knowledge*. Cambridge University Press.

Suggested Reading

Alvarado, C., Daane, A. R., Scherr, R. E., & Zavala, G. (2014). Responsiveness among peers leads to productive disciplinary engagement. In *2013 Physics Education Research Conference Proceedings* (pp. 57–60).

Barthelemy, R. S., Henderson, C., & Grunert, M. L. (2013). How do they get here? Paths into physics education research. *Physical Review Special Topics-Physics Education Research, 9*(2), 020107.

Barthelemy, R. S., McCormick, M., & Henderson, C. (2016). Gender discrimination in physics and astronomy: Graduate student experiences of sexism and gender microaggressions. *Physical Review Physics Education Research, 12*(2), 020119.

Blue, J., Traxler, A., & Cochran, G. (2019). Resource letter: GP-1: Gender and physics. *American Journal of Physics, 87*(8), 616–626.

Cochran, G. L., Gupta, A., Hyater-Adams, S., Knaub, A. V., & Roman, B. Z. (2019). Emerging reflections from the People of Color (POC) at PERC Discussion Space. arXiv preprint arXiv:1907.01655.

Cochran, G. L., Hodapp, T., & Brown, E. A. (2018, July 22–26). Identifying barriers to ethnic/racial minority students' participation in graduate physics In *PERC Proceedings*, Cincinnati, OH.

Daane, A. R., Decker, S. R., & Sawtelle, V. (2017). Teaching about racial equity in introductory physics courses. *The Physics Teacher, 55*(6), 328–333.

Hazari, Z., Cass, C., & Beattie, C. (2015). Obscuring power structures in the physics classroom: Linking teacher positioning, student engagement, and physics identity development. *Journal of Research in Science Teaching, 52*(6), 735–762.

Hazari, Z., Potvin, G., Tai, R. H., & Almarode, J. T. (2012). Motivation toward a graduate career in the physical sciences: Gender differences and the impact on science career productivity. *Journal of College Science Teaching, 41*(4), 90–98.

Hyater-Adams, S., Fracchiolla, C., Finkelstein, N., & Hinko, K. (2018). Critical look at physics identity: An operationalized framework for examining race and physics identity. *Physical Review Physics Education Research, 14*(1), 010132.

Hyater-Adams, S., Fracchiolla, C., Williams, T., Finkelstein, N., & Hinko, K. (2019). Deconstructing Black physics identity: Linking individual and social constructs using the critical physics identity framework. *Physical Review Physics Education Research, 15*(2), 020115.

Jerome, F., & Taylor, R. (2005). *Einstein on race and racism.* New Brunswick, NJ: Rutger University Press.

Maldonado-Torres, N. (2004). The topology of being and the geopolitics of knowledge: Modernity, empire, coloniality. *City, 8*(1), 29–56.

Patridge, E. V., Barthelemy, R. S., & Rankin, S. R. (2014). Factors impacting the academic climate for LGBQ STEM faculty. *Journal of Women and Minorities in Science and Engineering, 20*(1), 75–98.

Posselt, J. R., Hernandez, T. E., Cochran, G. L., & Miller, C. W. (2019). Metrics first, diversity later? Making the shortlist and getting admitted to physics PhD programs. *Journal of Women and Minorities in Science and Engineering, 25*(4), 283–306.

Prescod-Weinstein, C. (2020). Making Black women scientists under White empiricism: The racialization of epistemology in physics. *Signs: Journal of Women in Culture and Society, 45*(2), 421–447.

Rosa, K., & Martins, M. C. (2009). Approaches and methodologies for a course on history and epistemology of physics: Analyzing the experience of a Brazilian university. *Science & Education, 18*(1), 149–155.

Rosa, K., & Mensah, F. M. (2016). Educational pathways of Black women physicists: Stories of experiencing and overcoming obstacles in life. *Physical Review Physics Education Research, 12*(2), 020113.

CHAPTER 8

A Critical Feminist Approach for Equity and Inclusion in Undergraduate Biology Education

Ariel L. Steele

Key Terms and Definitions

Affective Learning	Feelings and emotions that arise during learning and the emotional state that is the result of learning. Affective learning can positively, neutrally, or negatively impact the learning process (Trujillo & Tanner, 2014).
Constructivism	Epistemological framework that believes individual learners build their own knowledge structures from experience and instruction on their current foundation of knowledge (Wood, 2009).
Self-efficacy	People's beliefs in their capabilities to produce desired effects (Trujillo & Tanner, 2014).

A. L. Steele (✉)
Auburn University, Auburn, AL, USA
e-mail: als0089@auburn.edu

© The Author(s), under exclusive license to Springer Nature Switzerland AG 2021
C. C. Ozaki and L. Parson (eds.), *Teaching and Learning for Social Justice and Equity in Higher Education*,
https://doi.org/10.1007/978-3-030-69947-5_8

Although women make up 60% of undergraduate biology majors, prompting the belief that the field of biology has overcome gender inequalities among the science, technology, engineering, and mathematics (STEM) disciplines, gaps in student achievement, academic performance, participation, sense of belonging, and persistence still exist within the field (Eddy et al., 2014). Moreover, gender and racial inequalities emerge at the postgraduate level, when fewer women and underrepresented minorities pursue postgraduate and academic positions than men (NSF, 2011). Introductory biology courses are a student's first exposure to their field of study and are notorious for being difficult "weed out" courses, with a large number of students leaving after taking an introductory class to pursue a non-STEM major (Barthelemy et al., 2015). This suggests that undergraduate students, particularly women[1] and underrepresented minoritized groups, may be experiencing a chilly or unwelcoming environment in introductory biology classes that makes them feel like they do not belong in STEM.

Fortunately, undergraduate biology educators and researchers have begun the process of restructuring courses using a constructivist framework and student-centered approaches to teaching and learning to improve performance and experiences of students in undergraduate biology education (Allen & Tanner, 2005; Connell et al., 2016; Freeman et al., 2014; Haak et al., 2011; Smith et al., 2005; Wood, 2009; Weir et al., 2019). However, constructivist approaches to teaching and learning are limited to how students acquire and construct knowledge and do not take into account the individual experiences of students or address structural inequality issues within STEM education (Klein, 1997; McPhail, 2015). As a result, although constructivist approaches may improve learning for some, they ultimately maintain the structural inequalities already present within STEM education (Klein, 1997; McPhail, 2015). Therefore, I suggest educators of undergraduate biology

---

[1] Current work in biology education/STEM education continues to use the male/female dichotomy to denote gender, however, male/female refers to an individual's sex rather than their gender identity. Throughout this chapter, I will refer to gender using man and woman instead of male and female. I recognize that gender is socially constructed identity that ranges from masculine identities to feminine identities and the words man and woman are not all inclusive to other gender identities that fall outside of that binary. Therefore, I acknowledge the limitation in my work and in the work of biology education research in the hopes that correct gendered terms are used and that future research involving gender includes more than just the man/woman binary.

courses combine constructivist approaches with feminist poststructural approaches in order to promote learning and social justice and create more equitable classroom.

In this chapter, I address the issue of inequity in undergraduate introductory biology courses by describing a framework for how feminist poststructuralism can be applied to improve the teaching and learning environment in a way that embraces diversity and acknowledges students as individuals with unique experiences that contribute to their learning. First, I define feminist poststructuralism and explore how the teaching and learning environment in introductory biology courses perpetuates inequity and a chilly climate. To illustrate this, I focused on women's experiences in introductory biology courses. Second, I describe how I used feminist poststructuralism as a framework to develop a course syllabus and lesson plan, and then I discuss empirically tested teaching and learning strategies that can be used to promote equity and inclusion in introductory biology courses. Finally, I conclude with how this framework can be adapted to other fields of study to promote equity, inclusion, and social justice in teaching and learning in higher education. The goal of this chapter is to provide an explicit framework that STEM educators can use to critically examine their current teaching practices and redesign their courses to be more equitable and inclusive to traditionally marginalized students.

Theoretical Framework

This chapter uses a feminist poststructural framework as a lens to view the current practice of teaching and learning in undergraduate biology education and develop a framework for equity in undergraduate biology education. Feminist poststructuralism as a paradigm seeks to identify and challenge oppressive practices against women by critiquing the dominant discourses, systems, and structures that socially privilege men and disadvantage women (Hesse-Biber, 2014; Lazar, 2007). Feminist postructuralism rejects objectivity and the notion of an absolute "Truth" or single reality, instead recognizing that there are different truths and that social systems are structured to allow members of privileged groups control what is considered knowledge (Hesse-Biber, 2014; Lazar, 2007; Tisdell, 1998). This rejection of objective truth challenges the notion of neutrality and objectivity in science, and illuminates how knowledge is subjective and constructed socially and historically (Lazar, 2007). Feminist post-structuralism also critically examines the intersections of identity and structural systems of privilege and oppression and how those systems can impact knowledge construction, experiences, and interactions with others (Tisdell, 1998). Therefore, examining teaching and learning in biology education with a feminist poststructuralist lens can provide insight into how structures and social systems within science continue to marginalize and disempower women despite efforts to improve diversity and inclusion in biology education.

LARGE-ENROLLMENT UNDERGRADUATE BIOLOGY EDUCATION

Introductory biology is a required course (or series of courses) for all biology majors and serves a gatekeeping function for access to a variety of upper-division courses (Barthelemy et al., 2015; Seymour & Hewitt, 1997; Sanabria & Penner, 2017). The purpose of introductory biology courses is to provide an overview of the different subfields of biology, prepare students for the upper-division courses, and teach students the foundations of scientific inquiry. Many introductory biology courses are large-enrollment and are taught in a lecture-only format that empha-size individual work and content-centered approaches to teaching and learning (Barthelemy et al., 2015; Armbruster et al., 2009). At most universities, introductory biology courses teach students from different backgrounds and educational experiences (Barthelemy et al., 2015).

Additionally, introductory biology courses are considered "high risk" and "weed out" courses intended to be competitive and difficult; a large majority of students fail or receive lower grades than expected in these courses (Barthelemy et al., 2015, p. 139; Sanabria & Penner, 2017). The difficult weed out culture of introductory courses maintains a competitive "sink or swim" environment and perpetuates the mentality that students are not academically prepared for the rigor of STEM fields (Sanabria & Penner, 2017, p. 2). This environment and mentality disproportionately impact women and minoritized students who are more likely to leave a STEM major after taking an introductory course (Barthelemy et al., 2015; Meaders et al., 2019; Mervis, 2011).

A growing body of literature suggests that the way introductory courses are being taught is contributing to this competitive environ-ment (Mervis, 2011). Traditionally, introductory science courses are taught in a lecture-only format and are content and instructor-focused. Students have reported feeling dissatisfied with their learning in introductory biology courses; passive listening and note taking are not optimal learning strategies for most students to develop critical thinking skills and make connections between the course materials (Wood, 2009; Seymour & Hewitt, 1997). Further, students have described feeling that the memorization and content-focused teaching makes introductory courses uninteresting and challenging (Seymour & Hewitt, 1997). Therefore, the teaching and learning environment in most introductory biology classrooms is not fostering a learning environment that is beneficial to all students.

However, instructors are beginning to restructure courses to incorporate pedagogical strategies that improve student engagement, achievement, and equity in large-enrollment introductory biology courses (Armbruster et al., 2009; Tanner, 2013; Weir et al., 2019; Wood, 2009). Over the last fifteen years, biology faculty have begun to focus on student-centered education over content- or teacher-centered education (Armbruster et al., 2009; Wood, 2009). Indeed, Wood (2009) highlighted the positive knowledge gains students experience when introductory courses are taught using research-based practices to teaching and learning, such as the formulation of student learning objectives, using formative assessments to evaluate student learning, and structuring class time around group work or small group discussions. These research-based practices shift the responsibility for learning from the instructor to the student by engaging students in an active learning process rather than the passive process traditionally used in introductory science courses (Wood, 2009). These student-centered practices are rooted in constructivism, the philosophical belief that knowledge is created by the learner and is built upon previous experiences or knowledge structures (Wood, 2009). Although research suggests using active learning strategies to transform the classroom from a passive space for learning to an active one increases student learning and achievement (Armbruster et al., 2009; Ballen, Salehi, and Cotner, 2017; Donovan et al., 2018; Freeman et al., 2014; Theobald et al., 2020; Styers et al., 2018; Wood, 2009), gender gaps still persist in introductory biology classrooms (Ballen, Salehi, and Cotner, 2017; Eddy & Brownell, 2016; Eddy et al., 2014; Koester et al., 2016).

Gender and Undergraduate Biology Education

When considering absolute numbers, there are more women than men pursing undergraduate biology in higher education, leading some to conclude that the gender gap is narrowing (Eddy et al., 2014). However, as women move along the STEM career track, fewer women pursue graduate biology education and academic or non-academic biology professional careers (Eddy et al., 2014; Miller & Wai, 2015). This phenomenon has been described as a "leaky pipeline" and suggests that as women progress along the STEM career pipeline, they "leak" out at different stages until there are fewer women exiting than had entered (Blickenstaff, 2005). Additionally, focusing on the number of women in undergraduate biology does not tell us anything about their experiences in the classroom or explain why women remain underrepresented post-graduation. Research has observed gender disparities in academic achievement, performance, participation, engagement, and sense of belonging in biology classrooms, which suggests that biology classrooms may still be unwelcoming to women (Eddy & Brownell, 2016).

Furthermore, research suggests that gender gaps persist in student achievement and performance in undergraduate biology classrooms (Ballen, Salehi, and Cotner, 2017; Eddy et al., 2014; England et al., 2019; Grunspan et al., 2016; Koester et al., 2016). Academic achievement is a strong predictor of retention in STEM fields, and researchers typically focus on exam scores and grades as measures of achievement and performance (Eddy et al., 2014; Koester et al., 2016; Matz et al., 2017). It has been reported that women students underperform compared to their man peers on high-stakes exams (Ballen, Salehi, and Cotner, 2017; Eddy et al., 2014), have lower overall grades in large lecture-based courses (Matz et al., 2017), and experience higher levels of anxiety and stereotype threat than their man peers when a course is perceived as difficult (Ballen, Salehi, and Cotner, 2017; Franceschini et al., 2014; Lauer et al., 2013; England et al., 2019). These studies suggest that anxiety, perceptions of difficulty, and grades impact the persistence of women students in undergraduate biology courses.

Students may perceive their introductory courses to be difficult because they are difficult; introductory science courses are typically designed to be challenging "weed out" courses that push students away from pursing STEM (Barthelemy et al., 2015; Parson, 2016). However, difficulty is a pervasive discourse in STEM education, such that the norms and values presented within syllabi and instructor attitudes present a discourse that is difficult and unwelcoming to students (Lindemann et al., 2016; Parson, 2016). The competitive "weed out" culture coupled with the difficult nature of STEM courses may lead to student feeling anxious or self-conscious about their abilities, and this disproportionately impacts women and minoritized groups (Barthelemy et al., 2015; Lindemann et al., 2016).

Gender bias also exists in perceptions of student performance in introductory biology courses. Women students are often viewed as less competent by faculty members and peers (Grunspan et al., 2016; Moss-Racusin et al., 2012). These biases can have negative impacts on women's self-efficacy and sense of belonging in STEM, which are both predictors of persistence in STEM education. The implicit gender bias that women are less competent in STEM domains can be attributed to the notion that scientific ability is considered a masculine characteristic and is indicative of the gendered nature of STEM education (Grunspan et al., 2016; Parson & Ozaki, 2017; Sallee, 2014).

When a classroom environment is perceived to be difficult and unwelcoming, women can experience a decreased sense of belonging and participate less in their introductory courses (Ballen et al., 2018; Crombie et al., 2003; Eddy et al., 2014). Indeed, research suggests women are less likely to participate in large enrollment introductory courses even if they make up a majority of the students in the courses (Ballen et al., 2018; Crombie et al., 2003; Eddy et al., 2014). Consequently, gender disparities in participation is a problem, especially since those who speak up can influence their peers and normalize who speaks and is viewed as more knowledgeable in classroom interactions (Ballen et al., 2018; Eddy et al., 2014). Namely, by calling on men students more often, instructors are unintentionally perpetuating the mentality that women students are less competent than their men peers (Moss-Racusin et al., 2012), that men are given more space to interact with instructors or faculty members (Ballen et al., 2018), or that women's voices are less valued. Indeed, this gendered bias in participation reduces the opportunity for women students to practice skills that are valued in STEM, such as critical thinking and sharing ideas (Eddy et al., 2014).

Overall, research has shown that the teaching and learning environment in introductory biology courses contribute to gender gaps in academic performance, achievement, and participation for women students. The teaching and learning environment for most introductory biology courses is largely lecture-based, with an emphasis on memorizing content and high-stakes exams. As such, the teaching and learning practices within these contexts are not conducive to optimal learning of all students and leads to these gendered experiences for women in biology. As evidenced by the existing gaps in achievement, participation, and performance of women students in introductory biology, it is imperative that changes to the structure and practices of introductory biology courses are inclusive and beneficial to all students. Therefore, the following sections will describe empirically tested teaching and learning strategies and propose a framework that uses feminist poststructuralism to develop courses to be more equitable and inclusive for all students.

EVIDENCE-BASED TEACHING STRATEGIES FOR EQUITY AND INCLUSION

Educators within science have been encouraged to adopt alternative teaching and learning strategies to traditional, uninterrupted lecture, such as active learning or problem-based learning (PBL), in order to model the skill of scientific inquiry and give students the opportunity to actively engage with content in a way that encourages cognitive growth and knowledge construction (Allen & Tanner, 2005). Recent studies have shown that using active learning and problem-based learning strategies in introductory biology classrooms have improved student performance, achievement, and learning (Armbruster et al., 2009; Ballen, Wieman et al., 2017; Freeman et al., 2014; Gouvea, 2019; Hewitt et al., 2019; Smith et al., 2005; Stanberry, 2018 for evidence of active learning in calculus). Implementing active learning pedagogy in introductory biology classrooms has been found to positively impact knowledge of course materials, increased confidence in science ability, and increased classroom social belonging for minoritized students when compared to traditional lecture-based courses (Ballen, Wieman et al., 2017). As such, courses that implement active learning strategies such as collaborative problem-solving, group work, and in-class activities are more beneficial to students that are typically underrepresented in STEM, such as women and minoritized students (Ballen, Wieman et al., 2017; Freeman et al., 2014).

Additionally, active learning in the form of group work has been found to improve student perseverance, establish connections and relationships with peers that are important for collaborations, and improve sense-making of content in biology courses (Gouvea, 2019). These are important skills for future biologists to learn, and active learning pedagogy aids in the development of these skills. Likewise, group gender composition has been found to positively impact overall course performance of all students regardless of gender (Sullivan et al., 2018). All-women groups had a positive impact on women students through the reduction of stereotype threat and improved sense of belonging and mixed-gender groups with a higher ratio of women to men also had a positive impact for both by reducing barriers to discussion (Sullivan et al., 2018). Thus, there is evidence that active learning pedagogy improves the experiences of women students and increases academic performance and sense of belonging.

Evidence-Based Teaching

Research on the implementation of new teaching practices involve using active learning strategies, formative and summative assessments, and inclusive teaching (Bathgate et al., 2019). However, as discussed above, these types of teaching practices are not commonly used in large-enrollment college courses, such as introductory biology courses. While there is insurmountable evidence that active learning and other evidence-based teaching practices are beneficial to student learning and are more inclusive to minoritized groups, faculty members are reluctant to implement evidence-based teaching practices because of the time commitment required to implement them, barriers to using evidence-based teaching, and motivations for using specific teaching practices (Bathgate et al., 2019). As such, discipline-based education research has provided frameworks for implementing evidence-based teaching practices that are manageable (Davidesco & Milne, 2019; Allen & Tanner, 2005; Wood, 2009; Smith et al., 2005; Eddy, 2019; Froyd, 2004; Armbruster et al., 2009). For example, Smith et al. (2005) developed an active learning course framework that redesigned an introductory biology course to center around case studies that engaged learners in concepts important to microbiology. The authors developed the course around three modules that used case studies as the core active learning tool and built class activities and learning objectives around those case studies (Smith et al., 2005). The active learning course framework was developed to shift student activity from memorization to making connections between course content and applying knowledge to solve problems (Smith et al., 2005). Similarly, Armbruster et al. (2009) redesigned an introductory undergraduate biology course to implement student-centered and active learning strategies and found that student attitudes toward learning and student performance improved. Furthermore, Hewitt et al. (2019) developed laboratory curriculum using a socio-scientific issues (SSI) framework that engaged students with science issues that were socially relevant to students. The authors found that students who participated in the SSI curriculum were more motivated and engaged, and were more likely to participate because the content was relevant to their lived experiences (Hewitt et al., 2019). While these course redesigns did not focus on gender performance or gender disparities, overall student performance and motivation improved and provide further support for the implementation of evidence-based teaching practices.

Innovations in Undergraduate Biology Education

The following studies have described innovations to the introductory biology classroom to improve student engagement and learning (Trujillo & Tanner, 2014; Wood, 2009; Tanner, 2013; Allen & Tanner, 2005). Allen and Tanner (2005) highlight simple and complex active learning strategies that can be used in large-enrollment introductory courses. Some of these strategies include bookending the standard lecture format with discussion questions, using classroom technology such as student response systems (clickers) to give students immediate feedback on multiple-choice questions or short quizzes, the use of learning-cycle instructional models, and problem-based learning or case study activities (Allen & Tanner, 2005). Trujillo and Tanner (2014) recommend affective learning activities in teaching and learning of undergraduate biology. There are three key constructs to affective learning: self-efficacy, sense of belonging, and science identity, and the authors also provide possible assessment tools for measuring these three constructs. Additionally, Tanner (2013) provides an overview of active learning teaching strategies that can be used in the classroom to promote engagement and cultivate equity. It is important to note that some of the strategies focus on cultivating equity and inclusion in the classroom by learning student names, integrating diverse, and relevant examples or increasing representation of students' lived experiences, working in small groups, using varied active learning strategies, and explicitly stating a commitment to access, equity, and inclusion for all students (Tanner, 2013). Furthermore, Tanner (2013) suggests setting clear expectations, establishing community norms, and recognize that all of the students in a course come from different backgrounds and experiences, and thus instructors should be aware of that and cultivate a classroom environment that embraces diversity and focuses on teaching the students currently in the classroom, instead of generalizing students and learning.

These are specific examples of how to implement evidence-based teaching practices in large-enrollment introductory biology courses in a way that is manageable for faculty members and improves student learning and persistence. Constructivist teaching practices that focus on student learning and construction of knowledge have shown to be beneficial to students in introductory biology courses by improving learning and metacognition. However, awareness of affective learning and diversity within the classroom is important for beginning the process of meeting students where they are at and implementing social justice in the classroom. For example, Trujillo and Tanner (2014) and Tanner (2013) provide explicit examples for improving diversity, equity, and inclusion in biology classrooms through evidence-based teaching practices in a way that is moving beyond constructivism and embracing critical and engaged pedagogy. While constructivism and critical pedagogies are similar in that they emphasize learning through student experiences and examine how knowledge is constructed and operationalized, this shift highlights how solely using constructivist approaches is insufficient for promoting social justice and that there is a need for the implementation of critical pedagogies within undergraduate biology education, such as feminist poststructuralism.

PROGRAM RECOMMENDATION

Feminist poststructuralism and discipline-based education research (DBER) in biology make up the framework for a program recommendation to improve the experiences of women and underrepresented minority students in undergraduate biology and create an inclusive and equitable teaching and learning environment for all students. The program recommendation uses feminist poststructuralism and evidence-based teaching strategies to develop a syllabus for an introductory biology course. This section will describe the process of how feminist poststructuralism informed the development of the syllabus to create an inclusive and equitable teaching and learning environment for an introductory biology course. The program recommendation also includes: (1) evidence-based strategies to use within the biology classroom to promote equity and inclusion, (2) a sample syllabus developed using a feminist poststructuralist framework (Appendix A).

Feminist Poststructuralism as a Pedagogical Framework

Feminist poststructural pedagogies require instructors to challenge unequal power relations within the classroom and proactively work toward social change (Tisdell, 1998). Challenging unequal power relations may look like actively seeking out contributions of those whose voices are not often heard or are traditionally marginalized within the classroom. For example, when asking questions, a professor can use random calling to call on students (Eddy et al., 2014) or actively call on women and students of color instead of white men.

Furthermore, feminist poststructural pedagogies also use "engaged pedagogy" (hooks, 1994) which takes into account emotion and affective learning as well as critical thinking in learning (Tisdell, 1998). Trujillo and Tanner (2014) described affective learning and how to monitor affective learning and emotions around learning in biology classrooms through the use of assessments. This is an important step in making biology education more inclusive and equitable because it recognizes that there is an emotional component to learning, and learning is more complex than just memorizing facts and taking exams. Specifically, instructors can implement the use of one-minute papers or metacognitive reflections to understand and assess where students are at affectively in their learning. Finally, the use of poststructural feminist pedagogies in college classrooms requires a level of problematizing the instructor's own positionality and recognizing the power differential between the instructor and the students (Tisdell, 1998). When instructors are aware of their positionality, they can understand how their positionality influences the decisions they make, the power dynamics within the classroom, how they teach, and how knowledge is constructed by students (Tisdell, 1998). Therefore, reflexively examining instructor positionality is crucial for awareness in how the course is taught and evaluated.

Pawley (2004) introduced feminist science studies to the field of engineering and discussed several aspects of feminist science studies that are relevant to biology education and STEM education in general. Feminist critiques of science focus on concerns about "who participates in the development, process, production, and dissemination of science and engineering" (Pawley, 2004, p. 4). Pawley (2004) highlights the need for students to recognize gendered relationships of power in science and challenge the notion of objectivity in science. From there, students can understand how knowledge is created, shared, and given power within the context of science. For biology, this may look like asking students to reflect on how knowledge within biology was discovered and by whom. A great example of this is the discovery of DNA by Rosalind Franklin and how Watson and Crick were given credit for Franklin's discovery. Exploring how knowledge is power can be turned into short writing assignments where students examine scientific literature or historical scientific discoveries and write about who the authors are, the context of the literature, and reflect upon how biological knowledge has historically been created and by whom for specific advances in knowledge. Examining power dynamics and systems of privilege and oppression within this example can show students how knowledge is constructed, and who benefits from science. While these tend to be difficult conversations, they are important to have to make biology and science education more equitable and inclusive to a diverse set of students.

Development of a Feminist Poststructuralist Syllabus and Lesson Plan

In this next section, I describe the process of creating a syllabus using feminist poststructuralism as a framework. Creating a syllabus and lesson plan using feminist poststructuralism requires thinking carefully about how you are approaching power and knowledge within your course. Instructors hold knowledge about their field of expertise and thus power. This includes the knowledge and power to make decisions about how the course is structured, what content is covered, what materials are used, how students are expected to engage with the course, and how students are assessed. The structure and organization of the syllabus is important. By including a diversity and inclusion statement early in my syllabus, I am letting students know I am aware of and support their identities and value them as much as the course itself. Because they make the course what it is, not just the content covered in the class.

Reflexivity. Reflexivity is an important practice for educators to understand their positionality, explicit and implicit biases, and power dynamics within and outside of the classroom (Hesse-Biber, 2014; Tisdell, 1998). Therefore, when I began the process of developing the syllabus for an introductory biology course, I reflected on my own positionality, the knowledge I have about education and biology, and how my biases may impact the decisions I made about the course I was developing. Reflexive practice can look like journaling, pausing, and/or thinking about how decisions may be impacted by the instructor's own bias and positioning in the world.

Use inclusive language. Developing a course syllabus through a poststructuralist feminist lens also requires being aware of how language can create barriers or impact belonging. When I developed my sample syllabus, I avoided language that created dichotomies about students, and instead chose language that was inclusive of the whole person and diverse individuals. This can be challenging because language is so integral to how we communicate and how we are taught to communicate. By avoiding gendered, ableist, racist, sexist, etc., language, I am writing a syllabus and lesson plan that challenges the structures within higher education that are marginalizing, and instead creating an inclusive environment. Typically, a syllabus is one of the first things a student sees about a class, and language that is marginalizing can impact a student's sense of belonging or even safety within a course.

Present knowledge as subjective and dynamic. As I worked on the introductory biology syllabus, I pulled from other publicly available syllabi and critically examined the course structure, the information on the syllabi, the course content, materials selected, and the language used throughout the syllabus. When designing a course and syllabus using a poststructuralist feminist lens, it is imperative to be mindful of the language you are using. Traditional STEM syllabi use language that reinforce the discourse that knowledge is static and unchanging by using words or phrases that suggest there are correct solutions or conclusions, or that there is only one approach to learning and problem-solving (Parson, 2016). Shifting the language around learning and knowledge from a static point of view to a dynamic process that is constructed through dialogue between the instructor and the students is a feminist approach to teaching and learning and promotes equity and inclusion in the classroom by signaling to students that there is no one right approach or way of thinking. Therefore, writing course learning outcomes and student learning outcomes that focus on constructing knowledge and making connections with the knowledge learned in class and the student's own knowledge and experiences is important for promoting a classroom that is inclusive. For example, removing definite articles like "the" from phrases and concepts such as "the scientific method" and replacing it with "skills in hypothesis creation, data collection, analysis, and writing" removes the idea that knowledge in science is static or that there is one right way to do things and instead helps students develop skills that they can use within scientific inquiry in creative ways (Appendix A).

Highlight diverse voices in course content. I also carefully selected course content and activities that highlight diverse voices. Students are diverse and come from a variety of backgrounds and interests, so it is important to select course materials and content that relates back to student lives and experiences while also fulfilling the knowledge and skill requirements they need to be successful in the course and move through a sequence. For example, I developed an activity called "Science Friday" where I assign students to read a primary research paper and summary written by an author that is not traditionally represented in biology textbooks or research and write a short biographical sketch of the authors. This activity engages the students with examining how knowledge is created in biology and exposes them to diverse scientists and experiences. Another aspect of using feminist poststructuralism as a framework is the ability to be critical of how assessments make your students feel and understand of how assessments can be marginalizing. I addressed this in my syllabus by designing smaller, low-stakes, and more frequent assessments to assess student knowledge, which is more likely to be inclusive and reduce student anxiety. Examples of this are frequent, low-stakes quizzes that test student understanding of the materials covered that week and using non-cumulative summative assessments such as exams. However, it is also important to continually practice and retrieve previous knowledge for students to make connections across the course content. Therefore, while the exams are not technically cumulative, the exams will still require students to retrieve and build upon past knowledge and content in the course to answer questions (Lang, 2016).

Select accessible course texts. For course materials, I selected the Integrating Concepts in Biology eTextbook because it is cheaper than traditional textbooks ($45 for students versus $200), is accessible to everyone, focuses on core concepts and information that students need to know instead of extra information that can be overwhelming, and is short and easy to read to keep students engaged in the material. I can also expect students to read and engage with the material before attending class and have set up active learning activities around the chapters and activities within this book so they are still learning the knowledge and skills they need to be successful in biology without expecting them to do 3+ hours of reading each week.

Develop intentional learning objectives. I developed student learning outcomes that align with the core competencies from the "Vision and Change" report (AAAS, 2011). The student learning outcomes use language from Bloom's taxonomy and explicitly state what students will learn and how they will demonstrate learning of each competency. For example, students should be able to "demonstrate the development of skills in hypothesis development, data collection and analysis, drawing conclusions from data, and written communication through lab activities and group activities." This student learning outcome describes the skills students should develop in the course and how they will be assessed through lab and group activities.

Co-create classroom rules. Finally, I created space for the instructor and students to develop expectations for the instructor, the students, and their peers. The intent of the activity is to engage students in the learning process and give them an opportunity to hold themselves accountable and be aware of how their voices and behaviors may impact others. This activity can be done on the first day of class while the instructor is going over the syllabus, and the instructor can use a web app such as Padlet that students can access online to send suggestions onto a projector screen to make the process more interactive and give students who may not feel comfortable speaking up a chance to participate. In Appendix A, I provided some sample expectations for the instructor and students.

CONCLUSION

Inequalities within undergraduate biology education persist for women; gender gaps in academic achievement, performance, sense of belonging, and participation persist in introductory biology classes. However, through the use of evidence-based teaching practices, such as active learning, affective learning, and feminist poststructuralist pedagogy, instructors of undergraduate biology can begin the process of making their classrooms a more equitable and inclusive space for students. This framework can also be used in other STEM and non-STEM fields in higher education. While the emphasis was on biology education, activities such as instructor reflexivity, critically examining language use in syllabi, and selecting course materials that are representative of non-dominant identities are important for other fields to consider as they are developing courses and syllabi. Feminist poststructuralist practices involve consistent reflexivity of one's own positionality and bias, how knowledge and power structures within higher education are maintained by common practices, and how content and knowledge within a course can be designed to be relevant to student's lived experiences. Feminist poststructuralism also involves challenging dominant ways of knowing and power structures within higher education and STEM education by shifting power to individual's whose voices are less heard. Although I used women's experiences with gender gaps as a way to illustrate inequalities within biology education, other systems of oppression such as racism, ablism, homophobia, transphobia, are still highly prevalent within STEM, and my hope is that this book chapter can be a springboard to guide further research and practice into this area within STEM education.

Appendix A: Sample Syllabus

Introduction to Biology (Majors)
Semester: Fall/Spring
Credits: 3 credit hours
Day and Time: MWF (1 h) or TR (1 h 15 min)
Class Location: Lecture Hall [Include information about location]
Co-requisites: Introduction to Biology Lab
Instructor Information

Name: [Your name and pronouns, if comfortable listing pronouns] Ariel L. Steele (she/her/hers)
Office: [office number and building]
Student Office Hours: [list hours students can come by for office hours or state if students need to make an appointment and how/where they can do that]
Contact Information: [list your contact information, how you prefer to be contacted (i.e., via email, Canvas, etc.), and any boundaries (i.e., I will respond to email inquiries within 24 h on weekdays and within 48 h on weekends, or I am not able to respond to email inquiries after 8 p.m. on weeknights and 5 p.m. on weekends, but will get back to you by the next day).

Course Overview

The purpose of this course is to provide an overview of the fundamental concepts, principles, and theories of modern biology. In this course we will use a variety of active learning methods such as group work, small and large group discussion, games, short writing activities, and student response to help students build foundational knowledge of biological concepts and encourage students to synthesize and apply information to real-world topics within and outside of biology. The key concepts of this course are organized into four units: (1) biochemistry and molecular biology, (2) cell biology and energetics, (3) genetics and inheritance, and (4) evolution and ecology.

Diversity, Equity, and Inclusion

As an educator, I am committed to diversity, equity, inclusion, and social justice within and outside of my courses to foster an environment that is welcoming and supportive of all students. I recognize that each student is a whole person with unique experiences, backgrounds, and identities and I strive to engage with each student in a way that is validating and empowering. In practice, this means centering on different student voices and creating a classroom community that is positive, welcoming, and respectful to the whole person. This includes respect for treatment of materials/issues/people with respect to gender/gender expression, sexuality, disability, age, religion, socioeconomic status, race, ethnicity, and culture. My approach to teaching and learning uses learner-centered activities that encourage students to engage with the course content and make connections with their own experiences. Meaning-making is unique to each individual, and I will facilitate learning through open dialogue, active learning strategies, and frequent reflection. Diversity in thought and experience is important for student development, and so to promote diversity, equity, and inclusion, I use a variety of activities that encourage a diverse and universal learning experience and I select course materials and content that is accessible and written by groups that are traditionally underrepresented in biology.

Required Texts and Materials

1. Integrating Concepts in Biology eTextbook (http://www.trunity.com/trubook-integrating-concepts-in-biology-by-campbell-heyer-paradise.html)

2. Web-enabled wireless device (laptop, tablet, etc.) to access Canvas or websites used in class
3. Additional primary and secondary readings (will be available on Canvas)
4. Calculator

Student Learning Outcomes

By the end of this course, students should be able to:

1. Explain and summarize fundamental concepts and principles of biology
2. Demonstrate the development of skills in hypothesis development, data collection, data analysis, drawing conclusions from data, and written communication through lab activities and group activities.
3. Apply quantitative analysis to interpret biological data collected from lab activities
4. Critically review primary scientific literature in biology by interpreting meaning and summarizing main ideas
5. Communicate biological concepts and interpretations effectively in written and oral format through short writing projects and group work
6. Evaluate the relevance of biological problems to social/cultural/political contexts

Technology

Canvas: Canvas will be used to post readings, instructions for activities/assignments, and your grades. I will also post links to valuable resources that will help you learn the material. It is your responsibility to keep up with the course content on the Canvas page.

Computers: Computers will be allowed to use in class with the understanding that it is your responsibility to use it appropriately. Computers are an amazing tool and we will use them frequently throughout the semester for in-class activities.

Assignments and Activities

Group Work/Activities: At the beginning of the semester, students will be assigned to groups to work with throughout the semester. Students within groups can share what they are comfortable with, but they are recommended to share contact information to work on assignments outside of class and to form study groups. Group activities during class can include question-call-response activities, worksheets, small group discussions, and games, and will depend upon the lesson planned for that class period. The goal of group work is to promote collaboration and cooperation, develop communication skills, practice understanding of biological concepts, and solve biological problems that are relevant to student's interests/experiences.

Think-Pair-Share: Think-pair-share is an example of small group activities that students can participate in. Student's will pair up (typically with their neighbor) and each spend one minute explaining their thoughts/experience/knowledge on the prompt and then spend 2 min synthesizing their discussion. Groups may then be asked to share their discussion with the class if they so choose.

Questions-Thoughts-Epiphanies/Know-Want to know-Learn: These two examples of activities ask students to reflect upon their current knowledge and learning. The instructor will ask students to think quietly for a minute or two and/or write down their responses to the prompt. Students may write down any questions, thoughts, or epiphanies they had after reading the materials they prepped before class or the Know-Want to know-Learn activity can be used at the beginning and end of the class to understand where students are starting at and how they developed by the end of the semester. The goal of these activities is to engage students in the learning process through reflection, and the instructor can use this reflection to evaluate lessons and course goals/objectives.

"Science Friday": At the end of each week, we will spend some time discussing current research and news in biology that is relevant to the topics covered in this course. The purpose of this activity is three-fold: (1) to demonstrate how biology is relevant to the world around us socially, politically, culturally, and personally, (2) to develop an understanding of scientific literature and research and build a foundation of scientific literacy, and (3) to highlight diversity in biology by selecting materials from diverse scientists and topics, with special attention to identities that are underrepresented in biology, such as Black, Indigenous, People of Color, LGBTQIA+, and women. At the beginning of each week, I will post an article, summary, and discussion questions on Canvas for you to read and discuss. Discussion questions can include questions about the main ideas of the article, the implications, understanding figures, and a biographical sketch of the authors. Please post your discussion answers to the Canvas discussion page before the last class of the week (Thursday or

Friday) as preparation for our discussion in class. Additionally, I encourage you send me any articles you find that might be interesting or fit with this activity! If you find an article that you want shared with the class, please send it to me no later than the week before the articles are posted. This means send me the article on Monday before I post them to Canvas to give me adequate time to review and summarize the article. Discussion posts will be worth 2 points each and are due on Friday of each week.

One-minute Papers: One-minute papers will be used throughout the semester as a way for students to engage with and process course content. The goal of these short writing assignments is to spend one-minute answering a prompt or question posed by the instructor and practice written communication skills, critical thinking, and synthesis of information. One-minute papers will be submitted on Canvas and will be worth 2 points.

Rubric	2 points	1 point	0 points
Demonstration of understanding of concept	Student demonstrates understanding of concept/question asked	Student demonstrates understanding of concept, but some (1–2) elements are missing	Student does not demonstrate understanding of concept (several elements are missing) or does not answer the question

Quizzes: Quizzes in this course will be short, low-stakes assessments that will be used to assess your understanding of course material and help you prepare for exams and are worth 2 points each. Quizzes will occur on the last class period of each week (with the exception of exam weeks) and include short answer questions and/or multiple-choice questions to help you process the content learned each week.

Exams: Exams in this course will not be cumulative and will occur after we complete each major unit, however, you may need to draw on older course content to answer some exam questions. Because biological concepts build upon each other, developing a comprehensive understanding of key concepts will be important for making connections to the course content throughout the semester. Exams will primarily be multiple choice and short answer questions and will be worth 75 points each.

Grading
Distribution
A: 100–90%
B: 89–80%
C: 79–70%
D: 69–60%
F: 59% or less

Breakdown

In-class activities and out of class assignments	25 points
Discussion posts	25 points
Quizzes	25 points
Exam 1	75 points
Exam 2	75 points
Exam 3	75 points
Exam 4	75 points
Total	375 points

Course Policies
Expectations (Instructor/Student):
[This is a space where the instructor and students can develop course expectations for the instructor, the students, and their peers. The intent is to engage students in the learning process and give them an opportunity to hold themselves accountable and be aware of how they may impact others. The instructor can use a web app such as Padlet that students can access to send suggestions to on the projector screen to make this process interactive. Some examples of expectations are listed below.]

- Respectful dialogue with peers and instructor
- Mutual respect and consideration for peers
- Preparing for class before class time by reading/watching/engaging with assigned materials, reviewing materials during the week, coming to class with questions
- Work collaboratively and cooperatively with group members
- Communicate in a timely manner
- Provide feedback in a timely manner
- Be empathetic and understanding of student's lived experiences, their experiences inside and outside of the classroom

References

AAAS. (2011). Vision & change in undergraduate biology education. In *American assocation for the advancement of science*. http://visionandchange. org/.

Allen, D., & Tanner, K. (2005). Infusing active learning into the large-enrollment biology class: Seven strategies, from simple to complex. *Cell Biology Education, 4*, 262–268. https://doi.org/10.1187/cbe.05-08-0113.

Armbruster, P., Patel, M., Johnson, E., & Weiss, M. (2009). Active learning and student-centered pedagogy improve student attitudes and performance in introductory biology. *CBE-Life Sciences Education, 8*, 203–213. https://doi. org/10.1187/cbe.09.

Ballen, C. J., Danielsen, M., Jørgensen, C., Grytnes, J., & Cotner, S. (2018). Norway's gender gap: classroom participation in undergraduate introductory science. *Nordic Journal of STEM Education, 1*(1), 262. https://doi.org/10. 5324/njsteme.v1i1.2325.

Ballen, C. J., Salehi, S., & Cotner, S. (2017). Exams disadvantage women in introductory biology. *PLoS ONE, 12*(10), 1–14. https://doi.org/10.1371/ journal.pone.0186419.

Ballen, C. J., Wieman, C., Salehi, S., Searle, J. B., & Zamudio, K. R. (2017). Enhancing diversity in undergraduate science: self-efficacy drives performance gains with active learning. *CBE Life Sciences Education, 16*(4), 1–6. https:// doi.org/10.1187/cbe.16-12-0344.

Barthelemy, R. S., Greenberg, A., McKay, T., & Hedberg, G. (2015). The climate experiences of students in introductory biology. *Journal of Microbiology & Biology Education, 16*(2), 138–147. https://doi.org/10.1128/jmbe. v16i2.921.

Bathgate, M. E., Aragón, O. R., Cavanagh, A. J., Frederick, J., & Graham, M. J. (2019). Supports: A key factor in faculty implementation of evidence-based teaching. *CBE Life Sciences Education, 18*(2), ar22. https://doi.org/ 10.1187/cbe.17-12-0272.

Blickenstaff, J. C. (2005). Women and science careers: Leaky pipeline or gender filter? *Gender and Education, 17*(4), 369–386. https://doi.org/10.1080/ 09540250500145072.

Connell, G. L., Donovan, D. A., & Chambers, T. G. (2016). Increasing the use of student-centered pedagogies from moderate to high improves student learning and attitudes about biology. *CBE Life Sciences Education, 15*(1), 1–15. https://doi.org/10.1187/cbe.15-03-0062.

Crombie, G., Silverthorn, N., Jones, A., Piccinin, S., & Pyke, S. W. (2003). Students' perceptions of their classroom participation and instructor as a function of gender and context. *Journal of Higher Education, 74*(1), 51–76 + i. https://doi.org/10.1080/00221546.2003.11777187.

Davidesco, I., & Milne, C. (2019). Implementing cognitive science and discipline-based education research in the undergraduate science classroom. *CBE Life Sciences Education, 18*(3), es4. https://doi.org/10.1187/cbe.18-12-0240.

Donovan, D. A., Connell, G. L., & Grunspan, D. Z. (2018). Student learning outcomes and attitudes using three methods of group formation in a nonmajors biology class. *CBE Life Sciences Education, 17*(4), 1–14. https://doi.org/10.1187/cbe.17-12-0283.

Eddy, S. L. (2019). Recent research in science teaching and learning. *CBE Life Sciences Education, 18*(1), 1–3. https://doi.org/10.1187/cbe.18-12-0250.

Eddy, S. L., & Brownell, S. E. (2016). Beneath the numbers: A review of gender disparities in undergraduate education across science, technology, engineering, and math disciplines. *Physical Review Physics Education Research.* https://doi.org/10.1103/PhysRevPhysEducRes.12.020106.

Eddy, S. L., Brownell, S. E., & Wenderoth, M. P. (2014). Gender gaps in achievement and participation in multiple introductory biology classrooms. *CBE Life Sciences Education, 13*(3), 478–492. https://doi.org/10.1187/cbe.13-10-0204.

England, B. J., Brigati, J. R., Schussler, E. E., & Chen, M. M. (2019). Student anxiety and perception of difficulty impact performance and persistence in introductory biology courses. *CBE Life Sciences Education, 18*(2), ar21. https://doi.org/10.1187/cbe.17-12-0284.

Franceschini, G., Galli, S., Chiesi, F., & Primi, C. (2014). Implicit gender-math stereotype and women's susceptibility to stereotype threat and stereotype lift. *Learning and Individual Differences, 32,* 273–277. https://doi.org/10.1016/j.lindif.2014.03.020.

Freeman, S., Eddy, S. L., McDonough, M., Smith, M. K., Okoroafor, N., Jordt, H., & Wenderoth, M. P. (2014). Active learning increases student performance in science, engineering, and mathematics. *Proceedings of the National Academy of Sciences, 111*(23), 8410–8415. https://doi.org/10.1073/pnas.1319030111.

Froyd, J. E. (2004). *White paper on promising practices in undergraduate STEM education introduction decision-making framework for course/curriculum development.* Retrieved from http://sites.nationalacademies.org/cs/groups/dbassesite/documents/webpage/dbasse_072616.pdf.

Gouvea, J. S. (2019). Learning in a group, as a group, and between groups. *CBE Life Sciences Education, 18*(2), fe4. https://doi.org/10.1187/cbe.19-03-0067.

Grunspan, D. Z., Eddy, S. L., Brownell, S. E., Wiggins, B. L., Crowe, A. J., & Goodreau, S. M. (2016). Males under-estimate academic performance of their female peers in undergraduate biology classrooms. *PLoS ONE, 11*(2), 1–16. https://doi.org/10.1371/journal.pone.0148405.

Haak, D. C., HilleRisLambers, J., Pitre, E., & Freeman, S. (2011). Increased structure and active learning reduce the achievement gap in introductory biology. *Science, 332*(3), 1213–1216.

Hesse-Biber, S. N. (2014). *Feminist research practice: A primer*. Thousand Oaks, CA: Sage.

Hewitt, K. M., Bouwma-Gearhart, J., Kitada, H., Mason, R., & Kayes, L. J. (2019). Introductory biology in social context: The effects of an issues-based laboratory course on biology student motivation. *CBE—Life Sciences Education, 18*(3), ar30. https://doi.org/10.1187/cbe.18-07-0110.

hooks, b. (1994). *Teaching to transgress: Education as the practice of freedom*. New York, NY: Routledge.

Koester, B. P., Grom, G., & McKay, T. A. (2016). Patterns of gendered performance difference in introductory STEM courses, 1–9. Retrieved from http://arxiv.org/abs/1608.07565.

Klein, M. (1997). Looking again at the 'supportive' environment of constructivist pedagogy: An example from preservice teacher education in mathematics. *Journal of Education for Teaching, 23*(3), 277–292. https://doi.org/10.1080/0267479720015.

Lang, J. M. (2016). *Small teaching: Everyday lessons from the science of learning*. San Francisco, CA: Jossey-Bass.

Lauer, S., Momsen, J., Offerdahl, E., Kryjevskaia, M., Christensen, W., & Montplaisir, L. (2013). Stereotyped: Investigating gender in introductory science courses. *CBE Life Sciences Education, 12*(1), 30–38. https://doi.org/10.1187/cbe.12-08-0133.

Lazar, M. M. (2007). Feminist critical discourse analysis: Articulating a feminist discourse Praxis. *Critical Discourse Studies, 4*(2), 141–164.

Lindemann, D., Britton, D., & Zundl, E. (2016). "I don't know why they make it so hard here": Institutional factors and undergraduate women's STEM participation. *International Journal of Gender, Science, and Technology, 8*(2), 221–241.

Matz, R. L., Koester, B. P., Fiorini, S., Grom, G., Shepard, L., Stangor, C. G., … McKay, T. A. (2017). Patterns of gendered performance differences in large introductory courses at five research universities. *AERA Open*. https://doi.org/10.1177/2332858417743754.

McPhail, G. (2015). The fault lines of recontextualization: The limits of constructivism in education. *British Educational Research Journal, 42*(2), 294–313. https://doi.org/10.1002/berj.3199.

Meaders, C. L., Toth, E. S., Lane, A. K., Shuman, J. K., Couch, B. A., Stains, M., Stetzer, M. R., Vinson, E., & Smith, M. K. (2019). "What will I experience in my college STEM courses?" An investigation of student predictions about instructional practices in introductory courses. *CBE Life Sciences Education, 18*(4), ar60.

Mervis, J. (2011). Undergraduate science: Weed-out courses hamper diversity. *Science, 334*(6061), 1333.

Miller, D. I., & Wai, J. (2015). The bachelor's to Ph.D. STEM pipeline no longer leaks more women than men: A 30-year analysis. Frontiers in Psychology, 6(FEB), 1–10. https://doi.org/10.3389/fpsyg.2015.00037.

Moss-Racusin, C. A., Dovidio, J. F., Brescoll, V. L., Graham, M. J., & Handelsman, J. (2012). Science faculty's subtle gender biases favor male students. *Proceedings of the National Academy of Sciences, 109*(41), 16474–16479.

Parson, L. (2016). Are STEM syllabi gendered? A feminist critical discourse analysis. *Qualitative Report, 21*(1), 102–116.

Parson, L., & Ozaki, C. C. (2017). Gendered Student Ideals in STEM in Higher Education. *NASPA Journal About Women in Higher Education, 11*(2), 171–190. https://doi.org/10.1080/19407882.2017.1392323.

Pawley, A. L. (2004). The feminist engineering classroom: A vision for future educational innovations. *ASEE Annual Conference Proceedings.*

Sallee, M. W. (2014). Performing masculinity: Considering gender in doctoral student socialization. *International Journal for Researcher Development, 5*(2), 99–122. https://doi.org/10.1353/jhe.2011.0007.

Sanabria, T., & Penner, A. (2017). Weeded out? Gendered responses to failing calculus. *Social Sciences, 6*(2), 1–14.

Seymour, E., & Hewitt, S. (1997). *Talking about leaving: Why undergraduates leave the sciences.* Boulder, CO: Westview Press.

Smith, A. C., Stewart, R., Shields, P., Hayes-Klosteridis, J., Robinson, P., & Yuan, R. (2005). Introductory biology bourses: A framework to support active learning in large enrollment introductory science courses. *Cell Biology Education, 4*(2), 143–156. https://doi.org/10.1187/cbe.04-08-0048.

Stanberry, M. L. (2018). Active learning: a case study of student engagement in college Calculus. *International Journal of Mathematical Education in Science and Technology.* Taylor & Francis. https://doi.org/10.1080/0020739X.2018.1440328.

Styers, M. L., Van Zandt, P. A., & Hayden, K. L. (2018). Active learning in flipped life science courses promotes development of critical thinking skills. *CBE Life Sciences Education, 17*(3), 1–13. https://doi.org/10.1187/cbe.16-11-0332.

Sullivan, L. L., Ballen, C. J., & Cotner, S. (2018). Small group gender ratios impact biology class performance and peer evaluations. *PLoS ONE, 13*(4), 1–14. https://doi.org/10.1371/journal.pone.0195129.

Tanner, K. D. (2013). Structure matters: Twenty-one teaching strategies to promote student engagement and cultivate classroom equity. *CBE Life Sciences Education, 12*(3), 322–331. https://doi.org/10.1187/cbe.13-06-0115.

Theobald, E. J., Hill, M. J., Tran, E., Agrawal, S., Nicole Arroyo, E., Behling, S., Chambwe, N., Cintrón, D. L., Cooper, J. D., Dunster, G., Grummer, J. A., Hennessey, K., Hsiao, J., Iranon, N., Jones, L., Jordt, H., Keller, M., Lacey, M. E., Littlefield, C. E., ... Freeman, S. (2020). Active learning narrows achievement gaps for underrepresented students in undergraduate science, technology, engineering, and math. *Proceedings of the National Academy of Sciences of the United States of America, 117*(12), 6476–6483. https://doi.org/10.1073/pnas.1916903117.

Tisdell, E. J. (1998). Poststructural feminist pedagogies: The possibilities and limitations of feminist emancipatory adult learning theory and practice. *Adult Education Quarterly, 48*(3), 139–156.

Trujillo, G., & Tanner, K. D. (2014a). Considering the role of affect in learning: Monitoring students' self-efficacy, sense of belonging, and science identity. *CBE Life Sciences Education, 13*(1), 6–15. https://doi.org/10.1187/cbe.13-12-0241.

Weir, L. K., Barker, M. K., McDonnell, L. M., Schimpf, N. G., Rodela, T. M., & Schulte, P. M. (2019). Small changes, big gains: A curriculum-wide study of teaching practices and student learning in undergraduate biology. *PLoS ONE, 14*(8), 1–16. https://doi.org/10.1371/journal.pone.0220900.

Wood, W. B. (2009). Innovations in teaching undergraduate biology and why we need them. *Annual Review of Cell and Developmental Biology, 25*(1), 93–112. https://doi.org/10.1146/annurev.cellbio.24.110707.175306.

Recommended Readings

Allen, D., & Tanner, K. (2005b). Infusing active learning into the large-enrollment biology class: Seven strategies, from simple to complex. *Cell Biology Education, 4*, 262–268. https://doi.org/10.1187/cbe.05-08-0113.

Course Source: a website built for STEM educators that publishes peer-reviewed studies and teaching strategies. https://www.coursesource.org/.

Dewsbury, B., & Brame, C. J. (2019). Inclusive teaching. *CBE Life Sciences Education, 18*(2), fe2 1–5.

Evidence-Based Teaching Guides—CBE Life Sciences Education: a website that includes resources for educators for group work, inclusive teaching, peer instruction, and modeling. https://lse.ascb.org/.

hooks, b. (1994). *Teaching to transgress: Education as the practice of freedom.* New York, NY: Routledge.

Lang, J. M. (2016b). *Small teaching: Everyday lessons from the science of learning.* San Francisco, CA: Jossey-Bass.

Roychoudhury, A., Tippins, D. J., & Nichols, S. E. (1995b). Gender-inclusive science teaching: A feminist-constructivist approach. *Journal of Research in Science Teaching, 32*(9), 897–924.

Smith, A. C., Stewart, R., Shields, P., Hayes-Klosteridis, J., Robinson, P., & Yuan, R. (2005b). Introductory biology bourses: A framework to support active learning in large enrollment introductory science courses. *Cell Biology Education, 4*(2), 143–156. https://doi.org/10.1187/cbe.04-08-0048.

Tanner, K. D. (2013b). Structure matters: Twenty-one teaching strategies to promote student engagement and cultivate classroom equity. *CBE Life Sciences Education, 12*(3), 322–331. https://doi.org/10.1187/cbe.13-06-0115.

Trujillo, G., & Tanner, K. D. (2014b). Considering the role of affect in learning: Monitoring students' self-efficacy, sense of belonging, and science identity. *CBE Life Sciences Education, 13*(1), 6–15. https://doi.org/10.1187/cbe.13-12-0241.

Wood, W. B. (2009b). Innovations in teaching undergraduate biology and why we need them. *Annual Review of Cell and Developmental Biology, 25*(1), 93–112. https://doi.org/10.1146/annurev.cellbio.24.110707.175306.

Teaching Race and Racism in Social Work Education

Ebony Nicole Perez

DEFINITIONS OF KEY TERMINOLOGY

Cultural Competence	As defined by CSWE refers to the ability to integrate and apply social work knowledge, values, and skills to practice situations in a *"purposeful, intentional, and professional manner to promote human and community well-being"* (CSWE, 2015, p. 6).
Institutional Racism	Is defined as norms, policies, laws, and rules that advantage White people as a whole and oppress Communities of Color. This type of racism seeks to maintain the existing power structure thus benefitting White communities often at the expense of Communities of Color.

E. N. Perez (✉)
Saint Leo University, St. Leo, FL, USA
e-mail: ebony.perez@saintleo.edu

© The Author(s), under exclusive license to Springer Nature Switzerland AG 2021
C. C. Ozaki and L. Parson (eds.), *Teaching and Learning for Social Justice and Equity in Higher Education*,
https://doi.org/10.1007/978-3-030-69947-5_9

177

People of Color	A term utilized to collectively represent ethnic peoples who are often placed into subordinated status in the United States (i.e., African/Black American, American Indian or Native American, Asian American, Latinx).
Race	A socially constructed, shifting, and imprecise phenomenon that uses morphology (skin color, hair texture, facial features, etc.) as visible markers of difference that are influenced by time, space, and power (Haney Lopez, 1994, Omi & Winant, 1994; Smedley & Smedley, 2011). There is no biological basis for race and more variation within the same racial group rather than between them (Smedley & Smedley, 2011).

In 2013 the #BlackLivesMatter movement came on the scene in response to the murder of Trayvon Martin. The Black Lives Matter movement continued to develop throughout 2013–2014 as communities across the nation protested the killings of Tamir Rice, Tanisha Anderson, Philando Castile, and other Black Americans without consequence. This violence sparked a national conversation that found its way into social work classrooms with faculty and students (Davis, 2016). As faculty and students in social work programs engaged in such discussions, the need to more critically examine the role of race and racism in social work education and practice became evident (Nakaoka & Ortiz, 2018).

Social workers serve in racially diverse communities and work with clients who are experiencing virtually every social ill, including disparities in health and healthcare made evident by the COVID-19 pandemic, education, child welfare, and poverty. The continued police and vigilante violence against Black persons in 2020, with the killings of Ahmaud Arbery, George Floyd, and Breonna Taylor, underscored the need for skilled social workers who are knowledgeable about how race and racism operate within the United States. It is imperative that social work education facilitates critical learning opportunities attuned to the impact of race and racism on the outcomes of both individuals and communities. Two key aspects of social work practice are advocacy and intervention. In order to effectively advocate, social workers must engage in studying individual, institutional, and systemic racism and how race has been woven into public policy, law, health and mental health, housing, and education systems.

Further, the racially charged sociopolitical U.S. landscape adds to the difficulty social work educators must contend with as they adapt their educational approaches to prepare students to understand race and racism and their influences on practice. Because experiences with racially diverse populations present both opportunities and challenges for personal, professional, and organizational growth, the social work educational context must provide opportunities for students to develop within these varied areas of growth. Specifically, undergraduate education programs combine theory with mandatory field hours that allow students to integrate academic and practical knowledge. This composition of theory and practice can be instrumental in helping students to meet their professional responsibilities and mobilize advocacy efforts. Yet, to begin to realize the standards advanced by CSWE, social work educators must create teaching and learning environments that engage all participants through being intentional and critical about their pedagogical choices. To this end, this chapter outlines three areas social work educators must explicitly teach through the lens of developing cultural competence: (1) the historical context of race and racism and how it impacts current social work practice in the United States, (2) the development of skills to engage in productive dialogue around race, and (3) the cultivation of knowledge and skills to challenge disparities to contribute to greater racial harmony and justice. The chapter concludes with specific curriculum recommendations that integrate learning goals with pedagogical strategies that encourage both reflection and action.

HISTORY OF SOCIAL WORK AND RACE

Social workers engage with individuals, groups, and communities to help assess needs, strengths, support networks, respond to crisis situations, and advocate for social justice. A guiding principle of social work is the person-in-environment perspective which highlights the reciprocity of the person–environment relationship (Mizrahi, 2009). This perspective incorporates the idea that social, economic, political, historical, familial, and cultural environments can exert a conducive or oppressive influence on behavior and life experiences.

Social work is poised to research and assess the impact of race on systems and advocate for social change. Racism has proven to be foundational, pervasive, and persistent in the United States. Racism impacts People of Color through overt and covert challenges that create and maintain enduring racial disparities and inequities. Thus, the onus of the social work profession to strengthen its efforts to understand both individual and institutionalized racism is central to addressing the call to "promote sensitivity to and knowledge about oppression and cultural and ethnic diversity" (NASW, 2017, p. 5, Ethical Principles section, para. 3). A social worker's ability to understand the role of race and racism on life experiences is a critical component of cultural competency and social work praxis.

As racial diversity rapidly grows, this expansion challenges the Master Narrative of who is and is not American, particularly in cities around the United States—Boston, New York, San Francisco, Atlanta, and others— already showing a majority of the population being People of Color (U.S. Census Bureau, 2015). Takaki (2008) posits the "Master Narrative of American History" of our country being "settled by Europeans and Americans are white," is simultaneously popular and inaccurate (p. 4). Recent Census Bureau projections indicate that by 2043 more than half of the United States population will belong to a group other than non-Hispanic[1] White (U.S. Census Bureau, 2015). Thus the question: "how can we prepare ourselves for this future, when the Master Narrative is such a powerful force in our thinking about the past?" is timely and relevant for social work educators to consider (Takaki, 2008, p. 5). It is reasonable to acknowledge that this line of thinking impacts each social worker's knowledge, values, skills, as well as their cognitive and affective processing with regards to the function of race and impact of racism in contemporary U.S. society.

Further, the continued diverse demographic shift of the U.S. population serves as notice to social workers that this change can mean increased exposure to the richness and complexities of race and racism within the life experiences their clients encounter. For social workers and other helping professionals experiences with racially diverse populations

---

[1] Analyst will often utilize Hispanic over Latinx or use the two interchangeably. I solely employ Latinx as the pan-ethnic term "Hispanic" is rooted in conquest, colonialization, and European oppression. The exception is when the referenced data employs the term "Hispanic" only.

presents both opportunities and challenges for personal, professional, and organizational growth. Social work education programs do not isolate thinking and doing. They require both. By blending theory with mandatory field hours, undergraduate social work education requires students to put classroom knowledge into practice prior to graduation. Therefore, the expectation at the baccalaureate level is that students will have the basic cultural competency skills to practice entry-level social work. By tending to crucial tasks such as case management, biopsychosocial interviews, community outreach, and advocacy, caseworker, and juvenile court liaisons undergraduate social work (BSW) degrees are both useful and flexible. Consequently, the opportunity for someone with a BSW degree to encounter the nuances of race and racism even prior to graduation in a professional setting is highly likely.

The primary mission of the NASW is to "enhance human well-being and to help meet the basic human needs of all people, with particular attention to the needs and empowerment of people who are vulnerable, oppressed, and living in poverty," where "Social workers are sensitive to cultural and ethnic diversity and strive to end discrimination, oppression, poverty, and other forms of social injustice". Guided by the value of social justice, each social worker's activities should seek to promote knowledge about and sensitivity to power and oppression, thus change efforts should be focused on social injustice through the development of cultural competence. Traditionally, cultural competency frameworks have emphasized a heightened awareness of cultural backgrounds and the knowledge and skills to deliver services to a diverse clientele. Staying true to the profession's mission, values, and standards, social workers should be leading the charge to implement social changes focused on racial equity. Regardless if they want to or not, social workers operate as agents of social control often holding powerful positions over their clients. Additionally, social workers can identify and positively impact agencies and policies thus having an overall impact on society. By working with those who are marginalized and oppressed, social workers are also accountable to the agencies that hire them and government contracts that fund their services. This paradoxical relationship may be further complicated by racial and ethnic differences. Thus, the need to develop beyond the current cultural competency frameworks to an actionable racial equity framework that challenges institutional racism is evident (NASW, 2014).

The Social Construction of Race

Race is a powerful, yet unstable, social signifier absent of any biological foundation with meaning deeply embedded in law, history, geography, and sociopolitical contexts (Haney Lopez, 1994; Omi & Winant, 1994, 2015; Patton, 2016). While not "real," the ideology of race has a significant impact on social relations through implicit beliefs as well as social practices; therefore, the outcome of being racialized has concrete consequences (Bell, 2016; Garner, 2017). Haney Lopez (1994) remarked the meaning of race is directly related to the social structure of a society in which it came to exist. Race is a relatively recent invention in human history, developed with colonialism and capitalism to create hierarchies of greater than and less than (Haney Lopez, 1994; Takaki, 2008). In the United States, legal definitions of race became a way to create and maintain a racial caste system, a system that continues to impact the current sociopolitical landscape of the country (Haney Lopez, 1994). Although not biological, race holds both meaning and power in the United States (Haney Lopez, 1994; Leonardo, 2009). Race continues to influence whether one is free or imprisoned, determines one's economic and education prospects, impacts health outcomes, permeates U.S. sociopolitical landscape, and politics (Brach & Fraserirector, 2000; Bonilla-Silva, 2018; National Urban League, 2013).

Race, ideologically and as a phenomenon, can be critiqued and analyzed through social science methodology. It is an attempt to link people's physiological appearance to their behavior and status. Haney Lopez (1994) argues that although few seem to know what race is or is not, the U.S. racial codes make sense only because of the meaning attached to morphology and pigmentation (e.g., Asians are good at math or Mexicans are criminals). Within everyday U.S. society, "race" is often used to refer to non-white people; however contemporary scholars argue white people are racialized beings as well (Bonilla-Silva, 2018; Garner, 2017). Garner (2017) insists, "how we think about 'race' is to assume, that Person X belongs to group A, therefore, she behaves in a certain way" (p. 3). As Garner (2017) contends, and I agree, "we hold these truths to be self-evident that all men [*sic*] are created racially" (p. 3).

Understanding the assumptions tied to race is a foundational block of cultural competency. According to Michael Omi (2001), "the meaning of race in the United States has been and probably always will be fluid and subject to multiple determinations" (p. 244). How white Americans engage race has rendered whiteness in America virtually invisible, and white people have little understanding of the effects of race and racism in their own lives (Davis & Gentlewarrior, 2015; McIntosh, 1988 [2004]; Omi & Winant, 2015; Robbins & Jones, 2016; Robinson-Wood, 2016). A common misperception is that racism is only evident in the most extreme cases, particularly those that are violent or vile acts (Garner, 2017; Robinson-Wood, 2016). Altogether, racism operates in society with consequences for both the oppressed and the privileged (Robinson-Wood, 2016; Garner, 2017). However, Rahill et al. (2016) note that social work students often fail to connect how diverse life experiences impact their lives or the experiences of their clients.

CULTURAL COMPETENCY MODEL (CCM) IN SOCIAL WORK EDUCATION

Within the social work profession key practices, beliefs, and policies direct the socialization of how educators, practitioners, and students engage race and racism. As previously stated, both the CSWE and NASW continue to emphasize self-awareness as a key component of cultural competency. The policies for obtaining and maintaining accreditation require social work programs to create curricula that specifically address self-awareness (CSWE, 2015). Existing cultural competency models only focus on assisting practitioners to become more comfortable with "others" (Fisher-Borne et al., 2015). The focus on the "other" normalizes white, Western culture and directs all else to be treated as obscure or abnormal (Garner, 2017; Jeyasingham, 2012). Further, white people (i.e., the dominant group) only need to learn about People of Color to label behavior as a manner of understanding (Fisher-Borne et al., 2014). This proclivity to characterize behavior may facilitate stereotypes as it assumes race is both knowable and monolithic (Dunn, 2002; Fisher-Borne et al, 2014).

Further, currently within social work education, there is a tendency to avoid critical engagement when addressing racial differences (Davis, 2016; Mensah Moore, 2016). Cultural competency and multiculturalism frames comprise the existing conceptual framework for meeting the mandate to engage diversity and difference in social work education and eventual practice. This chosen model highlights micro-level change and is largely focused on exposure, cultural awareness, and attitude readjustment of social work students (Campbell, 2014; Constance-Higgins,

2012). It allows for the development of cultural appreciation and recognition of clients (Constance-Higgins, 2012), as well as the realization that clients may possess a cultural wealth that is absent from the practitioner's purview. For all of its good, this culturally relevant, micro-level approach is limited in its ability to make a significant impact when engaging diversity, particularly race and racism (Campbell, 2014). Relying on socially constructed U.S. categories the existing CCM does little to promote anti-racist activism. Abrams and Moio (2009) challenged social work educators to engage in developing a more relevant model and work toward anti-racist pedagogy.

Additionally, the CCM framework traditionally ignores the historical legacies of race and how differences were, and continue to be, used to justify inhumane policies and practices (Adams & Zuniga, 2016; Deepak et al., 2015). Furthermore, it does not consider the emotional toll of learning new knowledge associated with race, racism, and anti-racism as well as the emotional stamina required to engage in such work. Without attention to the emotional component of learning, students may become discouraged or fatigued and therefore cannot fully engage in dismantling whiteness (Matias & Mackey, 2015). As Sue (2001) asserts, racial identity holds a primary position over other socio-demographic identifiers mainly due to many social work provider's "greater discomfort" addressing race (p. 792). Providers who identify with any of the dominant U.S. statuses (i.e., white, man, and heterosexual) must acknowledge and contend with the deeply ingrained values which enable the existence of both separation and discrimination (Dunn, 2002; Fisher-Borne et al., 2015). Racial competency, as defined by Campbell (2014) entails that "educators or practitioners [have an] advanced understanding of the social construction, significance, and functionality of race in today's 'post racial' society" (p. 17). In other words, racial competency involves educators and practitioners being able to acknowledge the existing power hierarchies and mechanisms that have been constructed by race.

Jeffery (2005) argues,

1. whiteness as a set of practices very much resembles social work as a set of practices;
2. when we teach people to be self-reflexive and critical of whiteness, we are, at the same time, inviting them to be critical of social work.

However, this is not usually an explicit component of the social work curriculum (p. 410).

As Abrams and Moio (2009) challenged, there is an opportunity for social work education to develop a cultural competence model that contradicts stereotypes and moves beyond "comfort" to understanding, empathy, and activism. This model should allow for the development of self-awareness and prompt students to engage with diversity and difference while working toward anti-racist pedagogy in social work education. The strategies outlined in this chapter work to create recognition and build awareness of how race operates in society. In the subsequent section, I discuss both the challenges and pedagogical strategies to support faculty and students in this journey.

SOCIAL WORK EDUCATION AND TEACHING RACE

There is consensus within education and social work scholarship that the very nature of teaching about race and oppression is likely to evoke strong emotions, strongly held opinions, and create conflict (Abrams & Gibson, 2007; Jeyasingham, 2012; Hikido & Murray, 2016; Matias et al., 2016). The fields of sociology and education have a long history of dealing with issues of race and racism that can be incorporated into social work education (see Adams & Bell, Eduardo Bonilla- Silva, and Eileen O'Brien). In the following sections, I suggest strategies to facilitate the development of cultural competence in the social work classroom by highlighting social work classroom challenges and a review of implicit bias.

Working Amidst Discomfort

Social workers need to be cognizant of the differential effect of social policies that disadvantage Communities of Color while benefiting others. However, scholars suggest educators and students alike report feeling uncertain, insecure, angry, and other negative sensations when engaging with race-specific content and whiteness in the classroom (Jones, 2008; Matias et al., 2016; Mensah Moore, 2016; Quaye, 2012, 2014; Robbins & Jones, 2016; Robbins, 2017; Tatum, 1992). Robbins and Jones (2016) reported many educators have difficulty overcoming student resistance when discussing racial content. Yet, a fundamental component of addressing institutional racism is social workers' ability to comprehend the effect of racism on their clients and their communities. This cannot be accomplished by only teaching tolerance or avoiding explicit discussions on racism.

One strategy to help assuage resistance to participate in conversations about racism is to invite students to create class rules for discussions. This can be done in a combination of small and large group activities. First, students work in small groups and create two or three classroom rules. Next, each group shares their rules with the entire class and, after a large group discussion, the class should come to a consensus about which rules to keep. While facilitating this discussion, the instructor should also capture these rules and distribute them to the class. This activity helps students to develop cultural competence by modeling how to have conversations about race and racism. Professional social workers must initiate both formal and informal discussions about race with colleagues and constituents. The conversations may involve either general discussions or be in response to specific policies, practices, behaviors, and attitudes observed in a professional context. Due to the nature of institutional racism such discussions are often experienced as threatening. Self-awareness, critical judgment, and skills in initiating and maintaining discussions about institutional racism evolve over time. These skills are essential components to move cultural competency to an anti-racist praxis.

A Look in the Mirror

In 2015 the Council of Social Work Education (CSWE) implored educators to prepare students to "engage in diversity and difference in practice" and "advance human rights, social, economic, and environmental justice" (p. 7). In order to fulfill this mandate, it is important for educators, students, and professionals to recognize the assumptions, biases, and stereotypes, both conscious and unconscious, they have about cultural groups. Campbell (2014) notes unconscious assumptions may involve personal constructions to lead to biases, assumptions, and stereotypes based on professional misinterpretations. For example, white professionals are more likely to develop negative views of marginalized racial populations based on differing dialects, which contributes to the perception of lack of knowledge or education (Campbell, 2014, Patton, 2016).

Social work educators, therefore, must assess their personal level of cultural competence and the impact it may have on pedagogical strategies they choose. An educator's lack of personal knowledge is the most frequently identified obstacle to the inclusion of race-specific and culturally relevant content, along with feelings of discomfort in exploring these issues with their students (Mishna & Bogo, 2007; Saunders et al., 2015). By exploring cultural competency, educators can develop an understanding of their own cultural heritage, beliefs, and values. This understanding can allow educators to identify areas of discomfort which may impact the interactions they have with individuals of another identity (e.g., race, culture, gender) which may unknowingly impact pedagogical choices (Campbell, 2014; CSWE, 2015; Garran & Rozas, 2013; Mishna & Bogo, 2007). One way to do this is to include a statement in the syllabus that notifies students about course assignments that focus on being intentionally self-reflexive about race. This statement gives students time to start the deeper reflective work required to complete those assignments and makes the educator's expectation that students be prepared to discuss the topics of race and racism. Students often have had little experience or development that would prepare them to discuss race and racism reflectively; all social workers need to dedicate time to personal and professional growth to be effective in dismantling institutional racism. Thus, this syllabus statement should also orient students to the professional expectation of self-reflection as a continuous process throughout their career.

Discussing the Impact of Sociohistorical Context on Practice

To talk about race without its historical legacy is to talk about it out of context (Omi & Winant, 1994). Understanding the history of race is essential to combatting racism (Adams & Zuniga, 2016), yet the dominant rhetoric of color-blindness and post-racialism had largely been silenced since 2016, until the Black Lives Matter protests began again in June 2020. During that time, not only had racial disparities persisted, the gaps between racial groups have steadily increased (Kochhar & Cilluffo, 2017). Yet, most students continue to be inept in their understanding of the history of race and the significance of racial categorization and hierarchy. It is important to understand the history of race and racism and how that history informs the present and, therefore their social work practice behaviors. Through awareness of the sociohistorical context of race allows students to begin to understand the impact of race on life experiences, policies, systems, and laws.

One foundational premise needed to increase a student's awareness is understanding of the construction of race as a social category used to organize people hierarchically. Citing "science," race was operationalized in the United States as proof of inherent, biological differences that justified the exploitation of Indigenous land and the forced labor of enslaved Africans. Initially, race was not the most salient classification marker in the United State, religion and class were. As Europeans, Italian, Jewish, and Irish people began to fuse into U.S. society and "became" white, race was used to reinforce ideals of who had property rights, voting rights, and the ability to fully participate in society (Haney Lopez, 1994). Haney-Lopez (1994) argues the social construction of race has deep historical roots in the legal system. As the United States developed, the law reified the social meanings of race to sustain class delineations between the wealthy and the poor (Alexander, 2012; Haney-Lopez, 1994) as well as physical and intellectual differences (Bell et al., 2016). This idea was reinforced as Native Americans were forced off their land and chattel slavery developed a permanent racial caste system in the United States.

Understanding the unique history of race in the context of the United States is critical to being able to analyze the contemporary function of race (Adams 2016; Bell, 2016; Bell et al., 2016; Deepak et al., 2015). Significant engagement with the history of race is often left out of higher education (Patton, 2016). As students graduate college without their racist ideologies being challenged, racism continues within everyday lives. Racist graduates lead to racist professionals and the cycle persists (Patton, 2016). Within social work education, understanding the dynamic nature of race enables social workers to unpack how privilege and disadvantage are ingrained into legal and social systems and continue to reinforce contemporary racism. Being able to adapt practice approaches in consideration of these factors, increases student cultural competence and moves them toward anti-racist social work.

Social work educators need to include strategies and assignments that will center race and challenge existing white supremacist ideologies. In the classroom, one assignment could prompt students to apply social work skills to advocate for characters in a television series or on a movie. With a television show or movie, students could follow characters and practice completing real-world social work responsibilities and taking notes. One way to approach this as an assignment might include group work, where students are directed to operate as a "treatment team" and develop plans for their "clients". Working with media allows the opportunity for students to practice their social works, practice critical thinking skills, demonstrate social work knowledge, and be able to discuss social work values around the function of race in a significant manner. This also creates a more positive way for students to meaningfully engage the role of race in a lower stakes classroom situation. Without the chance to practice these skills, social workers may misapply principles and become a "white savior," which negates their culpability in maintaining contemporary racism (Matias & Mackey, 2015). Social workers need to better understand the relationship between the problems a client needs help with and the role of racism in the genesis of those problems.

For example, one television show to guide students to explore such a relationship is the remake of Party of Five. Party of Five depicts a Mexican American family dealing with the result of the post-2016 immigration law changes in the United States. Doing the activities described previously also provides a chance for students to discuss the emotional aspects of social work practice. In crafting discussion questions, faculty should develop questions that interrogate the affective processing surrounding the issues that are depicted in the television series. Discussions can be focused on helping the client(s) deal with their emotions and identify potential emotional triggers, as well as teaching students how to utilize self-regulation to work with families in such crisis. In addition to practicing their practice skills, this pedagogical strategy allows for the exploration of the unique strengths that Communities of Color inherently have as part of their culture. Oftentimes, these communities are depicted from a deficit view, and it is difficult for students who are not part of the culture to identify the strengths. Yosso's (2005) Community Cultural Wealth frame is pivotal in providing a framework to acknowledge that Communities of Color have a cultural benefit that can add to the richness of assessment and treatment. However, that framework has been insufficiently applied to social work education, and it provides an important lens to help instructors develop assignments and activities that more fully develop the knowledge, skills, and awareness required to engage anti-racist activism on all levels.

Increasing Self-Awareness Around Race and Racism

Within the United States, white people are not socialized to see themselves as "raced". This mechanism allows white people to be able to see race as something that exists outside of them, thereby making *racism* someone else's issue (DiAngelo, 2018). Social work educators can assist students through this process by helping students not only develop external strategies to challenge racism but to also develop internal strategies to resist racism. The Council on Social Work Education (CSWE) calls for students to be able to apply self-awareness and self-regulation in praxis to manage their personal bias. It is irresponsible and unreasonable to expect social work students to critically apply self-awareness without knowledge of themselves as a "raced" being. Students need to recognize, accept, and discuss the importance and impact of race to engage in competent social work practice. Yet, it is difficult to effectively have a dialogue about race or racism when the topic is only seen as belonging to People of Color. As such, Quaye (2014) argues that educators who engage in racial dialogues must contend with "students' preconceived notions ... as well as accept that even talking about race is challenging a dominant ideology, an ideology that asserts students are to remain silent about race" (p. 5).

Learning about the historical underpinnings of contemporary racism often leaves students feeling guilty or helpless to enact true social change (Bell et al., 2016; DiAngelo, 2018; Leonardo, 2009). Zembylas (2015) asserts that to create an opportunity for individual and social transformation alike, discomforting feelings are important for challenging the dominant beliefs. Yet, Harris et al. (2012) assert that when race and racism are not explicitly incorporated into the curriculum it can leave students feeling unsure and disoriented. The ability to challenge worldviews in a manner that holds the greatest possibility for learning and lasting change cannot be accomplished in an environment of worry and mistrust. This means that faculty need to consider and address anxiety around race in order to facilitate productive learning about race (Garcia & Van Soest, 2000; Rodenborg & Boisen, 2013; Tatum, 1992).

To help address anxiety, research suggests several strategies to facilitate critical conversations that facilitate a "pedagogy of discomfort" (Boler, as cited by Nadan & Stark, 2016). This critical education approach encourages students and educators both to abandon their "comfort zone" and to critically investigate "Self" (p. 12). Tatum (1992) argues that when allowed to explore race-related content in the classroom where both the affective and intellectual responses are given space and addressed, student understanding is significantly improved. Therefore, providing students the opportunity to learn about and discuss race in the classroom requires educators to avoid conflating safe with comfortable and to work instead to foster an environment of trust and support. The opportunity to be guided through a critical process that engages in self-reflection around race starts with the student. While white students may easily recognize overt racism, they are less likely to detect more subtle forms of racism. By having students examine seemingly benign aspects of their lives such as talking about their neighborhood or school early in the term students are set up to analyze the more commonplace covert or unintentional racist actions. For example, students may be unaware of the true foundation of the Black Lives Matter (BLM) movement. Educators can create affirmative opportunities for discussions between students who have experienced firsthand the effect of institutional racism and facilitate, through reflection and discussions, connection-making between student experiences and the BLM movement. These discussions require students to listen; the intended outcome of these discussions is the realization that racism effects everyone—two key components of developing cultural competence.

Practical Activity

This activity could be included in a diversity or multi-cultural issues course, and be adapted as an introductory activity in a microlevel social work course. The purpose of this module is to provide the opportunity for students to appraise and advance their understanding of race and racism. It is important for students to unpack the role race has played in their lives as a starting point to anti-racist practice. Educators must also take care to avoid the assumption that Students of Color are well versed in issues of race and racism.

1. Learning Objectives: At the conclusion of the lesson, students will be able to
2. Examine the concept of race;
3. Highlight the role race plays in development and society;
4. Extrapolate the impact of racial difference;
5. Evaluate the origins and attitudes associated with race; and
6. Demonstrated an increased awareness of how unconscious cultural stereotypes impact on future clients and practice.

This activity works best if given within the first two to three weeks of the course before there is a great deal of content delivered. Students are to engage in a 25–30 min, recorded self-interview (either audio or video).

Students should be advised only the instructor will view the video. Sample questions for the self-interview may include:

1. Tell me about yourself.
2. Why do you want to be a social worker?
3. Please describe your friends growing up.
4. Tell me about your neighborhood growing up.
5. What messages have you received about your heritage? (From family/friends/society, etc.).
6. What messages have you received about the heritage of others? (From family/friends/society, etc.).
7. How do you define social justice?
8. How do you define diversity?
9. What is oppression?
10. Describe one thing people would say about your appearance? How does that make you feel? Are they correct?
11. Which of your identities have shaped you the most?
12. Discuss race and culture.

Assessing whether students have met the intended learning outcomes includes evaluating the interview content focusing on the quality of student content, the insightfulness of their discussion of racial positionality, and their ability to analyze and evaluate the impact of race on their lived experiences presented in the interview. As a part of the formative assessment process, the instructor can identify specific gaps in knowledge about race and racism revealed by the students. In response, instructors can then add in resources as well as develop meaningful opportunities for students to dialogue and work to develop as allies in the quest toward anti-racist praxis. Through this activity, the instructor can identify cultural competency areas for development and, then, move to anti-racist action and socially-just social work that promotes larger change at the individual, agency, community, and societal levels.

Conclusion

The miasmic nature of racism persists in part due to its invisibility as a systemic issue. Social work education is inimitably positioned to impact education, social services, social policy, the criminal justice system, while simultaneously attending to the micro-level needs of clients and constituents. It is incumbent for social work educators to more critically attend to race and racism both inside and outside of the profession given their sphere of influence and as they train future practitioners to engage in an increasingly diverse world. The weight of dismantling institutional racism belongs to everyone. Fundamental to this task is the need for professional social workers to understand the effect of racism on their clients, communities, and the larger society. In order to be effective in addressing racism, educational institutions must commit to incorporating content related to institutional racism into the curriculum and all forms of education. For social work education programs, the goal is to graduate social workers who are committed to addressing institutional racism throughout their careers. This requires that instructors explore ways in which the current curriculum supports practices that foster institutional racism and then actively working to dismantle and rebuild systems with an anti-racist lens.

The desire to take knowledge and skills, developed through education and practice, and participate in society as a change agent begins within oneself. Social work educators are trained practitioners who have taken up the challenge to provide the next generations with better tools for addressing race and racism. Educators should attend critically to their pedagogical choices, challenge racist teaching practices, and develop strategies (as well as support) when dealing with student resistance and backlash. This is the art of teaching from a framework that incorporates social justice pedagogy.

REFERENCES

Adams, M. (2016). Pedagogical foundations for social justice education. In M. Adams & L. A. Bell (Eds.), *Teaching for diversity and social justice* (pp. 27–54). Routledge.

Abrams, L. S., & Gibson, P. (2007). Teaching notes: Reframing multicultural education: Teaching white privilege in the social work curriculum. *Journal of Social Work Education, 43*(1), 147–160. https://doi.org/10.5175/jswe.2007.200500529.

Abrams, L. S., & Moio, J. A. (2009). Critical race theory and the cultural competence dilemma in social work education. *Journal of Social Work Education, 45*(2), 245–261.

Adams, M., & Zuniga, X. (2016). Getting started: Core concepts for social justice education.In M. Adams & L. A. Bell (Eds.), *Teaching for diversity and social justice* (pp. 95–130). Routledge.

Alexander, M. (2012). *The new Jim Crow: Mass incarceration in the age of colorblindness*. New York, NY: New Press.

Bell, L. A. (2016). Theoretical foundations for social justice education. In M. Adams & L. A. Bell (Eds.), *Teaching for diversity and social justice* (pp. 3–26). Routledge.

Bell, L. A., Funk, M. S., Joshi, K. Y., & Valdivia, M. (2016). Racism and white privilege. In M. Adams & L. A. Bell (Eds.), *Teaching for diversity and social justice* (pp. 133–182). Routledge.

Bonilla-Silva, E. (2018). *Racism without racists: Color-blind racism and the persistence of racial inequality in America*. Lanham, MD: Rowman & Littlefield.

Brach, C. & Fraserirector, I. (2000). Can cultural competency reduce racial and ethnic health disparities? *Medical Care Research and Review, 57*(1), 187–217.

Campbell, E. (2014). Using critical race theory to measure racial competency among social workers. *Journal of Sociology and Social Work, 2*(2).

Constance-Huggins, M. (2012). Critical race theory in social work education: A framework for addressing racial disparities. *Critical Social Work, 13*(2), 2–16.

Council on Social Work Education. (2015). *Educational policy and accreditation standards*.

Davis, L. E. (2016). Race: America's grand challenge. *Journal of the Society for Social Work and Research, 7*(2), 395–403.

Davis, A., & Gentlewarrior, S. (2015). White privilege and clinical social work practice: Reflections and recommendations. *Journal of Progressive Human Services, 26*(3), 191–208.

Deepak, A. C., Rountree, M. A., & Scott, J. (2015). Delivering diversity and social justice in social work education: The power of context. *Journal of Progressive Human Services, 26*(2), 107–125.

DiAngelo, R. J. (2018). *White fragility : Why it's so hard for white people to talk about racism*. Beacon Press.

Dunn, A. M. (2002). Cultural competence and the primary care provider. *Journal of Pediatric Health Care, 16*, 105–111.

Fisher-Borne, M., Cain, J. M., & Martin, S. L. (2014). From mastery to accountability: Cultural humility as an alternative to cultural competence. *Social Work Education, 34*(2), 165–181.

Garcia, B., & Van Soest, D. (2000). Facilitating learning on diversity: Challenges to the professor. *Journal of Ethnic and Cultural Diversity in Social Work, 9*(1–2), 21–39.

Garran, A. M., & Werkmeister Rozas, L. (2013). Cultural competence revisited. *Journal of Ethnic and Cultural Diversity in Social Work, 22*(2), 97–111.

Garner, S. (2017). *Racisms: An introduction*. Los Angeles, CA: Sage.

Haney Lopez, I. F. (1994). The social construction of race: Some observations on illusion, fabrication, and choice. *Harvard Civil Rights-Civil Liberties Law Review*.

Harris, A. P., Crenshaw, K., Gotanda, N., Peller, G., & Thomas, K. (2012). Critical race theory. *International Encyclopedia of the Social & Behavioral Sciences*.

Hikido, A., & Murray, S. B. (2016). Whitened rainbows: How white college students protect whiteness through diversity discourses. *Race Ethnicity and Education, 19*(2), 389–411.

Jeffery, D. (2005). What good is anti-racist social work if you can't master it? Exploring a paradox in anti-racist social work education. *Race Ethnicity and Education, 8*(4), 409–425. https://doi.org/10.1080/13613320500324011.

Jeyasingham, D. (2012). White noise: A critical evaluation of social work education's engagement with whiteness studies. *British Journal of Social Work, 42*(4), 669–686.

Jones, S. R. (2008). Student resistance to cross-cultural engagement: Annoying distraction or site for transformative learning? In S. R. Harper (Ed.), *Creating inclusive campus environments for cross-cultural learning and student engagement* (pp. 67–85). Washington, DC: NASPA.

Kochhar, R., &Cilluffo, A. (2017). *How wealth inequality has changed in the U.S. since the great recession, by race, ethnicity and income*. Washington, DC: Pew Research Center.

Leonardo, Z. (2009). *Race, whiteness, and education*. New York, NY: Routledge.

Matias, C. E., & Mackey, J. (2015). Breakin'down whiteness in antiracist teaching: Introducing critical whiteness pedagogy. *The Urban Review, 48*(1), 32–50.

Matias, C.E., Henry, A., & Darland, C. (2016). The twin tales of whiteness exploring the emotional roller coaster of teaching and learning about whiteness. *Taboo: The Journal of Culture and Education, 16*(1).

McIntosh, P. (1988 [2004]). White privilege and male privilege: A personal account of coming to see correspondences through work in women's studies. In M. L. A. P. H. Collins (Ed.), *Race, class and gender: An anthology* (pp. 70–81). Belmont, CA: Wadsworth Publishing Company.

Mensah Moore, F. (2016). *Preparing for discussions on race and racism: The critical voices in teacher education course*. NARST Annual Conference, Baltimore, MD.

Mishna, F., & Bogo, M. (2007). Reflective practices in contemporary social work classrooms. *Journal of Social Work Education, 43*, 529–541.

Mizrahi, T. (2009). *Encyclopedia of social work*. [Electronic resource]. Oxford University Press.

Nadan, Y., & Stark, M. (2016). The pedagogy of discomfort: Enhancing reflectivity on stereotypes and bias. *British Journal of Social Work, 47*(3), 683–700.

National Associations of Social Workers (NASW). (2017). *NASW code of ethics.* Washington, DC: Author.

National Association of Social Work. (2014). *Achieving racial equity: Calling the social work profession to action.* http://www.antiracistalliance.com/SWPIRacia lEquityReport.pdf.

Omi, M. (2001). The Changing Meaning of Race. In N. Smelser, W. J. Wilson, & F. Mitchell (Eds.), *America becoming: Racial trends and their consequences* (pp. 243–263). National Academy Press.

Omi, M. A., & Winant, H. (1994). *Racial formation in the United States: From the 1960s to the 1990s* (2nd ed.). New York, NY: Routledge.

Omi, M., & Winant, H. (2015). *Racial formation in the United States.* New York, NY: Routledge and Taylor & Francis.

Patton, L. D. (2016). Disrupting postsecondary prose: Toward a critical race theory of higher education. *Urban Education, 51*(3), 315–342.

Quaye, S. J. (2012). White educators facilitating discussions about racial realities. *Equity & Excellence in Education, 45*(1), 100–119.

Quaye, S. J. (2014). Facilitating dialogues about racial realities. *Teachers College Record, 116*(8), n8.

Rahill, G. J., Joshi, M., Lucio, R., Bristol, B., Dionne, A., & Hamilton, A. (2016). Assessing the development of cultural proficiency among upper-level social work students. *Journal of Social Work Education, 52*(2), 198–213.

Robinson-Wood, T. (2016). *The convergence of race, ethnicity, and gender: Multiple identities in counseling.* Thousand Oaks, CA: Sage.

Robbins, C. (2017). College experiences that generated racial dissonance: Reflections from cisgender white women in graduate preparation programs. *College Student Affairs Journal, 35*(2), 57–69.

Robbins, C. K., & Jones, S. R. (2016). Negotiating racial dissonance: White women's narratives of resistance, engagement, and transformative action. *Journal of College Student Development, 57*(6), 633–651.

Saunders, J. A., Haskins, M., & Vasquez, M. (2015). Cultural competence: A journey to an elusive goal. *Journal of Social Work Education, 51*(1), 19–34.

Smedley, A., & Smedley, B. D. (2011). *Race in North America: Origin and evolution of a worldview.* Boulder, CO: Westview Press.

Sue, D. W. (2001). Multidimensional facets of cultural competence. *The Counseling Psychologist, 29,* 790–821.

Takaki, R. (2008). *A different mirror: A history of multicultural America* (Revised edition). New York, NY.

Tatum, B. (1992). Talking about race, learning about racism: The application of racial identity development theory in the classroom. *Harvard Educational Review, 62*(1), 1–25.

U.S. Census Bureau. (2015). *New census bureau report analyzes U.S. population projections.* Release Number: CB15-TPS.16.

Yosso, T. J. (2005). Whose culture has capital? A critical race theory discussion of community cultural wealth. *Race Ethnicity and Education, 8*(1), 69–91. https://doi.org/10.1080/1361332052000341006.

Zembylas, M. (2015). 'Pedagogy of discomfort' and its ethical implications: The tensions of ethical violence in social justice education. *Ethics and Education, 10*(2), 163–174.

Suggestions For Further Reading

Constance-Huggins, M. (2012). Critical race theory in social work education: A framework for addressing racial disparities. *Critical Social Work, 13*(2), 2–16.

DiAngelo, R. J. (2018). *White fragility: Why it's so hard for White people to talk about racism.* Beacon Press.

Haney Lopez, I. F. (2007). 'A nation of minorities': Race, ethnicity, and reactionary colorblindness. *Stanford Law Review, 57*, 985–1063.

Nakaoka, S., & Ortiz, L. (2018). Examining racial microaggressions as a tool for transforming social work education: The case for critical race pedagogy. *Journal of Ethnic & Cultural Diversity in Social Work, 27*(1), 72–85.

Nakaoka, S., Ortiz, L., & Garcia, B. (2019). Intentional weaving of critical race theory into an MSW program in a hispanic-serving institution. *Urban Social Work, 3*(1), S115–S128.

National Urban League. (2013). *2013 State of Black America.* New York, NY: Author.

Wagaman, A. M., Odera, S. G., & Fraser, D. V. (2019). A pedagogical model for teaching racial justice in social work education. *Journal of Social Work Education, 55*(2), 351–362. https://doi.org/10.1080/10437797.2018.1513878.

Werman, A., Adlparvar, F., Horowitz, J. K., & Hasegawa, M. O. (2019). Difficult conversations in a school of social work: Exploring student and faculty perceptions. *Journal of Social Work Education, 55*(2), 251–264. https://doi.org/10.1080/10437797.2018.1520665.

Teaching and Learning for LGBTQ Justice: An Examination of a Professional Learning Series for Faculty Development in Health and Helping Fields

Annemarie Vaccaro, Jessica A. Adams, and Howard L. Dooley Jr.

KEY TERMS AND DEFINITIONS

Cisgender	A social identity that describes someone whose sense of gender (e.g., gender identity) matches the sex they were assigned at birth. Can be abbreviated as **cis**.
Cultural Competence	The combination of an individual's awareness, knowledge, and skills that allow them to effectively teach and/or work with individuals who are culturally diverse.

A. Vaccaro (✉) · J. A. Adams · H. L. Dooley Jr.
University of Rhode Island, Kingston, RI, USA
e-mail: avaccaro@uri.edu

© The Author(s), under exclusive license to Springer Nature Switzerland AG 2021
C. C. Ozaki and L. Parson (eds.), *Teaching and Learning for Social Justice and Equity in Higher Education*,
https://doi.org/10.1007/978-3-030-69947-5_10

199

Heterosexism	A system of oppression against individuals who are not heterosexual that can manifest as a dominant societal ideology that suggests heterosexuality is the norm.
LGBTQ	Common acronym used to refer to the lesbian, gay, bisexual, transgender, and queer community.
Gender Identity	A person's internal sense of their gender which may or may not correlate with their sex assigned at birth. Gender identity is shaped by roles, behaviors, activities, and characteristics that society socially constructs.
Gender Expression	The manner in which an individual externally represents their gender (e.g., clothes, hairstyle, pronouns, chosen name).

Decades of research suggest that lesbian, gay, bisexual, transgender, and queer (LGBTQ) students face hostile campus climates because of their sexuality, gender identity, and/or gender expression. Research in health and helping fields also suggest that LGBTQ clients and patients often experience marginalization (Burch, 2008; Green et al., 2010; Knochel et al., 2011; Shields et al., 2017). This chapter highlights the important role that university faculty in the health and helping professions can play in creating climates of inclusion in college learning spaces (e.g., classrooms, training clinics) as well as future professional settings where their students (e.g., practitioners-in-training) will treat LGBTQ people. We describe a Professional Development Learning Series designed to increase the cultural competence of university faculty regarding LGBTQ issues and people. Cultural competence can be defined in various ways (Camphina-Bacote, 2002; Sue, 2001). For the purposes of this project, we viewed cultural competence as the combination of awareness, knowledge, and skills needed to work effectively with LGBTQ people (e.g., students, clients) in a U.S. society where oppression for LGBTQ people is an everyday reality. In this chapter, we delve into faculty motivations to participate in this unique professional development series.[1] The chapter also offers rich insight into the variety of ways faculty attempted to transform their teaching practices and improve the professional socialization of students as a result of the LGBTQ Professional Learning Series.

We contend that practitioners-in-training must be taught by multiculturally competent instructors. If educators do not have sufficient awareness, knowledge, and skills to enact LGBTQ inclusion, they cannot foster it in their students. Through the LGBTQ Professional Learning Series, university faculty increased their cultural competence and capacity to develop transformative classroom and clinical education for college students preparing to enter the health and helping fields of nursing, pharmacy, physical therapy, speech therapy, and counseling.

University faculty who participated in the LGBTQ Professional Learning Series were the primary socializers for emerging psychologists, physical therapists, speech therapists, nurses, pharmacists, and other helping professionals in training. Faculty participated in the LGBTQ Professional Learning Series so they could: (1) better support their LGBTQ identified practitioners-in-training; (2) learn to disrupt and challenge LGBTQ exclusion in curriculum and classroom/clinical interactions; and (3) develop skills to create transformative and LGBTQ inclusive classroom and clinical learning experiences. In essence, faculty came to the LGBTQ Professional Learning Series in hopes of transforming health and helping practice by sending more LGBTQ inclusive practitioners into their fields. Faculty understood that they needed to increase their own LGBTQ competence in order to provide transformative and inclusive education for their undergraduate and graduate students who would soon serve LGBTQ clients and patients in clinical settings.

LITERATURE REVIEW

A growing body of research details the lack of cultural competence of most current health professionals. Javaherian, Christy, and Boehringer (2008) reported that only 4% of practitioners had four or more hours of education about gay, lesbian, and bisexual issues while 64% received none. Further, a recent study found that 80% of emergency department practitioners will not even ask LGBTQ patients to identify themselves as

---

[1] Elsewhere, we offer an analysis of the cultural competence (i.e., awareness, knowledge, skills) self-reported by LGBTQ Professional Learning participants (Vaccaro et al., 2019).

LGBTQ even though national standards prescribe they do so (Haider et al., 2017). This is a cause for concern; low self-efficacy[2] in treating culturally diverse populations is proven to have direct and indirect negative correlations to the quality of healthcare patients receive (Burch, 2008; Green et al., 2010; Javaherian et al., 2008; Knochel et al., 2010; Shields et al., 2017). Fortunately, many of these studies also suggest effective courses of action to remedy these deficiencies. One strategy is to develop the cultural competence of faculty who train professionals and another is to assist them in creating more inclusive curricula and learning environments for health and helping pre-professionals (Case et al., 2009; Haider et al., 2017; Horton-Ikard et al., 2009). An additional strategy is to provide professional development opportunities regarding LGBTQ inclusion in the workplace (Burch, 2008; Haider et al., 2017; O'Hanlan, 2010; Shields et al., 2017).

LGBTQ patients and clients comprise a collection of related communities that suffer the effects of cultural incompetence (Case et al., 2009; Shields et al., 2017). These populations experience tolerance versus respect as well as societal oppression (e.g., heterosexism, cissexism) (Burch, 2008; Green et al., 2010; Shields et al., 2017); "lifelong experiences of discrimination in the broader community lead LGB people to expect similar treatment" (Knochel et al., 2011, p. 371) from their healthcare providers. While most professionals agree cultural competence will improve patient interactions and quality of service, few providers actively seek out opportunities to learn, and institutional policies often serve as barriers to learning (Clark et al., 2001; Javaherian et al., 2008). It is important to note that a significant number of agencies still hold the belief that there is no need for tailoring services to the LGBTQ clients as everyone is treated equally. This stance perpetuates heterosexism and gender identity discrimination (Javaherian et al., 2008; Knochel et al., 2011).

There is hope, however. A small but growing body of literature has identified best practices for use in the health and helping professions. First, relevant LGBTQ resources and information should be obtained, as a patient or client's sexual identity has relevance to service provision (Haider et al., 2017; O'Hanlan, 2010; Shields et al., 2017). Moreover, culturally inclusive content should be infused into lectures, readings, and

---

[2] Self-efficacy is one's perception of their ability to succeed in accomplishing a specific goal.

discussions (Case et al., 2009) used to teach and train emerging professionals. In the field, cultural competence and skill building should occur at the provider level while the development of advocacy strategies can occur at the consumer level (Clark et al., 2001). Altogether, targeted LGBTQ educational activities can result in significant effects on diversity self-efficacy, which is a pre-cursor to behavior change (Burch, 2008). As such, we contend faculty who train health and helping professionals should seek to increase their own cultural competence and self-efficacy in order to create inclusive classrooms. Faculty should also make conscious efforts to eliminate instructor bias, use appropriate terminology, and refer to students by their chosen names and pronouns (Vaccaro et al., 2012).

Recent literature suggests LGBTQ inclusive training is direly needed in healthcare fields (Shields et al., 2017). The small, but growing body of literature on cultural competence training and best practices for health and helping professionals suggest that LGBTQ inclusion is not, but could become, more prevalent in clinical practice. The infusion of such works into faculty development and clinical training suggests LGBTQ inclusion might someday become part of the normative socialization process for emerging clinicians, researchers, and scholars. We contend LGBTQ cultural competence training can align well with the identity trajectories of practitioners who are committed to the health and wellbeing of all patients. In an article about the development of professional identity for medical professionals, Goldie (2012) argued that the identity development process is socially situated and deeply influenced by faculty, role models, and hands on practice. In this chapter, we explicate how an LGBTQ Professional Learning Series served as a transformational experience for university faculty. These faculty members used their increased cultural competence to design inclusive LGBTQ curriculum and clinical training for their university students. As the primary socializers of future health and helping professionals, university faculty also serve as role models for enacting LGBTQ inclusion as part of one's professional identity.

OVERVIEW OF THE LGBTQ
PROFESSIONAL LEARNING SERIES

The LGBTQ Professional Learning Series was conceptualized, designed, and implemented at a mid-sized research university in the northeastern United States. In 2011, students at the university engaged in an eight-day protest which drew attention to issues of bullying and harassment faced by LGBTQ students. Protesters composed a list of demands for the university that included provisos like: "stronger responses to harassment and bullying, better and more training for residence staff and others on campus, hiring of an upper level administrator responsible for diversity and equity issues, and a new, better-staffed GLBT Center" (Pantalone, 2011). While many of these responses fell under the purview of university administrators—especially student affairs professionals—academic administrators also took steps to create more affirming LGBTQ climates. In 2011, the Dean of the College of Human Sciences (CHS) reached out to two faculty members, one from human development and one from nursing, with experience conducting diversity training, climate work, and faculty development. The Dean invited them to create an LGBTQ Professional Learning Series for faculty members in the college. They crafted a college-specific LGBTQ Professional Learning Series and delivered it to CHS faculty. Building upon the success of the CHS series, a university-wide LGBTQ Professional Learning Series was implemented the following academic year. Faculty from all colleges and departments at the institution were eligible to participate in that university-wide series.

Similar recruitment strategies were used for the CHS and university-wide LGBTQ Professional Learning Series. In both cases, the senior administrator (e.g., Dean, Provost) constructed a letter to the faculty describing the LGBTQ Professional Learning Series. The Dean (year one) and Provost (year two) offered a small incentive in the form of professional development funding for faculty who agreed to complete all four workshops in the LGBTQ Professional Learning Series. To encourage in-depth discussions, space in each series was limited to 12 participants. Faculty were required to submit an application which included a one-page description of their interest in the program. In total, seven faculty members participated in the first CHS series and 11 participated in the university-wide series. This chapter focuses on the motivations, experiences, and outcomes related to a sub-set of 10 attendees who were faculty members (as well as researchers and clinicians) in the health and helping professions of nursing, pharmacy practice, speech therapy, physical therapy, counseling/psychology, and human development.

The LGBTQ Professional Learning Series was comprised of four, two-hour workshops offered over the course of the academic year. The goals of the workshop were to increase faculty: (1) awareness and knowledge of LGBTQ issues; (2) skills at including LGBTQ issues and topics into their curriculum and pedagogy; and (3) confidence addressing instances of LGBTQ exclusion. Inspired by the concepts of transformative learning, the LGBTQ Professional Learning Series facilitators wanted to do more than provide new knowledge to faculty attendees. The co-facilitators hoped to inspire faculty to reflect upon their cultural competence, enact change in their spheres of influence (e.g., classrooms, clinics), and influence the professional socialization of health and helping professionals in training. As Taylor (2006, 2009) noted, teaching for transformation is about teaching for change. Each participant was required to compose an action plan by the end of the series. Faculty action plans were intended to create small- and large-scale changes to improve the current campus climate for LGBTQ students and future clinical climates for LGBTQ patients and clients. Throughout the series, faculty were encouraged to read best practices from their professions, dialogue about effective inclusion strategies, and apply relevant strategies to their work. Through discussions of LGBTQ best practices, faculty gave and received feedback on their LGBTQ inclusion strategies (successes and challenges).

Sessions

Session one began with introductory activities to foster connections among faculty, many whom did not know one another. After brief introductions, participants were invited to share their motivations and hopes for the LGBTQ Professional Learning Series. These sharing activities were followed by a PowerPoint presentation about cultural competence models from multiple fields like psychology (Sue, 2001) and nursing (Camphina-Bacote, 2002). Facilitators attended to the commonalties among the models, namely the importance of awareness, knowledge, and skill development. At the end of the session one, faculty participated in an activity where they reflected upon their cultural competence (see Appendix A).

Session two focused specifically on increasing faculty awareness and knowledge of LGBTQ people and issues. A brief PowerPoint presentation provided an overview of empirical research about the experiences of LGBTQ students in higher education settings. Some content included information about the ways curriculum can exclude or demonize LGBTQ people and normalize heterosexuality and cisgenderism (Vaccaro et al., 2012). The presentation was interspersed with small group dialogues where faculty were prompted to apply LGBTQ research to their work with students in their programs.

For session three, faculty were required to conduct a homework assignment. Their task was to locate and review an article about LGBTQ inclusion (or exclusion) in their health or helping profession. Most selected articles describing best practices for LGBTQ inclusive clinical care in their profession. Half of session three was dedicated to faculty sharing highlights from their articles. The remainder of the session was dedicated to skill building (the third component of cultural competency development). Faculty were given scenarios related to LGBTQ exclusion in the classroom, the clinic, and advising settings (see Appendix B). In small groups, they role played each scenario and then discussed the pros and cons of various responses. Through discussion, faculty garnered a myriad of ways that effectively and ineffectively address LGBTQ exclusion.

As a culminating project for the LGBTQ Professional Learning Series, faculty were required to develop an action plan for LGBTQ inclusion in their classrooms, clinics, and/or research. Session four was dedicated to faculty sharing their action plans. Faculty described their plans and asked for feedback from their peers. Through this discussion, participants learned about the diverse LGBTQ inclusion strategies peers planned to use in their classrooms and clinics and, thus, gained additional ideas. The remaining time was used for collection of program evaluation materials.

Data

Data for this chapter were gleaned from a variety of sources. First, we used information from the initial faculty applications for the LGBTQ Professional Learning Series. Second, we drew rich data from faculty action plans. Third, program evaluation data were collected via a short questionnaire. Additional program evaluation data were accumulated through an audio-recorded focus group at the conclusion of the LGBTQ Professional Learning Series. Finally, five years after the LGBTQ Professional Learning Series, faculty were invited to complete a brief on-line questionnaire about long-term influences of their learning. Rich qualitative data from all of these sources were initially analyzed using two types of analytic methods: a priori (e.g., codes predetermined) and posteriori (e.g., unexpected codes emerge). First, we used an a priori coding frame that mirrored the diversity, inclusion, and cultural competence literatures. The five major priori themes we searched the data for included teacher awareness, knowledge, skills, motivations, and classroom and curricular inclusion strategies. During the coding process, we also allowed for unexpected or a posteriori major themes to emerge. Those include reflections on professional socialization in their classrooms and clinics, ideas about enacting LGBTQ justice via specific pedagogical practices, and evaluations of the usefulness of the LGBTQ Professional Learning Series.

FINDINGS

The findings are presented in two sections. The first section details health and helping faculty member motivations for their participation in the LGBTQ Professional Learning Series. Data suggest that these motivations were inherently tied to the professional identity development of faculty and their students. Building upon the first section, the second section delves more deeply into faculty motivation to, and strategies for, transforming professional socialization to be more LGBTQ inclusive. In both sections, we discuss the transformative learning that occurred in the LGBTQ Professional Learning Series. Taylor (2006, 2009) believed that teaching for transformation was synonymous with teaching for change. Correspondingly, workshop facilitators sought to deliver professional learning that would result in campus and community change. Through transformative learning within the LGBTQ Professional Learning Series, faculty members learned to recognize and challenge LGBTQ-bias in curriculum and clinical training. In turn, they enacted transformative and authentic pedagogy (Taylor, 2006), because LGBTQ inclusion aligned with their professional identities, which were constructed upon a basic desire to be caring, compassionate, and inclusive educators and scholars.

Participant Motivations and Professional Identity Development

LGBTQ Professional Learning Series participants described themselves as professionals whose moral compass pointed them toward a deep desire to value and care for all human beings. This included their LGBTQ university students and patients/clients who might present with unique needs. Faculty participants exhibited the values of care, compassion, and inclusion in their work. These cornerstones of their professional identities shaped their initial motivations to apply to the LGBTQ Professional Learning Series. These cornerstones of care, compassion, and inclusion were also the driving forces behind their work as educators of future generations of health and helping professionals.

Sometimes faculty members were prompted to join the LGBTQ Professional Learning Series after witnessing the struggles of LGBTQ college students or loved ones. Kristina was inspired to be more inclusive of LGBTQ college students after hearing of "heartbreaking" experiences of LGBTQ students in her clinical mental health program. She also sought professional development so she could learn how to help a lesbian professionals-in-training "feel more comfortable in our program." Another professor explained how her commitment to LGBTQ inclusion stemmed from very personal experiences. In her application for the LGBTQ Professional Learning Series, Carina shared:

> My youngest son is gay and being gay has made life more difficult for him in many ways. I would like to be considered for the (LGBTQ Professional Learning Series) because I have a keen interest in LGBT[Q] issues. I am a strong advocate for persons who are gay and lesbian ... Those who are lesbian, gay or transgender–they want and need the support of family and others ... I want others, particularly students ... to know that I [am] a safe person they could come to if they needed to talk or were looking for help some way.

Carina's initial awareness of LGBTQ oppression was born from her experiences as a mother and prompted her to apply care and compassion in support of LGBTQ students learning to be healthcare professionals.

Another reason faculty applied to the program was to learn (or further develop) specific skills to support LGBTQ students and clients. Faculty wanted to learn how to address bullying, harassment, and more subtle forms of LGBTQ exclusion in the classroom. Many admitted that despite their commitment to care and compassion for all, they felt ill prepared to enact LGBTQ inclusion. Abby discussed an incident where a gay student was outed in front of peers. She admitted:

> I "was winging it" in trying to deal with what could have potentially become a terrible situation for all of the students involved. As teachers, we are not trained in how to address diversity and all of its glories and the unknowns for some in a society where every student's world view has been formed by different life experiences.

As Abby's quote suggests, despite deep levels of care, compassion, and inclusion, faculty often felt unprepared when LGBTQ exclusion occurred in classroom and clinical laboratory settings.

Participants recognized that ineffective responses to LGBTQ exclusion caused harm to students in their classrooms and training clinics. Allowing harm to occur and/or lacking the skills to address was incongruent with their professional identities as caring, compassionate, and inclusive health and helping educators. As such, many participants sought the LGBTQ Professional Learning Series to learn skills to effectively address subtle (and not so subtle) forms of exclusion. Abby described her motivation to join the LGBTQ Professional Learning Series: "I want to develop the skills to create a safe, comfortable classroom, field, or lab environment for all while also feeling confident with how to address issues of discrimination should they arise." Similarly, Rachel said:

> I am often confronted by students who are openly homophobic and bigoted, and become acutely distressed in the classroom when expected to discuss issues regarding sexual orientation, gender identity, and gender expression ... [I] would like to think about, reflect on, and discuss how to handle the interactions in other, constructive ways in the future ... and become better prepared for what I have come to see as inevitable resistance and challenges [to LGBTQ inclusion].

While Rachel believed resistance to LGBTQ people and topics was inevitable, it was not acceptable. In her opinion, future psychologists needed to learn to be accepting and affirming of LGBTQ people in general, and future clients in particular. Indeed, the professional standards and ethical statements in the field of psychology have long affirmed this perspective (American Psychological Association, 1993). Carina felt similarly. She firmly believed that the speech therapists needed to exude care and compassion and learn how to effectively support LGBTQ clients. She explained: "I think it is imperative for all of us to learn how to best provide that support."

Workshop attendees were responsible for the socialization and training of the next generation of psychologists, physical therapists, speech therapists, nurses, pharmacists, and other helping professionals. As such, another reason why faculty joined the LGBTQ Professional Learning Series was to develop strategies for enacting transformative learning in their undergraduate and graduate classrooms, laboratories, and training clinics. They felt a moral and professional obligation to engage in peda-gogy, design curriculum, and supervise practical training in ways that were LGBTQ inclusive. Alicia said:

> I am the lead teacher for a Community Health Nursing Program in which we cover LGTBQ health issues ... The students tell me this is the only course touching on the LGTBQ issues, so I know we have a long way to go. I believe this program could help me integrate LGTB issues into the [nursing] curriculum.

Mary explained her motivation to join the LGBTQ Professional Learning Series as follows:

> I teach a [speech therapy] course that needs an infusion of informa-tion about providing non-biased service delivery to persons in the LGBT community. Although I have made several attempts to provide this perspec-tive to my students, I could use some assistance in further developing this curricular change and making it a reality.

Ellie similarly shared: "Through the [series], I feel I would be able to enhance our college's curriculum by including relevant case discussions of health disparities and issues that LGBT persons may encounter within healthcare."

For all participants, classrooms and clinical training grounds were the primary venue for socialization of novice health and helping pre-professionals. As such, faculty came to the Professional Learning Series hoping to gain cultural competence (i.e., awareness, knowledge, and skills) to provide more LGBTQ inclusive training grounds for future health and helping professionals. Ellie summed up the sentiments of fellow participants when she said: "The LGBT workshops would augment my knowledge in the classroom as well as my practice to improve our student's learning and help to support essential skills of empathy and respect for LGBT patients." Through the LGBTQ Professional Learning Series another participant realized that in order for her students to learn the importance of LGBTQ inclusion in health and helping practice, she needed to role model inclusive perspectives and behaviors. She concluded: "It is important for me to be a leader for students who look up to me."

We show how values of care, compassion, and inclusion influenced faculty motivation to take part in the LGBTQ Professional Learning Series. These values have historically been cornerstones of effective health and helping practice (Camphina-Bacote, 2002; Horton-Ikard et al., 2009; Irby & Hamstra, 2016). We contend that faculty participants who engaged in this transformative learning process affirmed their learner orientation and desire to constantly become more inclusive educators, scholars, and practitioners. The experience influenced their identity development as educators, scholars, and leaders in their professions and prompted ongoing reflection, which aligns with notions of resilient identity (Epstein & Krasner, 2013; Mansfield et al., 2016). Participants adopted a lifelong and transformative learner stance, saying things like: "there's always more to learn!" This perspective aligns with Camphina-Bacote's (2002) view of cultural competence as the "ongoing process in which the health care provider continuously strives to achieve the ability to effectively work within the cultural context of the client (individual, family, community)" (p. 181). Moreover, Camphina-Bacote (2002) suggested that culturally competent practitioners "want to" versus "have to" become more culturally competent (p. 182).

To close this section, we use a quote from Rachel. Rachel explained that participation in the LGBTQ Professional Learning Series:

> introduced me to new language and concepts, helped me think deeply about my educational practices ... [and] to look more carefully at the literature I read that informs my work as an educator and scholar and investigate LGBTQ related information to include in my courses.

Rachel's quote speaks to complicated identities of faculty members in the health and helping fields. They are simultaneously educators, scholars, and practitioners who are responsible for the socialization of future professionals. The LGBTQ Professional Learning Series influenced the way participants thought about each of these aspects of their professional identity. They strove to be more reflective and inclusive educators to their LGBTQ students, more insightful scholars in their research, and more influential socializers of the next generation of practitioners.

Transforming Professional Socialization and Praxis

In this section, we provide examples of the actual strategies faculty used to enact LGBTQ inclusion. In an effort to train future healthcare workers more inclusively, they enacted change in their curriculum, clinical training, and departmental environments.

In the LGBTQ Professional Learning Series, participants learned about the hostile, unwelcoming and, and chilly campus climates faced by LGBTQ students (Nicolazzo, 2016; Nicolazzo & Marine, 2015; Rankin et al., 2010). They also learned strategies to design campus microclimates (e.g., offices, classrooms, clinics) to be more LGBTQ inclusive (Vaccaro et al., 2012). As a result, faculty developed personalized strategies to implicitly and explicitly convey the following messages: LGBTQ people are welcome in this classroom; it is clinically necessary to understand LGBTQ topics and issues; and it is good professional practice to respect, accept, and effectively address the needs of LGBTQ clients and patients. Kristina believed that her syllabus was an important place to begin conveying these messages of LGBTQ inclusion. Therefore, she drafted an inclusion statement and posted a "safe zone" image in her syllabus. When she shared this idea during session four, many colleagues were impressed. On the five year follow up survey, a number of faculty mentioned adopting inclusion statements on their syllabi. For instance, Mary explained how her "syllabus has changed to state up front ... the importance to acknowledge that differences of sexual orientation and identity must be appreciated in a classroom learning environment."

Another way participants attempted to infuse LGBTQ inclusion into the socialization of future practitioners was by increasing student awareness and knowledge of LGBTQ issues. Most did this by adding LGBTQ content into their curriculum. Rachel spoke generally about the way the LGBTQ Professional Learning Series influenced her faculty work. On the five-year evaluation, she explained how she has "increased the amount of time" she spends on LGBTQ topics across all of her courses. Other faculty, like Jane, increased the number of required readings with LGBTQ content. She "expanded coverage of gender development and sexual orientation in the required readings." Jane also fostered "more detailed discussion of gender development and sexual orientation through lectures."

In the Professional Learning Series, faculty learned about, reflected upon, and challenged hidden discipline-specific curriculum that excluded or demonized LGBTQ people and normalized heterosexuality and the gender binary (Vaccaro et al., 2012). Therefore, many faculty found that they had to augment traditional textbooks, videos, exam questions, and case studies to be more inclusive of LGBTQ people and issues. For instance, Ellie increased the number of "cases and exam questions to include LGBTQ inclusion." In classroom discussions, Mary constantly challenged her students to consider if, and how, clinical diagnoses might be rooted in stereotypical or exclusionary assumptions. Mary explained: "I prompt students to consider case studies from both majority and minority population perspectives. That is: 'Would your conclusions about assessment or treatment planning change if you knew that the client identified as [lesbian, gay, bisexual, transgender, queer]?'"

Many of the participants taught in professional preparation programs that required significant practical training, often in the form of clinical practice. As such, faculty felt it was imperative to foster LGBTQ inclusion in clinical training spaces. Two pharmacy professors (Jennifer and Ellie) realized that there was not a single LGBTQ affirming clinical case study in their curriculum for professionals-in-training. The only instance where LGBTQ issues emerged were in case studies related to gay patients with HIV/AIDS. They wanted to challenge the hidden curriculum that portrayed LGBTQ people as deviant. These pharmacy professors sought to normalize LGBTQ people and issues in all aspects of the curriculum but especially in the skill building portion that relied heavily on case studies. In response, Jennifer and Ellie crafted new case studies with more positive images of LGBTQ people and issues so that their students could learn to be more affirming and inclusive of LGBTQ clients. One newly designed case study included a sick child who was accompanied to the pharmacy with gay parents. They believed this case normalized gay and lesbian families.

Curricular and clinical changes, however, were not without challenge. On the five year follow up survey, Jennifer explained how she continued to infuse LGBTQ issues and topics into her practical training. One of the ways she did this was teaching clinical students not to assume all patients were heterosexual or cisgender. She now requires pharmacists-in-training to ask patients how they self-identify. However, they sometimes resisted these inclusion efforts. She shared:

[I've] changed the amount of LGBTQ health disparities topics covered in ... the [pharmacy] program ... There has been quite a bit of resistance to asking patients about gender/sexuality/identity/expression. While I have included it in my skills lab it is not supported throughout the curriculum consistently.

Jennifer's students are not unique. Recent research elucidates provider discomfort and unwillingness to ask patients about their sexuality or gender identity (Haider et al., 2017; Shields et al., 2017). Despite the fact that students resisted, and colleagues did not include LGBTQ issues in their courses, Jennifer felt it was important to keep training students inclusively so that they would not marginalize patients in the future.

Another workshop participant recognized exclusionary patient intake forms were being used in the campus clinic where graduate students practiced counseling psychology. As a result of the LGBTQ Professional Learning Series, Kristina was inspired to design more inclusive gender and sexuality-related demographic questions on clinic forms. This change not only impacted clients, but it was also a transformative learning experience for psychologists in training. They learned how seemingly simple things—like exclusionary demographic categories—sent unwelcoming messages and, in turn, could negatively impact clients.

In the five year follow up survey, we asked participants: "What effects on students, colleagues, and/or administration have you witnessed because of your LGBTQ inclusion efforts?" Rachel responded: "Students are better informed, may be more open, more accepting of others." Annette believed that increasing LGBTQ content in her courses helped her foster deeper connections with students. She specifically noted "some increased willingness of students to come to see me in office hours." As part of her class, Annette required students to submit anonymous response cards related to the topic for each day. She noted that "inclusion of LGBTQ material increased awareness among all students. Evidence came in the comments students made on their response cards." Faculty who participated in the LGBTQ Professional Learning Series seemed to have accomplished their goal to increase the cultural competence of their pre-professional students.

Five-year follow up data suggested that faculty successfully designed and implemented inclusive education for positive change (Taylor, 2006, 2009). As scholars have noted, LGBTQ oppression is pervasive in higher education (Nicolazzo, 2016; Nicolazzo & Marine, 2015; Rankin et al., 2010) as well as health and helping clinical settings (Burch, 2008; Camphina-Bacote, 2002; Case et al., 2009; Haider et al., 2017; Horton-Ikard et al., 2009; Javaherian et al., 2008; O'Hanlan, 2010; Shields et al., 2017). While faculty participants could not end pervasive and systemic LGBTQ exclusion in their fields, they could, however, make real change within their spheres of influence—namely their classrooms and clinical training grounds. Faculty hoped their efforts would have a trickle-down effect in their health and helping professions. By setting standards of

LGBTQ inclusion in their classrooms and clinics, faculty influenced the professional socialization of emerging health and helping practitioners who would interact with LGBTQ clients and patients throughout their careers.

RECOMMENDATIONS FOR HIGHER EDUCATION INSTITUTIONS

In this section, we discuss the implications of our work for higher education institutions.

We offer recommendations to post-secondary institutions considering LGBTQ professional development for health and helping faculty members.

The LGBTQ Professional Learning Series was an interdisciplinary and inter-professional learning community or a community of practice (Lave & Wenger, 1991). Both the college-specific and university-wide LGBTQ Professional Learning Series were comprised of faculty from a variety of disciplines and professional backgrounds. The diversity of faculty backgrounds made for rich discussions and learning across fields. Participants discussed many ways LGBTQ inclusive best practices could transcend their disciplinary and professional boundaries. The LGBTQ Professional Learning Series became a community where faculty developed personal and professional connections with colleagues outside their departments. Connections garnered in the LGBTQ Professional Learning sessions were especially important for faculty in small departments and/or departments that were resistant to LGBTQ inclusion, as they found allies and collaborators through the LGBTQ Professional Learning Series.

Although there are many benefits of interdisciplinary communities of practice, there can also be benefits for discipline-specific professional development structures. For instance, faculty may have had deeper and more targeted discussions if they had all come from a single profession or discipline. In discipline-specific series, case studies, scenarios, and conversation topics can be tailored specifically for each discipline. Discussions and experiential learning activities might have more impact if tailored specifically for classroom and clinical realities of mental health counselors, pharmacists, speech therapists, physical therapists, or nurses. In sum, there is value in both profession-specific *and* interdisciplinary LGBTQ professional development. Depending on the size of a campus and its faculty, one approach might be more appropriate than another.

The LGBTQ Professional Learning Series was optional. Therefore, faculty volunteers were the proverbial "choir." They attended the year-long series because their professional identities included a commitment to care, compassion, and inclusion. We recognize that it will be much more difficult to recruit faculty who harbor anti-LGBTQ sentiments or those who do not see LGBTQ exclusion as an issue in their field. However, recruiting such faculty members is not impossible. In fact, given the important role health and helping faculty play in shaping the future of their professions, we suggest institutions require LGBTQ professional development for all university faculty. One way to garner buy-in from skeptics is to tap into faculty professional identities as caring, compassionate, and inclusive professionals. The ethics statements and professional standards in most health and helping fields include care, compassion, and inclusion. Drawing connections between professional standards and expectations might make it easier for faculty to understand why LGBTQ inclusion in teaching, research, and clinical work is good practice (Haider et al, 2017; Shields et al., 2017).

One overarching criticism of the LGBTQ Professional Learning Series was that it was too short. Facilitators and participants agreed that four, two-hour workshops were not sufficient for the kind of in-depth skill building they desired. In their evaluative comments, faculty requested more time for case studies and role playing. They wanted more opportunities to practice LGBTQ inclusion (especially responding to bullying and harassment) in a safe environment of like-minded peers. Given these suggestions, we recommend that any LGBTQ professional development for faculty includes sufficient time for skill building. Such sessions can begin with experienced faculty members role playing tough scenarios so that less skilled (or less confident) faculty can observe effective techniques.

A final suggestion to higher education institutions is to ensure that LGBTQ faculty development sessions are structured as communities of practice (Lave & Wenger, 1991) whereby learners give and receive feedback with the intention of individual and group growth. To accomplish this, facilitators must create atmospheres of respect and trust (Vaccaro, 2019). Participants are unlikely to admit their lack of LGBTQ competence and/or confidence if they perceive the professional development environment to be hostile or judgmental. Nor is transformative learning likely to occur unless the learning space is a welcoming and affirming one. It is not easy, but it is imperative, to craft LGBTQ Professional Learning

Series to be communities of practice where transformative learning for change can occur.

APPENDIX A: LGBTQ CULTURAL COMPETENCE SELF-REFLECTION ACTIVITY

What strengths do you bring to the classroom? What strengths do you bring to your departmental curriculum and/or environment? What LGBTQ-related awareness, knowledge, skills, and encounters do you need to be a more culturally competent teacher, researcher, advisor, colleague?

Competence area	My strengths	Areas where I can grow
LGBT awareness		
LGBT knowledge		
LGBT skills		
LGBT encounters		

APPENDIX B: LGBTQ SCENARIOS

Read the following scenarios. In small groups discuss how you would respond to the situation. As you discuss the scenarios consider the following questions:

- What types of cultural competencies (awareness, knowledge, skills, etc.) might be needed to effectively address this situation?
- What would your immediate or short-term response be?
- What long-term, if any, strategies might you use to support this student?
- How might your responses differ from those of your peers? What strategies can you learn from your faculty colleagues?

Scenario #1
You are setting up for class and students are talking amongst themselves before the class officially begins. You hear a student remark to another: "Wow, that's so gay!" How, if at all, do you respond?
Scenario #2

A student comes up to you before the first class session and says, the roster has my legal name as Brian. However, I go by Skyler and I use they/them pronouns. Can you refer to me by these chosen identities and make sure my peers do too? How do you respond?

Scenario #3

You have a student who "comes out" as queer during a class discussion. How do you respond?

Scenario #4

A student comes out to you during an advising session. They admit that they are struggling with telling friends and family about their gender or sexual identity. The stress seems to be impacting their academic success. How do you respond?

Scenario #5

At the beginning of your clinical or classroom lesson, you explain how LGBTQ inclusion is the topic for today's session. A student raises their hand and says that they do not think it is appropriate for you (or any faculty) to push a gay agenda. They just want to learn the "facts" of your discipline. How do you respond?

REFERENCES

American Psychological Association. (1993). Guidelines for providers of psychological services to ethnic, linguistic, and culturally diverse populations. *American Psychologist, 48*(1), 45–48. https://doi.org/10.1037/0003-066X.48.1.45.

Bernstein, D. (2010). Finding your place in the scholarship of teaching and learning. *International Journal for the Scholarship of Teaching and Learning, 4*(2). https://doi.org/10.20429/ijsotl.2010.040204.

Burch, A. (2008). Health care providers' knowledge, attitudes, and self-efficacy for working with patients with spinal cord injury who have diverse sexual orientations. *Physical Therapy, 88*(2), 191. https://doi.org/10.2522/ptj.20060188.

Camphina-Bacote, J. (2002). The process of cultural competence in the delivery of healthcare services: A model of care. *Journal of Transcultural Nursing, 13*(3), 181–184. https://doi.org/10.1177/10459602013003003.

Case, K. A., Stewart, B., & Tittsworth, J. (2009). Transgender across the curriculum: A psychology for inclusion. *Teaching of Psychology, 36*(2), 117–121. https://doi.org/10.1080/00986280902739446.

Clark, M. E., Landers, S., Linde, R., & Sperber, J. (2001). The GLBT Health Access Project: A state-funded effort to improve access to care. *American Journal of Public Health, 91*(6), 895–896. https://doi.org/10.2105/AJPH. 91.6.895.

Epstein, R. M., & Krasner, M. S. (2013). Physician resilience: What it means, why it matters, and how to promote it. *Academic Medicine, 88*(3), 301–303. https://doi.org/10.1097/ACM.0b013e318280cff0.

Gilpin, L., & Liston, D. (2009). Transformative education in the Scholarship of Teaching and Learning: An analysis of SoTL literature. *International Journal for the Scholarship of Teaching and Learning, 3*(2). https://eric.ed.gov/?id= EJ1136663.

Goldie, J. (2012). The formation of professional identity in medical students: Considerations for educators. *Medical Teacher, 34*(9), 641–648. https://doi. org/10.3109/0142159X.2012.687476.

Green, M. S., Murphy, M. J., & Blumer, M. L. (2010). Marriage and family therapists' comfort working with lesbian and gay male clients: The influence of religious practices and support for lesbian and gay male human rights. *Journal of Homosexuality, 57*(10), 1258–1273. https://doi.org/10.1080/00918369. 2010.517072.

Haider, A. H., Schneider, E. B., Kodadek, L. M., Adler, R. R., Ranjit, A., Torain, M., ... Lau, B. D. (2017). Emergency department query for patient-centered approaches to sexual orientation and gender identity: The EQUALITY study. *Journal of American Medical Association: Internal Medicine. 177*(6), 819–828. https://doi.org/10.1001/jamainternmed.2017.0906.

Horton-Ikard, R., Munoz, M. L., Thomas-Tate, S., & Keller-Bell, Y. (2009). Establishing a pedagogical framework for the multicultural course in communication sciences and disorders. *American Journal of Speech-Language Pathology, 18*(2), 192–206. https://doi.org/10.1044/1058-0360(2008/07-0086).

Irby, D. M., & Hamstra, S. J. (2016). Parting the clouds: Three professionalism frameworks in medical education. *Academic Medicine, 91*(12), 1606–1611. https://doi.org/10.1097/ACM.0000000000001190.

Javaherian, H., Christy, A. B., & Boehringer, M. (2008). Occupational therapy practitioners' comfort level and preparedness in working with individuals who are gay, lesbian, or bisexual. *Journal of Allied Health, 37*(3), 150–155.

Knochel, K. A., Quam, J. K., & Croghan, C. F. (2011). Are old lesbian and gay people well served? Understanding the perceptions, preparation, and experiences of aging services providers. *Journal of Applied Gerontology, 30*(3), 370–389. https://doi.org/10.1177/0733464810369809.

Lave, J., & Wenger, E. (1991). *Situated learning: Legitimate peripheral participation.* Cambridge University Press.

Leibowitz, B., & Bozalek, V. (2016). The scholarship of teaching and learning from a social justice perspective. *Teaching in Higher Education, 21*(2), 109–122. https://doi.org/10.1080/13562517.2015.1115971.

Mansfield, C. F., Beltman, S., Broadley, T., & Weatherby-Fell, N. (2016). Building resilience in teacher education: An evidenced informed framework. *Teaching and Teacher Education, 54,* 77–87. https://doi.org/10.1016/j.tate.2015.11.016.

Nicolazzo, Z. (2016). "Just go in looking good": The resilience, resistance, and kinship-building of trans* college students. *Journal of College Student Development, 57*(5), 538–556. https://doi.org/10.1353/csd.2016.0057.

Nicolazzo, Z., & Marine, S. B. (2015). It will change if people keep talking: Trans* students in college and university housing. *Journal of College and University Student Housing, 42*(1), 160–177.

O'Hanlan, K. (2010). Homophobic jokes and patient care. *AMA Journal of Ethics: Virtual Mentor, 12*(8), 618. https://doi.org/10.1001/virtualmentor.2010.12.8.ccas3-1008.

Pantalone, J. (2011, April 6). Making URI a place where everyone feels safe, respected, and valued. *Quadangles: URI Alumni Magazine.* https://web.uri.edu/quadangles/making-uri-a-place-where-everyone-feels-safe-respected-and-valued/.

Rankin, S. Weber, G. Blumenfeld, W., & Frazer, S. (2010). *The state of higher education for lesbian, gay, bisexual and transgender people.* Campus Pride.

Shields R., Lau B., & Haider A. H. (2017). Emergency general surgery needs for lesbian, gay, bisexual, and transgender patients: Are we prepared? *JAMA: Surgery, 152*(7), 617–618. http://doi.org/10.1001/jamasurg.2017.0541.

Sue, D. W. (2001). Multidimensional facets of cultural competence. *The Counseling Psychologist, 29*(6), 790–821. https://doi.org/10.1177/0011000001296002.

Taylor, E. W. (2006, Spring). The challenge of teaching for change. In E. W. Taylor (Ed.), *Teaching for change: Fostering transformative learning in the classroom* (special edition), 109, 91–95.

Taylor, E. W. (2009). Fostering transformative learning. In J. Mezirow, E. W. Taylor, & Associates (Eds.), *Transformative learning in practice: Insights from community, workplace, and higher education* (pp. 3–17). Jossey-Bass.

Vaccaro, A. (2019). Developing culturally competent and inclusive curriculum: A comprehensive framework for teaching multicultural psychology. In K. Quina & J. Mena (Eds.), *Teaching a multiculturally-informed psychology of people* (pp. 23–35). American Psychological Association.

Vaccaro, A., August, G., & Kennedy, M. S. (2012). *Safe spaces: Making schools and communities welcoming to LGBT youth.* Praeger.

Vaccaro, A., Dooley Jr., H. L., &Adams, J. A. (2019). Developing LGBTQ competence in faculty: The case of a faculty development series. In R. Jeffries (Ed.), *Diversity, equity and inclusivity in contemporary higher education* (pp. 122–140). IGI Global.

CHAPTER 11

Problematize, Theorize, Politicize, and Contextualize: A Social Justice Framework for Postsecondary Integrated Reading and Writing Instruction

Mariko L. Carson, Cynthia A. Brewer, Jeanine L. Williams, and Sonya L. Armstrong

It has become commonplace that the nightly news offers snapshots of symbolic violence, police brutality, and hegemonic power, which demonstrates the increasingly hostile cultural and racial climate within the U.S. Given this toxic climate and the trauma it wreaks, now, more than ever before, social justice education is desperately needed. As Bell (2007) has argued, "the goal for social justice education is to enable people to develop the critical analytical tools necessary to understand oppression

M. L. Carson (✉) · J. L. Williams
University of Maryland Global Campus, Adelphi, MD, USA
e-mail: mariko.carson@umgc.edu

C. A. Brewer · S. L. Armstrong
Texas State University, San Marcos, TX, USA

C. C. Ozaki and L. Parson (eds.), *Teaching and Learning for Social Justice and Equity in Higher Education*, https://doi.org/10.1007/978-3-030-69947-5_11

221

and their own socialization within oppressive systems and to develop a sense of agency and capacity to interrupt and change oppressive patterns and behaviors in themselves and in the institutions and communities in which they participate" (p. 2). Recent reform efforts in higher education offer an opportunity to re-envision social justice education within these spaces.

One key site for higher education reform is within developmental education, a field of study and of practice that has traditionally offered course- and non-course-based interventions intended to support student transitions to college-level work. Central to state-mandated reform in developmental education coursework is a focus on shortening the pipeline to college-level, credit-bearing coursework through acceleration. Acceleration is "the reorganization of instruction and curricula in ways that facilitate the completion of educational requirements in an expedited manner," which involves "a departure from the multi-course sequence in favor of a streamlined structure that ultimately better supports students' college-level degree program learning objectives" (Edgecombe, 2011, p. 4). Specifically related to developmental literacy courses, acceleration emphasizes academic literacy through integrated courses where developmental reading, writing, and critical thinking are taught in one course with reduced hours (Edgecombe, 2011; Hern, 2011, 2012). For many states and systems, integrated reading and writing (IRW) courses have been a focus of policy-driven developmental education reform (Armstrong et al., 2018). However, as Hayes and Williams (2016) point out, "very few of these new, integrated courses actually address the curricular, pedagogical, and affective barriers that have stifled the success of students in traditional developmental reading and writing courses" (p. 13).

Developmental-level integrated reading and writing (IRW) classrooms in community colleges are a particularly meaningful vehicle for a social justice framework because many students enrolled in developmental education courses are classified in the minoritized groups most affected by social injustices (Schak et al., 2017). Despite its recent resurgence in the midst of developmental education reform that focuses on acceleration, IRW is not a new curriculum model, as it has origins at the University of Pittsburgh in the 1980s (Bartholomae & Petrosky, 1986). The original instantiation of the model was rooted in pedagogical and theoretical perspectives that view reading and writing as interrelated communication processes (e.g., Emig, 1982; Graham & Hebert, 2010; Kucer, 1985; Langer, & Flihan, 2000; Parodi, 2013; Rosenblatt, 2013; Shanahan,

1990; Tierney & Shanahan, 1991). However, as noted, this grounding may not be reflective of current practice within the reform era:

> From an acceleration perspective, the benefit of such a structure is that it often combines multiple developmental reading and writing courses into a single course, thereby reducing time in developmental education (Saxon et al., 2016a). However, from a literacy perspective, the benefits are pedagogical with potential to better support students' transitions to college literacy practices. Unfortunately, despite IRW's long history and rich theoretical base, in its current reconceptualization across the field, principle-driven, theoretically sound models are not being emphasized. (Armstrong et al., 2019, p. 1)

For our own curriculum design and instruction, we adopt a theoretically driven approach rooted in language and literacy theory, as opposed to one that privileges acceleration as a curricular driver. Thus, in this manuscript, we describe IRW as a curricular structure that values reading and writing as literacy practices that are bound by sociocultural, identity, contextual, and power constraints. In practice, this curricular structure often takes the form of a course that includes both reading and writing foci.

Given the nature of such instruction—at the outset of a college transition where tacit literacy practices are both high-stakes and prevalent, IRW becomes a significant site for the present social justice framework. Emphasizing the importance of literacy curriculum and pedagogy that reflect the racialized identities and experiences of students, Gay (2000) asserts that literacy "is a powerful medium through which students can confront social injustices, visualize racial inequities and find solutions to personal and political problems" (p. 131). This includes providing learners with opportunities to develop tools to navigate media-based text for both academic and non-academic reasons. Of course, classroom conversations about racial violence and social and economic inequities are challenging to initiate and navigate; however, the trauma that students are experiencing as a result of this violence and these inequities is undeniable. As educators, we also enter the classroom space with our own traumas, as well as with our own privileges. This chapter offers theoretically based, practical recommendations for navigating these conversations by checking our own traumas—and privileges—while ensuring that learner voices are primary.

On a surface level, such a revisioning entails offering meaningful texts reflective of students' social identities and experiences (Gay, 2000;

Tatum, 2009; Williams, 2013); however, this is but a single step toward a literacy-focused social justice framework. Indeed, social justice pedagogy is much larger than only text selection, and begins with theoretically sound, evidence-based curriculum and instruction that make learning purposes transparent for students. Toward that end, this chapter presents a social justice focused curricular and pedagogical framework that we can use as literacy instructors and that aims to problematize, theorize, politicize, and contextualize language, text, and *thinking* about language and text (literacies). The structure we adopt for this manuscript mirrors our assumptions about effective curricular design in that it foregrounds philosophy and theory and works outward from there toward curriculum and actual instruction. As instructors problematize literacies, we set the stage for students to consider the power tension between and among literacy issues. Next, as instructors theorize literacy, we lay a foundation for students to meaningfully engage with literacy issues. Taken together, problematization and theorization form the basis for the more practical aspects of this framework—politicization and contextualization. As we politicize literacies, instructors urge students to consider the larger implications of literacy issues by asking questions like "who benefits from current literacy structures?" And finally, as instructors contextualize literacies, we support students in considering literacy issues through the lens of various identities/positions/roles. This approach to social justice education can play a critical role in students examining root causes of inequalities with the goal of recognizing (North, 2006) and providing corrective solutions (Freire, 1970b).

PROBLEMATIZE

Enacting a social justice framework for literacy instruction requires that we first acknowledge and problematize the political nature of education in general and literacy more specifically. Patton et al. (2007) cite that "the classroom—where knowledge is constructed, organized, produced and distributed—is a central site for the construction of social and racial power" (p. 49). They further explain that too often, college faculty ignore the role and systematic complexities of race, class, gender, and other social identities. This is echoed by Grayson (2017) who points out that, despite the impact of institutional racism on student lives, there are too few opportunities for them to discuss their racialized experiences or the social and cultural ideologies that shape these experiences. Specifically related to literacy, Willis (2008) illuminates issues of power that ungird traditional literacy research and practice. Based on her extensive study of the historical, social, and political foundations of literacy testing and instruction, she concludes that literacy instruction in the U.S. "was used to inculcate dominant ideologies as natural, commonsensical, and universal" (p. xi). In doing so, traditional literacy instruction validates and privileges the literacy practices of some and negates and marginalizes the literacy practices of others. This stratification of literacy occurs along racial, gender, and class differences. When the role of race, class, gender, and other social identities and their systematic complexities are ignored, all students, especially those from marginalized groups, are disadvantaged.

To address the inequality and injustice inherent to traditional literacy instruction, a large body of research points to the value of a critical sociocultural approach where reading, writing, and thinking skills are contextualized by the student's diverse social, linguistic, and cultural identities and experiences (i.e., de Kleine & Lawton, 2015; Delpit, 2006; Freire, 1970a, 1991; Gay, 2000, 2010; Hale, 2001; Lesley, 2001; Wenger, 1998; Williams, 2008, 2009). This critical sociocultural conception of literacy instruction emerges from studies of the social, political, cultural, economic, and historical contexts in which literacies are practiced (Gee, 2001; Lankshear & Knobel, 2006; New London Group, 1996; Street, 2003). Specifically related to college literacy, Paulson and Armstrong (2010) argue that faculty must "stress the importance of including an understanding of identity in postsecondary literacy educational contexts" (p. 3). They emphasize that students do not meet their academic goals by simply mastering basic skills through a linear process. Instead, literacy has a variety of purposes that are dependent upon a variety of academic and discourse-community contexts. Students must need to be able to recognize and navigate these contexts; this recognition and navigation involves "sophisticated matters of socialization and acculturation" (p. 3) that are ultimately linked to students' identities (Paulson & Armstrong, 2010). A critical sociocultural approach to literacy instruction acknowledges, values, and engages the diverse ways of knowing, being, and doing that serve as the basis for students' literacy practices. For example, Gay (2010) argues for instruction that uses "the cultural knowledge, prior experiences, frames of reference, and performative styles of ethnically diverse students to make learning encounters more relevant to and effective for students" (p. 31). Likewise, Ladson-Billings (2009) calls for "a pedagogy that empowers students intellectually, socially, emotionally, and politically by using cultural referents to impart knowledge, skills, and attitudes" (p. 20). At the heart of this critical sociocultural approach to literacy instruction is social justice.

According to Bell (2007), social justice is both a goal and a process. The goal of social justice is "equal participation of all groups in a society that is mutually shaped to meet their needs... in which distribution of resources is equitable and all members are physically and psychologically safe and secure" (Bell, 2007, p. 1). Witnessing increasing symbolic violence, a steady encroachment of women's rights, inhumane treatment of immigrants seeking asylum, flagrant racism and hateful rhetoric, and the recurring experience of literally watching life leave the bodies of unarmed Black men on social media undoubtedly take a huge mental and emotional toll. Although classroom conversations about these occurrences are challenging to initiate and navigate, the trauma that students are experiencing should not be ignored. Given this reality, postsecondary literacy classrooms can and should provide a space for students to process their trauma. Using a social justice education framework, reading, writing, and critical thinking can be used to perform meaningful reflection and healing.

By infusing a social justice perspective in literacy instruction, students are provided with an opportunity to problematize and grapple with critical issues and the impact that they have on their lives. They are given an opportunity to call out and question the power dynamics within literacy that privileges some literacies, while marginalizing and negating others. They have the space to call out and question unequal distributions of power and privilege in all areas of their lives and in larger society. More importantly, students have an opportunity to imagine and enact remedies to all forms of injustice. Problematization is not only pivotal to the student's personal development, it is an integral part of their postsecondary literacy acquisition. The power of social justice-oriented literacy instruction has the potential to help students navigate and ultimately dismantle oppression of all kinds in all areas of their lives and in society at large.

Theorize

Having problematized literacy, the next phase in this framework is to theorize. Although not new to postsecondary contexts, and particularly to developmental education (see Armstrong et al., 2018), across the past ten years or so, IRW has been reemerging as a curricular approach (especially in co-requisite and other reform-era models). Whereas a holistic approach to English language arts is already a staple of PK-12 curricula, at the college level, reading and writing have held separate, siloed spaces for years. Although there are volumes of theoretical support for integration (i.e., Clifford, 1988; Emig, 1982; Fitzgerald & Shanahan, 2000; Nelson & Calfee, 1998; Rosenblatt, 2013; Shanahan, 1990, 2006, 2016; Shanahan & Tierney, 1990; Tierney & Shanahan, 1991), that literature has not prompted the two coming back together at the college level in recent years. Instead, a focus on acceleration has been the impetus (Saxon et al., 2016a, 2016b). As one major reform in a much-larger college-completion agenda, acceleration models have largely been imposed rather than developed in purposeful, pedagogically sound ways.

Given the description above regarding the historical theoretical grounding for IRW juxtaposed with the current models rooted in a principle of acceleration rather than literacy theory, the current climate has further complicated the development of a social justice-oriented perspective in what is currently a theory-less or otherwise theory-ambiguous curricular model. Given our frustration with the theory-less state of most IRW curriculum and instruction presently, as we conceptualize a social justice-oriented IRW (SJ-IRW) model, it is all the more important to us to be explicit about our foundational assumptions that inform curriculum and pedagogy. The present SJ-IRW model is informed by three major literacy-based assumptions:

1. literacy-development is a lifelong endeavor and instruction is therefore warranted at the postsecondary level;
2. literacy instruction at the college level must be rigorous and challenging, providing authentic academic literacy experiences;
3. beginning college students bring language and literacy expertise, experiences, goals, and potential that must be honored within the curriculum.

First, we adopt a perspective that literacy is context-dependent, and thus that learners require focused literacy support across contexts. Further, because contextual differences across a lifetime are not isolated to only the primary grades, literacy instruction across a lifetime of contexts is warranted. As endorsement of this assumption, we rely upon Alexander's (2005, 2006) argument that we are always developing as readers and learners. Extending this to the postsecondary level, we also acknowledge that beginning college students are faced with a number of transitions, including personal, social, cultural, geographical, linguistic, and academic ones. In addition, most beginning college students also face a literacy transition, which becomes an enculturation process that involves discovering and then adopting the appropriate academic literacy practices and expectations of multiple discourse communities across higher education (Armstrong, 2007; Jolliffe & Brier, 1988; Rafoth, 1988). Students are thus forced to "invent the university," to "learn to speak our language, to speak as we do, to try on peculiar ways of knowing, selecting, evaluating, reporting, concluding, and arguing that define the discourse of our community" (Bartholomae, 1985, para. 2; see also Bartholomae & Schilb, 2011). Such a significant transition clearly warrants explicit, focused, and informed literacy instruction within that context.

Second, a learner-centered, theory-supported SJ-IRW curriculum could, at least in part, draw upon the work of Bartholomae and Petrosky (1986), whose postsecondary-specific model was holistic in nature, emphasizing whole texts and authentic academic discourse practices. On a pedagogical level, such a model "could easily be imagined as an honors course and not a remedial or developmental one" (Bartholomae & Petrosky, 1986, Preface). In other words, IRW curricula can be simultaneously rigorous and deliberately scaffolded. One way to accomplish this is to better align IRW curricula to the next-level academic literacy practices students will encounter, providing authentic literacy experiences truly reflective of the rigors students will face in their next-level courses. Recent research exploring literacy practices within introductory-level general education (Armstrong et al., 2015a, 2016) and career technical education courses (Armstrong et al., 2019) may provide a model (Armstrong et al., 2015b) for the types of "reality checks" that Simpson (1996) described. Providing experiences that allow access to otherwise-tacit and highly specialized literacy practices is, in and of itself, a social justice concern; however, it also provides a space for querying and critique regarding why such literacies are so tightly held in the first place.

Third, a key assumption in the model we describe is that both curriculum and instruction in an SJ-IRW course would honor the language and literacy expertise and potential that students bring with them to college contexts (Harklau, 2001; Hoff, 2020; Rose, 1985; Young, 2020; Young et al., 2014). Although such a perspective has been a staple of theoretical scholarship in both composition and literacy for many years, it warrants an explicit position within our model as far less work of a practical nature has been done to demonstrate how to employ such an approach in practice. Acknowledging and honoring students' existing literacies happens both on a curricular and pedagogical level. For each to happen, however, SJ-IRW curriculum designers and educators must first do the work of understanding what students bring as they enter the academy.

Although the three key assumptions presented here serve as foundational principles for the SJ-IRW we envision, it is clear that the field needs a postsecondary-specific theoretical model of academic literacy development (see also Paulson & Armstrong, 2010). Even if other assumptions and perspectives are incorporated and blended, employing theory to drive curricular models ensures that our work in support of students is purposeful.

POLITICIZE

Having problematized and theorized literacy, we can now move into one of the more practical aspects of this proposed framework: politicize. As many social justice education scholars have argued, for effective implementation of social justice instruction, it is necessary for us to first acknowledge our privilege and understand how those privileges impact how we perceive and interact with the world around us (e.g., Bell, 2007; Carter, 2018; Delpit, 2006; Gay, 2000; Ladson-Billings, 2009). Additionally, we should respect the traumas and experiences that students bring to the classroom and understand how those experiences influence the growth and learning of students and instructors alike. By acknowledging our privileges and understanding the issues that affect the students we serve, we are forced to become comfortable with the discomfort of allowing constructive dialogue to occur within a safe space. The primary question becomes how do we—all at once, and with care and grace—allow ourselves to recognize our privilege, acknowledge the social injustices of the students we serve, and ensure that we are meeting the learning objectives as outlined in the curriculum?

The answer to this question is simple in that it means that we, as instructors, must first acknowledge the privileges that exist at multiple levels. It is no secret that educational inequalities exist at the macro-, meso-, and micro-levels (Carter, 2018). It can be argued that privilege is manifested at these same levels within educational settings. We observe these manifestations at the macro-level in the campus culture and with the decision-making of executive administrators and content experts. It is displayed at the meso-level through the adoption of the culturally biased curriculum and assessment models that currently exist at all levels of education. At the micro-level, our own personal privilege is on display in the way that we conduct our instruction and assessment of student performance. It is at this micro-level that we have the ability to begin to deconstruct the deeply rooted injustices that exist within these institutions by recognizing how our privilege is exhibited in our own instructional methods, shifting the focus from our own desired teaching methods to instead allowing our students to take a self-directed approach to their learning. There are two assumptions that are arguably pertinent to college students: (1) the student's experiences should serve as one of the core elements to learning, and (2) instructors should engage in a process of mutual inquiry with students rather than engaging in the transmission of knowledge and evaluating a student's conformity to that knowledge (Lindeman, 1989). In aligning our instructional practices with these assumptions, we empower our students to enlighten us on their individualized experiences and traumas resulting from a multitude of injustices. With the adoption of such an approach, our sole responsibility is to establish the framework for how this process will occur. The curricular inclusions with this framework should consist of clear learning objectives, identification of appropriate topics, relevant reading materials, and congruous writing prompts.

The process for implementing social justice instruction rests with the ideals of the desired learning outcomes. In conventional IRW courses, some of the common learning outcomes include application of active reading and writing practices to identify and incorporate key ideas, evaluation and analysis of sources, and utilization of rhetorical strategies to effectively convey messages. These elements are no different in SJ-IRW classrooms. However, the divarication from traditional reading and writing instructional approaches is that the student has the authority to control the narrative as it relates to how those learning outcomes are achieved. With this in mind, it is necessary for us to place value in the experiences of our students and recognize how those experiences contribute to our overall enlightenment and understanding. Additionally, we must relinquish our role as *sage on the stage* for *guide on the side* and exhibit a willingness to establish ourselves as mutual learners within the classroom and provide students with the platform to impart knowledge based on their individual experiences, in this case, as they relate to social issues.

In providing students with this platform to share their experiences and promote self-direction in their learning, it is also necessary to be flexible with the topics that students choose to address. Instructors should provide students with the opportunity to select topics with which they are personally connected. When students are given the freedom to choose topics that are personally relevant, they are more inclined to invest an appropriate and genuine energy into their work while also potentially drawing connections to their issues beyond the classroom (Knowles, 1975). Some students may be able to connect their topics to their respective programs of study. For example, someone studying criminal justice might choose to examine the discrepancies in how law enforcement handles situations with white individuals in comparison to their non-white counterparts. Similarly, a student pursuing business-related or social science majors might decide to research the role that implicit bias plays in decision-making practices. This type of flexibility also affords the opportunity for more cross-curricular instruction to be incorporated so that reading and writing are not taught in isolation. Some common topics related to social justice include criminal justice reform, human trafficking, LGBTQ+ issues, sizeism, colorism, gender equity, sexual harassment or assault, climate change, and immigration reform.

With social justice being ubiquitous in our media, identifying exigence for such issues is effortless. One can simply turn on the television or computer screen, pick up a newspaper, or scroll through the news feed on the cell phone to identify social issues that are relevant in some capacity to many of the students we serve. The available literacies related to social justice issues are endless. In addition to class texts that reference such topics, instructors can access news and journal articles (from credible outlets), and transcripts from TED Talks. Therefore, it is only fair to allow students the autonomy to discuss what is personal to them in order for their learning to be meaningful and their concerns to be shared.

CONTEXTUALIZE

Having problematized, theorized, and politicized literacy, we engage in the final and most practical aspect of the proposed framework: contextualize. Being able to provide authentic literacy experiences for students in an SJ-IRW environment is critical as it helps bring relevance to their personal and academic experiences, and allows for greater potential transference of these experiences within the differentiation of academic content and contexts (Voge, 2011). Contextualization, defined as teaching essential communication modes in a disciplinary context, has been proven to increase the transference of these skills in a variety of contexts and content areas while offering students authentic literacy experiences that can be both relevant to their personal and academic needs (Zimmerer et al., 2018).

Bringing lived experiences into the classroom can be a navigational landmine, particularly where developmental education and content-area instructors may not be fully aware of the subsequent daily reading and writing requirements that students find challenging in their credit-bearing coursework. Furthermore, faculty may be unwilling to utilize contextualization in the classroom due to the overwhelming commitment to the skill-and-drill implementation of instruction that has been engrained in much of a student's prior educational experiences.

In the current racialized climate that has been so pervasive in the day-to-day lives of students, they may not have the discourse opportunities in which to examine the social justice issues that are being lived out in a culture that has been desensitized. Further, they may be seeking safe spaces in which to express their voices as well as their trauma. Thus, building from the foundation of contextualization may ultimately serve as a way to inform students' literacies as well as give them the opportunity to develop the academic reading and writing skills necessary for college and life success.

However, the implementation of contextualized learning can be intimidating and overwhelming for some faculty, so included are some best practices for making the delivery a not-so-complicated undertaking along with some curriculum resources that have proven multiple ways to integrate the issues while developing the skills needed to engage in the discourse. According to Andriotis (2017) and Berns & Erickson (2001), curriculum design should be:

1. Relevant. This can include knowledge-based, cognitive, and skills-based.
2. Effective. Design activities that go beyond just achieving the learning objective but also that teach processes and procedures, as well as the application of the knowledge and content.
3. Transferable. The contextualized content can be organized in a conceptual framework in order to allow for greater transference of knowledge and skills.
4. Socially conscious. Factor in social and cultural nuances when developing contextualized learning activities.
5. Iterative. Focus on broad contextualized learning content.
6. Learner-focused. Design with interdependent learners in mind. Students will be working for others and their learning should reflect their ability to do so.
7. Appropriately assessed. Evaluate learners based on authentic assessments.

Other ways that contextualized teaching and learning can be accomplished include infusing academic courses, linking courses, and team teaching of integrated academic and career technical education courses (Baker et al., 2009; Perin, 2010). Further, faculty should maintain regular and on-going communication with each other as well as synchronize those syllabi that include a progression of skills and joint projects (Baker et al., 2009).

Designing effective contextualized learning experiences for students in integrated reading and writing classrooms helps to build bridges across various disciplinary departments. This allows for a more formal structure that enables the development of a framework from which to help students to understand complex issues and processes while being engaged in a meaningful way where they will be able to create their own narrative in how they view and interpret the world around them.

Examples of Contextualized Learning Experiences and Activities

For cultivating student understanding of their situations and validation of their struggles:

1. Construction of a formal, critical notebook in which they create a catalog of short journal entries (1–2 paragraphs) that translate the assigned readings and helps to focus on their practice of reading. Utilization of prompts that ask students to provide summaries in their words that include identifying key things and explain how it helps them to better understand the concepts of literacy (Listoe, 2015).

2. Use of popular culture as pedagogical tools to aid in student learning to examine and unpack existing stereotypes, perceptions, and prejudices because it often mimics the social, political, and economic times in real time (Gaynor, 2014). For example, the HBO TV Series *The Wire* can be used to build culturally competent curriculum and teach the concepts to students (Gaynor, 2014).

Resources for Developing Contextualized Content Involving Social Justice Issues

Although themes for SJ-IRW-based curricula are many, here we identify one focal topic, police brutality, as an exemplar for compiling resources en route to contextualized curricular design. We recommend identifying sources from different modes and media, as well as sources that offer particular opportunities for literacy instruction (development of an academic argument, integration of text evidence, various rhetorical approaches, etc.).

Books

Crump, B. (2019). *Open Season: Legalized Genocide of Colored People.* HarperCollins Publisher.

Films

Coogler, R., Bongiovi, N. Y., Whitaker, F., Chow, M. Y., Jordan, M. B., Diaz, M., Spencer, O., et al. (2014). *Fruitvale Station* [Film]. Anchor Bay Entertainment. DuVernay, A. (Director) (2016). *13th* [Film]. Netflix.

Print News

Kelly, J., & Nichols, M. (2019, October 14). We found 85,000 cops who've been investigated for misconduct. Now you can read their records. *USA Today*. https://www.usatoday.com/in-depth/news/invest igations/2019/04/24/usa-today-revealing-misconduct-records-police-cops/3223984002/.

Richmond, K. (2016, July 7). *Philando Castile's mother: He was 'black in the wrong place'.* CNN. https://www.cnn.com/2016/07/07/us/philando-castile-family-new-day/index.html.

TED Talks

Robinson, I. (2019). *Social media's impact on cases of police brutality* [Video]. YouTube. https://www.youtube.com/watch?v=Z_Y3_y_hzp8.
Russell, M. (2015). *We police have become great protectors, but forgot how to serve* [Video]. YouTube. https://www.youtube.com/watch?v=KIMWf_e7ZJI.

Television

Noah, T. (2016, July 7). The fatal shootings of Alton Sterling and Philando Castile. *The Daily Show* [Video]. YouTube. https://www.youtube.com/watch?v=tP0awqth0XI.

This list of resources is, of course, partial, as the topic of racially motivated police brutality could (and should) necessarily extend into many arenas, including academic areas such as history, sociology, criminal justice, and psychology. Those charged with curriculum design should proceed with resource-selection based on their program- and institution-level outcomes and goals, as well as the interests and needs of their students.

CONCLUSION

We argue that acceleration of developmental education coursework and the subsequent shift away from theoretical approaches has deviated from the intended purpose to equip students with the skills they need to persist in their postsecondary studies. However, such reform has simultaneously provided an opportunity for professionals to re-examine current pedagogical practices and re-envision how to establish a more holistic approach to literacy instruction in the reading and writing classroom. Specifically, as part of the acceleration movement, integration of previously separated courses has reignited the premise that reading and writing are interconnected and should not be taught in isolation. Academic goals are not met by linear processes. Instead, pedagogy that allows for recognition and navigation of contexts with which students can identify and are empowered to integrate their own experiences and identities into their learning yield more fruitful results to knowledge retention.

Revisioning the design of IRW that offers a contextualized approach to instruction and is reflective of the identities and experiences of the students it is meant to serve, while also addressing social justice issues existent both within and beyond the classroom has endless possibilities. The infusion of social justice instruction in IRW courses offers a platform upon which students can reflect, analyze, synthesize, and confront issues that impact them. This process extends beyond traditional text selection, and is inclusive of multiliteracies such as television, movies, music, and social media. An SJ-IRW classroom encourages instructors to acknowledge the systematic complexities that privileges some and marginalizes others. Most importantly, this model adopts a more inclusive approach to learning by allowing students a space to express their views on a variety of social issues from their own perspectives.

REFERENCES

Alexander, P. A. (2005). *The path to competence: A lifespan developmental perspective on reading.* Paper commissioned by the Literacy Research Association. http://www.literacyresearchassociation.org/assets/docs/Websitedocs/thepathtocompetence.pdf.

Alexander, P. A. (2006). The path to competence: A lifespan developmental perspective on reading. *Journal of Literacy Research, 37*(4), 413–436.

Andriotis, N. (2017). *Contextualized learning: Effective elearning.* EfrontLearning.com/blog. https://www.efrontlearning.com/blog/2017/06/contextualized-learning-effective-elearning.html.

Armstrong, S. L. (2007). *Beginning the literacy transition: Postsecondary students' conceptualizations of academic writing in developmental literacy contexts.* Unpublished dissertation, University of Cincinnati, Cincinnati, OH.

Armstrong, S. L., Stahl, N. A., & Kantner, M. J. (2015a). *What constitutes "college-ready" for reading? An investigation of academic text readiness at one community college.* Center for the Interdisciplinary Study of Language and Literacy [CISLL] Technical Report. http://www.niu.edu/cisll/_pdf/reports/TechnicalReport1.pdf.

Armstrong, S. L., Stahl, N. A., & Kantner, M. J. (2015b). Investigating academic literacy expectations: A curriculum audit model for college text readiness. *Journal of Developmental Education, 2–4, 6, 8–9, 12–13, 23.*

Armstrong, S. L., Stahl, N. A., & Kantner, M. J. (2016). Building better bridges: Understanding academic text readiness at one community college. *Community College Journal of Research and Practice, 40,* 1–24.

Armstrong, S. L., Stahl, N. A., & Lampi, J. P. (2019). All the best-laid plans: A content analysis of textbooks driving integrated reading and writing courses in community college contexts. *Community College Journal of Research and Practice*. https://doi.org/10.1080/10668926.2019.1616633.

Armstrong, S. L., Williams, J., & Stahl, N. A. (2018). Integrated reading and writing. In R. F. Flippo & T. Bean (Eds.), *Handbook of college reading and study strategy research* (3rd ed., pp. 143–167). Routledge.

Baker, E., Hope, L., & Karandjeff, K. (2009). *Contextualized teaching and learning: A faculty primer.* RP Group.

Bartholomae, D. (1985). Inventing the university. In M. Rose (Ed.), *When a writer can't write: Studies in writer's block and other composing process problems* (pp. 134–175). Guilford.

Bartholomae, D., & Petrosky, A. (Eds.). (1986). *Facts, artifacts and counterfacts: Theory and method for a reading and writing course.* Boynton/Cook.

Bartholomae, D., & Schilb, J. (2011). Reconsiderations: "Inventing the University" at 25: An interview with David Bartholomae. *College English, 73*(3), 260–282.

Bell, L. A. (2007). Theoretical foundations for social justice education. In M. Adams, L. A. Bell, & P. Griffin (Eds.), *Teaching for diversity and social justice.* Routledge.

Berns, R. G, & Erickson, P. M. (2001). *Contextual teaching and learning: preparing students for the new economy.* National Dissemination Center for Career and Technical Education.

Carter, P. L. (2018). The multidimensional problems of educational inequality require multidimensional solutions. *Educational Studies, 54*(1), 1–16. https://doi.org/10.1080/00131946.2017.1409225.

Clifford, G. J. (1988). *A Sisyphean task: Historical perspectives on the relationship between writing and reading instruction.* University of Illinois at Urbana-Champaign, Center for the Study of Reading.

de Kleine, C., & Lawton, R. (2015). *Meeting the needs of linguistically diverse students at the college level.* Executive summary and paper commissioned by the College Reading and Learning Association. https://www.crla.net/images/whitepaper/Meeting_Needs_of_Diverse_Students.pdf.

Delpit, L. (2006). *Other people's children: Cultural conflict in the classroom.* Oxford Press.

Edgecombe, N. (2011). *Accelerating the academic achievement of students referred to developmental education* (CCRC Working Paper, No. 30). Community College Research Center.

Emig, J. (1982). Writing, composition, and rhetoric. In H. E. Mitzell (Ed.), *Encyclopedia of educational research* (5th ed., pp. 2021–2036). Free Press.

Fitzgerald, J., & Shanahan, T. (2000). Reading and writing relations and their development. *Educational Psychologist, 35*, 39–50. https://doi.org/10.1207/S15326985EP3501_5.

Freire, P. (1970a). *Pedagogy of the oppressed*. Continuum.

Freire, P. (1970b). Cultural action and conscientization. *Harvard Educational Review, 40*(5), 452–477. https://doi.org/10.17763/haer.40.3.h76250x720j43175.

Freire, P. (1991). The adult literacy process as cultural action for freedom. In M. Minami & B. P. Kennedy (Eds.), *Language issues in literacy and bilingual/multicultural education* (pp. 248–265). Cambridge: Harvard Educational Review (Reprinted from *Harvard Educational Review, 40*(2), 205–225, 1970). http://doi.org/10.17763/haer.40.2.q7n227021n148p26.

Gay, G. (2000, 2010). *Culturally responsive teaching: Theory, research and practice*. Teachers College Press.

Gaynor, T. S. (2014). Through "The Wire": Training culturally competent leaders for a new era. *Journal of Public Affairs Education, 20*(3), 369–392.

Gee, J. P. (2001). Literacy, discourse, and linguistics: Introduction and what is literacy? In E. Cushman et al. (Eds.), *Literacy: A critical sourcebook* (pp. 525–544). Bedford/St. Martin's.

Graham, S., & Hebert, M. (2010). *Writing to read: Evidence for how writing can improve reading. A Carnegie Corporation Time to Act Report*. Alliance for Excellent Education.

Grayson, M. L. (2017). Race talk in the composition classroom: Narrative song lyrics as texts for racial literacy. *Teaching English in the Two-Year College, 45*(2), 143–167.

Hale, J. E. (2001). *Learning while black: Creating educational excellence for African American children*. The Johns Hopkins University Press.

Harklau, L. (2001). From high school to college: Student perspectives on literacy practices. *Journal of Literacy Research, 33*(1), 33–70. https://doi.org/10.1080/10862960109548102.

Hayes, S. M., & Williams, J. L. (2016). ACLT 052: Academic literacy—An integrated, accelerated model for developmental reading and writing. *NADE Digest, 9*(1), 13–22.

Hern, K. (2011). *Accelerated English at Chabot College: A synthesis of key findings*. California Acceleration Project.

Hern, K. (2012). Acceleration across California: Shorter pathways in developmental English and math. *Change*. https://doi.org/10.1080/00091383.2012.672917.

Hoff, M. (2020). *"But it's hard for a refugee": Transitioning to postsecondary literacy practices after forced migration*. Unpublished dissertation, Texas State University, San Marcos, TX.

Jolliffe, D. A., & Brier, E. M. (1988). Studying writers' knowledge in academic disciplines. In D. A. Jolliffe (Ed.), *Advances in writing research, volume two: Writing in academic disciplines* (pp. 35–87). Ablex Publishing.

Knowles, M. S. (1975). *Self-directed learning: A guide for learners and teachers.* Association Press.

Kucer, S. L. (1985). The making of meaning: Reading and writing as parallel processes. *Written Communication, 2*(3), 317–336. https://doi.org/10.1177/074108838500200006.

Ladson-Billings, G. (2009). *The dreamkeepers: Successful teachers of African American children.* Wiley.

Langer, J. A., & Flihan, S. (2000). Writing and reading relationships: Constructive tasks. In R. Indrisano & J. R. Squire (Eds.), *Writing: Research/theory/practice* (pp. 112–139). International Reading Association.

Lankshear, C., & Knobel, M. (2006). Sampling "the New" in new literacies. In C. Lankshear & M. Knobel (Eds.), *A new literacies sampler* (pp. 1–24). Peter Lang Publishing, Inc.

Lesley, M. (2001). Exploring the links between critical literacy and developmental reading. *Journal of Adolescent and Adult Literacy, 45*(3), 180–189.

Lindeman, E. C. (1989). *The meaning of adult education.* New Republic.

Listoe, D. (2015). Reading the scene: Discourse, literacy and pedagogy through the wire. In N. Crummey & K. Dillon (Eds.), *The wire in the college classroom: Pedagogical approaches in the humanities.*

Nelson, N., & Calfee, R. C. (Eds.). (1998). *The reading-writing connection. Ninety-seventh Yearbook of the National Society for the Study of Education.* National Society for the Study of Education.

New London Group. (1996). A pedagogy of multiliteracies: Designing social futures. *Harvard Education Review, 66*(1), 60–92.

North, C. E. (2006). More than words? Delving into the substantive meaning(s) of "social justice" in education. *Review of Educational Research, 76*(4), 507–535.

Parodi, G. (2013). Reading-writing connections: Discourse-oriented research. In D. E. Alvermann, N. J. Unrau, & R. B. Ruddell (Eds.), *Theoretical models and processes of reading* (6th ed., pp. 957–977). International Reading Association.

Patton, L. D., McEwan, M., Rendon, L., & Howard-Hamilton, M. F. (2007). Critical race perspectives on theory in student affairs. *New Directions in Student Services, 120,* 39–53.

Paulson, E. J., & Armstrong, S. L. (2010). Postsecondary literacy: Coherence in theory, terminology, and teacher preparation. *Journal of Developmental Education, 33*(3), 2–13.

Perin, D. (2010). Academic-occupational integration as a reform strategy for the community college: Classroom perspectives. *Teachers College Record, 103.* http://doi.org/10.1111/0161-4681.00117.

Rafoth, B. A. (1988). Discourse community: Where writers, readers, and texts come together. In B. A. Rafoth & D. L. Rubin (Eds.), *The social construction of written communication* (pp. 131–146). Ablex Publishing.

Rose, M. (1985). The language of exclusion: Writing instruction at the university. *College English, 47,* 341–359. https://doi.org/10.2307/376957.

Rosenblatt, L. M. (2013). The transactional model of reading and writing. In D. E. Alvermann, N. J. Unrau, & R. B. Ruddell (Eds.), *Theoretical models and processes of reading* (6th ed., pp. 923–956). International Reading Association.

Saxon, D. P., Martirosyan, N. M., & Vick, N. T. (2016a). Best practices and challenges in integrated reading and writing: A survey of field professionals, part 1. *Journal of Developmental Education, 39*(2), 32–34.

Saxon, D. P., Martirosyan, N. M., & Vick, N. T. (2016b). Best practices and challenges in integrated reading and writing: A survey of field professionals, part 2. *Journal of Developmental Education, 39*(3), 34–35.

Schak, O., Metzger, I., Bass, J., McCann, C., & English, J. (2017). *Developmental education: Challenges and strategies for reform.* U.S. Department of Education, Office of Planning, Evaluation and Policy Development. https://www2.ed.gov/about/offices/list/opepd/education-strategies.pdf.

Shanahan, T. (1990). Reading and writing together: What does it really mean? In T. Shanahan (Ed.), *Reading and writing together: New perspectives for the classroom* (pp. 1–21). Christopher Gordon Publishers, Inc.

Shanahan, T. (2006). Relations among oral language, reading, and writing development. In C. A. MacArthur, S. Graham, & J. Fitzgerald (Eds.), *Handbook of writing research* (pp. 171–183). Guilford.

Shanahan, T. (2016). Relationships between reading and writing development. In C. A. MacArthur, S. Graham, & J. Fitzgerald (Eds.), *Handbook of writing research* (pp. 194–207). Guilford.

Shanahan, T., & Tierney, R. J. (1990). Reading-writing connections: The relations among three perspectives. In J. Zutell & S. McCormick (Eds.), *Literacy theory and research: Analyses from multiple paradigms. Thirty-ninth Yearbook of the National Reading Conference* (pp. 13–34). National Reading Conference.

Simpson, M. L. (1996). Conducting reality checks to improve students' strategic learning. *Journal of Adolescent and Adult Literacy, 41*(2), 102–109.

Street, B. (2003). What's "new" in new literacy studies? Critical approaches to literacy in theory and practice. *Current Issues in Comparative Education, 5*(2).

Tatum, A. W. (2009). *Reading for their life: Rebuilding the textual lineages of African–American adolescent males.* Heinemann.

Tierney, R. J., & Shanahan, T. (1991). Research on the reading-writing relationship: Interactions, transactions, and outcomes. In R. Barr, M. L. Kamil, P. Mosenthal, & P. D. Pearson (Eds.), *Handbook of reading research* (vol. 2, pp. 246–280). Erlbaum.

Voge, N. (2011). Teaching developmental reading requires teaching students to read contexts as well as texts. *Research and Teaching in Developmental Education, 27*(2), 82–86.

Wenger, E. (1998). *Communities of practice: Learning, meaning, and identity.* Cambridge University Press.

Williams, J. (2008). Aligning developmental reading pedagogy with persistence research. *LLC Review, 8*(2), 71–84.

Williams, J. (2009). Teaching the revolution: Critical literacy in the college reading classroom. *LLC Review, 9*(1), 36–47.

Williams, J. (2013). Representations of the racialized experiences of African Americans in developmental reading textbooks. *Journal of College Reading and Learning, 43*(2), 39–69.

Willis, A. (2008). *Reading comprehension research and testing in the US: Undercurrents of race, class, and power in the struggle for meaning.* Lawrence Erlbaum.

Young, V. A. (2020). Black lives matter in academic spaces: Three lessons for critical literacy. *Journal of College Reading and Learning, 50*(1). https://doi.org/10.1080/10790195.2019.1710441.

Young, V. A., Barrett, R., Young-Rivera, Y., & Lovejoy, K. B. (2014). *Other people's English: Code meshing, code switching, and African American literacy.* Teachers College Press.

Zimmerer, M., Skidmore, S., Chuppa-Cornell, K., Sindel-Arrington, T., & Beilman, J. (2018). Contextualizing developmental reading through information literacy. *Journal of Developmental Education,* 1–7.

CHAPTER 12

What Is My Educational Experience? The Use of Autoethnography as an Instructional Tool in an Online Introduction to Educational Leadership Course

Henrietta Williams Pichon

Definitions Terms and Definitions

Social justice: Briscoe and Khalifa (2015) defined social justice as the "praxis of bringing about greater social, political, and economic equity" (p. 10).

Critical thinking skills:

- raising vital questions and problems, formulating them clearly and precisely;

H. W. Pichon (✉)
New Mexico State University, Las Cruces, NM, USA
e-mail: pichon@nmsu.edu

243
C. C. Ozaki and L. Parson (eds.), *Teaching and Learning for Social Justice and Equity in Higher Education*,
https://doi.org/10.1007/978-3-030-69947-5_12

- gathering and assessing relevant information, using abstract ideas to interpret it effectively, making well-reasoned conclusions and solutions, testing conclusions against relevant criteria and standards;
- thinking open-mindedly within alternative systems of thought, recognizing and assessing, as need be, their assumptions, implications, and practical consequences; and
- communicating effectively with others in figuring out solutions to complex problems.

Critical thinking: Critical thinking is self-directed, self-disciplined, self-monitored, and self-corrective thinking. It presupposes assent to rigorous standards of excellence and mindful command of their use. It entails effective communication and problem-solving abilities and a commitment to overcome our native egocentrism and sociocentrism (The Foundation for Critical Thinking, 2019). It is often synonymous with separate knowing (Belenky et al., 1986; Clinchy, 1989).

Connected knowing: Connected knowing is a way of thinking that is based on empathy and trying to understand information by making connections to own experiences (Belenky et al., 1986; Clinchy, 1989; Galotti, 1998). Clinchy (1989) noted that connected knowers "deliberately bias themselves in favor of what they are examining. They get inside it and form an intimate attachment to it" (p. 32). According to Clinchy (1989), connected knowing requires a personal connection with the material; separate knowers take a more detached, impersonal approach to analyzing information.

Autoethnography: A form of qualitative research inquiry that asks the primary question: "How does my own experience of this culture connect with and offer insights about this culture, situation, event, and/or way of life?" (Patton, 2002, p. 84). According to Glesne (2006), "the autoethnography begins with the self, the personal biography. Using narratives of the self, the researcher goes on to say something about the larger cultural setting" (p. 199). Increasingly, researchers (Pichon, 2010, 2013; Smith, 2005; Wall, 2006) see a need to better incorporate self into research as a means of exploring socio-cultural issues, as well as to relieve the researchers from having to speak for others, because self is the source of data. Briscoe and Khalifa (2015) argue that autoethnographies allow for different knowledges to be represented, especially those that do not fit in mainstream literature paradigms (which often silences the voices of minoritized and/or marginalized groups in education).

In Horace Mann's 1848 "Twelfth Annual Report to the Secretary of the Massachusetts State Board of Education," he postulated that public education can do great things to move society forward:

> Education, then, beyond all other devices of human origin, is the great equalizer of the conditions of men...I mean that it gives each man the independence and the means, by which he can resist the selfishness of other men. ...The spread of education, by enlarging the cultivated class or caste, will open a wider area over which the social feelings will expand; and, if this education should be universal and complete, it would do more than all things else to obliterate factitious distinctions in society. (Mann, 1848, p. 9)

More than 170 years later, education's ability to "equalize" has dwindled (Growe & Montgomery, 2003; Rhode et al., 2012). There remains an education achievement divide that needs to be explored from varying perspectives including gaps for between economic and racial groups (Growe & Montgomery, 2003; Rhode et al., 2012). Overall, in 2016–2017, the high school graduation rate was 85%, and the dropout rate declined from 9.7 to 5.4% in 2017 (McFarland et al., 2019). However, during that time, Latino and Black students had the highest dropout rates at 8.2 and 6.5%, respectively (McFarland et al., 2019). The same report showed that ninth graders from a high SES household (78%) were more likely to enroll in college four years later than those from a lower SES household (28%). Furthermore, the baccalaureate degree attainment numbers mirrored those of the high school completion rates. According to Kena et al. (2015), "about 59 percent of students who began seeking a bachelor's degree at a 4-year institution in fall 2007 completed that degree within 6 years." Although this number has slightly risen over the years, there remained a significant attainment-rate gap among different race/ethnicities per the 2014 completion rate data: Asian/Pacific Islander (61%), White (41%), Black (22%), Hispanic (15%), and American Indian/Alaskan Native (5%). If all things were equitable, we would expect that all students would complete at or around the same rate. These completion rates in k-12 and postsecondary education are part of the evidence showing that there is still work to do to make education across levels more equitable.

As Dr. Martin Luther King, Jr. (1963) stated in *Letter from the Birmingham Jail*: "Injustice anywhere is a threat to justice everywhere. We are caught in an inescapable network of mutuality, tied in a single garment of destiny. Whatever affects one directly, affects all indirectly." Dr. King's words resonate the most in education, especially today. Educators are constantly challenged to help students, parents, employers, legislators, and other constituencies understand the relationship between education and multiple inequalities in society. Not only that, college students as consumers and products of education need knowledge of how the current system is working or not for underrepresented and minoritized persons and to critique claims that education is "the great equalizer." Inequity in the educational system is clearly a social justice issue. Educational leaders have to figure out ways to make education accessible to all by understanding the factors that negatively impact student participation.

Thus, the work that I do in my Introduction to Educational Leadership course serves as an excellent backdrop for understanding teaching and learning for social justice and equity. In this class, students explore inequities in the current educational system and offer suggestions for improvement using a four-prong framework for educational leadership: social justice, critical thinking, connected knowing, and autoethnography. A social justice framework examines the inequities in education while critical thinking allows students to fine-tune skills required to systematically examine those inequities. Additionally, connected knowing allows students to use their own experiences as a means of understanding inequities while autoethnography provides the vehicle for which the students systematically explore inequities using self as a source of data. Combined, this four-prong framework allows students to fully immerse themselves in understanding social justice and equities in education.

Thus, this book chapter contributes to this volume of work by using autoethnography as an instructional tool for helping students think critically about social justice issues in the educational system through connected knowing. It includes a context section which explains the Educational Leadership and Administration department and the Introduction to Educational Leadership course. Additionally, I discuss the four-prong approach to educational leadership (i.e., social justice, critical thinking, connected knowing, autoethnography) noting what the content is and how it is used in the course. Furthermore, I provide details regarding the course assignment before making recommendations for introducing teaching and learning for social justice and equity in other courses.

CONTEXT

Educational Leadership and Administration Department

The Educational Leadership and Administration (ELA) division at New Mexico State University (NMSU) is dedicated to teaching and learning for social justice and equity in higher education. The mission of the division is to seek "...to prepare and graduate capable, skillful and dynamic educational leaders for a diverse society. Through the use of theory and practice we aim to develop change agents and role models for socially-just educational systems." Our department has a 63–78 credit hours doctoral degree program in educational leadership and administration, two 33 credit hours master's degree programs in educational leadership (k-12 administration and university/community college administration), and a 120 bachelor's degree program in educational leadership and administration (one of few in the country). As a part of the undergraduate programs, the division offers a general elective in educational leadership, the Introduction to Educational Leadership course, which can be taken by undergraduate students from across the university to fulfill a "viewing the wider world" elective. According to Eckel and King (2004), "The purpose general education is to provide students with broad knowledge and prepare them to be engaged and informed citizens" (p. 9). This holds true at NMSU. The foundation of the leadership course informs citizens. The "viewing the wider world" designation also gives the course another layer of responsibility. According to the university catalog, a "viewing the wider world" elective "strongly emphasize the international character and multicultural influences in the fields of study and strengthen information retrieval skills." The viewing the wider world course that is the subject of this book chapter is entitled "Introduction to Educational Leadership in a Global Society." Both the general education and viewing the wider world designations make this an excellent course for teaching and learning for social justice and equity.

Introduction to Educational Leadership in a Global Society Course

The Introduction to Educational Leadership is a three-credit hour elective course. The catalog description is as follows: "Multinational educational systems covered through knowledge of the U.S. system of education promoting critical leadership roles every citizen plays in the success of educational systems." This course can be taught in a 16-week or eight-week course format and is taught both face-to-face or online. Instructors are allowed to teach their educational leadership sections as they like. As such, topics have varied and have included leadership, change in education, service learning, and comparative education. I focus on exploring inequities in education and ways in which educational leaders can address them using the social justice, critical thinking, connected knowing, and autoethnography framework.

Using this four-prong framework, I seek to prepare and graduate the next generation of critical leaders and educational consumers. I would like to ensure that they know how education influences them and impacts their communities, our society, and others in different countries around the world. This requires that students answer four questions:

- What do inequities in education look like?
- How do I fit into this educational system?
- What works and what does not work within this educational system?
- How can I and others learn from my experiences in order to affect change education?

Students are encouraged to critically explore the current state of education (kindergarten to postsecondary; k-16) in the United States and beyond while juxtaposing their own experiences through connected knowing, culminating in an autoethnography. Using principles and concepts of social justice, critical thinking, connected knowing, and autoethnography, the students develop ways in which educational leaders can improve k-16 experiences for all students (see Fig. 12.1 for Venn diagram of course content).

Over the years, I have encountered challenges in exploring these questions with students. Those challenges have included a lack of interest in course topics, not fully understanding education as a system, historical inequities, institutionalized "isms," and time management. As many university administrators are concerned about whether or not students are getting the tools they need to function within a diverse, information-based, market-driven society (Eckel & King, 2004), New Mexico's Higher Education Department (NMHED) mandates that all universities are to ensure that students are taught how to think critically (NMHED, n.d.). The NMHED has defined critical thinking as problem-solving (i.e.,

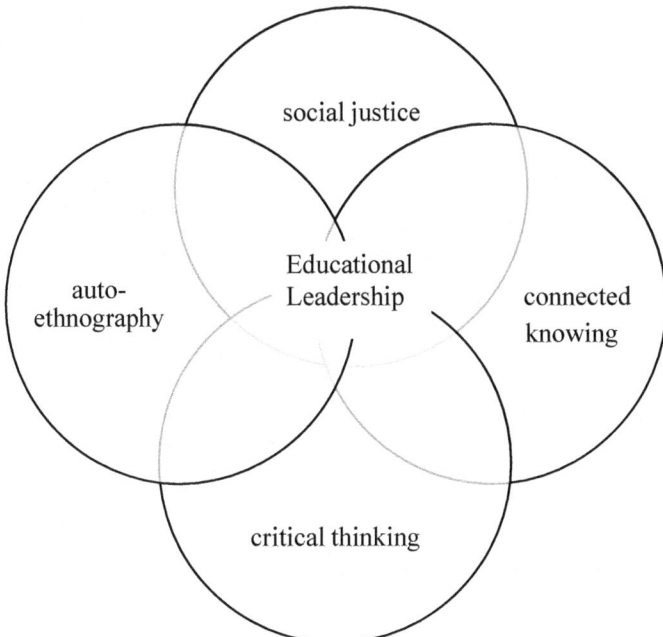

Fig. 12.1 Venn diagram of course content

delineate a problem or question: students state problem/question appropriate to the context), evidence acquisition (i.e., identify and gather the information/data necessary to address the problem or question), evidence evaluation [i.e., evaluate evidence/data for credibility (e.g., bias, reliability, and validity), probable truth, and relevance to a situation], and reasoning/conclusion (i.e., develop conclusions, solutions, and outcomes that reflect an informed, well-reasoned evaluation). Thus, this focus on critical thinking is an excellent foundation both to discuss social justice in the Introduction to Educational Leadership course and to address NMHED mandates.

The Introduction to Educational Leadership course I teach is offered online and allows student to engage with the material, the environment, and people offline as well. There are three events that students may attend. Each week, students are responsible for completing a Learning Module. Each Learning Module will require that students read assigned articles, as well as review YouTube and TED Talk videos, mini lectures prepared by the instructor, and/or presentation prepared by peers. Each Learning Module also includes information-processing exercises that allow students to demonstrate their understanding of course content and to engage with the instructor and their peers. Several activities include but are not limited to the following: discussion board responses, handouts/scavenger hunts, collaboration, reflections, observations, and quizzes. All assignments are scaffolded to help students develop skills and/or acquire information that may be used for the autoethnography research assignment.

Overview of Course Content

In Introduction to Educational Leadership course, students must understand factors that negatively impact their ability to participate in education. Readings topics include comparative educational systems (United States and abroad), sustainable, ethical, and global leadership, and cultivating community change. The readings are not easy for students to grasp; therefore, it is important for students to engage with the material in meaningful ways. One way to do this is to have them write about it. According to a website dedicated to Doing Collaborative Learning (National Institute for Science Education, 1997), "writing is an effective method to teach content as well as to test knowledge and can be combined with collaborative learning structures" (para 1). Writing aids in critical thinking and is an active process of discovery (National Institute for Science Education, 1997), which is extremely important when attempting to move students beyond awareness to action with regard to social justice and equity. In teaching the Introduction to Educational Leadership course, the four-prong framework was chosen based on the following reasons:

1. Social Justice: The department's mission to "develop change agents and role models for socially-just educational systems";
2. Critical thinking: The state's mandate that all universities ensure that students are taught how to think critically;
3. Connected Knowing (Belenky et al., 1986): Connected knowing is a way of facilitating voice in marginalized students (or students who feel silenced), because they do not understand how their own experiences are connected to theoretical concepts and thinking traditionally prioritized in the classroom;

4. Autoethnography: My belief that autoethnography as an instructional tool would be able to bring together these notions of self as data, connected knowing, and critical thinking about inequities in education (social justice) as way of reimagining education.

Ultimately, writing an autoethnography is a means of developing critical thinking skills.

Thus, for this class, concepts related to social justice, critical thinking, connected knowing, and autoethnography were used as pedagogical tools that allowed students to develop a richer understanding of educational leadership within the context of creating a more equitable education system and world.

Social Justice

Although we often discuss how to "develop change agents and role models for socially-just educational systems" as ELA faculty, we did not have a consistent definition for social justice. When posing the same question to the students ("What is social justice?") answers varied as well. Searches via library databases, YouTube, and Google found that social justice descriptions shared multiple meanings. Thus, one of the first assignments in the class was to explore that question. Because of the ever-inclusive and varying definitions of social justice, one aim of the Introduction to Educational Leadership course was not to convince students of one reductionistic definition of social justice but to expose them to the varying definitions in hopes that they would connect with a definition or perspective.

Ultimately, students are provided with the opportunity to understand and connect with different definitions of social justice by relying on a number of scholars (i.e., Bell, 2013; Briscoe & Khalifa, 2015; Jean-Marie et al., 2009; Taylor, 2015). First, Bell (2013) defined social justice as:

> ...full and equal participation of all groups in a society that is mutually shaped to meet their needs...[It includes] a vision of society in which the distribution of resources is equitable, and all members are physically and psychologically safe and secure. Social justice involves social actors who have a sense of their own agency as well as a sense of social responsibility toward and with others, their society, and the broader world in which we need. (p. 21)

Jean-Marie et al. (2009) added that social justice should call for equitable education while focusing on issues of race, class, gender, and other marginalized identities. Finally, Briscoe and Khalifa (2015) asserted that social justice is necessary in order to be a critical leader. They identify social justice as the "praxis of bringing about greater social, political, and economic equity" (p. 10). This is a lofty charge for undergraduates who are future leaders and current educational consumers. Thus, students need experience practicing social justice, especially because focusing on race, class, gender, and other marginalized identities can create some anxieties for students who have never discussed those issues, especially those whose privileges might be uncovered in those conversations.

Faculty who teach social justice often approach it using multiple and varied pedagogical approaches. According to Cooper and Gause (2007), these educators often co-create with students, have democratic classrooms, engage in constructive debate, and help all students feel valued in the process. Further, Taylor (2015) noted that when social justice is introduced by educators, it is best done as an intellectual and moral virtue.

> In developing an ethics of teaching for social justice that uses this virtue framework, we need to identify intellectual and moral virtues that contribute to the aim of social justice. For each relevant virtue, the first task is to understand its characteristic motive, and the second is to consider the conditions needed for teachers to successfully follow through on this motive across different contexts, attending to both internal and external conditions for success. (p. 3)

Because of these nuances in teaching social justice, faculty often encounter resistance on multiple fronts (Cooper & Gause, 2007). First, teaching social justice "requires that educators possess clarity about themselves and their commitments. It entails infusing dialogue, reflection, and critique in our teaching methods" (p. 213). Additionally, faculty have to be willing to allow students to explore, which requires creating a space where students can be vulnerable and take risk thinking through open discourse related to inequities (Cooper & Gause, 2007). This asks students to reflect on their own educational experiences; it is through their own experiences that they are able to practice the virtues of social justice.

Critical Thinking

In attempting to meet the state requirements for *critical thinking*, students have to be introduced to what it means. Readings such as Defining Critical Thinking (The Foundation for Critical Thinking, 2019) and Critical thinking: Why is it so hard to teach? (Willingham, 2007) were selected to introduce to students to varying perspectives and ways of operationalization it. My goal was to help students to attain Paul and Elder's (2008) description of a critical thinker as described in *The Miniature Guide to Critical Thinking Concepts and Tools*:

- raises vital questions and problems, formulating them clearly and precisely;
- gathers and assesses relevant information, using abstract ideas to interpret it effectively comes to well-reasoned conclusions and solutions, testing them against relevant criteria and standards;
- thinks open-mindedly within alternative systems of thought, recognizing and assessing, as need be, their assumptions, implications, and practical consequences; and
- communicates effectively with others in figuring out solutions to complex problems.

Critical thinking is self-directed, self-disciplined, self-monitored, and requires self-corrective thinking. It presupposes assent to rigorous standards of excellence and mindful command of their use. It entails effective communication and problem-solving abilities and a commitment to overcome our native egocentrism and sociocentrism.

This definition seemed the most apropos for the course teaching for social justice and equity in education, because it provided a guide for students to engage with the readings by asking questions, gathering information, thinking about alternatives, and communicating effectively.

Willingham (2007) noted that teaching critical thinking can be quite a challenge for faculty. For the most part, individuals use their own frames of reference and knowledge when seeking to solve issues. According to Willingham, this can prevent individuals from moving beyond the surface structure of the issue to a deeper structure of the issue. Individuals have to be able to determine what type of thinking is required to solve which issues. The more information and knowledge the individual has about a particular topic, the better able they are at employing the best kind of thinking to resolve the issue. Thus, the goal is to provide the students with as much information about education in order for them to begin the best kind of thinking to make the most productive connections. The same holds true for other disciplines. Read and Mathison (2019) found that even when writing to improve critical thinking skills in engineering students, instructors had to be more intentional about providing students with the correct information in order for the teaching for social justice and equity to occur, especially as it related to making connections to engineering concepts and writing assignments. The key to improving critical thinking skills, no matter the discipline, is practice.

Connected Knowing

As individuals are likely to rely on their own frame of reference and knowledge when seeking to resolve an issue, it is important to know how students make connections to the information. In *Women's Ways of Knowing*, Belenky et al. (1986) posited that women may learn differently from men; women were likely to move through a five stage process of learning that began with silence (i.e., reliant on others, not confidant in own words), received knowledge (i.e., receive and give back as learning), subjective knowledge (i.e., personal constructs, listener, watcher), procedural knowledge (i.e., objective, seek truth) to constructed knowledge (i.e., contextual; relativity). As one constructs procedural knowledge, Belenky et al. (1986) found that two distinct ways of knowing: connected knowing and separate knowing. Separate knowing is viewed as objective, often makes no connections or relationships about information, and seeks to disconnect feelings and emotion from knowledge. Connected knowing is characterized by trying to understand information by making connections to own experiences (Belenky et al., 1986; Clinchy, 1989; Galotti, 1998). Clinchy (1989) also noted that connected knowers "deliberately bias themselves in favor of what they are examining. They get inside it and form an intimated attachment to it" (p. 32). According to Clinchy, connected knowing is a personal connection with the material, while separate knowers take nothing at face value and attempt to take on more of a detached, impersonal approach to analyzing information. Building on these definitions, Galotti (1989) found that connected and separate knowing were not necessarily two opposite ends of a procedural knowing continuum but instead could be seen equally in learners. That is, an individual could be fluent in both connected knowing and separate knowing. This finding was important because it did not relegate women to a particular way of knowing and was evidence that all students were capable of the "empathetic, appreciative thinking" required for rigor and logical thinking (p. 282).

In many ways, connected knowing becomes not only a gateway for students to develop voice but to also to think critically about the course content. In a critical piece that provided a connection between connected knowing and critical thinking, Clinchy (1989) offered that connected knowing was simply a different kind of critical thinking. Clinchy explained that although they (Belenky et al., 1986) found that women were more likely to use connected knowing, it did not mean that they were not thinking critically. Instead, the author argued "against an unnecessarily constricted view of thinking as analytic, detached, divorced from feeling" (p. 32). Because colleges should be places for students to think through the things they care about, Clinchy identified a connected teacher as someone who is able to help students understand what is good and point out what needs to be considered to make it better all while using the assignments to help understand the learners and what they need.

Thus, if working with students to think through social justice and equity issues is important for instructors, they need to approach it from a connected knowers perspective. Creating opportunities for connected knowing is appropriate for the instructor as well as the student so both can work through the nuances of social justice and equity. Oftentimes the lived experiences of students are not reflected in the literature. Therefore, it is important to talk through experiences and juxtapose them against the experiences discussed in the existing literature. This connected knowing is both an internal and external process as students engage with the literature and connect it to their own lives and the lives of their peers.

Autoethnography
For the Introduction to Educational Leadership course, I used autoethnography as an instructional tool that would allow students to tell their story. Increasingly, researchers (Briscoe & Khalifa, 2015; Pichon, 2010, 2013; Smith, 2005; Wall, 2006) see a need to better incorporate the self into research as a means of exploring socio-cultural issues as well as relieve the researchers from the responsibility of having to speak for others, because the self is the source of data. An autoethnography is a form of qualitative research inquiry that asks the primary question: "How does my own experience of this culture connect with and offer insights about this culture, situation, event, and/or way of life?" (Patton, 2002, p. 84). According to Glesne (2006), "the autoethnography begins with the self, the personal biography. Using narratives of the self, the researcher goes on to say something about the larger cultural setting" (p. 199).

Autoethnographies allow for different knowledges to be represented, especially those to do not fit in mainstream literature paradigms, which often silences the voices of minoritized and/or marginalized groups in education (Briscoe & Khalifa, 2015). When teaching for social justice and equity in the Introduction to Educational Leadership course, the autoethnographies illuminated issues not widely studied in education and provided counter-narratives that forced students to question whether or not education really was a "great equalizer" (Mann, 1848).

Further, the use of autoethnography in this classroom allowed students to truly immerse themselves in their own sense of knowing, vis a vis connected knowing. That is, autoethnography allowed students to use the self as a source of data. In doing so, students were asked to make connections between theoretical concepts, research, and the self by noting how their experiences were similar and dissimilar and whether or not the theoretical concepts explained, described, or predicted their experiences in education. Thus, autoethnography and connected knowing converged in one space.

The ethnographic aspect of the course assignment must be grounded in authentic research to uncover each student's educational experiences. Data collected included correspondences, journals, pictures, question-naires, test results, and other important artifacts (Duncan, 2004; Patton, 2002; Wall, 2006). That data was presented in the form of a story; the use of narrative analysis allowed stories to stand alone as a worthy documentary of experience to be analyzed for connections between cultural and social patterns. Each student's story provided insight into the cultural meaning and social significance of a particular event. In teaching for social justice and equity in the Introduction to Educational Leadership course, student experiences became the foundation for discussions about how to make education more equitable.

THE ASSIGNMENT

The autoethnography was the culminating assignment in the Introduction to Educational Leadership course. This helped students think critically about social justice issues in the educational system through connected knowing. Because this class was a part of the Writing to Learn initiative at the institution, writing was used as a means to end to develop critical thinking skills. Writing has been found to build critical thinking skills and provides a process to synthesize new knowledge (Writing to Learn, n.d.), and therefore chosen as the vehicle I used to help students understand the course content.

The use of autoethnography was a great way to fulfill my goal of teaching and learning for social justice and equity. In doing the autoethnography assignment, students were able to do the following: (a) explore how personal experiences influenced their understanding of educational leadership in a global society, (b) identify gaps in mainstream literature by asking "is this story being told?," (c) evaluate data from various sources (e.g., document analysis, journals, interviews), and (d) write up findings of their study in a scholarly format (Pichon, 2013). The use of autoethnography allowed students to critically examine equity issues in k-16 education, starting with the self.

For the autoethnography assignment, students were asked to write an eight to ten page paper that included the following components:

1. Identify an issue of equity and social justice in education grounded in research on education;
2. Discuss their relationship to the issue and define why that issue is important to discuss;
3. Tell their own students and detail how their story is consistent or inconsistent with the existing literature; and
4. Define implications for practice, which was a call for action in which students were encourage to pull lessons learned from their exploration of how other countries work with inequities in their educational systems.

I provided examples of autoethnographies to students (e.g., Briscoe & Khalifa, 2015; Chavez, 2012; Pichon, 2010; Sykes, 2014), and I provided directions on how to write them (Pichon, 2013; Smith, 2005). Students were required to use a minimum of eight different resources of which only some could be course readings. The final project was assessed using a rubric in which varying points were assigned for criteria assessing each of the required components (See Table 12.1).

First, students were asked to articulate notions of social justice, especially as it related to education, which allowed me to understand which meanings resonated most with students. Second, students identified a social justice in education issue, which allowed me to determine which issues of inequity most resonated with them. Examples included issues

Table 12.1 Autoethnography grading rubric

Description	90–100% Mastery; complete with minor to no errors	80–89% Approaching mastery; complete, however, one or two items were incorrect	70–79% Satisfactory; partially completed; missing one or two key items (not addressed)	60–69% Approaching satisfactory; missing key items; not able to demonstrate a satisfactory understanding of requirement	59% or below Missing and/or absent; not enough present to demonstrate understanding of requirement	Score
Social Justice Articulate notions of social justice, especially as it relates to education (10 points) Identify social justice in education issue (8 points) Clearly explain interest in topic and why it is important to explore (why is this important to educational leaders? 8 points) *Their Story*						

Description	90–100%	80–89%	70–79%	60–69%	59% or below	Score
	Mastery; complete with minor to no errors	Approaching mastery; complete, however, one or two items were incorrect	Satisfactory; partially completed; missing one or two key items (not addressed)	Approaching satisfactory; missing key items; not able to demonstrate a satisfactory understanding of requirement	Missing and/or absent; not enough present to demonstrate understanding of requirement	
Tell their story (focus on k-12, postsecondary, and/or k-16 experiences; 20 points)						
Literature and Connection to Story						
Evaluate literature-related issues with social justice, critical thinking, and connected knowing (8 points)						
Connect experiences (connected knowing) to existing literature (be able to discuss similarities and differences; 16 points)						

(continued)

Table 12.1 (continued)

Description	90–100%	80–89%	70–79%	60–69%	59% or below	Score
	Mastery; complete with minor to no errors	Approaching mastery; complete, however, one or two items were incorrect	Satisfactory; partially completed; missing one or two key items (not addressed)	Approaching satisfactory; missing key items; not able to demonstrate a satisfactory understanding of requirement	Missing and/or absent; not enough present to demonstrate understanding of requirement	
Call for action Identify implications for practice (these should include ideas learned from other countries and things that they think that they will address the issue(s); 10 points) Writing Mastery of APA or writing style preferences in college (10 points) Eight references (10 points)						

such as the achievement gap, standardized testing, low-income communities, women in STEM, gifted/accelerated programs, and special education services. To meet this criterion, students had to explain what makes this a social justice issue. Third, students were asked to clearly explain their interest in the topic and why it was important to explore, which allowed me to assess how they connected what they learned to their call to action. Students were assessed on their ability to articulate how this information could be used to help others. Fourth, students evaluated the scholarly literature-related issues with social justice, critical thinking, and connected knowing, which allowed me to determine if the student had researched the topic and understood issues related to the topic beyond their own experiences. Fifth, I asked students to tell their own story, which allowed them to share their experiences that impacted their education. Students often shared vignettes or chronicled their journey, noting "this is what happened to me." Sixth, students connected their experiences (connected knowing) to existing literature, which allowed me to determine how students made sense of their experiences in conjunction with the existing literature. In meeting this criterion, students needed to answer the question, "are my experiences in education reflected in the existing literature?" Seventh, I asked students to identify implications for practice, which should include ideas learned from other countries and fields that they think will address the issue(s). Evaluating this criterion allowed me to determine if students were able to develop implications based on their experiences situated within the existing literature to improve education for all students. Often, students made similar recommendations: "develop more inclusive loan forgiveness programs," "make psychological testing more accessible to families," "assign school districts with a sufficient number of social workers," "offer year-round school," "move general education courses to junior colleges," and "free tuition." Eighth, I assessed student mastery of APA (or MLA, Chicago, or Turabian), which allowed me to assess student understanding of professional writing standards. At this stage in their academic career (usually a junior or senior), they should have mastered a professional writing. Finally, I required students to use at least eight references, which allowed me to assess whether or not students had done enough research to substantiate their autoethnography.

TEACHING SOCIAL JUSTICE AND EQUITY IN THE FUTURE

My experience using autoethnography as an instructional tool for helping students think critically about social justice issues in the educational system through connected knowing has major implications for teaching social justice and equity in the future across multiple disciplines using different teaching different modalities (face-to-face, online, hybrid). Specifically, lessons were learned from course evaluations and correspondences with students over a three-year period. I identified five themes from student feedback. Students (1) found that the readings were unmanageable; (2) had trouble making connections between readings and assignments and scaffolded assignments; (3) needed frequent and early feedback; (4) found that learning outcomes were not always clear; and (5) experienced unique challenges per the online teaching and learning modality. From those themes, I made adjustments to the next iteration of the course to enhance student learning experiences with regard to using autoethnography as an instructional tool for teaching social justice and equity. Future iterations of this course and, potentially, other courses seeking to teach with and through a social justice lens should do the following: focus on understanding social justice and equity issues, use low-stakes writing to help students make connections, and clearly describe course expectations.

Focus on Understanding Social Justice and Inequities in Society

First, when using autoethnography as an instructional tool to teach social justice, it is important to focus on student understanding of that concept. Instructors need to be prepared to explain and help students process information related to inequities in society and how all of us are affected by it. For example, readings associated with social justice and inequities in society can be difficult for students to understand or they may have negative response to them that can create a cognitive barrier to understanding or discussing those issues. One statement I have often used in class is that "none of us in this room are responsible for the current state of education in these United State, but all of us are responsible for what the future will look like." Although some students may have first-hand experiences with inequities in society, others may not. Ebbitt (2015) provides guidelines for discussing privilege and encourages students to lead with empathy, understand relativity of privilege, know that systematic injustice can hurt anyone, avoid guilty or defensive responses, and consider ways to equalize power. Those guidelines have seemed to resonate with students and resulted in more productive discussions.

Therefore, when teaching for social justice and equity, begin with common notions of our "inalienable rights." Second, ask students to consider how access to these rights is different for different people. Finally, ask students with identifying patterns that emerge among those differences. Although it is not likely that all students will agree on the reasons for the differences, acknowledging the differences can be a beginning step for a number of students who then have to think through ways of addressing those differences. To help students critically think about these differences continue to press them by encouraging them to ask questions, gather information, think about alternatives, and communicate effectively (Paul & Elders, 2008; Willingham, 2007). An instructor needs to be prepared to help students understand how all of their experiences help our understanding of social justice. In doing so, this allows students to see social justice in action in the classroom through the co-creation of knowledge, democratic decision-making, constructive debate, and feeling valued (Cooper & Gause, 2007).

One assignment that can help students co-create knowledge together is to have students work on a single wiki-page (using Google Docs, for example) together on a particular question. Although this book chapter has focused on teaching educational leadership, questions that could be asked to guide the creation of these wiki-pages could be pulled from varying disciplines. Sample questions might include: What is social justice? What are inalienable rights? How has the "War on Drugs" affected different communities? What is the role of social justice in the code of ethics for engineers? How does society benefit when persons have access to healthcare (e.g., prenatal care, preventive care, timely intervention, medication)? What is the difference between inductive and deductive reasoning? To complete this assignment, students work in groups (no more than five students) to answer different aspects of the question and use references (cited per professional style) to support assertions. Once they finalize their answer, other groups provide peer feedback on the wiki-pages by asking different questions, providing different perspectives, and assessing the page for its ability to effectively communicate ideas. This assignment has been consistently highly rated over years. It allows students to engage in social justice as facilitators of learning, which allows for a critical examination of their work and others.

Use Low-Stakes Writing to Help Students Make Connections

Second, when using autoethnography as an instructional tool to teach for social justice and equity it is important to allow students opportunities to write freely about their understanding of the course readings and their personal connections to those readings. Largely, these notions of writing to improve critical thinking can be found in Writing-Across-the-Curriculum and Writing-Across-the-Disciplines (Bean, 2011; Doing Critical Learning, n.d.; Read & Mathison, 2019; Writing to Learn, n.d.) of their own experiences. Specifically, a Writing-Across-Curriculum Clearinghouse at Colorado State (Colorado State, n.d.) is dedicated to Writing to Learn. This website provides a number of different writing activities to include in classroom that promote critical thinking about the course topic. Because learning about social justice can be a personal experience, that learning requires dialogue, reflection, and critique (Cooper & Gause, 2007).

Free writing (also known as low-stakes writing) can be a good way to get students to connect with the readings in a meaningful way. I use journal entries to allow for this low-risk exchange of dialogue, reflection, and critique. These journals allow students to practice "summarizing particular arguments, identifying main issues, noting key details, and choosing pertinent quotes" (Colorado State, n.d.). Students then try to understand information by making connections to their own experiences (Belenky et al., 1986, Clinchy, 1989; Galotti, 1998). By reflecting on all of these skills, students are more likely to be able to make meaning of content and are able to generate higher-level questions and connections (Cooper & Gause, 2007; "The Reading Journal", n.d.). This is extremely important when teaching for social justice and equity because students need a safe space to explore ideas and notions that have not been well developed. These writings do not have to be graded by the instructor, instead, they can be an assignment in which students self-assess their ability to make connections to the readings while providing specific examples relevant for their autoethnography (Cooper & Gause, 2007; Jean-Marie et al., 2009; Taylor, 2015).

Further, using low-stakes grading encourages completion and honest dialogue because the emphasis is on providing feedback and not critique. Again, this allows students to make meaningful connections among self, research, and society as a whole.

Clearly Identified Course Expectations

When using autoethnography as an instructional tool to teach for social justice and equity, it is important to have clearly identified course expectations for students. Over the years, students have struggled with readings and making connections between readings and assignments. To address this, I presented clear expectations of course objectives, course organization, readings, assignments, and communication. Course objectives should clearly identify learning goals specific to social justice and equity. Let students know how they will be expected to practice principles of social justice and equity, such as co-creating knowledge, participating in a democratic classroom, engaging in constructive debate, and acting as a valued member of the class (Briscoe & Khalifa, 2015; Cooper & Gause, 2007; Taylor, 2015).

Further, I provide students with clear expectations of how the course is set up. For example, the following is an excerpt from my syllabus:

> Each week, students will be responsible for completing a Learning Module. Each Learning Module will require that students read assigned articles, as well as review YouTube videos, mini lectures prepared by the instructor, and/or presentation prepared by peers. Each Learning Module also includes information-processing exercises that allow students to demonstrate their understanding of course content and to engage with the instructor and their peers; several activities include but is not limited to discussion board responses, handouts, collaboration, or observations.

By providing students with clear understanding of the organization of the course, students are able to understand what is expected of them within the course modality. If the course is delivered face-to-face, the instructor should also explain to the students what they may expect when they enter the classroom. This can be assessed by checking in with students early (see Fig. 12.2).

Course Expectations

Because students struggle with the readings and assignments related to social justice and equity, it is important for them to be able to allow students space to process readings and make connections to the assignments. Instructors should help students understand how to complete the assignment and how they will be graded. In doing so, it helps students know that their grade is less reliant on their thinking like the instructor

Now that you have had a chance to review the syllabus and take the online readiness quiz, please respond to the following questions:

1. Identify assignments that you believe you will be able to complete with ease.

2. Identify any assignments in which you believe will be challenging for you or will require more directions.

3. Since this course is taught completely online, please identify at least 3 things that you will do to ensure your success.

4. What are the best instructional ways you believe may assist you with meeting the objectives of this course?

Fig. 12.2   Assessing students' understanding

and more reliant on their ability to meet assignment criteria. Because resisters (Cooper & Gause, 2007) do not necessarily believe inequities may be addressed by taking a critical look at the educational system that creates these conditions, they tend to write to the instructor. Having clear grading expectations can guide students, instead, to write to the assignment expectations. Similarly, when discussing the weekly readings and assignments, communicate the associated weekly/lesson learning objectives. This could be communicated to students using a Course Map (see https://www.coursemapguide.com). Although course maps were designed for online instruction, they work equally well in face-to-face classes.

Finally, course expectations should be communicated to students in multiple ways. In communicating expectations, instructors could include this information in the course syllabus, on the first day of class, or in a welcome video on the home page of an online course. Additionally, course maps with weekly learning expectations could be presented in class or posted in the designated Learning Management System (LMS). In teaching for social justice and equity, it is important that help students understand how they will be required to demonstrate their learning. If our goal is for students to be able to understand social justice and equity and apply that lens to thinking about education, course expectations should communicate that students need to demonstrate that they know what social justice is, can explain principles, concepts, notions, and practices associated with social justice, can explain social justice to others, and use course content to benefit others. Finally, students need to be able to draw conclusions and make connections about social justice to key concepts within the academic discipline (e.g., engineering, nursing, social work, education, biology, sociology) as well as take a stand based on the understanding of principles, concepts, notions, and practices associated with social justice while creating new and co-constructed knowledge that address equity issues. Communicating these expectations clearly at the beginning of the course can help students to meet those learning objectives.

Conclusion

I hope that my experiences of using autoethnography as an instructional tool for helping students think critically about social justice issues in the educational system through connected knowing may help others consider autoethnography as a way to approach a class and/or lessons that seek to develop student's capacity for critical thinking about social justice. In classrooms where co-creation of knowledge, democratic decision-making, constructive debate, and affirmation is practiced, promoting critical self-evaluation through an autoethnography assignment can be an effective way to help students connect theory to practice in ways that result in more equitable schools.

References

Bean, J. C. (2011). *Engaging ideas: The professor's guide to integrating writing, critical thinking, and active learning in the classroom* (2nd ed.). San Francisco, CA: Wiley.

Belenky, M. F., Clinchy, B. M., Goldberger, N. R., & Tarule, J. M. (1986). *Women's ways of knowing: The development of self, voice, and mind*. New York: Basic Books.

Bell, L. (2013). Theoretical foundations. In M. Adams, W. J. Blumenfeld, C. Castañeda, H. W. Hackman, M. L. Petrs, & X. Zúñiga. (Eds.), *Readings for diversity and social justice*. New York: Routledge.

Briscoe, F. M., & Khalifa, M. A. (2015). *Becoming critical: The emergence of social justice scholars*. Albany, NY: State University of New York Press.

Chavez, M. S. (2012). Autoethnography, a Chicana's methodological research tool: The role of storytelling for those who have no choice but to do critical race theory. *Equity & Excellence in Education, 45*(2), 334–348.

Clinchy, B. M. (1989). On critical thinking and connected knowing. *Liberal Education, 75,* 14–19.

Cooper, C. W., & Gause, C. P. (2007). "Who's afraid of the big bad wolf?" Facing identity politics and resistance when teaching for social justice. In D. Carlson & C. P. Gause (Eds.), *Keeping the promise: Essay on leadership, democracy, and education* (pp. 197–216). New York, NY: Peter Lang.

Duncan, M. (2004). Autoethnography: Critical appreciation of an emerging art. *International Journal of Qualitative Methods, 3*(4), Article 3. Retrieved from http://www.ualberta.ca/~iiqm/backissues/3_4/pdf/duncan.pdf.

Ebbitt, K. (2015, February 27). *Why it's important to think about privilege and why it's hard.* Retrieved from Global Citizen at https://www.globalcitizen.org/en/content/why-its-important-to-think-about-privilege-and-why/.

Eckel, P. D., & King, J. E. (2004). *An overview of higher education in the United States: Diversity, access, and the role of the marketplace.* Atlanta, GA: American Council on Education. Retrieved from https://www.acenet.edu/Documents/Overview-of-Higher-Education-in-the-United-States-Diversity-Access-and-the-Role-of-the-Marketplace-2004.pdf.

Galotti, K. M. (1989). Approaches to studying formal and everyday reasoning. *Psychological Bulletin, 105*(3), 331–351.

Galotti, K. M. (1998). Valuing connected knowing in the classroom. *The Clearing House, 71*(5), 281–283.

Glesne, C. (2006). *Becoming qualitative researchers: An introduction* (3rd ed.). Boston: Pearson Education, Inc.

Growe, R., & Montgomery, P. S. (2003). Educational equity in America: Is education the great equalizer. *The Professional Educator, 25*(2), 23–29. Retrieved from https://files.eric.ed.gov/fulltext/EJ842412.pdf.

Jean-Marie, G., Normore, A. H., & Brooks, J. S. (2009). Leadership for social justice: Preparing 21st century school leaders for a new social order. *Journal of Research on Leadership Education, 4*(1), 1–31.

Kena, G., Musu-Gillette, L., Robinson, J., Wang, X., Rathbun, A., Zhang, J., Wilkinson-Flicker, S., Barmer, A., & Dunlop Velez, E. (2015). *2015* (NCES 2015–144). U.S. Department of Education, National Center for Education Statistics. Washington, DC. Retrieved [date] from http://nces.ed.gov/pub search.

King, M. L., Jr. (1963). *Letter from a Birmingham jail.* Retrieved from https://www.africa.upenn.edu/Articles_Gen/Letter_Birmingham.html.

Kirby, K., et al. (1986). The Reading Journal: *A Bridge between Reading and Writing. Forum for Reading, 18*(1), 13–19.

Mann, H. (1848). *Twelfth annual report to the secretary of the Massachusetts state board of education.* https://genius.com/Horace-mann-twelfth-annual-report-to-the-secretary-of-the-massachusetts-state-board-of-education-1848-annotated.

McFarland, J., Hussar, B., Zhang, J., Wang, X., Wang, K., Hein, S., Diliberti, M., Forrest Cataldi, E., Bullock Mann, F., & Barmer, A. (2019). *The condition of education 2019* (NCES 2019–144). U.S. Department of Education. Washington, DC: National Center for Education Statistics. Retrieved [date] from https://nces.ed.gov/pubsearch/pubsinfo.asp?pubid=2019144.

National Institute for Science Education. (1997). *Writing to learn.* Retrieved from http://www.wcer.wisc.edu/archive/cl1/cl/doingcl/writing.htm.

New Mexico Higher Education Department. (n.d). *New Mexico general education curriculum.* Retrieved from https://hed.state.nm.us/resources-forsch ools/public_schools/general-education.

OECD. (2017). *Education at a galance 2017: OECD indicators.* Paris: OECD Publishing. http://dx.doi.org/10.1787/eag-2017-en.

Patton, M. Q. (2002). *Qualitative research and evaluation methods* (3rd ed.). Thousand Oaks, CA: Sage Publications.

Paul, R., & Elder, L. (2008). *The miniature guide to critical thinking concepts and tools, foundation for critical thinking press.* Retrieved from https://www.criticalthinking.org/pages/defining-critical-thinking/766.

Pichon, H. W. (2010). Transitioning into the professoriate: The pursuit of power in the academy. *Journal on Excellence in College Teaching, 27*(1), 5–27.

Pichon, H. W. (2013). Telling their stories: The use of autoethnography as an instructional tool in an introductory research course. *The Qualitative Report, 18*(2), 1–8. Retrieved at http://www.nova.edu/ssss/QR/QR18/pic hon2.pdf.

Read, S., & Mathison, M. A. (2019). Locating common ground for diplomacy: Using critical thinking to teach writing. In M. A. Mathison's, *Sojourning in disciplinary cultures: A case study for teaching writing in engineering.* Fort Collins, CO: University Press of Colorado.

Rhode, D., Cooke, K., & Ojha, H. (2012, December 12). The decline of the great equalizer. *The Atlantic.* Retrieved from https://www.theatlantic.com/business/archive/2012/12/the-decline-of-the-great-equalizer/266455/.

Smith, C. (2005). Epistemological intimacy: A move to autoethnography. *International Journal of Qualitative Methods, 4*(2), Article 6. Retrieved at http://www.ualberta.ca/~ijqm/backissues/4_2/pdf/smith.pdf.

Sykes, B. (2014). Transformative autoethnography: An examination of cultural identity and its implications for learners. *Adult Learning, 25*(1), 3–10.

Taylor, R. M. (2015). The ethics of teaching for social justice: A framework for exploring the intellectual and moral virtues of social justice educators. *Democracy and Education, 23*(2), 1–5.

The Foundation for Critical Thinking. (2019). *Defining critical thinking.* http://www.criticalthinking.org/pages/defining-critical-thinking/766.

Wall, S. (2006). An autoethnography on learning about autoethnography. *International Journal of Qualitative Methods, 5*(2), 1–12.

Willingham, D. T. (2007). Critical thinking: Why is it so hard to teach? *American Educator,* 8–19.

Suggestions for Future Readings

Bean, J. C. (2011). *Engaging ideas: The professor's guide to integrating writing, critical thinking, and active learning in the classroom* (2nd ed.). San Francisco, CA: Wiley.

Bloom, B. (2001). *A taxonomy for teaching, learning, and assessment.* Retrieved from Vanderbilt University Center for Teaching at https://cft.vanderbilt.edu/guides-sub-pages/blooms-taxonomy/.

Brookhart, S. M. (2010). *How to assess higher-order thinking skills in your classroom.* Alexandria, VA: ASCD.

DuBois, W. E. B. (1935, 1962). Black reconstruction in America (The Oxford W. E. B. Du Bois): An essay toward a history of the part which Black folk played in the attempt to reconstruct democracy in America, 1860–1880.

Inclusive Teaching. (2017, August 29). *An instructor's guide to understanding privilege.* Retrieved from https://sites.lsa.umich.edu/inclusive-teaching/2017/08/29/an-instructors-guide-to-understanding-privilege/.

McIntosh, P. (2020). *On privilege, fraudulence, and teaching as learning: Selected essays 1981–2019.* New York, NY: Routledge.

Read, S., & Mathison, M. A. (2019). Locating common ground for diplomacy: Using critical thinking to teach writing. In M. A. Mathison's *Sojourning in disciplinary cultures: A case study for teaching writing in engineering.* Fort Collins, CO: University Press of Colorado.

Teaching Social Justice Education. (n.d.). Retrieved from Teaching Social Justice Education website at https://socialjusticeteaching.weebly.com.

Writing-Across-Curriculum Clearinghouse. (n.d.). Retrieved from https://wac.colostate.edu/resources/wac/intro/wtl/wtlactivities/#wtl_a.

Narratives of Bystanding and Upstanding: Applying a Bystander Framework in Higher Education

Amanda Sugimoto and Kathy Carter

KEY TERMS AND DEFINITIONS

Bystander Effect	Named by Latané and Darley (1969), the bystander effect is a psychological phenomenon where the more witnesses there are to an emergency and/or crime, the less likely they are to intervene.
Upstander	Someone who intervenes in an injurious event, whether or not the intervention was successful. The term "active bystander" can also be used, but we intentionally use the term upstander with

A. Sugimoto (✉)
Portland State University, Portland, OR, USA
e-mail: asugimo2@pdx.edu

K. Carter
University of Arizona, Tucson, AZ, USA

© The Author(s), under exclusive license to Springer Nature Switzerland AG 2021
C. C. Ozaki and L. Parson (eds.), *Teaching and Learning for Social Justice and Equity in Higher Education*,
https://doi.org/10.1007/978-3-030-69947-5_13

271

	students to clearly differentiate bystanding from intervention.
Narrative Inquiry	An epistemology that involves studying the human phenomenon of how a person narrates or stories particular experiences, and, in turn, how this storying shapes a person's beliefs, knowledge, and/or actions.

Over the past decades, institutions of higher education and the individuals within those institutions have explored issues of social justice in the hopes of advancing equity within and outside campus boundaries. Increasingly, social justice considerations are embedded within institutional vision statements, admissions, and curricular policies, campus culture efforts, as well as programs and coursework. One example of this work is the bystander intervention programs that some institutions have implemented to educate students about the bystander effect and prepare them to intervene in instances of violence and/or sexual assault (e.g., Coker et al., 2011). Yet, social justice efforts in higher education have often been inhibited by underdeveloped theoretical framings and a lack of a shared vision of practices and programs that support this work (Davis & Harrison, 2013). This challenge is not surprising given that social justice and equity work is deeply intertwined with the beliefs and lived experiences of the individuals who are leading or taking part in these efforts, and these beliefs and storied experiences may fundamentally differ based on a person's power, authority, context, and/or culture (Davis & Harrison, 2013; Fischer, 1998; Guba & Lincoln, 1994; Latz et al., 2017; Patton, 2010; Phillips & Burbules, 2000). Scholars and practitioners continue to interrogate and explore established theories (e.g., the bystander effect; Latané & Darley, 1969) in an effort to bridge the theory to practice divide and to contribute to more socially just and equitable institutions of higher education.

The bystander effect is the psychological phenomena that individuals are more likely to intervene in potentially injurious events when they are alone rather than in the company of others (Garcia et al., 2002; Latané & Darley, 1969). Within higher education institutions, faculty and staff have explored how the bystander effect influences an individual's decision of whether or not to intervene in instances of violence and/or sexual assault on campus (e.g., Banyard et al., 2009; Burn, 2009; Chekroun & Brauer, 2002; Coker et al., 2011; Katz, 1994). As teacher educators, we look to expand this exploration of the bystander effect beyond instances of violence on higher education campuses to the K-12 institutions where our students, as preservice teachers, will be working. Specifically, we explore how instances of bystanding may be connected to larger societal narratives related to social injustice (e.g., when an aggressor(s) may be motivated by racism, linguicism, homophobia, sexism, xenophobia, and/or classism) in an effort to better prepare preservice teachers to upstand in moments where they may feel the pull to bystand.

We define upstander as an individual who witnesses an injurious event and does something to intervene, whether or not the invention actually ends the event. This chapter details a "soft intervention" that we have used to support preservice teachers in higher education in considering how, or even if, to move from bystanding to upstanding in future events both inside and outside of the classroom. Our particular intervention and concomitant study uses narrative inquiry as pedagogy to explore how previous instances of bystanding shape preservice teachers' current thinking about historically marginalized student populations in schools (i.e., emergent bilinguals and students from the LGBTQ community). We use narrative as pedagogy to explore both the storied knowledge that preservice teachers bring into their higher education program from their K-12 studenting days as well as their developing storied knowledge from their current field-based practicum placements (Carter et al., 2019; Sugimoto et al., 2017). The goal of this particular analysis was to explore how these remembered events of bystanding from K-12 schools shaped preservice teachers' understandings of how teaching, learning, and social justice are intertwined. In this chapter we explore the following questions: (1) how do preservice teachers narrate their experience(s) where they were a bystander to the marginalization and/or bullying of an emergent bilingual, and (2) how might bystander narratives be used in higher education classrooms to explore issues of social (in)justice through a student's previous experiences and decisions?

Background

This instructional initiative and accompanying study was grounded in the post-positivist paradigm that asserts absolute truth does not exist; therefore, research should explore the varied perspectives that can influence human knowledge through multiple research tools and paradigms (Clark, 1998; Fischer, 1998; Guba & Lincoln, 1994; Phillips & Burbules, 2000). In alignment with this paradigm, we explore the bystander effect through narrative inquiry.

Bystander Effect

Latané and Darley (1970) argued that individuals engage in an internal decision-making model when deciding whether or not to intervene during a potentially injurious event. This decision-making model involves individuals: (1) noticing that something is wrong, (2) defining the event as a situation in which someone needs help, (3) deciding to take personal responsibility in the event, (4) deciding to intervene, and (5) implementing an intervention. If at any point in this model an individual deviates from these steps, then they will in effect remain a bystander. Yet, deciding to upstand can be complicated by social, emotional, and psychological factors that can lessen the likelihood that an individual will intervene.

A multitude of factors can influence an individual's decision to remain a bystander. Firstly, a crowd mentality can contribute to a diffusion of responsibility, or a belief that someone else in the group will intervene thereby alleviating one's personal responsibility to intervene (Darley & Latané, 1968). Secondly, individuals often look to other witnesses as models for how or even if they should intervene, and if no intervention is present from others, it is more likely that they will remain a bystander (Bierhoff, 2002; Clark & Word, 1974; Manning et al., 2007). Thirdly, "apprehension evaluation" makes individuals less likely to intervene because they do not want to look foolish or embarrass themselves in front of other witnesses if they did decide to intervene (Bierhoff, 2002; Hall et al., 2013). Conversely, the more confident an individual is in their ability to effectively intervene, the more likely they are to intervene (Goldman & Harlow, 1993; Latané & Darley, 1970). Finally, an individual's relationship to the person being harmed can influence their decision of whether or not to intervene (Hall et al., 2013).

Classrooms and schools are unique social environments because one inherent feature of these spaces is that one is educated within a crowd (Jackson, 1990). Therefore, it is more likely that at least one person will witness the most injurious events within these school spaces. Further, Banyard and colleagues (2004) recognized that the bystander effect in colleges and universities was not just an individual issue but closely related to social and cultural norms in the community. Concomitantly in K-12 schools, a growing body of research has documented similar patterns of teacher and student inaction with respect to intervention in bullying events (e.g., Barnes et al., 2012; Yoon & Kerber, 2003). These separate but relatable phenomena should be of particular concern to faculty in higher education, particularly teacher educators, if we hope to better prepare preservice teachers to become upstanders in future injurious events.

Narrative Inquiry

Nearly 30 years ago, Nell Noddings argued that "stories have the power to direct and change our lives" (1991, p. 157). Yet, historically marginalized student populations continue to be marginalized and/or bullied in all levels of education from preschool to higher education (e.g., Espelage, 2015; Osanloo & Boske, 2015). Following in the hope of Nell Noddings's words and undergirded by a growing body of research in narrative inquiry, we have used narrative inquiry as a framework for a story-based intervention initiative and study in our teacher preparation programs. Based on what we have learned, we believe that this initiative has the potential to explore the narrated knowledge that students bring with them to their colleges and universities, as this storied knowledge may shape their future decisions of whether to bystand or upstand.

Narrative inquiry explores the ways in which people narrate and make meaning of their lives and the larger world. Within a narratological framework, an individual's choices, thoughts, and perceptions are shaped by their individual expectations, experiences, and the larger cultural norms through which they interpret their ongoing experiences (Bruner, 1985; Carter, 1993; Chafe, 1990; Sarbin, 1986; Clandinin et al., 2006; Sugimoto et al., 2017). As an individual moves through life, they weave their experiences into an ongoing storyline that can shape their interpretations and choices. These narrative fragments can then be recalled and reflected upon during moments in one's life and can provide a sense of unity or discontinuity that further shapes one's storied knowledge and actions (Clandinin & Connelly, 2000).

Narrative inquiry involves studying the human phenomenon of experiences and how one stories particular experiences (Carter, 1993; Clandinin & Connelly, 2000; Clandinin et al., 2006). In this sense, narrative inquiry is both the phenomena, the act of storytelling, and the methodology, structured inquiry into narratological patterns. In other words, when individuals narrate their lives, they are both (re)living their stories as well as reflecting on and explaining their lives to others (Connelly & Clandinin, 1990). Therefore, narrative is a means of exploring an individual's life experiences, how an individual makes sense of their experiences, and how they explain their sense-making to others. Further, this sense-making is often intertwined with socio-cultural norms and can provide insight into these norms (Chafe, 1990).

Narrative inquiry can also be a tool to explore the tensions or challenges that individuals negotiate and renegotiate as part of their storied lives (Huber et al., 2006). Clandinin and colleagues (2009) conceptualized these challenges as "bumping places" where "individuals' lived and told stories bumped against the lived and told stories of others who had been shaped by different social, cultural, linguistic, and institutional narratives" (p. 83). In our work as teacher educators, we focus on these bumping places where an individual negotiates their ongoing storied knowledge alongside the storied knowledge and experiences of others.

As a pedagogical tool, narrative has a long tradition in teacher education (Chafe 1990; Coulter et al., 2007; Egan, 1988; Tate, 1997; Wood, 2000). However, the act of storytelling as curriculum is not unique to teacher education. Fields such as art, psychology, and drama also use forms of narrative inquiry as a pedagogical strategy. Narrative as curricular activity can support students in reflecting on and critically questioning their lived experiences in relation to higher education coursework (Conle, 2003). To this end, narratives have been used as a means of engaging students in recalling, retelling, and potentially recasting their storied knowledge in order to identify directions for their personal and professional growth (Clandinin & Connelly, 2000; Connelly & Clandinin, 1994; Wood, 2000). In teacher education, Connelly and Clandinin (1988) argued that teachers integrate theory and practice through their unique "narrative unity of experience" (p. 48). Therefore, a preservice teachers' storied knowledge can be thought of as part of their larger learning to teach journey, and can uniquely shape their beliefs and practices (Lortie, 1975; Coulter et al., 2007).

By attending to the developing storied knowledge of preservice teachers in a teacher preparation program, faculty have the opportunity to better understand how past experiences may influence preservice teachers' developing professional understandings of how teaching, learning, and diverse learners are connected (Carter, 1993; Coulter et al., 2007; Sugimoto et al., 2017). Therefore, we have designed a line of narrative inquiry to investigate preservice teachers' experiences as bystanders to potentially deleterious events during their *own* K-12 studenting days as well as their field-based practicums in order to explore how these previous experiences shape their current storied knowledge related to bystanding and/or upstanding.

METHODS

This analysis comes from a larger, multiyear project aimed at exploring preservice teachers' developing storied knowledge about schools, schooling, and students. The larger study explores preservice teachers' personal and professional narratives regarding multiple aspects of schools and teaching, as well as the concomitant shaping force that these narratives have on preservice teachers' learning to teach journey. Participants in this initiative were sampled from a course taught by the authors, which is one of the first courses that the preservice teachers complete in their teacher preparation sequence. Most of the preservice teacher participants in the course self-identified as white, woman, and native English speakers, which aligns with ongoing national trends (Ingersoll et al., 2014).

Instructional Sequence to Explore Preservice Teachers' Bystander Narratives

The instructional sequence described herein was implemented in a course that we both taught with different sections of undergraduate students. Students in the course were enrolled in an elementary teacher preparation program and this course was one of their introductory, foundational courses. The course content focused on classroom management and models of instruction. As instructors, we embedded a diversity and inclusion strand in the course to support preservice teachers in making their classroom management and instruction more inclusive. Attached to this course was a 45-hour fieldwork component where preservice teachers observed and worked with teachers and students in elementary or middle schools.

As part of their coursework, both instructors assigned preservice teachers a pair of narratives, called bystander Well-Remembered Events (WRE) (Carter, 1994; Carter et al., 2019; Sugimoto et al., 2017) (see Appendix A for assignment). In their WREs, preservice teachers described and reflected upon an event within which they observed or participated in where a student was marginalized or bullied. The instructors explicitly directed preservice teachers to focus on an event involving an emergent bilingual student or student from the LGBTQ community based on their contextualized knowledge. This means that preservice teachers may not have had official knowledge of whether or not a student was classified as an English Language Learner (ELL) by the school, but they drew upon their knowledge of the student to decide whether or not they could be considered an emergent bilingual.

For the bystander WRE, preservice teachers described: (1) an event from their K-12 studenting days and (2) an event from their fieldwork observations as part of their teacher preparation coursework. The goal of the initiative was to explore how past and current events may be influencing preservice teachers' developing storied knowledge of bystanding and upstanding. All bystander WREs followed a format where preservice teachers narrated an event with a rich description, analyzed the event from varied perspectives, and reflected on the implications of the event for their future teaching. The first part of the WRE included a detailed description of the event with contextual information including grade level, location where the event occurred, participants present during the event (both observers and active participants), and a detailed description of the entirety of the event. Next, the preservice teachers analyzed the event(s) by explaining their internal dialogue and sense-making during the event, speculating about the reasons for why they and others chose to bystand or upstand and provided a description of not only their reaction to the event but also the reactions of the other individuals present. In the concluding section of their WREs, preservice teachers described their current understandings of the event, and what, if anything, they would want to change about the event, as well as how this reflection on the event(s) shaped their thinking about how teaching and issues of social (in)justice are connected.

Data Collection and Analysis

For this chapter, we analyzed a subset of 108 WREs (54 from preservice teachers' K-12 studenting days and 54 from their field-based practicums) that particularly focused on events involving emergent bilinguals (for analyses of other narrative sets see Carter et al., 2019). Our goal throughout this analysis was to provide a sense of the patterns in responses that preservice teachers crafted during their writing of their bystander WREs, how we used the bystander WRE as pedagogy, and how the WREs became the basis for further instruction. We analyzed the bystander narratives in order to understand and explore standard analytical narrative elements: (1) characters, (2) temporality of events, (3) place, (4) patterns of action, and (5) sociality or the dialectic interplay between one's inner and outer worlds (Clandinin et al., 2009).

Using iterative qualitative analysis techniques, including constant comparison methods (Bogdan & Biklen, 2006; Lichtman, 2012), we identified and coded patterns in the narratives. We used a combination of etic and emic codes (Goulding, 2005) to lift off the particulars of each narrative. Etic codes came from current literature about the bystander effect and narrative inquiry. Example etic codes included: the role of specific characters in the narrative, decision points in the plot, and/or a diffusion of responsibility contributing to one's decision to bystand (Clandinin et al., 2009; Darley & Latané, 1968). Emic codes resulted from a process of open coding across the corpus of narratives to identify patterns. For example, one prominent and recurring emotional pattern identified across the narratives was feelings of regret over not having intervened. Given the prevalence of this feeling in the retellings, we analyzed this subset of narratives to identify themes related to why these narrators continued to feel regret even, in some instances, many years after the event took place. Consistent with a narrative focus, we summarize the major findings into distinct thematic plot patterns that characterized the cumulative set of narratives. All names in the provided narrative excerpts are pseudonyms.

PLOT PATTERNS: HOW PRESERVICE
TEACHERS NARRATE THEIR DECISION(S)

We framed this chapter with the following questions: (1) how do preservice teachers narrate their experience(s) where they were a bystander to the marginalization and/or bullying of an emergent bilingual? And (2) how might bystander narratives be used in higher education classrooms to explore issues of social (in)justice through students' storied knowledge? In response, we first detail the three major plot patterns that we identified during our analyses. These plot patterns were titled with preservice teachers' own words taken from their narratives. Within each plot pattern, we provide illustrative narratives from preservice teachers' K-12 studenting days and/or field-based observations to illustrate the larger plot pattern before providing an analysis of preservice teachers' sense-making of the recalled events. Following this, we detail how we used these narratives as pedagogy in our higher education courses to engage preservice teachers in exploring bystander moments through a social justice lens.

Plot Pattern 1 "It Seemed so Complicated at the Time": Expressions of Regret and Self Protection

This plot pattern focused on 24 narrated events from the preservice teachers' own K-12 studenting days where the narrators were bystanders to the verbal and/or physical bullying of an emergent bilingual. In this plot pattern, there were stories about bullying events where the preservice teachers reported standing mute for a variety of reasons. While a majority of the preservice teachers were afraid of becoming targets of bullying themselves, others felt underprepared to effectively intervene.

Illustrative Narratives from Preservice Teachers' Remembered K-12 Schooling

In one illustrative incident, a preservice teacher (who was a fourth-grade student at the time) witnessed her peers physically bully an emergent bilingual while her class was on the playground. As the emergent bilingual was walking around the perimeter of the playground equipment, a group of native English-speaking boys ran up and pushed the student repeatedly into the mud while saying, "Go back to where you come from." The preservice teacher described feeling "horrified" but also unwilling to intervene because she did not want to become a target of the bullies. In her reflection on the event, she expressed regret by saying, "It seemed so complicated at the time, but it really was not" (Roxanne).

In another narrative, a preservice teacher (who was a third-grade student at the time) described an event involving her best friend during elementary school. María and her family had recently emigrated from Mexico and, reportedly, María quickly became a target for peers who would tease her for "her accent, her car, and the way she dressed" (Heather). The preservice teacher relating this story expressed sadness and regret over not having spoken up for her friend during the course of the year. However, the preservice teacher cited her own challenges with an ongoing speech impediment as being the motivating factor for her decision not to intervene because she was unsure of "what to do or say."

Preservice Teacher Sense-Making of Bystanding Then and for the Future

These narratives, taken together, portrayed a puzzling predicament for preservice teachers both in their past position as K-12 students and their current position in their teacher preparation programs. As preservice teachers reflected in their writing upon these events from their K-12 studenting days, their conflicting emotions were evident. While preservice teachers clearly expressed regret over their decision to remain a bystander, they often questioned if they would be able to intervene in similar events in their future pedagogy and practice with emergent bilinguals. In this set of narratives, preservice teachers' decision to bystand appeared to be related to their own desire for self-preservation and/or feelings of apprehension evaluation, or a lack of confidence in their ability to effectively intervene (Bierhoff, 2002; Hall et al., 2013). Looking forward, preservice teachers still continued to question whether or not they would know how to intervene in similar future events.

Plot Pattern 2 "The Teachers Were Not Doing Anything, Who Was I to Step In?" Looking in Vain for Teacher Intervention

This subset of 27 narratives came from the preservice teacher's K-12 studenting days and field-based experiences. A prominent pattern of teacher inaction existed in this data set as preservice teachers looked to teachers or other staff members as a model of how to react to events where emergent bilingual students were marginalized and/or bullied;

however, there was no witnessed intervention on the part of the adults present. Ultimately, these preservice teachers wondered if "the teachers were not doing anything, who was I to step in" (Jennifer).

Illustrative Narratives from Preservice Teachers' Remembered K-12 Schooling

Recalling their K-12 studenting days, preservice teachers wrote about looking to nearby teachers, monitors, staff, or any adult for intervention during marginalizing events involving their emergent bilingual peers. Preservice teachers wrote about their uncertainty in how they should react, and remembered hoping that nearby adults would take action and intervene. In one recalled narrative, a preservice teacher (in high school at the time) waited in vain for a teacher to "walk by" and intervene in the bullying of an emergent bilingual peer during lunchtime. Reportedly, a group of native English-speaking students verbally harassed the emergent bilingual and repeatedly called her "a stupid wetback." As the preservice teacher watched this event unfold, she continually looked to nearby teachers and monitors to intervene, but no adult came over. The harassment did not end until the emergent bilingual and her friends retreated to a nearby bathroom.

Illustrative Narratives from Preservice Teachers' Remembered Fieldwork

Similarly, when preservice teachers were in their field placements, they reported looking to their mentor teachers, and possibly other teachers present, for guidance on how to react. One preservice teacher recalled such an incident as the students in her placement classroom were returning from a fire drill. The school where the preservice teacher was completing her observations was set up with four classroom doors facing each other in an alcove. The preservice teacher recalled that all four fourth-grade teachers were busy at their doors directing students into their respective classrooms. As the preservice teacher helped her mentor teacher usher her students back into class, the preservice teacher noticed an interaction unfolding between a native English-speaking boy and an emergent bilingual student from Africa. The native English-speaking boy repeatedly advanced on the emergent bilingual saying, "You can't even talk right. No one likes you. Speak English." The emergent bilingual attempted to repel his aggressor by lightly pushing him away and saying, "cruel...stop." The preservice teacher recalled looking to the teachers who were ushering their students back into their own classrooms, but even though the preservice teacher felt the teachers were aware of the event, no one intervened. The preservice teacher attempted to explain this lack of intervention in terms of distraction, as "all of the teachers appeared to be engaged with returning their own students to their classrooms" (Angela).

Prospective Teacher Sense-Making of Bystanding Then and for the Future

This set of narratives echoed previous findings that individuals often look to others to model how to react to deleterious events (e.g., Bierhoff, 2002; Clark & Word, 1974; Manning et al., 2007). Adding to this work, this narrative pattern highlights the potential influence that teachers in schools can have when modeling how or even if to intervene in events where students are marginalized and/or bullied. Unfortunately, in these narratives, teacher intervention often did not appear. In reflecting on the event after the fact, preservice teachers reported that they were still unsure of whether or not they could and should intervene given that the teachers and monitors present during these past events remained bystanders as well. As Angela, the preservice teacher who witnessed the bullying of the African emergent bilingual during the fire drill, said, "This (bullying of an emergent bilingual) did not appear to be as high an issue on the social justice scale," therefore, the preservice teacher questioned whether or not she would intervene in similar events in her future practice.

Plot Pattern 3 "Better if He Remained Clueless to the Fact That He Was Being Mocked"

This final plot pattern illustrated the complicated emotions and thoughts that bystanders can experience when deciding whether or not to intervene in an injurious event involving individuals who are emergent bilinguals. In these 21 narrated events, drawn from preservice teachers' K-12 studenting days and teacher preparation programs, the decision to intervene in the verbal harassment of an emergent bilingual was all the more complicated because of the students' supposed "limited English" proficiency. These bystanders questioned if these events even warranted intervention given that the emergent bilingual "probably did not completely understand, so what they (aggressors) were saying was not as hurtful" (Gwen).

Illustrative Narratives from Preservice Teachers' Remembered K-12 Schooling

In one illustrative narrative from a participant's K-12 studenting days, a preservice teacher (high school student at the time) witnessed the very public and prolonged taunting of an emergent bilingual who was running for class president. The prolonged harassment culminated in a group of "popular varsity players" verbally assaulting the emergent bilingual during his campaign speech in front of the entire student body and teaching staff. The preservice teacher was sitting in the audience next to the bullies as they mocked the emergent bilingual who was attempting to give his campaign speech from the stage of the auditorium. She explained her own decision to not intervene in the moment by saying, "He (the student classified as an English Language Learner) thought these boys were his friends. Perhaps it would be better if he remained clueless" (Alex).

Illustrative Narratives from Preservice Teachers' Remembered Fieldwork

During their field-based observations, preservice teachers again explained their reluctance to intervene in terms of the emergent bilinguals' supposed English proficiency. In a final illustrative event, a preservice teacher observed a group of four elementary students, three of whom were native English-speakers and one who was an emergent bilingual student from China. The emergent bilingual student in the group repeatedly attempted to contribute ideas to the group project; however, his group mates consistently expressed misunderstanding and gave him "blank stares." Eventually, the three native English-speaking students decided to move on without the emergent bilingual, reportedly saying "he will just have to figure it out on his own; he can't even talk to us." The preservice teacher who observed this event reported being unsure of whether or not it would be appropriate to intervene because she was not sure if the emergent bilingual student understood his classmates' rebuke. Even though the preservice teacher reported "empathizing" with the student, she ultimately decided not to intervene because she felt that her intervention might have made the emergent bilingual student realize just how "hurtful" his peers' comments were.

*Prospective Teacher Sense-Making of Bystanding Then
and for the Future*

In this final plot pattern, the desire to intervene was further complicated for the narrators based on their perceptions of the emergent bilingual students' English proficiency. The uniqueness of the actors in these events (i.e., students who are learning English in schools with native English-speakers) provides a richer understanding of how the bystander effect can be heightened based on the perceived language proficiency of the marginalized or harassed individual. For these preservice teachers, an ascribed lack of English proficiency appears to have temporarily mitigated the potential harm that verbal harassment could have on emergent bilingual students. While some preservice teachers reported that they felt their previous lack of intervention as K-12 students made them more likely to intervene in future marginalizing events, the majority of the narrators in this plot pattern reported that they still felt their responsibility to intervene was negated because the emergent bilingual students themselves "did not understand what was happening" (Olivia).

In summary, across the three plot patterns preservice teachers shared their storied knowledge of why they decided to bystand during a potentially injurious event involving an emergent bilingual student. Our goal in this work with preservice teachers was not to call out or shame their past "decision-making model" (Latané & Darley, 1970). Rather, our goal was to engage preservice teachers in making sense of how these narrated events may be shaping their developing professional knowledge about emergent bilingual students and when, or even if, they should upstand in future injurious events. Therefore, we shift our focus from our use of narrative as a methodological tool for this study to narrative as pedagogy in the higher education classroom (Chafe 1990; Coulter et al., 2007; Egan, 1988; Tate, 1997; Wood, 2000).

Continuing the Conversation in Higher Education Settings: Using Narratives to Explore Issues of Social Justice

Through multiple rounds of course revision, the instructors sought to refine how they introduced and engaged preservice teachers in making sense of the bystander effect in relation to larger issues of social justice in and out of schools. Initially, the instructors assigned the bystander narratives as a course assignment and then had unstructured small group discussion time for preservice teachers to discuss what they wrote. However, it became clear that preservice teachers often continued to feel unsure of their ability to intervene in future events. Therefore, the instructors created the following instructional sequence where the bystander narratives became a starting point for discussion about ways to potentially upstand in the future.

During the class session that followed preservice teachers writing the bystander WREs, the instructors first focused on collectively unpacking why the preservice teachers decided to bystand or upstand during the events. By design, these small and whole group discussions connected the bystander effect to these preservice teachers' decision-making processes. The instructors then presented research about factors that could influence a person's decision to bystand or upstand. For preservice teachers, learning about this research appeared to be a "bumping place" (Clandinin et al., 2009) with their own narratives as they discovered resonance or dissonance with their own prior decisions. The instructors then introduced the question of whether or not individuals, and particularly teachers, had a responsibility to disrupt the marginalization and/or bullying of others, particularly historically marginalized students. As Banyard and colleagues (2004) argue, the bystander effect is often closely related to the socio-cultural norms of a community, and these bystander narratives became a tool for encouraging students to explore what norms may have been present in their school, and how they may have impacted their decision-making processes. For example, in the case of WREs involving emergent bilingual students, the classroom discussion connected to themes of racism, xenophobia (e.g., "Go back to where you come from" and linguicism, e.g., "You can't even talk right. No one likes you. Speak English"). By connecting these individual events to larger patterns of social injustice in society, preservice teachers explored how societal beliefs could have impacted their own thinking in the moment and possibly in the future.

Finally, the classroom discussion moved to brainstorming and sharing ways that preservice teachers could move from bystanders to upstanders in the future. The University of Arizona's facilitator guide, "Step Up: A prosocial behavior/bystander intervention program for students," was a useful reference for this discussion (see Suggestions for Further Readings). One example of a preservice teacher-generated idea that came up across the courses was the idea of setting an intention to intervene within the group. This intention could involve specific actions, such as to say something to the aggressor, walk over and start talking to the student being marginalized, or just a more generalized statement of preservice teachers' intention to attend to these potentially injurious events more closely in the future.

To summarize, this instructional sequence intentionally started with eliciting preservice teachers' storied knowledge (Huber et al., 2006; Sarbin, 1986) of bystanding, then connected to the larger research on the bystander effect, and finally moved to exploring how these individual instances might connect to larger themes of social (in)justice. In alignment with narrative inquiry as pedagogy, we grounded this work firmly in the actual lived experiences of preservice teachers in order to connect, question, and possibly redirect how the bystander effect impacts their decision-making process when witnessing potentially injurious events.

Next Steps and Future Directions

Based on extant scholarship regarding the bystander effect as well as our own findings, it is clear that upstanding is a complicated action. However, we hope that this instructional sequence helps provide a pathway for preservice teachers to explore how to move from regret to responsible intervention in higher education spaces *and* in the elementary schools where they will work. We believe that this exploration of previous bystander decisions may better attune preservice teachers' attention to potentially marginalizing or bullying events involving historically marginalized students, and prepare them to negotiate the potential influences of the bystander effect in the future.

Participant selection for this study and initiative focused on one group of higher education students, preservice teachers. Yet, the bystander WRE format (see Appendix A) could be revised to suit other academic disciplines and/or more general campus programming designed to disrupt the bystander effect on and off campus. For example, in STEM fields the bystander narrative format could be used to explore the marginalization of women in the STEM classroom, and possibly in the field at large, in an effort to attune students' vision to this marginalization and possibly encourage them to upstand in the future. Or, more general campus workshops could use the bystander narrative format to explore the marginalization of students of color on campus, and how an individual could productively disrupt marginalizing events in the future.

To do this, an instructor would first need to decide whether a bystander narrative was appropriate for their course and content. For example, the instructor could identify a relatively common phenomena of marginalization in their course or field where an individual or groups of individuals were treated deleteriously. Then, the instructor would have to decide whether or not a narrative methodology would be an appropriate pedagogical tool. For example, an instructor could ask themself if their students would benefit from critically analyzing and questioning their lived experiences in an effort to understand their decision-making during these deleterious events (Clandinin & Connelly, 2000; Connelly & Clandinin, 1994; Conle, 2003; Wood, 2000). If an instructor decides to implement the bystander narrative assignment, we have found that it can be helpful to explicitly explain that marginalization and discrimination can occur on a variety of scales and in different contexts. Therefore, it is important for students to think about deleterious interactions that involved overt aggression as well as interactions that involved microaggressions (Pierce, 1970). From there, students engage in individually writing their bystander narrative to recall and reflect on their past decisions. This individual writing lays the foundation for subsequent classroom discussions. During these discussions, the instructor(s) could intentionally plan to have students collectively discuss their previous bystander decisions, the lingering emotional, mental, and possibly physical reminders from these past decisions for both themselves and others involved, and how they might become upstanders in future events. We have found that these classroom discussions are important as they help students to collectively focus and refine their plans for future action and upstanding.

In our work with undergraduate preservice teachers, we have also found that naming the bystander phenomena and how it may have shaped students' prior decisions can be an agentive move as it attunes student vision to the influence of the bystander effect in deleterious interactions. In the future, more work and research are needed to explore how this intentional exploration of higher education students' narratives of previous decisions to bystand or upstand continues to shapes their current knowledge, beliefs, and potential actions. Ultimately, it is our hope that this work will support students as they reflect on often regret-laden bystander events in an intentional effort to become upstanders in the future.

Appendix A: Bystander/Upstander Well-Remember Event Assignment

Background

This assignment will help us develop our knowledge of issues of social (in)justice in our teaching, classrooms, and schools. For this assignment, you will focus on two separate but potentially relatable well-remembered events where you witnessed an emergent bilingual student being embarrassed, marginalized, shamed, and/or humiliated by others in a classroom or school setting. Your assignment is to write a paper of two well-remembered events, one from your own experience as a K-12 student and one from your field-based practicum placements. For your paper, you will include the following five parts (see write-up description section for specific prompts):

1. Description 1: A detailed description of the well-remembered event in which you were a witness to marginalization of a student. Please focus on an event where the student was an emergent bilingual and/or English Language Learner;
2. Analysis 1: An analysis of the event using the format below;
3. Description 2: A detailed description of a field-based well-remembered event in which you were a witness to the marginalization of a student who was an emergent bilingual and/or English Language Learner;
4. Analysis 2: An analysis of the event using the format below;
5. Implications: A reflection on the implications of these two events have on your thinking.

Write-Up Description

You will describe one personal well-remembered event and one field-based well-remembered event that focuses on an event you witnessed involving an emergent bilingual student. The events are ones that have stuck with you, likely for a myriad of reasons.

1. Event Description: Your description should be detailed and focused on the sequence of events and all participants in the event (the person who was shamed, humiliated, or bullied, you, as a witness/bystander, and others who also were witnesses to the event. Your description should provide a thorough description of the event

via rich, factual information pertinent to the event. You are to include contextual information (grade level, approximate number of student and/or teacher witnesses, physical location, and duration of the event).

2. Analysis of the Event: After *each* description revisits the event now thinking about the observers, yourself, and others, to the event. You should have two analyses sections, one for each event. In your analyses, please address each of the following areas:

   a. Verbalize your internal dialogue; i.e., witnessing the event, what were you thinking? What were you feeling? What were you worried about it? What did you anticipate would happen?
   b. How would you describe the reaction of others to this event, both verbal and non-verbal reactions? In other words, what did you hear and see?
   c. How many other people were witnesses to the event? What, if anything, did they do?
   d. What or whom were you attending to or focused on during this event?
   e. How did you decide whether or not to intervene and why? Please attempt to lay out the rationale for your decision.
   f. What do you think complicated the event for other witness who remained a bystander to the event?

3. Implications: Taking this pair of narratives in conjunction, how are you making sense of your thoughts, challenges, and/or beliefs related to teaching emergent bilingual students. Answer the following:

   a. Recalling these events, are you thinking about specific areas as you continue your journey in learning to teach? If so, please describe your thoughts.
   b. What, if anything, would you change about the event(s)?
   c. How have these events and your subsequent reflections affected, if at all, your thinking about teaching in a socially just way?
   d. What knowledge or skills do you wish to gain in order to teach all of your students more equitably?

References

Banyard, V. L., Moynihan, M. M., & Crossman, M. T. (2009). Reducing sexual violence on campus: The role of student leaders as empowered bystanders. *Journal of College Student Development, 50,* 446–457. https://doi.org/10.1353/csd.0.0083.

Banyard, V. L., Plante, E. G., & Moynihan, M. M. (2004). Bystander education: Bringing a broader community perspective to sexual violence prevention. *Journal of Community Psychology, 32,* 61–79. https://doi.org/10.1002/jcop.10078.

Barnes, A., Cross, D., Lester, L., Hearn, L., Epstein, M., & Monks, H. (2012). The invisibility of covert bullying among students: Challenges for school intervention. *Australian Journal of Guidance and Counseling, 22*(02), 206–226. https://doi.org/10.1017/jgc.2012.27.

Bierhoff, H. W. (2002). *Prosocial behaviour.* Psychology Press. https://www.kobo.com/us/en/ebook/prosocial-behaviour-1.

Bogdan, R. C., & Biklen, S. K. (2006). *Qualitative research for education: An introduction to theories and methods.* Pearson. https://eric.ed.gov/?id=ED419813.

Bruner, J. (1985). Narrative and paradigmatic modes of thought. In E. Eisner (Ed.), *Learning and teaching the ways of knowing* (pp. 97–115). University of Chicago Press. https://www.tcrecord.org/Content.asp?ContentId=19134.

Burn, S. M. (2009). A situational model of sexual assault prevention through bystander education. *Sex Roles, 60,* 779–792. https://digitalcommons.calpoly.edu/cgi/viewcontent.cgi?article=1030&context=psycd_fac.

Carter, K. (1993). The place of story in the study of teaching and teacher education. *Educational Researcher, 22*(1), 5–18. https://doi.org/10.3102/0013189X022001005.

Carter, K. (1994). Preservice teachers' well-remembered events and the acquisition of event-structured knowledge. *Journal of Curriculum Studies, 26*(3), 235–252. https://doi.org/10.1080/0022027940260301.

Carter, K., Sugimoto, A. T., Stoehr, K., & Carter, G. (2019). (Re)Storying school experience and transforming teacher education: Writing a new narrative for LGBTQ students. In L. Wilcox & C. Brant (Eds.), *Teaching the teachers: LGBTQ issues in teacher education.* American Educational Research Association. https://www.infoagepub.com/products/Teaching-the-Teachers.

Chafe, W. (1990). Some things that narrative tells us about the mind. In B. K. Britton & A. D. Pellegrini (Eds.), *Narrative thought and narrative language* (pp. 79–98). Erlbaum. http://dx.doi.org/10.4324/9781315808215.

Chekroun, P., & Brauer, M. (2002). The bystander effect and social control behavior: The effect of the presence of others on people's reactions to norm violations. *European Journal of Social Psychology, 32,* 853–867. https://doi.org/10.1002/ejsp.126.

Clandinin, J., & Connelly, M. (2000). *Narrative inquiry: Experience and story in qualitative research.* Jossey-Bass. https://www.wiley.com/en-us/Narrat ive+Inquiry%3A+Experience+and+Story+in+Qualitative+Research-p-978078 7972769.

Clandinin, D. J., Huber, J., Huber, M., Murphy, M. S., Orr, A. M., Pearce, M., & Steeves, P. (2006). *Composing diverse identities: Narrative inquiries into the interwoven lives of children and teachers.* Routledge. http://dx.doi.org/10.4324/9780203012468.

Clandinin, D. J., Murphy, M. S., Huber, J., & Orr, A. M. (2009). Negotiating narrative inquiries: Living in a tension-filled midst. *The Journal of Educational Research, 103*(2), 81–90. https://doi.org/10.1080/00220670903323404.

Clark, A. M. (1998). The qualitative-quantitative debate: Moving from positivism and confrontation to post-positivism and reconciliation. *Journal of Advanced Nursing, 27*(6), 1242–1249. https://doi.org/10.1046/j.1365-2648.1998. 00651.x.

Clark, R. D., III, & Word, L. E. (1974). Where is the apathetic bystander? Situational characteristics of the emergency. *Journal of Personality and Social Psychology, 29,* 279–287. https://doi.org/10.1037/h0036000.

Coker, A. L., Cook-Craig, P. G., Williams, C. M., Fisher, B. S., Clear, E. R., Garcia, L. S., et al. (2011). Evaluation of Green Dot: An active bystander intervention to reduce sexual violence on college campuses. *Violence Against Women, 17*(6), 777–796. https://doi.org/10.1177/1077801211410264.

Conle, C. (2003). An anatomy of narrative curricula. *Educational Researcher, 32*(3), 3–15. https://doi.org/10.3102/0013189X032003003.

Connelly, F. M., & Clandinin, D. J. (1990). Stories of experience and narrative inquiry. *Educational Researcher, 19*(5), 2–14. https://doi.org/10.3102/001 3189X019005002.

Connelly, F. M., & Clandinin, D. J. (1994). Telling teaching stories. *Teacher Education Quarterly, 21*(1), 145–158. https://www.jstor.org/stable/234 75539.

Connelly, F. M., & Clandinin, D. J. (1988). Teachers as curriculum planners: Narratives of experience. *Teachers College Press.* https://doi.org/10.1177/019263658907351318.

Coulter, C., Michael, C., & Poynor, L. (2007). Storytelling as pedagogy: An unexpected outcome of narrative inquiry. *Curriculum Inquiry, 37*(2), 103–122. https://doi.org/10.1111/j.1467-873X.2007.00375.x.

Darley, J. M., & Latane, B. (1968). Bystander intervention in emergencies: Diffusion of responsibility. *Journal of Personality and Social Psychology, 8*(4, Pt.1), 377–383. https://doi.org/10.1037/h0025589.

Davis, T., & Harrison, L. M. (2013). *Advancing social justice: Tools, pedagogies, and strategies to transform your campus.* Wiley. https://www.wiley.com/en-us/.

Egan, K. (1988). *Teaching as storytelling: An alternative approach to teaching and the curriculum.* London: Routledge. ISBN-13: 978-0226190327.

Espelage, D. L. (2015). Bullying and k-12 students. In G. L. Wimberely (Ed.), *LGBTQ issues in education: Advancing a research agenda* (pp. 105–120). American Educational Research Association. http://dx.doi.org/10.3102/978-0-935302-36-3.

Fischer, F. (1998). Beyond empiricism: Policy inquiry in post positivist perspective. *Policy Studies Journal, 26*(1), 129–146. https://doi.org/10.1111/j.1541-0072.1998.tb01929.x.

Garcia, S. M., Weaver, K., Moskowitz, G. B., & Darley, J. M. (2002). Crowded minds: The implicit bystander effect. *Journal of Personality and Social Psychology, 83*(4), 843–853. https://doi.org/10.1037/0022-3514.83.4.843.

Goldman, J. A., & Harlow, L. L. (1993). Self-perception variables that mediate AIDS-preventive behavior in college students. *Health Psychology, 12,* 489–498. https://doi.org/10.1037/0278-6133.12.6.489.

Goulding, C. (2005). Grounded theory, ethnography and phenomenology: A comparative analysis of three qualitative strategies for marketing research. *European Journal of Marketing, 39*(3/4), 294–308. https://doi.org/10.1108/03090560510581782.

Guba, E. G., & Lincoln, Y. S. (1994). Competing paradigms in qualitative research. In N. K. Denzin & Y. S. Lincoln (Eds.), *Handbook of qualitative research* (pp. 105–117). Sage. https://psycnet.apa.org/record/1994-98625-000.

Hall, A., Wooton, K., & Hutton, A. (2013). Bystander experiences at and after a motor vehicle accident: A review of the literature. *Australasian Journal of Paramedicine, 10*(4), 1–10. http://dx.doi.org/10.33151/ajp.10.4.54.

Huber, M., Clandinin, D. J., & Huber, J. (2006). Relational responsibilities of narrative inquirers. *Curriculum and Teaching Dialogue, 8,* 209–223. https://www.jstor.org/stable/24641962.

Ingersoll, R., Merrill, L., & Stuckey, D. (2014). Seven trends: The transformation of the teaching force. *Consortium for Policy Research in Education, 4,* 31. https://repository.upenn.edu/cpre_researchreports/108.

Jackson, P. W. (1990). *Life in classrooms.* Teachers College Press. https://lccn.loc.gov/2007001061.

Katz, J. (1994). *Mentors in Violence Prevention (MVP) trainer's guide.* Center for the Study of Sport in Society, Northeastern University. http://www.mvpstrat.com/.

Latané, B., & Darley, J. M. (1969). Bystander "apathy." *American Scientist, 57*(2), 244–268. https://www.truthaboutnursing.org/research/orig/latane_and_darley/bystander_apathy.pdf.

Latané, B., & Darley, J. M. (1970). *The unresponsive bystander: Why doesn't he help?* Prentice Hall. https://trove.nla.gov.au/work/21268623.

Latz, A. O., Ozaki, C. C., Royer, D. W., & Hornak, A. M. (2017). Student affairs professionals in the community college: Critically examining preparation programs from a social justice lens. *Community College Journal of Research and Practice, 41*(11), 733–746. https://doi.org/10.1080/10668926.2016.1222507.

Lichtman, M. (2012). *Qualitative research in education: A user's guide.* Sage. https://us.sagepub.com/en-us/nam/qualitative-research-in-education/book235144#contents.

Lortie, D. (1975). *Schoolteacher: A sociological study.* University of Chicago Press. https://doi.org/10.1177/002248717502600425.

Manning, R., Levine, M., & Collins, A. (2007). The Kitty Genovese murder and the social psychology of helping: The parable of the 38 witnesses. *American Psychologist, 62*(6), 555–562. https://doi.org/10.1037/0003-066X.62.6.555.

Noddings, N. (1991). Stories in dialogue: Caring and interpersonal reasoning. In C. Witherell & N. Noddings (Eds.), *Stories lives tell: Narrative and dialogue in education* (pp. 157–170). Teachers College Press. http://dx.doi.org/LB1027.3.S76.

Osanloo, A. F., & Boske, C. (Eds.). (2015). *Living the work: Promoting social justice and equity work in schools around the world.* Emerald Group Publishing.

Patton, L. D. (2010). *Culture centers in higher education: Perspectives on identity, theory, and practice.* Stylus Publishing. https://eric.ed.gov/?id=ED515056.

Phillips, D. C., & Burbules, N. C. (2000). *Postpositivism and educational research.* Rowman & Littlefield. https://psycnet.apa.org/record/2000-08253-000.

Pierce, C. M. (1970). Black psychiatry one year after Miami. *Journal of the National Medical Association, 62*(6), 471. https://www.ncbi.nlm.nih.gov/pmc/articles/PMC2611929/.

Sarbin, T. (1986). The narrative as a root metaphor for psychology. In T. R. Sarbin (Ed.), *Narrative psychology: The storied nature of human conduct* (pp. 3–21). Praeger. https://psycnet.apa.org/record/2001-18244-001.

Sugimoto, A. T., Carter, K., & Stoehr, K. (2017). Teaching "in their best interest": Preservice teachers' narratives regarding linguistically diverse students. *Teaching and Teacher Education, 67,* 179–188. https://doi.org/10.1016/j.tate.2017.06.010.

Tate, W. (1997). Critical race theory and education: History, theory, and implications. In M. Apple (Ed.), *Review of research in education* (pp. 195–247). American Educational Research Association. https://doi.org/10.3102/0091732X022001195.

Wood, D. R. (2000). Narrating professional development: Teachers' stories as texts for improving practice. *Anthropology & Education Quarterly, 31*(4), 426–448. https://doi.org/10.1525/aeq.2000.31.4.426.

Yoon, J. S., & Kerber, K. (2003). Bullying: Elementary teachers' attitudes and intervention strategies. *Research in Education, 69,* 27–35. https://doi.org/10.7227/RIE.69.3.

Suggestions for Further Reading

Caine, V., Steeves, P., Clandinin, D. J., Estefan, A., Huber, J., & Murphy, M. S. (2018). Social justice practice: A narrative inquiry perspective. *Education, Citizenship and Social Justice, 13*(2), 133–143. https://doi.org/10.1177/1746197917710235.

The University of Arizona CATS Life Skill Program. (2018). *Step UP: A prosocial behavior/bystander intervention program for students: Facilitator guide.* http://stepupprogram.org/docs/guides/18_StepUP_Guidebook-Print.pdf.

CHAPTER 14

Incorporating Antiracist Education Using Aspects of Asian American Studies to Teach About Race and Discrimination

Catherine Ma

KEY TERMS

Antiracist or antiracism education   An approach toward education where focus lies in examining power structures that promote and sustain racism within educational systems. Antiracist education originated in the United Kingdom in response to right-wing conservatives fighting against immigration. In the United States, antiracist

C. Ma (✉)
Kingsborough Community College,
The City University of New York, New York, NY, USA
e-mail: Catherine.Ma@kbcc.cuny.edu

© The Author(s), under exclusive license to Springer Nature
Switzerland AG 2021
C. C. Ozaki and L. Parson (eds.), *Teaching and Learning
for Social Justice and Equity in Higher Education*,
https://doi.org/10.1007/978-3-030-69947-5_14

	education originated from the Civil Rights Movement (Carr & Lund, 2008).
Antiracist	Anyone who actively supports antiracism through their thoughts, behaviors, and actions (Kendi, 2019).
Asian American Studies	An academic interdiscipline that focuses on the history, lived experiences, identities, politics, culture and current concerns of Asian Americans and people of Asian ancestry around the world (Wikipedia, 2020).
Black Lives Matter	The murder of Trayvon Martin in 2013 sparked the formation of the Black Lives Matter movement whose aim was to provide support for all Black lives while rallying against white supremacy, oppression, and violence. For more information please visit: https://blackl ivesmatter.com/about/.
Colin Kaepernick	A former National Football League quarterback known for his activism by kneeling during the national anthem to protest against police brutality against Black Americans and people of color. His activism has often been misconstrued by others as being un-American (Branch, 2017).
Residential school	An effective form of ethnic cleansing where Aboriginal children from Canada were separated from their families and forced to assimilate into Canadian society with a heavy emphasis on a Christian upbringing. These children

	were beaten for speaking in their native tongues, separated from siblings, sexually abused, psychologically damaged, starved, in addition to other atrocities. The last residential school closed in the late 1980s but their legacy of harm has continued to plague survivors in many ways. For more information, please visit: https://indigenousfoundations.arts.ubc.ca/the_residential_school_sys tem/.
Structural racism	This system can be viewed as a continuum of privilege where those who are afforded privilege are usually white and have access to opportunities, power, and benefits while the opposite is true for those who lie on the low end of this spectrum who are often people of color and disproportionately economically disadvantaged, lack power with little or no opportunities for advancement (Lawrence et al., 2004).
White privilege	Refers to the growing list of unearned benefits such as increased opportunities for advancement, access to quality education and healthcare, gainful employment, accruement of political representation, etc. that has historically been granted to white people to secure their legacy of power and influence (Lawrence et al., 2004).
The Yellow Peril	A danger to Western civilization from the expansion of the

	power and influence of Eastern Asian people; a threat to Western living standards from the influx of Eastern Asian laborers willing to work for very low wages (Merriam-Webster, n.d.).
1882 Chinese Exclusion Act	Stemming from anti-Chinese sentiment in 1882, this act enforced a decades-long moratorium restricting Chinese laborers from immigrating to the United States and denied current Chinese resident aliens the right to apply for citizenship (U.S. National Archives & Records Administration, n.d.).

As academics, we cannot turn a blind eye to racism in academia. The effects of white supremacy have been made more evident since Donald Trump became president in 2016, and the COVID-19 pandemic has only further exacerbated already racist policies that increase the disparities between the rich and poor. These tensions came to a head in 2020 when protests against police brutality after the deaths of George Floyd and Breonna Taylor spread across the United States. Those protests reignited the Black Lives Matter (BLM) movement and, perhaps for the first time for some white Americans, brought to the forefront the blatant racial disparities and inequities experienced by communities of color (Brown, 2020). Discussions about race have often been fraught. As children, many grew up being hushed by our parents or told it was rude to discuss race. Yet, the events of 2020 and the associated momentum emphasize the pressing need to address the racism inherent in our educational system now. We can no longer ignore the longstanding racist history of our education system and the growing evidence of the disparities in how people of color are treated.

The idea for this chapter came about from my psychology of immigration course where I teach about race and discrimination. Through teaching this course, I found that students wanted and needed a safe space to discuss their experiences with race in not just this class but in all my classes. It seems ironic that I teach about race and discrimination in the US higher education system, an institution that has a long history of racist policies. Due to this irony, the application of an antiracist standpoint seems fitting for the task at hand. Choosing not to be racist is woefully inadequate. Instructors must work toward learning how to be antiracist, which requires them to take a close look at their biases and commit to being antiracist by changing thoughts, behaviors, and actions (Kendi, 2019). In this chapter, I apply elements of antiracism education and aspects of Asian American Studies (AAS) to teach my students about race and discrimination. There has never been a time when this book has been more needed in the fight toward social justice and equity, and I hope educators who read this chapter will make that commitment with me as we use our power as faculty to steadily chip away at racism.

WHY ANTIRACISM?

To support a social justice and equity model of education, this chapter takes an antiracist approach where the focus is on dismantling racist policies that favor dominant groups with educational advantages, structural racism, and political power over groups that do not share these benefits (e.g., marginalized and people of color; Carr & Lund, 2008). In this sense, structural racism is defined as a robust system that maintains racial hierarchies, public policies, and institutional practices that propagate racial inequalities and inequities for people of color (Lawrence et al., 2004). History is at a crossroad in 2021, and educators can play a crucial role in teaching students and colleagues ways to make society a more inclusive space through an antiracist curriculum (Henry & Tator, 1994).

To make the biggest impact with the limited space in this chapter, I emphasize three elements of antiracist education: (1) creating a classroom that is conducive to discussing race by fostering open dialogues and inclusive spaces, (2) promoting civic engagement as a path to awareness and activism, and (3) incorporating current events into lesson plans. In some sections, narratives from students, who have all given me permission to use their words, have been included to offer their perspectives. These narratives are from an Institutional Review Board-approved (IRB File #2017-0546) research project to assess what students learned from participating in my psychology of immigration course. I hope that by sharing my experiences in the classroom, other academics can learn how to integrate aspects of an antiracist pedagogy into their curriculum to transform our educational systems to be more inclusive.

Fostering Open Dialogues to Discuss Race

A key element of antiracist education is to foster open dialogues because there is a long history of marginalized voices being silenced and excluded. This is a valid concern among many academics who teach in racially diverse universities that tout the merits of diversity and inclusion but often fail to support faculty in creating a safe environment to teach these topics (Booker & Campbell-Whatley, 2018; Merryfield, 2000). According to the National Center for Education Statistics, academia is still overwhelmingly homogenous with 75% of full-time faculty identifying as white; the statistics are especially bleak for Asian/Pacific Islander associate professors, who represent a paltry 5% of all professors (Hussar et al., 2020). As a Chinese associate professor who falls into that aggregate category, I know that the percentage of associate professors like me is just a fraction of that 5%. I find it bittersweet to hear from students that I am their very first Asian professor.

This underrepresentation means that faculty of color have added service expectations both as a consequence of and a cause of their underrepresentation in higher education. Maton et al. (2011) found that students of color prefer mentors who share similar cultural backgrounds, which overextends professors of color by taking time away from their research and publications which are critical for promotion and tenure. Further, as discussed by Williams (2019), racial climates in academia consistently create challenges for faculty of color. Those challenges range from partialities in student evaluations against women faculty of color, ignoring the history of marginalized groups, micro/macroaggressions from students and faculty, to departmental climates that are governed by dominant groups who obstruct all attempts at structural change. Some faculty are even bullied by students resulting in uncomfortable classroom settings (May & Tenzek, 2018; Ozkilic & Kartal, 2012). One semester, a threatening white student argued with me during class, challenging me as he yelled, "Honey, you can't teach!" Women professors of color are often viewed as intellectually inferior and more likely to be disrespected in class by their white students (Yancy, 2014). The class was stunned silent as I looked him dead straight into his menacing eyes and told him sternly, "Never call me honey, and there is no law that requires you to take this class with me." He stormed out of the classroom, I continued teaching my lesson, and he dropped my class the following day. Yet, I know colleagues whose students did not drop their classes and continued their harassment. Being Chinese I also have the exhausting task to continually debunk Asian stereotypes of being demure and submissive to students and faculty, but I use these experiences in class to highlight antiracism by examining the origins of these stereotypes, how race influences one's attitudes, and ways to counter these biases and racial tensions—when I do that, I seek to create and foster open dialogues about race.

The rationale for encouraging open dialogue is tied to antiracism's focus on examining the history of excluding marginalized voices. Neider (2020) critiques how higher education has shrugged its responsibility to eradicate white supremacy and suggests ways educators can incorporate antiracism into their pedagogy. She proposes including readings and texts by authors of color and incorporating assignments that center on the experiences of marginalized groups. She also recommends examining the racial history of our disciplines to identify inequities that continue to exist (e.g., low percentages of tenured faculty of color in academia) and work to dispel racial stereotypes and misconceptions. She underscores the importance of confronting micro/macroaggressions as they occur in the classroom or on campus because ignoring racist comments shows students that such behavior is acceptable. Faculty can no longer be complicit with silence and must incorporate ways to give voice to those who have been continually ignored to be actively antiracist. We must also relieve faculty of color of the burden of teaching everyone on issues related to race and racism and hold individuals responsible for educating themselves, a major tenet of antiracism. Too often this invisible and time-consuming work takes away valuable time from the tenure and promotion files of faculty of color. Lastly, in light of significant budget cuts stemming from the pandemic, priority in funding must be set aside to protect faculty of color who are often the first to be let go (Neider, 2020). We cannot engage in truly open dialogues if everyone does not have a seat at the table. To begin incorporating antiracism into our classrooms, we start by creating a classroom environment where students feel safe and included.

CREATING AN INCLUSIVE CLASSROOM ENVIRONMENT

An inclusive classroom is a critical facet of antiracist education because students want and need a safe space to share their thoughts on race and discrimination—to have an open dialogue (Roberts et al., 2008). However, many students may feel afraid of being judged, and professors want to know how to keep discussions respectful. Creating this safe space entails strong classroom management skills and self-awareness to not take certain statements personally but to use them as pedagogic moments for discussion. Educators also need to embrace flexibility to stop a lesson and address issues as they arise. This section will highlight three ways to support faculty by focusing on how to address hate speech, building rapport in class, and detailing a lesson on inclusivity.

Civility Clauses in the Syllabus

First, it is imperative to firmly state in the syllabus that any form of hate speech will not be tolerated, and remind students that these are non-negotiable terms. Some universities may have civility clauses and professors can add those policies into their syllabi. Meires (2018) suggests that student incivility is a precursor to bullying faculty, so any attempts to curtail this behavior will protect professors. It may be helpful to distinguish between freedom of speech and hate speech to reinforce these rules. Although hate speech is protected by the first amendment, professors can remind students that universities are obligated to create an environment that fosters tolerance and mutual respect among members of the campus community (American Civil Liberties Union, 2020). In other words, students are free to express their freedom of speech but if it is infused with hate, there will be consequences such as a visit from our conduct officer and possible expulsion. Addressing civility and freedom of speech is most effective when done on the first day of class to set clear rules on classroom conduct. Professors should be assertive in tone to convey to students that these are hard rules with no room for negotiation.

An effective and logical lesson to follow these rules is one I use to teach critical thinking. This lesson is the first scheduled lecture in my psychology of immigration class. During this lecture, students and I discuss the definition of critical thinking, its importance, differences between equality/equity and facts/opinions, and engage in small group exercises that encourage students to think outside of the box. For many students, critical thinking can help them be more comfortable negotiating the grey areas, such as seeing that loved ones can espouse racist views. Teachers whose pedagogy promoted critical thinking resulted in students who relied less on stereotypes and showed lower levels of anti-immigrant sentiment (Hjerm et al., 2018). In addition to a curriculum that incorporates critical thinking, small group work can also foster open dialogue by exposing students to others who are different from them.

Building Camaraderie

Secondly, ice-breaker exercises can create a safe and inclusive classroom where students can get to know one another by asking them to post an online introduction of who they are, their preferred learning style, and a goal for the semester. This exercise allows me to foster a sense of inclusion by adapting my pedagogy to help them learn more effectively. I also gently remind students to only post what they feel comfortable in sharing with the class, and I have noticed that many long-lasting friendships that have extended beyond the classroom from this exercise. I am always the first to post my introduction to encourage students to post theirs and offer them an example to follow. Although this exercise is voluntary, most students do comply, especially with a few points of extra credit. I often rely on these introductions to remember faces in the classroom which helps build rapport.

As a Chinese immigrant, first generation college graduate, and woman professor, I find using my personal experiences of discrimination and racism as teaching opportunities sets an important tone in the class. Many students are shocked to learn that I am not immune to racism and hearing my own accounts helped validate their personal experiences. Andersen (1988) notes how the curriculum needs to be more inclusive of women of color as a radical way to decentralize the white man Eurocentric standard that is still prevalent in the academy. Often students mentioned how grateful they were that we discussed a particular topic or when I shared some of my difficulties in school because they were able to relate to similar circumstances. Each professor will have their own level of comfort in sharing personal details about their lived experiences, and each semester may entail a different dynamic between students. I have noticed that sharing a little bit of my life has had a positive impact on generating a sense of inclusion among my students.

Sharing personal experiences in dealing with racism also has cultivated a greater understanding and helped students process emotionally-laden topics. To put a face on racism reassured students who experienced similar acts and educated those who had not experienced this hatred. One student shared "*I always knew racism existed but was never exposed to it myself. After taking this class and hearing how my classmates of different races were exposed to different situations of racism really opened my eyes.*" One semester, I had an older white student in my immigration class who mentioned that learning about the topics in class led to his own antiracist awakening where he changed the way he viewed his behaviors and thoughts toward others who were different from him. His reaction led me to be aware of my own biases of older students. I have changed the way I view older students and often share my experience with other colleagues who share similar biases. Making conscious and equitable decisions to be self-aware of our own biases is a key element of antiracism and can transform not only students but also faculty.

Lesson on Inclusivity

Thirdly, a lesson that helped foster inclusion was inviting students to describe ways to create a fundamental sense of safety in their home or community. This exercise consisted of having students share two pictures—one that made them feel safe and another that made them feel unsafe. I began by sharing my own pictures of an Asian supermarket that questioned my authenticity as a Chinese person who speaks English without an accent, and my favorite restaurant in Chinatown that is very welcoming, knows my favorite dishes, and treats my children with respect. As students shared their pictures, we discussed the commonalities of safe and unsafe spaces, and they felt more comfortable revealing acts of discrimination in their unsafe spaces. One African American student shared how she was stopped by a Caucasian police officer as she drove through a white neighborhood, who accused her of running a red light when she knew she had stopped. For students to hear these testimonies from their peers can be more powerful than any lecture from faculty (Edwards, 2014). Hearing firsthand accounts of racism helped students who have little experience with discrimination gain a fuller understanding of the daily micro/macroaggressions people of color face and encouraged them to feel comfortable in sharing their own experiences of discrimination (Sue et al., 2009). Creating a space for students to share these experiences can become a constructive starting point in how to encourage a more tolerant and inclusive classroom environment. This starting point requires the instructor to reinforce the aspects of antiracism that value lived experiences and validate to marginalized populations that their experiences of discrimination are real. One student remarked that my immigration class *"was a respected environment from the professor on down to the students. I felt it gave people a platform who thought they didn't have a voice and encouraged them to be themselves, despite the naysayers."* Her narrative suggests that students need and want classes that tackle these difficult subjects, because it may be their only chance to have their experiences of marginalization be validated. Once a safe and inclusive foundation is established, it becomes easier to discuss race and discrimination in class, and a potential outcome is a heightened sense of civic engagement.

Encouraging Civic Engagement

Exposing students to antiracism may empower them to challenge the status quo as they learn the history of oppression in education and become adept at discussing topics related to race. Hearing how their peers experienced numerous acts of injustice created a class dynamic that empowered them to fight as a unified front. Cole and Zhou (2014) found a positive effect between student diversity experiences and their development of civic engagement that included increased cultural awareness, reduction in prejudicial views, and greater racial consciousness. The benefits of diversity-related curricula are not new, and its growing research has found that students reap the most benefits with improved racial and cultural engagement (Denson & Chang, 2009).

Diversify Course Readings

To include authors of color in one's course required reading list is a small yet impactful decision faculty can implement into their curriculum that is vital to practicing antiracism. Readings that have been helpful in this area in my courses have focused on minority advocacy groups and how immigrants survive in America while openly discriminated against. One student noted how my immigration class empowered him and instilled a sense of civic engagement to help Bangladeshi people who do not have a voice—"*I motivated myself to work with them because I am a legal immigrant and I thought [helping others] is my duty as well.*" This student advocated for immigrants who lacked healthcare and found numerous agencies/foundations that sought to remedy this problem. Readings and lectures that focus on the struggles of marginalized individuals and the privileges we take for granted can have a transformative effect on our students making them more civically engaged and sensitive to the needs of others. This mirrors aspects of antiracism.

Choosing readings by authors of color or videos with people of color encourages critical thinking and highlights ways to deal with racial tensions. For example, in my psychology of immigration class, learning about residential schools where Indigenous children were forcibly assimilated into the dominant culture led to a critical examination of how the American educational system is based on Western society, culture, and values. After this lesson, a student asked, "*Why don't Indigenous people assimilate into American culture?*" This student's reaction is not new; there are numerous viral videos of white English speakers harassing people speaking in their native language and yelling at them to speak English because they are living in America (Levenson et al., 2018). Kendi (2019) classified assimilationist thinking as racist because it places white people as the standard everyone should strive toward and measure oneself against. I used this student's question as a teaching moment by stating that the real question we should be asking is why we ask this of Indigenous people when they were here first and once the dominant culture. This critique helped students recognize how structural racism stemming from a Eurocentric perspective has shaped our educational system for so long that we have forgotten that Indigenous people were our predecessors (Sue, 2010).

Lesson on Civic Engagement

A lesson that was effective in encouraging civic engagement began by asking students why the popular online shopping platform, eBay shuts down for approximately two weeks around the end of January through early February. To further engage their curiosity, I showed the documentary, Last Train Home by Lixin Fan (2009) which centers on the lives of migrant workers in China. Due to poverty and a lack of local jobs, many parents in China leave their children and become migrant workers who live in the cramped quarters of their factories for 50 weeks out of the year. It is only during the two weeks of Chinese New Year are they allowed to return home to spend time with their families. This film underscored many of the privileges we take for granted living in America, and students saw with more clarity how seeing their family on a daily basis was indeed a luxury. One student wrote, "*This semester in my Psychology class, I've learned many important things that have opened my eyes. [sic] I learned so much more about the lives of Asians and all the struggles they have gone through just to support their kids so they can live a better life than they did. I will use this information to go out [of] my way and use the privileges that I have, that some don't and help others. Even if it means donating to families that are struggling with supporting their family here or if their [they're] back home. Or just by visiting the programs and organizations that help immigrant kids and volunteer there.*" Learning about the struggles of immigrants can ignite a strong sense of civic engagement while encouraging students to gain a broader understanding of the struggles of different cultures.

In addition, faculty can support antiracism in their classrooms by using examples of injustice to teach about the origins of many grassroots advocacy groups that continue to fight for minority rights. I've taught about the murder of Vincent Chin which was the catalyst in forming the Committee Against Anti-Asian Violence which still mobilizes and advocates against institutional racism in the United States.

Incorporating Current Events into Lesson Plans

With the increasing number of racist events on the news that include African countries called derogatory names and COVID-19 referred to as a Chinese virus, educators can use these events as teaching opportunities to emphasize the enduring effects of racism (Chapman, 2020; Rogers et al., 2020). To teach about stereotypes, prejudice, and discrimination, I used two key social issues that were prevalent in the news at that time—Colin Kaepernick's silent protest and the Black Lives Matter (BLM) movement in my introduction to psychology course. These topics provided a great opportunity to teach about white privilege and structural racism, address the concerns of many students under the Trump presidency, and encourage students to think critically while instilling in them hope that the current racial climate can change.

By bringing up the Yellow Peril, the 1882 Chinese Exclusion Act and tying them to the current view of Chinese Americans as the Model Minority (although the students and I discussed the inherent problems of being labeled as such), I sought to give students insight into the trajectories of other groups of color who have also been historically oppressed, openly discriminated against, and killed because of the color of their skin (Lee, 2015; Wu, 2014). Integrating the history of Chinese Americans into this lesson on discrimination provided a concrete example for marginalized students to see that stereotypes can change and shift to serve the purposes of those in power. For example, Chinese people can be labeled as the Model Minority and in an instant, be vilified as harborers of COVID-19 (Rogers et al., 2020). Linking these historical and current events can be an empowering act for many students as shown by their suggestions on how to challenge robust negative stereotypes through higher education, political consciousness, civic engagement, and lobbying for just laws. Unpacking these current events can help students comprehend the world around them while empowering them to use their knowledge to work toward change. One student stated, "*I also feel like the timing that I took this class was good because now that Trump is president I feel like it was good I got to hear how other students in my class feel and are handling it and how it may have affect[ed] their lives and it kind of gives me hope knowing that someone from my generation will eventually be running for president and hopefully try to abolish race issues within America.*" This response highlights the civic mindedness of taking an antiracist stand and motivating students to advocate for themselves and others based on injustices occurring around them.

Colin Kaepernick, Ferguson Is Everywhere, and Black Lives Matter

To highlight recent events and introduce students to structural racism, students were assigned to read "Colin Kaepernick's real problem: He's not white" (Maxwell, 2016), and the chapter, "Ferguson is Everywhere" (Iyer, 2015). The reading on Kaepernick highlights how a football player's silent protest could evoke so much hostility while Trump's blatant criticism of America was considered an acceptable rhetoric. The chapter, "Ferguson is Everywhere" enabled students to see that Black lives are on the lowest rung of the racial hierarchy. My goals with assigning these readings were to nurture civic engagement, connect the historical struggles of marginalized groups, understand systemic racism, and value the unification of marginalized voices. As a note of caution, it is imperative for educators to be nonjudgmental and allow students to voice their beliefs/opinions because this is where the greatest learning opportunities lie. Do not be alarmed when students dissent. Indeed, as I explore next, student responses to each reading provided opportunities to challenge traditional notions of race and racism.

Colin Kaepernick's Real Problem: He's Not White

Kaepernick was a quarterback for the National Football League and fired for refusing to stand during the national anthem which is played before every game. His actions have been misconstrued by many as contempt for the American flag. While we discussed Kaepernick after reading the article, one white student said it was disrespectful to not stand for the Star-Spangled Banner. A student of color countered that opinion with the fact that the lyrics were written during a historical period that reeked of racial inequality (Campisi & Willingham, 2018). As a class, I facilitated a discussion that sought to reinforce the differences between facts and opinions, and we discussed how a silent and nonviolent protest could be twisted as "un-American" when Kaepernick's intention was never to disrespect the American flag but to underscore the unfair treatment of Black Americans. As a result of our discussions and the reading, students learned how his personal beliefs resulted in the loss of numerous sponsors and the end of his football career but sparked the beginning of his political consciousness. As the instructor, it was critical that I allowed that student to voice what most people were thinking regarding the misinterpretation of Kaepernick's protest and, then, taking the time to dissect, examine, and discuss. This is also evidence of how much educators are needed to clarify these inaccuracies and teach students how race intersects every aspect of our lives.

Ferguson Is Everywhere and Black Lives Matter

The BLM movement continues to be an excellent exemplar to teach about structural racism in all my classes. To begin a conversation on the BLM movement, students read Iyer's (2015) chapter, which attests to the robustness of a racial hierarchy where Black lives are on the lowest rung; Iyer emphasizes the value of uniting people of color to fight for structural changes in a system that is unfair to them. To rally against this racist hierarchy and promote antiracism, students need to focus on attributing disparities not to individual racial-ethnic groups but to racist policies that continually keep marginalized groups oppressed (Kendi, 2019). After reading the chapter, students were asked to share their reactions to the name, Black Lives Matter, and they conflated the BLM movement with Blue Lives Matter and All Lives Matter. It was critical for me to allow students to respond openly where educators and fellow students can address why people respond in this manner and help students understand the effects of racist policies. For example, one student noted how BLM recognized that people of color never had the same opportunities as white people because racism is so ingrained in our daily living that people do not realize these structural inequalities even exist, and that is why we hear people say Blue/All Lives Matter. Another student responded that blue is not a skin color, that being a police officer is a choice, and cops can take off their uniforms at the end of their shifts. In discussing racial hierarchies, students recognized the value of supporting the BLM movement because when the lives of the individuals at the lowest rung of the social ladder truly matter, that is the only way all lives will matter (Iyer, 2015). These responses provided evidence of how students can discuss and provide insight into common misapprehensions and stereotypes, but to have those conversations, it is vital for professors to open the dialogue and provide a safe space for those discussions.

While discussing race and racism, be prepared for students with white privilege to feel discomfort, but do not feel obligated to assuage their guilt because a part of antiracism is to learn how to feel uncomfortable with racist policies. Lee (2014) suggests that allowing white students to feel guilt and unease for a longer period can evoke lasting behavioral change. An effective follow-up to a difficult discussion about racism can be a writing exercise where students are prompted to address how they feel about the dialogue. Professors can make this an anonymous writing assignment or break students up into small groups for a discussion. With the COVID-19 pandemic, there have been many more exemplars of structural racism especially communities of color facing increased mortality rates. Immigrant communities, low income, and people of color have suffered disproportionately from COVID-19, and many of these inequities can be used as examples of racist policies that continue to reinforce this disparity (Correal & Jacobs, 2020; Kendi, 2019). It is vital for professors to utilize an antiracist education where we examine racist policies that devalue Black lives and work on challenging our biases in how we interpret current events that disproportionately harm certain racial-ethnic groups over others.

Conclusion

These are unprecedented times. We are witnessing real structural change; racist progress leads to racial change (Kendi, 2019). Throughout this chapter, I have offered a glimpse into the impact of how using an antiracist pedagogy can create a deeper understanding of the complexities regarding race and discrimination. By incorporating readings on AAS and race into my psychology classes, students developed a deeper view of racism and discrimination, connected the historical oppression of Asian Americans to current events of structural racism, and became more civic-minded. Through sharing my own experiences of discrimination and marginalization, students felt safer to divulge their experiences, which validated their own familiarities with racism. For academics who feel uncomfortable addressing issues of race and discrimination, the suggestions in this chapter can provide a useful roadmap of how to tackle these topics in their classrooms. Using an antiracist framework, educators can facilitate open dialogues that acknowledge the history of racist policies that blind us to Eurocentric biases that disregard marginalized voices. We can also learn to see with more clarity our own biases and make a commitment to change our own world views. On the receiving end, antiracism education benefits our students by broadening their pluralistic experiences, fostering their critical thinking, and clarifying how racist power structures continue the divide between the haves and the have-nots. Lastly, academics must remember how critical it is to incorporate an antiracist pedagogy in our curriculum because we are shaping the next generation of students to fight for social justice and equity. Applying an antiracist curriculum allows both educators and students to see how racism is embedded into the very core of American society and resistant to change but it also gives us hope that racist identities are not fixed. With each change we make in our daily lives toward antiracism, we slowly change ourselves and our students for the better.

References

American Civil Liberties Union. (2020, June). *Speech on campus*. https://www. aclu.org/other/speech-campus?redirect=other/hate-speech-campus.

Andersen, M. (1988). Moving our minds: Studying women of color and reconstructing sociology. *Teaching Sociology, 16*(2), 123–132.

Asian American Studies. (2020, June 11). In *Wikipedia*. https://en.wikipedia. org/wiki/Asian_American_studies#cite_ref-5.

Black Lives Matter. (2020, June). https://blacklivesmatter.com/about/.

Booker, K. C., & Campbell-Whatley, G. D. (2018). How faculty create learning environments for diversity and inclusion. *InSight: A Journal of Scholarly Teaching, 13*, 14–27.

Branch, J. (2017). The awakening of Colin Kaepernick. *The New York Times*. https://nyti.ms/2xedUYz.

Brown, D. (2020, June). 'It was a modern-day lynching': Violent deaths reflect a brutal American legacy. *National Geographic*. https://www.nationalgeog raphic.com/history/2020/06/history-of-lynching-violent-deaths-reflect-bru tal-american-legacy/.

Campisi, J., & Willingham, A. J. (2018, July). Behind the lyrics of 'The Star-Spangled Banner'. *CNN*. https://www.cnn.com/interactive/2018/07/us/national-anthem-annotated/.

Canadian Broadcasting Corporation. (2015). *Stolen children | Residential school survivors speak out*. [Video]. *YouTube*. https://www.youtube.com/watch?v=vdR9HcmiXLA.

Carr, P., & Lund, D. (2008). Antiracist education. In *SAGE Encyclopedia of Cultural and Social Foundations of Education* (pp. 48–52). Sage.

Chapman, B. (2020, April 2). New York City sees rise in Coronavirus hate crimes against Asians. *The Wall Street Journal*. https://www.wsj.com/articles/new-york-city-sees-surge-incoronavirus-hate-crimes-against-asians-11585828800.

Cole, D., & Zhou, J. (2014). Do diversity experiences help college students become more civically minded? Applying Banks' multicultural education framework. *Innovative Higher Education, 39*(2), 109–121.

Correal, A., & Jacobs, A. (2020, April 9). 'A tragedy is unfolding': Inside New York's virus epicenter. *The New York Times*. https://nyti.ms/2JTeUFO.

Denson, N., & Chang, M. J. (2009). Racial diversity matters: The impact of diversity-related student engagement and institutional context. *American Educational Research Journal, 46*(2), 322–353.

Edwards, K. T. (2014). "The whiteness is thick": Predominantly white classrooms, students of color voice, and Freirian hopes. In G. Yancy & M. del Guadalupe Davidson (Eds.), *Exploring race in predominantly white classrooms: Scholars of color reflect* (pp. 17–30). Routledge.

Fan, L. (Director). (2009). *Last train home*. [Film]. Zeitgeist Films.

Henry, F., & Tator, C. (1994). Racism and the university. *Canadian Ethnic Studies, 26*(3), 74–90.

Hjerm, M., Johansson Sevä, I., & Werner, L. (2018). How critical thinking, multicultural education and teacher qualification affect anti-immigrant attitudes. *International Studies in Sociology of Education, 27*(1), 42–59.

Hussar, B., Zhang, J., Hein, S., Wang, K., Roberts, A., Cui, J., Smith, M., Bullock Mann, F., Barmer, A., & Dilig, R. (2020). *The condition of education 2020* (NCES 2020-144). U.S. Department of Education. Washington, DC: National Center for Education Statistics. https://nces.ed.gov/pubsearch/pubsinfo.asp?pubid=2020144.

Iyer, D. (2015). *We too sing America: South Asian, Arab, Muslim, and Sikh immigrants shape our multiracial future*. The New Press.

Kendi, I. X. (2019). *How to be an antiracist*. One World.

Lawrence, K., Sutton, S., Kubisch, G., & Fulbright-Anderson, K. (2004). *Structural racism and community building*. The Aspen Institute, Roundtable on Community Change.

Lee, E. (2015). *The making of Asian America: A history*. Simon & Schuster.

Lee, J. (2014). Teaching white settler subjects antiracist feminism. In G. Yancy & M. del Guadalupe Davidson (Eds.), *Exploring race in predominantly white classrooms: Scholars of color reflect* (pp. 62–78). Routledge.

Levenson, E., Murphy, P., & Mezzofiore, G. (2018, May 17). New York attorney in racist rant has history of confrontations. *CNN*. https://www.cnn.com/2018/05/17/us/aaron-schlossberg-attorney-racist-rant/index.html.

Maton, K. I., Wimms, H. E., Grant, S. K., Wittig, M. A., Rogers, M. R., & Vasquez, M. J. (2011). Experiences and perspectives of African American, Latina/o, Asian American, and European American psychology graduate students: A national study. *Cultural Diversity and Ethnic Minority Psychology, 17*(1), 68.

Maxwell, F. (2016). Colin Kaepernick's real problem: He's not white. *The Huffington Post*. http://www.huffingtonpost.com/entry/colin-kaepernicks-real-problem-hes-not-white_us_57c6f912e4b0b9c5b7361eef.

May, A., & Tenzek, K. E. (2018). Bullying in the academy: Understanding the student bully and the targeted "stupid, fat, mother fucker" professor. *Teaching in Higher Education, 23*(3), 275–290.

Meires, J. (2018). Workplace incivility: When students bully faculty. *Urologic Nursing, 38*(5), 251–255.

Merriam-Webster. (n.d.). Yellow peril. *Merriam-Webster*. https://www.merriam-webster.com/dictionary/yellow%20peril.

Merryfield, M. M. (2000). Why aren't teachers being prepared to teach for diversity, equity, and global interconnectedness? A study of lived experiences in the making of multicultural and global educators. *Teaching and Teacher Education, 16*(4), 429–443.

National Museum of African American History and Culture. (n.d.). Talking about race. *Smithsonian*. https://nmaahc.si.edu/learn/talking-about-race/topics/being-antiracist.

Neider, X. N. (2020, June 14). The responsibility of higher education to eradicate white supremacy. *Grouchyinparadise*. https://grouchyinparadise.com/2020/06/14/the-responsibility-of-higher-education-to-eradicate-white-supremacy/.

Ozkilic, R., & Kartal, H. (2012). Teachers bullied by their students: How their classes influenced after being bullied? *Procedia-Social and Behavioral Sciences, 46*, 3435–3439.

Roberts, R., Bell, L., & Murphy, B. (2008). Flipping the script: Analyzing youth talk about race and racism. *Anthropology & Education Quarterly, 39*(3), 334–354.

Rogers, K., Jakes, L., & Swanson, A. (2020, March 19). Trump defends using 'Chinese Virus' label, ignoring growing criticism. *New York Times*. https://nyti.ms/33spVXu.

Sue, D. W. (2010). *Microaggressions in everyday life: Race, gender, and sexual orientation*. John Wiley & Sons.

Sue, D. W., Bucceri, J., Lin, A. I., Nadal, K. L., & Torino, G. C. (2009). Racial microaggressions and the Asian American experience. *Asian American Journal of Psychology, S(1)*, 88–101.

U.S. National Archives & Records Administration. (n.d.). *Chinese Exclusion Act (1882)*. https://www.ourdocuments.gov/doc.php?flash=true&doc=47.

Williams, M. T. (2019). Adverse racial climates in academia: Conceptualization, interventions, and call to action. *New Ideas in Psychology, 55*, 58–67.

Wu, E. D. (2014). *The color of success: Asian Americans and the origins of the Model Minority*. Princeton University Press.

Yancy, G. (2014). White crisis and the value of losing one's way. In G. Yancy & M. del Guadalupe Davidson (Eds.), *Exploring race in predominantly white classrooms: Scholars of color reflect* (pp. 1–16). Routledge.

SUGGESTIONS FOR FURTHER READING

Asian American Writers' Workshop, *Xenophobia since 9/11: A primer by Deepa Iyer*. https://www.youtube.com/watch?v=PVtv0viiTrQ.

Ben & Jerry's. (n.d.). *7 ways we know systemic racism is real*. https://www.ben jerry.com/home/whats-new/2016/systemic-racism-is-real.

Iyer, D. (2017). *We too sing America: South Asian, Arab, Muslim, and Sikh immigrants shape our multiracial future*. The New Press.

Kendi, I. X. (2019). *How to be an antiracist*. One World.

National Museum of African American History and Culture. (n.d.). *Being antiracist*. https://nmaahc.si.edu/learn/talking-about-race/topics/being-ant iracist.

Schlund-Vials, C. J., Võ, L. T., & Wong, K. S. (Eds.). (2015). *Keywords for Asian American studies*. New York University Press.

Sue, D. W. (2016). *Race talk and the conspiracy of silence: Understanding and facilitating difficult dialogues on race*. Wiley.

Learning for Justice. (n.d.). https://www.learningforjustice.org/.

CHAPTER 15

Open Educational Resources as Tools to Foster Equity

Virginia Clinton-Lisell, Elizabeth M. Legerski, Bri Rhodes, and Staci Gilpin

KEY TERMS AND DEFINITIONS

Open educational resources (OER)	"Teaching, learning and research materials in any medium—digital or otherwise—that reside in the public domain or have been released under an open license that permits no-cost access, use, adaptation and

V. Clinton-Lisell (✉) · E. M. Legerski · B. Rhodes · S. Gilpin
University of North Dakota, Grand Forks, ND, USA
e-mail: virginia.clinton@und.edu

B. Rhodes
Mount Holyoke College, South Hadley, MA, USA

S. Gilpin
The College of St. Scholastica, Duluth, MN, USA

C. C. Ozaki and L. Parson (eds.), *Teaching and Learning for Social Justice and Equity in Higher Education*,
https://doi.org/10.1007/978-3-030-69947-5_15

	redistribution by others with no or limited restrictions." (William & Flora Hewlett Foundation, 2019, para. 7).
Open textbooks	OER in textbook form that are typically available without access fees online. These usually can be printed or ordered as bound, hard copies.
Course withdrawal	When students remove themselves from courses after the drop deadline but before the term is complete.
First-generation college students	Students whose parents or guardians did not attend college or did not complete a college degree (definitions vary by study and institution).
Creative Commons	A nonprofit organization with a mission to promote tools for public sharing of knowledge and culture. Creative Commons licensing provides legal tools and guidelines for rights and restrictions on public use, attribution, and modifications (Creative Commons, 2020).

Traditionally, educational materials for postsecondary students, such as textbooks, have been developed by commercial publishers. However, the price of these materials has risen substantially over the past few decades (US Bureau of Labor Statistics, 2016). In addition, commercial materials often have restrictive licenses that impede instructors who wish to share, adapt, or remix materials. In response to the issues of high costs and inflexibility due to licensing, there has been a movement to develop and share Open Educational Resources (OER; Butcher, 2015). The term "open educational resources" was first coined by UNESCO (The United Nations Educational, Scientific and Cultural Organization) in 2002, who recognized OER as an important method for ensuring the right to an inclusive and quality education for all (Bliss & Smith, 2017; Hoosen & Butcher, 2019). OER are educational materials, such as textbooks, videos, graphics, and syllabi, "that reside in the public domain or have been released under an intellectual property license that permits their free use and re-purposing by others" (William & Flora Hewlett Foundation, 2019, para. 7). As a result, OER do not require paying fees in order to access them (Butcher, 2015) and their licensing allows for the editing and remixing of materials (see Green, 2017, for a thorough explanation of OER licensing).

While those in support of OER often imply such materials help support social justice goals, very few evaluations of OER pedagogies, materials, and outcomes utilize distinctly social justice frameworks. One exception to this is Lambert (2018) who explored the extent to which key OER texts are aligned with the social justice principles of redistributive justice, recognitive justice, and representational justice. The principle of redistributive justice involves allocating resources to support those who have less, while "recognitive justice involves recognition and respect for cultural and gender difference, and representational justice involves equitable representation and political voice" (Lambert, 2018, p. 227). We apply this framework to summarize research and scholarship showing how the social justice principles described above can be applied to OER. In doing so, we demonstrate the ability of OER to promote social justice by supporting more equitable access to higher education and by providing opportunities to increase the visibility and voices of marginalized communities and people.

OER Cost-Savings and Educational Access and Success

The price of commercial materials has negative repercussions on post-secondary students. On average, postsecondary students spend approximately $1200 on materials each year (The College Board, 2019). Students are often savvy about avoiding costs, particularly for textbooks, by sharing books with peers, finding pirated versions online, or simply not getting required materials (Jhangiani & Jhangiani, 2017; Moxley, 2013). According to one estimate, as many as two-thirds of postsecondary students decided not to purchase commercial materials due to the expense (USPIRG, 2014), even though they realize they may suffer academically without these materials (Florida Virtual Campus, 2018). Students often wait until they know for certain that the materials are truly necessary to perform well in a course, with 80% of students reporting not having the textbook on the first day of class due to the cost (Jenkins et al., 2020). Students also report that they enroll in fewer courses per term because of the financial cost of materials (Florida Virtual Campus, 2018). In addition, the time spent searching for cheaper versions of commercial materials diverts students' time away from academics (Katz, 2019).

Students who are historically underserved in higher education may be particularly affected by textbook costs. A recent survey indicated Latinx students, students who are dependent on financial aid, and first-generation students reported higher levels of stress due to textbook costs than their peers. Latinx and first-generation students also were more likely to report that they failed a course because of the high cost of the textbook (Jenkins et al., 2020). In addition, students who identified as both first-generation college students and of Black or Latinx background were more likely than their white peers to report that high textbook costs led to lower grades (Nusbaum et al., 2019).

There is clear empirical evidence that OER save students money. In one study comparing the same course taught using an OER textbook in one section and a commercial textbook in another section, students reported spending on average $80 less for course materials in the section with an open textbook compared to the section with the commercial textbook (Clinton, 2018). Institutions that have adopted OER initiatives also report substantial aggregate savings for their students. For example, the cost savings calculated as part of one community college's initiative to adopt OER in 11 courses saved students $34,000 (Ikahihifo et al., 2017). Students tend to reinvest money saved through OER into their education by enrolling in more courses in a given term, purchasing materials for courses that do not use OER, and for tuition (Ikahihifo et al., 2017).

There is also evidence that OER can save costs by lowering course withdrawal rates, which extend time-to-degree completion (Hall et al., 2003). In fact, one-fifth of students report having withdrawn from a course because of the cost of course materials (Florida Virtual Campus, 2018). Although the long-term costs of withdrawing are likely greater than the immediate costs of accessing required course materials, students may feel compelled to withdraw from courses if they do not have the means to access needed materials. When students withdraw from courses after the drop deadline, they are still responsible for the tuition for that course. The issue of commercial material costs contributing to course withdrawals appears to be particularly problematic for first-generation college students (Nusbaum et al., 2019).

Evidence suggests that courses using OER materials have substantially lower withdrawal rates. Based on a meta-analysis of 11 studies, the course withdrawal rate was 29% lower in courses with open textbooks compared to courses with commercial textbooks (Clinton & Khan, 2019). This overall quantitative effect size is consistent with the qualitative findings of document analyzes in which the theme of course material costs being an important factor shaping student withdrawals was identified (Michalski, 2014). In other studies, students have reported that having immediate access to an open textbook without fees enabled them to successfully complete a course rather than withdraw (Hardin et al., 2019). Not requiring expensive course materials may be particularly important for first-generation and low-income students. In fact, according to one study, first-generation college students viewed not requiring expensive materials as a form of faculty support (Ellis et al., 2019).

Given the demonstrated cost savings and impacts on course retention, a majority of instructors have not adopted OER materials in their courses. Often one of the primary concerns faculty have about adopting OER is that the quality is inferior to that of commercial materials (Belikov & Bodily, 2016; Seaman & Seaman, 2017). This concern is not supported by existing data. In a meta-analysis of 22 studies comparing courses with open textbooks to those with commercial textbooks, it was found that there was no difference in learning performance (Clinton & Khan, 2019). Furthermore, systematic reviews examining OER more broadly (i.e., beyond textbooks), have also concluded that OER and commercial materials are comparable in terms of learning outcomes (Hilton, 2016, 2019). These systematic reviews also indicate that the overwhelming majority of students and faculty who have actually used OER materials perceive the quality of OER to be as good or better than that of commercial materials (Hilton, 2016, 2019).

There is evidence that OER may be particularly beneficial in terms of learning outcomes for students who have traditionally been underserved in higher education. In a comparison of the grades of over 20,000 students in courses before and after OER adoption, students overall had higher grades in OER courses than those with commercial textbooks (Colvard et al., 2018). However, the increase was larger for students from lower socioeconomic backgrounds (as indicated by their Pell grant status).

This can be explained by the *access hypothesis*, which would suggest that OER benefit students who would not otherwise have access to necessary learning materials (Grimaldi et al., 2019).

OER Licensing for Recognitive and Representational Justice

The adoption of OER materials in postsecondary education may also contribute to more equitable learning in other ways beyond reducing financial barriers to student access. OER differ fundamentally from commercial materials and other non-OER materials that may be available online through the use of a Creative Commons copyright (Bissell, 2009). The restrictions on Creative Commons licensing vary, but at its most open level, it allows for permission to engage in what is termed the "5R" activities: retain, reuse, revise, remix, and redistribute (Wiley & Hilton, 2018). Retain activities include having the right to download, store, duplicate, and own personal copies of the OER. Reuse means that an OER created for one purpose could be used for another purpose. The rights to retain and reuse OER allow OER to be available without access fees. Simply having required materials available to each student at the beginning of the semester without cost to students can benefit pedagogy as instructors can plan activities knowing students have their materials (Watson et al., 2017).

Revise activities involve adapting and changing content to meet the needs of the course and/or students. Large-scale changes that are possible with the right to revise include the ability to easily translate materials into another language or create an audio version of texts. In this way, options for revising materials facilitate access to course content for diverse populations. Opportunities for revision also allow instructors to remove portions of materials that are irrelevant to course learning objectives. This is a feature students report appreciating about OER-enabled pedagogy because they know all of their materials are relevant to the course (DeCarlo, 2019).

Remix activities involve combining material from one source (either in its original or revised form) with material from other sources. For example, an instructor may like most of an introduction to psychology textbook from a particular source but prefer the cognitive psychology unit from another source. Remixing allows this instructor to easily remove the cognitive psychology chapter from one OER source and use one from another OER source in its place. Another example of remixing OER textbooks is adding links to videos or helpful web resources (Mason & Kimmons, 2018). The rights to revise and remix are key advantages of OER as they afford instructors the ability to adapt materials, which is a good teaching practice (Forbes, 2013; Remillard, 2005).

The rights to revise and remix can also improve inclusion and the diversity of materials. This is critical because content analyzes of textbooks across multiple disciplines have indicated a lack of diverse representation in textbooks (Sleeter & Grant, 1991; Woyshner & Schocker, 2015). Specifically, studies show that women, people of color, people of lower socioeconomic status, and differently-abled individuals often are underrepresented and/or are represented stereotypically in textbooks (Deckman et al., 2018; Parker et al., 2017; Rosa et al., 2016). While there have been some improvements over time, women, particularly women of color, are still not well represented in many textbooks (Bernabé-Villodre & Martínez, 2018; Eigenberg & Park, 2016; Woyshner & Schocker, 2015). OER are not inherently immune to issues with diverse representations, but, unlike commercial materials, the licensing of OER allows for editing to improve representation. For example, edits might include changing the names of individuals in examples to allow for a more diverse representation of ethnic identities,[1] removing exclusionary language and adding more inclusive language (e.g., replacing "consumer tribe" in a marketing textbook with "consumer fan club" or changing gendered pronouns to they/them[2]). Visual representations can also be changed to include a wider range of communities and people by using graphics licensed for reuse (Perez, 2017). Such practices support the social justice goal of facilitating recognition by providing opportunities to increase visibility and share the experiences of marginalized and under-represented populations (Lambert, 2018). Finally, redistribution allows for instructors and students to share their revisions and remixes of OER with others. This can foster networking and collaboration among instructors who may be interested in creating and/or using more inclusive and diverse OER materials (Nascimbeni & Burgos, 2016; Paskevicius, 2017).

These activities allow for what is termed "OER-enabled pedagogy" (also referred to as open pedagogy or open educational practices), which

[1] We thank Rajiv Jhangiani for posting this example on Twitter.
[2] We thank Andrea E. Niosi for posting these examples on Twitter.

are teaching practices that are only possible with OER licensing (Wiley & Hilton, 2018). OER-enabled pedagogy is characterized by collaboration, innovation, creation, and participation of both instructors and students (Karunanayaka et al., 2015). In one study, instructors worked with students to develop graphics and videos that they then shared with others to use in similar courses (using the rights to retain, remix, and redistribute; Wiley et al., 2017). In an American Literature course, students wrote introductions providing contexts to readings in an OER anthology as well as videos and discussion questions, which were then redistributed (DeRosa, 2016). These pedagogical practices would not have been possible with materials regulated by closed copyrights. In an evaluation of such practices, the majority of students reported that OER-enabled pedagogy was as effective, or better, than traditional pedagogy activities (e.g., writing essays and taking quizzes; Hilton et al., 2019). Such practices also have the potential to support representational justice by providing marginalized groups with the opportunity to co-construct texts and tell their stories, rather than having their stories told by others (Lambert, 2018).

OER Initiatives

Lambert (2018) argues that the affordability, accessibility, and openness components of OER are not sufficient in and of themselves for supporting social justice; rather, working toward social justice using OER requires intentionality and a commitment to address and design for principles of social justice. Institutional support of the implementation of OER and OER-enabled pedagogy is critical to realizing the transformative impact of OER (Conole & Brown, 2018). Proponents of OER have suggested several strategies to help embed open practices into higher education, such as offering institutional incentives to use OER, providing professional development opportunities such as workshops related to OER pedagogy, and providing practical support for the integration of OER materials into courses (Conole & Brown, 2018). Conole and Brown (2018) also argue that institutional leaders must have knowledge of open pedagogies and be committed to the implementation of OER. In addition, OER must be acknowledged and rewarded in metrics assessing teaching excellence (Conole & Brown, 2018). For example, some student government associations have awards they present to faculty at their institutions who champion OER. More granular advocacy for the adoption of

OER might also include considering faculty's use and creation of OER as evidence of excellence in teaching when establishing review, tenure, and promotion criteria.

OER initiatives have been developed across many institutions of higher education in the past two decades (Wesolek et al., 2018). Libraries have been largely on the vanguard of exploring, adopting, and producing OER materials as they are uniquely positioned in institutions to act as both repositories of knowledge as well as a resource to students to make such knowledge more accessible (Kleymeer et al., 2010). Library resources are available to all students, regardless of financial background. Increasingly, university information technology is being housed in campus libraries, uniting technological skills and resource compilation, making them a natural home for open access initiatives (Hess et al., 2016). Although libraries at larger, public institutions have been the most common starting points of OER initiatives (Smith, 2018; Waller et al., 2018; Ross et al., 2018), some smaller institutions and many student groups have also played a key role in the current landscape of college OER initiatives (Miller, 2018; Batchelor, 2018; Baker & Ippoliti, 2018). Organizations such as the National Endowment for the Humanities and the Museum and Library Services provide grant funding to support faculty and staff efforts designed to raise awareness of OER, create repositories of open materials, update existing materials, and in some cases generate entirely new materials. Cummings-Sauls and colleagues (2018) compiled examples of significant OER projects and repositories such as the Duke Endowment Libraries, the University of Minnesota's Open Textbook Network, and the University of Massachusetts' ScholarWorks. These networks enable the sharing of institutions' scholarly work with the public to vary degrees in a free and open way.

State system support has proven to be a significant resource for many OER initiatives. For example, the North Carolina State University (NCSU) foundation has funded projects to create, remix, and adapt free or significantly reduced cost course materials for their students. The first round of grants distributed $250,000 to faculty. The institution estimates the project has saved students around $300,000 in textbook costs. The grant also enabled awareness-raising projects such as Open Access Week, to help both students and faculty better understand the costs of academic copyrighting to the institution as well as to the students. This developed into an International Open Access Week in 2016, a documentary miniseries called the "Power of Open," and a North Carolina student leader conference, OpenCon (Rigling & Cross, 2018).

In addition to initiatives to encourage and train faculty to use and develop OER, there are also initiatives to improve the accessibility of OER. Although open textbooks are typically designed to be accessible for people with disabilities (Baker et al., 2009), many interactive digital resources, both OER and commercial, have been justifiably criticized for lack of accessibility for people with disabilities (Hashey & Stahl, 2014). In response, there have been several initiatives launched to evaluate or improve the accessibility of OER websites and interactive materials (Moreno et al., 2018). For example, the OERfAll website is designed to be personalized to each user's unique needs and offers accessibility features to meet those needs (Navarette & Luján-Mora, 2018). Another example includes the Open Course Ware initiative, which organizes a variety of OER for use in specific courses, and has developed a process for reviewing the accessibility of its resources and providing feedback to instructors so their accessibility can be improved (Rodrígez et al., 2017).

FUTURE DIRECTIONS FOR SOCIAL JUSTICE AND OER

OER has been hailed as a tool for creating a more just and equitable educational environment (Hartnett, 2017; Huitt & Monetti, 2017). However, the measures chosen to assess OER and equity matter. Historically, measures such as test score gaps or grades between different populations have been used as evidence of educational equality (or inequality) (Polat, 2011; Baraniuk et al., 2017). The underlying assumption is that high test scores and grades represent high education quality, while lower test scores and grades indicate lower education quality. Nevertheless, such generalizations can be problematic. While test scores and grades matter, they are often symptomatic of deeper inequalities—inequalities requiring agile, adaptable, and non-essentialized resources—rather than an accurate measure of knowledge and skill (Lambert, 2018; Landorf & Nevin, 2007). Without using measures such as test scores and grades as a proxy for education quality, there is a need to redefine success measures in regards to education materials. This need dovetails nicely with many OER goals, mainly by addressing areas of concern that are caused primarily by economic inequality. For example, making assessments less driven by numbers and more about skills would help to reduce the gap between students who can afford test preparation programs and those who cannot (McKenzie et al., 2008). OER can support these by making skill-based resources more accessible. However, a deeper understanding of justice, and the ways in which OER may inadvertently replicate injustice, are critical for educators seeking to use OER to support more just learning environments.

Drawing on work by Fraser (1995), Lambert defined social justice in a way that is salient to OER. Lambert (2018) conceptualized social justice generally as, "a process and also a goal to achieve a fairer society which involves actions guided by the principles of redistributive justice, recognitive justice or representational justice (pg. 227)." Often the argument for OER simply stops at "openness is good." This simplistic idea stops short of examining specifically who OER is good for. "Good" may not necessarily support the goal of redistributive, recognitive, and representational justice. For example, if "good" means "good for everyone equally," then such outcomes may further prop up existing inequalities. In this way, focusing exclusively on redistributive justice, may benefit privileged students in the same way as marginalized students, leaving a gap between these groups that remains difficult to bridge (Lambert, 2018).

Defining social justice in open education therefore should focus on assessing freedoms and capabilities that result from these initiatives (Sullivan, 2011). In consideration of these factors, Lambert (2018) came to define a more justice-oriented approach to open education: "the development of free digitally-enabled learning materials and experiences primarily by and for the benefit and empowerment of non-privileged learners who may be under-represented in education systems or marginalized in their global context (pg. 239)." Understanding how just programs should look is an essential step in infusing justice alignment throughout the curriculum. Given the difficulties many educators and students in the United States and around the world face in accessing technology and developing technological skills, OER initiatives should not be measured by technical sophistication, but rather how they support Fraser's three features of social justice (i.e., redistributive, recognitive, and representational).

In considering representational and recognitive justice, Polat (2011) notes that many initiatives have stated goals of promoting greater inclusion, but often mistake integration for inclusion. Inclusion requires a level of intentionality that not only invites diverse stakeholders to the table, but gives them equal voices in decision-making. In a field where decision-makers are often people of privilege, educators cannot lose sight of their own positionality in considering ways to remove bias and essentialism when considering universal material design (Hackman, 2008).

CONCLUSION

OER afford greater student access to education through removing financial barriers. Furthermore, the licensing of OER enables instructors to promote redistributive, recognitive, and representational justice in their courses in manners not feasible with traditional copyrights (Lambert, 2018). There have been a variety of initiatives to promote, develop, and share OER at the institutions that were reviewed in this chapter. However, it should be noted that OER is a developing movement that must consider the needs of diverse learners in order to truly contribute to social justice causes.

APPENDIX

Student Course Project Incorporating OER-enabled Pedagogy

Context

It can be difficult for instructors working in teacher preparation programs to locate OER textbooks and other resources that address broad foundational elements along with issues, legislation, and practices applicable at the local/state level. The IRIS Center supported by the U.S. Department of Education's Office of Special Education Programs and located at Vanderbilt University's Peabody College offers free online interactive resources, which are licensed by Creative Commons that "translate research about the education of students with disabilities into practice" (Vanderbilt University, 2020). Included in their comprehensive coverage of evidence-based topics are behavior and learning strategies along with data collections and analysis. However, IRIS Center resources do not address the implementation of practices and teacher licensure standards relevant to specific states. Thus, IRIS Center resources are ripe for OER-enabled pedagogy through revision/remixing.

To that end, in an Introduction to Special Education course, the instructor used IRIS Center resources as their primary course text/resource. To add the local/state context, they assigned students to create resource guides that went with each course topic using other OERs of their choosing. The student-produced resource guides were created in Google Sites (free of charge) and expanded upon IRIS Center resources by sharing local/state interpretations of legislation, supports, best practices, and examples. The resource guides contained interactive features such as hyperlinks to other websites, podcasts, and videos. Students were also encouraged to create and embed podcasts and videos. Throughout the term, the instructor scaffolded students by providing them with periodic feedback, suggestions for resources, and by creating time for them to workshop their resource guides with one another. At the end of the semester, student volunteers put together a "best of the best" Google Site that highlighted the student-created resources that students found to be most helpful. This Google Site then served as the foundation for future courses as the resource guide and the website continued to be reviewed and revised.

Instructions to students
Imagine that you are a parent/guardian, and your child is struggling in school. You are trying to navigate getting help for your child. The first thing many of us would do is open up a browser and start researching. Your task for this series of assignments is to take what you are learning in this course and channel it into something useful and practical—the creation of a web-based resource guide intended to inform parents about the why, what, and how of getting their child support, regardless of whether they have a disability or not, because if a student is struggling, this is a sign they need something.

Your resource guide will explain the special education process, working with students with disabilities, those that are gifted and talented and English language learners along with Sect. 504, the Individuals with Disabilities Education Act (IDEA), and other legislation that supports the success of all learners. In the spirit of Universal Design for Learning (UDL), you may include elements in your resource guides that are typed, video, and/or audio. The resource guides will be created in a Google Site (web site) that you will create free of charge using your student Google Account.

The goal is for you to leave this course with a resource guide that you can use in your future work. A secondary goal is to use the information you include in your resource guides to create a course Google Site that highlights the student-created resources that you found to be most helpful. This Google Site will then serve as the foundation for future courses as the resource guide project continues, and the website will be continuously reviewed and revised. Your instructor will need student volunteers to assist with the creation/updating of the course Google Site. Please let me know if you are interested. Course extra credit will be provided for anyone who volunteers.

Before you get started, it is imperative that you understand your audience as you are creating the content for your resource guide. Avoid educational jargon as much as possible while still maintaining a professional tone and including appropriate academic language. To that end, I would encourage you to do some research on your own and see what others in your state/region are putting on their district websites. In addition, review the respective state agency websites related to supporting students with disabilities. You might ask teachers you know and others who work in schools for feedback and/or ideas. You may direct your site to either elementary, middle school, or high school students and their parents/guardians. PLEASE be creative—the more professional, yet engaging, a site is, the more comforted a parent/guardian will feel!

References

Baker, A., & Ippoliti, C. (2018). Student-driven OER: Championing the student voice in campus-wide efforts. In A. Wesolek, J. Lashley, & A. Langley (Eds.), *OER: A field guide for academic librarians* (pp. 239–252). Pacific University Press.

Baker, J., Thierstein, J., Fletcher, K., Kaur, M., & Emmons, J. (2009). Open textbook proof-of-concept via connexions. *The International Review of Research in Open and Distributed Learning, 10*(5). https://doi.org/10.19173/irrodl.v10i5.633.

Baraniuk, R., Finkbeiner, N., Harris, D., Nicholson, D., & Williamson, D. (2017). Free is not enough. In R. S. Jhangiani & R. Biswas-Diener (Eds.), *Open* (pp. 219–226). Ubiquity Press; JSTOR. https://www.jstor.org/stable/j.ctv3t5qh3.21.

Batchelor, C. (2018). Transforming publishing with a little help from our friends: Supporting an open textbook pilot project with friends of the libraries grant funding. In *OER: A field guide for academic librarians* (pp. 415–432). Pacific University Press.

Belikov, O. M., & Bodily, R. (2016). Incentives and barriers to OER adoption: A qualitative analysis of faculty perceptions. *Open Praxis, 8*(3), 235–246. https://doi.org/10.5944/openpraxis.8.3.308.

Bernabé-Villodre, M. D. M., & Martínez-Bello, V. E. (2018). Analysis of gender, age and disability representation in music education textbooks: A research update. *International Journal of Music Education, 36*(4), 494–508. https://doi.org/10.1177%2F0255761418763900.

Bissell, A. N. (2009). Permission granted: Open licensing for educational resources. *Open Learning: the Journal of Open, Distance and E-Learning, 24*(1), 97–106. https://doi.org/10.1080/02680510802627886.

Bliss, T. J., & Smith, M. (2017). A brief history of open educational resources. In R. S. Jhangiani & R. Biswas-Diener (Eds.), *Open: The Philosophy and Practices that are Revolutionizing Education and Science* (pp. 9–27). London: Ubiquity Press.

Butcher, N. (2015). *A basic guide to open educational resources (OER).* British Columbia, Canada: Commonwealth of Learning, Vancouver and UNESCO. http://oasis.col.org/handle/11599/36.

Clinton, V. (2018). Savings without sacrifices: A case study of open-source textbook adoption. *Open Learning: the Journal of Distance and Open Learning, 33*(3), 177–189. https://doi.org/10.1080/02680513.2018.1486184.

Clinton, V., & Khan, S. (2019). Efficacy of open textbook adoption on learning performance and course withdrawal rates: A meta-analysis. *AERA Open, 5*(3), 1–20. https://doi.org/10.1177%2F2332858419872212.

Colvard, N. B., Watson, C. E., & Park, H. (2018). The impact of Open Educational Resources on various student success metrics. *International Journal of Teaching and Learning in Higher Education, 30*(2), 262–276. http://www.isetl.org/ijtlhe/pdf/IJTLHE3386.pdf.

Conole, G., & Brown, M. (2018). Reflecting on the Impact of the Open Education Movement. *Journal of Learning for Development, 5*(3), 187–203. https://jl4d.org/index.php/ejl4d/article/view/314.

Creative Commons. (2020). *What is Creative Commons?* Retrieved from https://creativecommons.org/faq/#what-is-creative-commons-and-what-do-you-do.

Cummings-Sauls, R., Ruen, M., Beaubien, S., & Smith, J. (2018). Open partnerships: Identifying and recruiting allies for open educational resources initiatives. *OER: A Field Guide for Academic Librarians. 72.* Retrieved from https://scholarworks.umass.edu/librarian_pubs/72.

DeCarlo, M. P. (2019, November 7). *Teaching note: Creating open textbooks for social work education.* https://doi.org/10.31235/osf.io/qf3t5.

Deckman, S. L., Fulmer, E. F., Kirby, K., Hoover, K., & Mackall, A. S. (2018). Numbers are just not enough: A critical analysis of race, gender, and sexuality in elementary and middle school health textbooks. *Educational Studies, 54*(3), 285–302. https://doi.org/10.1080/00131946.2017.1411261.

DeRosa, R. (2016). My open textbook: *Pedagogy and practice.* https://robinderosa.net/uncategorized/my-open-textbook-pedagogy-and-practic.

Eigenberg, H. M., & Park, M.S. (2016). Marginalization and invisibility of women of color: A Content analysis of race and gender images in introductory criminal justice and criminology texts. *Race and Justice, 6*(3), 257–279. https://doi.org/10.1177%2F2153368715600223.

Ellis, J. M., Powell, C. S., Demetriou, C. P., Huerta-Bapat, C., & Panter, A. T. (2019). Examining first-generation college student lived experiences with microaggressions and microaffirmations at a predominately White public research university. *Cultural Diversity and Ethnic Minority Psychology, 25*(2), 266–279. https://doi.org/10.1037/cdp0000198.

Florida Virtual Campus. (2018). *2018 Florida Student Textbook Survey.* Tallahassee, FL: Author.

Fraser, F. (1995). From redistribution to recognition? Dilemmas of justice in a "post-socialist" age. *New Left Review, 1*(212). https://newleftreview.org/I/212/nancy-fraser-from-redistribution-to-recognition-dilemmas-of-justice-in-a-post-socialist-age.

Forbes, C. T. (2013). Curriculum-dependent and curriculum-independent factors in preservice elementary teachers' adaptation of science curriculum materials for inquiry-based science. *Journal of Science Teacher Education, 24*(1), 179–197. https://doi.org/10.1007/s10972-011-9245-0.

Green, C. (2017). Open licensing and open education licensing policy. In: R. S. Jhangiani, & R. Biswas-Diener (Eds.), *Open: The philosophy and practices that are revolutionizing education and science* (pp. 29–41).

Grimaldi, P., Basu Mallick, D., Waters, A. E., & Baraniuk, R. G. (2019). Do open educational resources improve student learning? Implications of the access hypothesis. *PLoS ONE, 14*(3), e0212508. https://doi.org/10.1371/journal.pone.0212508.

Hackman, H. (2008). Broadening the pathway to academic success: The critical intersections of social justice education, critical multicultural education, and universal instructional design. In *Pedagogy and student services for institutional transformation: Implementing universal sesign in higher education.* University of Minnesota.

Hall, M., Smith, K., Boeckman, D., Ramachandran, V., & Jasin, J. (2003, October). *Why do students withdraw from courses?* Southern Association for Institutional Research, 01–11. San Antonio, TX.

Hardin, E. E., Eschman, B., Spengler, E. S., Grizzell, J. A., Moody, A. T., Ross-Sheehy, S., & Fry, K.M. (2019). What happens when trained graduate student instructors switch to an open textbook? A controlled study of the impact on student learning outcomes. *Psychology Learning & Teaching.* https://doi.org/10.1177/1475725718810909.

Hartnett, J. (2017). DIY open pedagogy: Freely sharing teaching resources in psychology. In R. S. Jhangiani & R. Biswas-Diener (Eds.), *Open* (pp. 245–254). Ubiquity Press; JSTOR. https://www.jstor.org/stable/j.ctv3t5qh3.24.

Hashey, A. I., & Stahl, S. (2014). Making online learning accessible for students with disabilities. *Teaching Exceptional Children, 46*(5), 70–78.

Hess, J., Nann, A. J., & Riddle, K. E. (2016). Navigating OER: The library's role in bringing OER to campus. *The Serials Librarian, 70*(1–4), 128–134. https://doi.org/10.1080/0361526X.2016.1153326.

Hilton, J. (2016). Open educational resources and college textbook choices: A review of research on efficacy and perceptions. *Educational Technology Research and Development, 64*(4), 573–590. https://doi.org/10.1007/s11 423-016-9434-9.

Hilton, J. (2019). Open educational resources, student efficacy, and user perceptions: A synthesis of research published between 2015–2018. *Educational technology research and development.* https://doi.org/10.1007/s11423-019-09700-4.

Hilton, J., Wiley, D., Chaffee, R., Darrow, J., Guilmett, J., Harper, S., et al. (2019). Student perceptions of open pedagogy: An exploratory study. *Open Praxis, 11*(3), 275.

Hoosen, S., & Butcher, N. (2019). *Understanding the impact of OER: Achievements and challenges.* https://iite.unesco.org/wp-content/uploads/2019/04/Understanding_the_impact_of_OER_2019_final.pdf.

Huitt, W. G., & Monetti, D. M. (2017). Openness and the Transformation of Education and Schooling. In R. S. Jhangiani & R. Biswas-Diener (Eds.), *Open* (pp. 43–66). Ubiquity Press; JSTOR. https://www.jstor.org/stable/j.ctv3t5qh3.8.

Ikahihifo, T. K., Spring, K. J., Rosecrans, J., & Watson, J. (2017). Assessing the savings from open educational resources on student academic goals. *International Review of Research in Open and Distributed Learning, 18*(7). https://doi.org/10.19173/irrodl.v18i7.2754.

Jenkins, J. J., Sánchez, L. A., Schraedley, M. A., Hannans, J., Navick, N., & Young, J. (2020). Textbook broke: Textbook affordability as a social justice issue. *Journal of Interactive Media in Education, 1*(3), 1–13. https://doi.org/10.5334/jime.549.

Jhangiani, R. S., & Jhangiani, S. (2017). Investigating the perceptions, use, and impact of open textbooks: A survey of post-secondary students in British Columbia. *The International Review of Research in Open and Distributed Learning, 18*(4). https://doi.org/10.19173/irrodl.v18i4.3012.

Karunanayaka, S., Naidu, S., Rajendra, J. C. N., & Ratnayake, H. U. W. (2015). From OER to OEP: Shifting practitioner perspectives and practices with innovative learning experience design. *Open Praxis, 7*(4), 339–350. https://www.learntechlib.org/p/161991/.

Katz, S., (2019). *Student textbook purchasing: The hidden cost of time.* CUNY Academic Works. https://academicworks.cuny.edu/le_pubs/251.

Kleymeer, P., Kleinman, M., & Hanss, T. (2010). *Reaching the heart of the university: Libraries and the future of OER* (Open ED 2010 Proceedings). UOC, OU, BYU. https://hdl.handle.net/10609/4866.

Lambert, S. R. (2018). Changing our (dis)course: A distinctive social justice aligned definition of open education. *Journal of Learning for Development, 5*(3), 225–244. https://orcid.org/0000-0003-2722-9684.

Landorf, H., & Nevin, A. (2007). Inclusive global education: Implications for social justice. *Journal of Educational Administration, 45*(6), 711. https://doi.org/10.1108/09578230710829892.

Mason, S. L., & Kimmons, R. (2018). Effects of open textbook adoption on teachers' open practices. *International Review of Research in Open and Distributed Learning, 19*(3). https://doi.org/10.19173/irrodl.v19i3.3517.

McKenzie, K. B., Christman, D. E., Hernandez, F., Fierro, E., Capper, C. A., Dantley, M., et al. (2008). From the field: A proposal for educating leaders for social justice. *Educational Administration Quarterly, 44*(1), 111–138. https://doi.org/10.1177/0013161X07309470.

Michalski, G. V. (2014). In their own words: A text analytics investigation of college course attrition. *Community College Journal of Research and Practice, 38*(9), 811–826. https://doi.org/10.1080/10668926.2012.720865.

Miller, J. (2018). Bringing OER to the liberal arts: An innovative grant program. In *OER: A Field guide for academic librarians* (pp. 399–413). Pacific University Press.

Moreno, N., Caro, E. T., & Cabedo, R. (2018). Systematic review: OER and disability. *2018 IEEE 5th International congress on information science and technology (CiSt)*, Marrakech, (pp. 428–431). https://doi.org/10.1109/CIST.2018.8596659.

Moxley, J. (2013). Open textbook publishing. *Academe, 99*(5), 40. https://www.aaup.org/article/open-textbook-publishing#.WNPuNRLyvq0.

Nascimbeni, F., & Burgos, D. (2016). In search for the open educator: Proposal of a definition and a framework to increase openness adoption among university educators. *International Review of Research in Open and Distributed Learning, 17*(6), 1–17. https://doi.org/10.19173/irrodl.v17i6.2736.

Navarrete, R., & Luján-Mora, S. (2018). Bridging the accessibility gap in open educational resources. *Universal Access in the Information Society, 17*(4), 755–774. https://doi.org/10.1007/s10209-017-0529-9.

Nusbaum, A. T., Cuttler, C., & Swindell, S. (2019). Open educational resources as a tool for educational equity: Evidence from an introductory psychology class. *Frontiers in Education, 14*, 152–200.

Parker, R., Larkin, T., & Cockburn, J. (2017). A visual analysis of gender bias in contemporary anatomy textbooks. *Social Science and Medicine, 180*, 106–113. https://doi.org/10.1016/j.socscimed.2017.03.032.

Paskevicius, M. (2017). Conceptualizing open educational practices through the lens of constructive alignment. *Open Praxis, 9*(2), 125–140. https://www.learntechlib.org/p/181424/.

Perez, J. E. (2017). Images and the Open Educational Resources (OER) movement. *The Reference Librarian, 58*(4), 229–237. https://doi.org/10.1080/02763877.2017.1346495.

Polat, F. (2011). Inclusion in education: A step towards social justice. *International Journal of Educational Development, 31*(1), 50–58. https://doi.org/10.1016/j.ijedudev.2010.06.009.

Remillard, J. T. (2005). Examining key concepts in research on teachers' use of mathematics curricula. *Review of Educational Research, 75*(2), 211–246. https://doi.org/10.3102%2F00346543075002211.

Rigling, L., & Cross, W. (2018). Getting to know you: How we turned community knowledge into open advocacy. In A. Wesolek, J. Lashley, & A. Langley (Eds.) *OER: A field guide for academic librarians* (pp. 351–380). Pacific University Press.

Rodríguez, G., Pérez, J., Cueva, S., & Torres, R. (2017). A framework for improving web accessibility and usability of Open Course Ware sites. *Computers & Education, 109,* 197–215. https://doi.org/10.1016/j.compedu.2017.02.013.

Rosa, N. M., Bogart, K. R., Bonnett, A. K., Estill, M. C., & Colton, C. E. (2016). Teaching about disability in psychology: An analysis of disability curricula in US undergraduate psychology programs. *Teaching of Psychology, 43*(1), 59–62. https://doi.org/10.1177%2F0098628315620885.

Ross, H., Lucky, S., & Francis, D. (2018). A grassroots approach to OER adoption: The University of Saskatchewan experience. In *OER: A field guide for academic librarians* (pp. 381–398). Pacific University Press.

Seaman, J. E., & Seaman, J. (2017). Opening the textbook: Educational resources in U.S. higher education, 2017. https://www.onlinelearningsurvey.com/oer.html.

Sleeter, C. E., & Grant, C. A. (1991). Race, class, gender, and disability in current textbooks. In M. W. Apple & L. K. Christian-Smith (Eds.), *The politics of the textbook* (pp. 78–110). New York, NY: Routledge.

Smith, J. (2018). Seeking alternatives to high-cost textbooks: Six years of the open education initiative at the University of Massachusetts Amherst. In *OER: A field guide for academic librarians* (pp. 333–350). Pacific University Press.

Sullivan, J. (2011). Free, open source software advocacy as a social justice movement: The expansion of F/OSS movement discourse in the 21st century. *Journal of Information Technology & Politics, 8*(3), 223–239. https://doi.org/10.1080/19331681.2011.592080.

The College Board. (2019). *Trends in higher education series: Trends in college pricing, 2018.* https://research.collegeboard.org/pdf/trends-college-pricing-2018-full-report.pdf.

U.S. Public Interest Research Group Education Fund and Student Public Interest Research Groups. (USPIRG). (2014). *Fixing the broken textbook market.* Washington, DC. http://www.uspirg.org/reports/usp/fixing-brokentextbook-market.

Vanderbilt University. (2020). *IRIS center.* https://iris.peabody.vanderbilt.edu/.

Waller, J., Taylor, C., & Zemke, S. (2018). From start-up to adolescence: University of Oklahoma's OER efforts. In A. Wesolek, J. Lashley, & A. Langley (Eds.) *OER: A field guide for academic librarians* (pp. 351–380). Pacific University Press.

Watson, C. E., Domizi, D. P., & Clouser, S. A. (2017). Student and faculty perceptions of openStax in high enrollment courses. *The International Review of Research in Open and Distributed Learning, 18*(5). https://doi.org/10.19173/irrodl.v18i5.2462.

Wesolek, A., Lashley, J., & Langley, A. (2018). *OER: A field guide for academic librarians.* Pacific University Press.

Wiley, D. & Hilton, JL, III. (2018). Defining OER-enabled pedagogy. *The International Review of Research in Open and Distributed Learning, 19*(4). https://doi.org/10.19173/irrodl.v19i4.3601.

Wiley, D., Webb, A., Weston, S., & Tonks, D. (2017). A preliminary exploration of the relationships between student created OER, sustainability, and student success. *The International Review of Research in Open and Distributed Learning, 18*(4). https://doi.org/10.19173/irrodl.v18i4.3022.

William and Flora Hewlett Foundation. (2019). *Open educational resources.* https://hewlett.org/strategy/open-educational-resources/.

Woyshner, C., & Schocker, J. B. (2015). Cultural parallax and content analysis: Images of Black women in high school history textbooks. *Theory & Research in Social Education, 43*(4), 441–468. https://doi.org/10.1080/00933104.2015.1099487.

Suggestions for Future Reading

Systematic Reviews and Meta-Analyzes on OER

Clinton, V., & Khan, S. (2019). Efficacy of open textbook adoption on learning performance and course withdrawal rates: A meta-analysis. AERA Open, *5*(3), 1–20. https://doi.org/10.1177%2F2332858419872212

Hilton, J. (2016). Open educational resources and college textbook choices: A review of research on efficacy and perceptions. *Educational Technology*

Research and Development,64(4), 573–590. https://doi.org/10.1007/s11 423-016-9434-9

Hilton, J. (2019). Open educational resources, student efficacy, and user perceptions: a synthesis of research published between 2015–2018. *Educational Technology Research and development.* https://doi.org/10.1007/s11423-019-09700-4

Overviews of OER and OER-Enabled Pedagogy

Jhangiani, R. S., & Jhangiani, S. (2017). Investigating the perceptions, use, and impact of open textbooks: A survey of post-secondary students in British Columbia. *The International Review of Research in Open and Distributed Learning, 18*(4). https://doi.org/10.19173/irrodl.v18i4.3012

Wiley, D. & Hilton, JL, III. 2018. Defining OER-Enabled Pedagogy. *The International Review of Research in Open and Distributed Learning, 19*(4). https://doi.org/10.19173/irrodl.v19i4.3601.

Websites with OER Collections or Other Resources

Minnesota Open Textbook Library (collection of open textbooks with faculty reviews): https://open.umn.edu/opentextbooks/.

OER Commons (online library of OER and network of educators to collaborate on open pedagogy): https://www.oercommons.org/.

Open Course Ware (collection of freely-available content from Massachusetts Institute of Technology courses): https://ocw.mit.edu/index.htm.

Open Education Group (website about an interdisciplinary research group focused on OER empirical research and sharing open pedagogy resources): http://openedgroup.org/.

US Bureau of Labor Statistics. (2016). College tuition and fees increase 63 percent since January 2006 on the Internet at https://www.bls.gov/opub/ted/2016/collegetuition-and-fees-increase-63-percent-since-january-2006.htm.

CHAPTER 16

The Role of Power and Oppression in the Classroom: Actualizing the Potential of Intersectionality in Teaching and Learning

Antonio Duran and Romeo Jackson

KEY TERMS AND DEFINITIONS

Intersectionality	An analytical framework that exposes how systems of power and oppression overlap and disenfranchise those with minoritized identities.
Intersectional erasure	Describes how the needs of those with multiple minoritized identities are overlooked when people solely view their experiences from a single-axis lens of oppression (e.g., racism or sexism).

A. Duran (✉)
Auburn University, Auburn, AL, USA
e-mail: aad0051@auburn.edu

R. Jackson
University of Nevada, Las Vegas, Las Vegas, NV, USA

339

College campuses across the United States continue to be transformed as those from minoritized backgrounds (e.g., Students of Color, LGBTQ+ individuals, people with disabilities) access postsecondary institutions (Quaye et al., 2019). This change is notable considering the reality that the founders of many colleges and universities intended for these institutions to solely cater toward dominant populations (e.g., white men; Museus et al., 2015). Additionally, these campuses were built on the anti-Black use of slave labor (Wilder, 2013) and benefited from an ongoing system of settler colonialism (Stein, 2017). Importantly, these historical legacies of oppression are still ever-present at higher education institutions, interwoven into the fabric of U.S. colleges and universities. Specifically, students experience these histories and structures in their perception of campus climates (Hurtado et al., 2012) and how they view microclimates like the classroom environment.

Knowing that academia mirrors the systemic inequities that exist in larger U.S. society, and does not exist separate from them, creates questions: how do institutional agents address these issues? How do faculty, for example, acknowledge and attend to systems of power in their teaching approaches (e.g., curriculum and pedagogy)? One such analytic that might serve useful to answer these questions is that of intersectionality, a framework that found its way into the academy by way of critical legal scholarship (Crenshaw, 1989, 1991) and has since developed into its own field of study (Cho et al., 2013). In particular, individuals employing intersectional theorizing seek to understand how overlapping systems of power shape the lives of those with multiple minoritized identities, honoring a long history of Women of Color who engaged in intersectional activism (Hancock, 2016). With intersectionality turning into a field of its own right, it is no surprise that scholars have started to imagine what it would mean to translate this framework into the study of teaching and learning (e.g., Case, 2017; Jones & Wijeyesinghe, 2011; Pliner et al., 2011). However, this area of scholarship is still relatively new and requires additional interrogation.

Thus, the purpose of this chapter is to imagine what it means to actualize the potential of intersectionality as a framework in teaching and learning. Namely, we hope to outline how educators can mobilize one of intersectionality's main theoretical interventions: attending to overlapping systems of power (Dill & Zambrana, 2009). To do so, we first provide an overview of intersectionality as it exists both within and beyond the academy. Setting this foundation then allows us to describe how intersectional erasure manifests across academic disciplines. That is, we are interested in how instructors fail to attend to interlocking structures of power and the ways they shape the classroom environment for those with multiple minoritized identities. We then discuss our own relationship to intersectionality in teaching and learning before generating implications for educators and researchers. Throughout our writing, we keep at the forefront the following question: how may teaching and learning be transformed using insights learned from intersectional theorizing? The answer, albeit not a simple one, is imperative in today's contemporary higher education landscape.

OVERVIEW OF INTERSECTIONALITY

To imagine how intersectionality can translate to the study of teaching and learning, it is vital to first articulate how we are operationalizing intersectionality as a field of study in its own right. Notably, scholars have referenced intersectionality as a traveling theory (Lewis, 2013), referencing how intersectionality has found its way across academic disciplines. Part of the reason intersectionality has been so "successful," to use the words of Davis (2008), is due to its ability to both simultaneous generalist and specialist. In other words, intersectionality has achieved popularity because it can be applied to a variety of different social issues.

The origins of intersectionality have long been contested by scholars, with theorists like Jennifer Nash (2016, 2019) arguing against a linear way of conceptualizing intersectionality's genealogy and meaning. However, one often-agreed upon reality is that intersectionality largely entered the academic lexicon as a result of the work of Kimberlé Crenshaw (1989, 1991). As a Black feminist legal scholar, Crenshaw (1989) explored the limits of rhetoric used in legal cases that failed to attend to the complexities of oppression that Black women experienced. In particular, she noted that looking at these situations through a single-axis view of oppression (e.g., racism *or* sexism) fell short of understanding how structures like racism and sexism inherently functioned in conjunction with, and not separately from, one another in turn producing a unique form of oppression for Black women and other Women of Color. Moreover, society (re)produces inequality so that those who are most minoritized are disproportionately disadvantaged and continue to be so due to the ways that systems work. Crenshaw's basement metaphor, in which she depicts those most minoritized at the bottom of a basement with a hatch door being located at the top, captures this idea—though this analogy is largely forgotten in intersectional theorizing (Carastathis, 2013). Her 1991 article then expanded upon this argument to reveal how intersectionality applies in three different domains: structural, representational, and political.

Important to acknowledge, however, is that Crenshaw's (1989, 1991) introduction of the term intersectionality in fact stemmed from a longer history of intersectional theorizing. Scholars like Hancock (2016) have discussed the contributions of Women of Color activists (e.g., Anna Julia Cooper, Sojourner Truth) who had always fought for the recognition of the ways that systems like racism and sexism intersect with one another. Furthermore, examples provided by the Combahee River Collective (1993) extended the lens to implicate other systems of oppression (e.g., heterosexism) in this analysis.

From this line of scholarship and activists, intersectionality now has developed several central contours that define its work as an analytic (Collins, 2015). One of these contours involves always centering an analysis of power and not separating it from its politicized aim to achieve social change (Bilge, 2013). Though potentially clear to many intersectional scholars, others have witnessed a watering down of the framework with some interpreting the analytic as exploring multiple identities instead of overlapping systems of power (e.g., Bilge, 2013; May, 2015; Moradi & Grzanka, 2017). Additionally, intersectionality inherently centers on the needs of those with multiple minoritized identities (Dill & Zambrana, 2009). Though this does not mean that issues with privilege are meaningless (Carastathis, 2008), intersectional theorizing has the aim of creating a more just world for those who experience multiple forms of minoritization. Keeping these central contours in mind, we will expand upon how scholarship on teaching and learning highlights the lack of engagement with intersectional thinking in the collegiate context.

INTERSECTIONAL ERASURE ACROSS DISCIPLINES

Within higher education, intersectionality has grabbed the attention of educators due to its potential to name how institutions perpetuate inequities, especially with changing student demographics (Byrd et al., 2019; Mitchell, 2019). Because of its far-reaching aims, it is unsurprising that McCall (2005) once described the framework as "the most important theoretical contribution that women's studies, in conjunction with related fields, has made so far" (p. 1771). Its ability to travel across disciplines (Lewis, 2013) means that intersectional theorizing can apply to numerous ways of thinking as long as it maintains its focus on systemic issues of power and oppression.

To demonstrate the potential for intersectionality to reshape the ways that educators approach the practice of teaching and learning, we explore brief examples in three disciplines to highlight how scholars and pedagogues have historically erased conversations pertaining to intersectionality. In other words, in the process of creating and co-creating knowledge, these disciplines have advanced objectivist schools of thought or relied upon single-axis ways of seeing power that are not in alignment with intersectional theorizing. The result of this being a form of intersectional erasure where structures of domination and the individuals they affect get overlooked in these curricular spaces. Though we only attend to the following disciplines—Science, Technology, Engineering, and Mathematics (STEM), higher education and student affairs, as well as social and cultural analyses (i.e., ethnic, gender, and disability studies)—this critique applies across the academy. It is hard to say that there is one discipline that has it "completely right" as it relates to integrating intersectionality into its fabric, meaning that every educator within that field of study always teaches from this vantage point. Thus, those who are in disciplines outside of the three provided should reflect upon the ways that their own field has produced intersectional erasure as well.

Science, Technology, Engineering, and Mathematics (STEM)

The hard sciences are often situated within a positivist framework that creates an environment that values notions of "trust," "objectivity," and "facts" (Hudson, 1995). STEM disciplines may seek to remove researcher/human bias through its methodology approach, leaving readers to think a non-intersectional approach is not needed. However, no discipline is apolitical and separate from power structures. For example, genetics has been deeply informed by race and racism (Roberts, 1997). The creation of races serves as a way of understanding the connection because of science, race, and power. Race is indeed socially constructed. Specifically, scholars historically used to justify the creation of racial categories that justifies the oppression of groups viewed as inferior based on race. Compelling research shows the biological and genetics reasoning used to support, for example, the enslavement of Africans, racist Jim Crow laws, the increased policing and surveillance of black families, mothers, and children all can be traced to STEM disciplines to justify Black death (Roberts, 1997). Furthermore, solely understanding the social construction of race as racist denies how sexism (and the combination of racism and sexism) informs the creation of racial categories. As Dorothy Roberts (1997) showed in *Killing the Black Body*, anti-Black racism and sexism intersected through scientific racism (see Hudson, 1995 for more information), public discourse supporting tropes of Black women, and public policy supported by racist IQ test research to support ideas of Black mothers as unfit to mother their children. Hence, though STEM disciplines are often taught in positivistic ways, examples such as those offered above showcase that these fields of studies are deeply connected to systems of power.

Higher Education and Student Affairs

As scholars within higher education studies, intersectional erasure is clear across the discipline. We specifically offer the example of the erasure that is present in research seeking to address LGBTQ student experiences in higher education based on our positionalities as researchers who center the lives of Queer and Trans People of Color. Lange et al. (2019) noted that LGBTQ research in higher education often centers on a single identity framework, meaning researchers historically framed LGBTQ experiences as solely a matter of sexual orientation or gender identity degrading other social identities like race or class. Furthermore, this non-intersectional approach was also troubling as researchers continued to fail to name systematic oppression in lieu of interpersonal interactions, such as macroaggressions (Lange et al., 2019). Moreover, in a forthcoming content analysis of research published in the last ten years about LGBTQ people in higher education, Duran et al. (2019) observed the following:

> ...only seven articles in our sample [of 83 articles] engaged critical race theoretical perspectives. This reproduces whiteness as the norm, starting, and ending place when working alongside LGBTQ+ people - one way that LGBTQ+ people of color become erased in higher education scholarship. (pp. 24–25)

In a practice-based field like higher education and student affairs, the implications of this intersectional erasure extend beyond the theoretical to the material—affecting interventions to support LGBTQ students rendering LGBTQ people of color invisibility. To be sure, several scholars are countering this intersectional erasure through the centering of LGBTQ people of color and frameworks (Duran, 2019; Blockett, 2017; Mobley & Johnson, 2015). However, much more work needs to be done to combat this in scholarship, as well as in teaching.

Social and Cultural Analyses

Gender, ethnic, and disability studies can be thought of as critical social justice projects when they arrived in higher education often through student activism (Ferguson, 2012, 2017). Their goal, in part, is to create space for scholarship and people excluded from higher education due to systematic oppression. The value added by these social and cultural disciplines to research, teaching, and learning cannot be understated by us as authors. Yet, intersectional erasure remains across these disciplines. Black feminists have articulated this erasure clearly. *All the Women Are White, All the Blacks Are Men, But Some of Us Are Brave* (Hull et al., 1982), for instance, made space for Black women studies due to Black women's erasure in Black *and* women's studies. To bell hooks (1981) articulation of the theoretical erasure of Black women,

> No other group in America has so had their identity socialized out of existence as have black women [...] When black people are talked about the focus tends to be on black men; and when women are talked about the focus tends to be on white women. (p. 7)

Both hooks and the editors of *But Some of Us Are Brave* seek to draw attention to the erasing of Black women's experiences and knowledge production while also creating space to center Black women. Black feminists continue to make intersectional interventions within disabilities studies. For instance, Bailey & Mobley (2019) proposed a Black Feminist disability framework "to acknowledge the need to consider disability in Black Studies and race in Disability Studies" (p. 19). All three of these interventions reflect ways that gender, ethnic, and disability studies produce intersectional erasure s and the ways that Black feminists resist such erasures through intentional theorizing.

Our Relationship to Intersectionality in Teaching and Learning

Before offering implications for educators to consider as they construct their classroom environments, we see it necessary to situate ourselves and our narratives within this particular investigation. In particular, we discuss the experiences and desires that brought us to intersectional theorizing. Such context is imperative for readers to consider as they reflect upon our recommendations for intersectional pedagogy.

Antonio

I first entered into a formal relationship with intersectionality during my time as a doctoral student at The Ohio State University. Though I had long been interested in addressing the role that systems of power play in shaping people's realities, I gained the language to discuss this phenomenon during a seminar focused on intersectionality in higher education. Learning about the ways that intersectionality had entered into the academy as a result of a long genealogy comprised of Women of Color activists piqued my interest as an emerging scholar. In particular, I began to wonder how intersectional theorizing would guide my research projects. However, it was not until that I had the opportunity to teach alongside Dr. Anne-Marie Nuñez, the very instructor who taught the seminar on intersectionality, that I started to see the connections of how this framework could inform my teaching approaches. Dr. Nuñez showed me how to structure a course in order to address the structural and material realities that minoritized individuals face on college campuses, while also acknowledging their agency and resilience. I consider this my scholarly awakening as it relates to constructing classroom environments in a manner centering intersectionality. From then on, it was not possible for me to turn off this lens as I planned out my courses and lesson plans. Yet, I acknowledge that I still am constantly learning how to do this work, to honor intersectionality, and to pay homage to the thinkers and activists that came before me.

Romeo

Teaching from an intersectional approach requires a great deal of self-reflection as a teacher. This reflection is deeply tied to power, privilege, and oppression and my location with these structures. How do I show up as a teacher with multiple marginalized identities? How has my power showed up? These are questions require deep consideration as a Black queer femme teaching in gender studies through intersectional framework because I am always already navigating social and political structures that are outside of my control, yet within the classroom, I have power as the person that has decided with readings to assign, the assignments, the point totals, when class when beheld, and where. Intersectionality is a dynamic, critical social justice project. My role as an educator in the classroom to also be dynamic and have an attention to power.

IMPLICATIONS FOR EDUCATORS

In reflecting upon our own journeys toward employing intersectionality in teaching, as well as the ways that disciplines may (re)produce issues of erasure as it relates to intersectionality, we now provide implications for educators thinking about employing this framework in their practices. Across disciplines, an intersectional approach calls attention to power, privilege, and oppression. This requires all pedagogues to engage the histories of subjections under their disciplines. For example, how may a biology instructor take up the racist and sexist history of their field (Martin, 1991; Roberts, 1997)? How may sociology—a field that has been entrenched in white and heterosexist norms (Ferguson, 2004)—attend to its anti-queer and racist canon? And, what of disciplines, such as ethnic, disability and gender studies, that are committed to understanding the experiences of marginalized communities that have developed in a non-intersectional way (Bailey & Mobley, 2019; Hull et al., 1982)? Though the strategies below are in no way exhaustive, we find these to be important starting points toward actualizing an intersectional pedagogical approach.

Engaging in Critical Reflexivity

To begin, we assert that it is essential that educators consciously engage in a process of critical reflexivity; any other practice that furthers intersectional perspectives in teaching and learning would be incomplete without this practice. Critical reflexivity, or an "understanding of the diversity and complexity of one's own social location," requires that people actively consider how they are situated within larger systems of oppression (Hesse-Biber, 2017, p. 45). In doing so, instructors are more likely to facilitate a mode of social-perspective taking, recognized as "the ability to understand another person's point of view and accurately infer the thoughts and feelings of others" (Kelly & Bhangal, 2018, p. 48). Within an intersectional realm, social-perspective taking allows educators to not only consider another person's point of view but the ways in which others navigate differentially power dynamics in society and in the learning process. For educators, critical reflexivity is crucial to engage in anti-oppressive education practices and to avoid relying upon any belief that teaching can be objective (Kumashiro, 2002).

Of note, critical reflexivity should occur at every point of the teaching process, from the construction of the class to how instructors assess student learning. What does a critically reflexive approach look like as it relates to intersectionality? For the two authors, it requires that we ask ourselves the following questions:

- In what ways do I experience privilege and oppression in the academy and in society? How have I benefited from/been disadvantaged within systemic issues of inequity?
- How do the answers to the question above shape how I approach the process of knowledge production?
- How does my standpoint affect the areas I am most in tune to in my teaching and how might it preclude me from noticing other dynamics concerning societal inequities? What effects does this have on each student's learning?
- What norms did my discipline teach me? How may I reinforce oppression?

This type of self-inquiry occurs throughout the semester in a deliberate fashion. It is not enough to *want* to engage in an intersectional pedagogical approach; educators must make a concerted effort to set time aside to participate in this critical self-reflexive practice. This is an important note to make across disciplines from STEM, to higher education and student affairs, to social and cultural analyses and beyond. Antonio, for instance, sets aside time weekly after his courses (taught in a higher education program) to ask himself these questions by writing in a journal.

This allows him to constantly consider how he may be hindering or facilitating student learning by being attentive to systems of power. Though critical reflexivity is a foundational step toward engaging intersectionality in teaching and learning, educators must make moves in other areas, such as constructing a syllabus.

Constructing a Syllabus

The creation of a syllabus has long been regarded as a political act (Dittmar, 1985). Who educators assign as readings communicates to students who should be considered valid contributors to knowledge production. This is why there is a problem when educators solely use readings from those who identify as white cisgender heterosexual men. The effect that is had is that students then associate these identities with those who are knowledgeable in a given discipline. As Ahmed (2017) described it, citations function as "academic bricks through which we create houses" and "when citational practices become habits, bricks form walls" (p. 148). For this reason, we assert that attending to intersectional erasure within teaching and learning requires educators to become attune to the walls that they can create through their citational practices in syllabi construction.

Although an intersectional analysis extends far beyond and should never be limited to representational diversity, the question of who is being included on syllabi remains an important one that counters the erasure of Women of Color. In fact, Crenshaw's (1991) own formative writing on intersectionality included the mention of representational intersectionality, questioning how cultural images produced for Women of Color inherently disadvantaged them in the social system. Therefore, we posit that the same attentiveness of representational intersectionality and the images that educators create in their courses are integral to incorporating this framework in teaching. The questions that we ask ourselves in this instance include:

- Who am I citing?
- What are their identities and backgrounds?
- What are their politics?
- How might the answer to the three questions above contribute to issues of intersectional erasure and oppression?

For Romeo teaching courses in social and cultural analyses, they maintain a policy of having 90% of their syllabus consisting of women; of the 90% women, 80% need to be Women of Color. Queer and Trans People of Color must be 50% of the assigned reading. This policy requires Romeo to continuously challenge their own reading practices. Romeo has often had to go in search of readings by Women and/or Queer People of Color to meet their policy. This often means moving beyond what may be considered by "canon," knowing that canon is often associated with systems of oppression and dominant populations (e.g., Ahmed, 2017; Ferguson, 2004). One line of questioning that may follow is what happens when someone cannot locate readings that would allow them to unequivocally center Queer and Trans People of Color. This question requires educators to reflect upon their own discipline and what bodies of knowledge currently exist.

Critiquing the Discipline

Part of the work of engaging intersectionality in teaching and learning involves educators thinking about the oppressive histories and contemporary legacies that are present in their respective disciplinary areas. In other words, instructors must challenge notions of objectivity that have long plagued many fields of study in the academy. What does this look like in practice?

An important step involves educators across disciplines naming the histories of people and events that led to certain innovations within a field. For example, what does it mean to acknowledge the ways that biologists have attempted to justify systems of racism (Saini, 2019)? To break down student assumptions that knowledge is neutral, it would behoove educators to articulate the potentially oppressive histories that have permeated the work of scholars before them. In order to do this work, instructors should consider asking themselves the following questions:

- How do I set up my lessons to provide background information to the formative concepts, ideas, and theories in my field?
- How do I have students reflect on how these histories relate to how these concepts, ideas, and theories came to be and how they have been received in the discipline?

In Antonio's courses, he attempts to mobilize these two questions above by routinely asking students to do quick internet searches in class about the biographies of formative theorists and scholars that they are reading in class. Additionally, when presenting concepts, ideas, and theories, he also encourages students to similarly present on the genealogies of individuals and the historical moments that led to their creation. These practices bring to light the ways in which power is always informing the process of knowledge production and how students receive information. It is dangerous to present information as value-neutral in one's teaching. Connected to this thinking, instructors must consider how these answers affect who and how individuals are socialized to enter a certain discipline.

Consider Student Engagement and Disciplinary Socialization

To acknowledge the historical legacies of oppression that undergird academic disciplines means to also wrestle with the ways in which these legacies manifest in contemporary times. Because certain types of knowledge production are privileged in fields of study, it creates the question of who is able to engage in this production and who is positioned as outsider? For instance, an often-spoken about crisis in academia is the lower numbers of People of Color, especially Women of Color, who enter into and persist through STEM majors (McNeely & Fealing, 2019). To address this issue from an intersectional pedagogical perspective means to consider what are the reasons why certain individuals may not see themselves represented in their field and to take intentional steps to address these realities. It also means moving away from focusing on individuals to considering how systems do or do not create possibilities for historically underserved groups with STEM.

For this reason, instructors must reflect upon how they are acting as socializing agents for students in the ways that they teach and how they set up their courses. Because students may experience issues related to stereotype threat—the fear of confirming stereotypes related to their social identities (see Steele, 2010)—based on how educators socialize them, it is necessary to think through one's pedagogical impact. Questions that might assist individuals in thinking about this include:

- How am I describing who a member of this academic community is (e.g., who is a scientist, academic, or statistician)? How are these descriptions inherently racialized, gendered, and classed?

- Who are the people I am inviting to guest lecture in classes? Who are those that we in my academic unit invite to offer professional advice to students? How might the answers to these questions reflect oppressive systems within the discipline?
- Who do I "relate" to and choose to mentor and support beyond and in the classroom?

Though matters of socialization extend far beyond the classroom, it is pivotal that instructors think about their own agency in addressing these problems within their curricular spaces. For instance, educators might have students do activities that have them think about how their social identities and how they are situated within systems of power are influencing their interactions with the course material and their fellow classmates. These kinds of intentional exercises show students that their engagement and performance in class is inherently tied to larger structures of domination and does not exist separate from them.

Integration

Necessarily, we underscore that doing the work of integrating intersectionality into the study of teaching and learning requires educators to engage the framework in all aspects of their teaching. Thus, it is not enough to simply engage one aspect of the teaching and learning experience (e.g., considering who is cited in syllabi) while also ignoring the ways that their lessons, for example, may further the same problematic norms that have often existed across disciplines. Relatedly, nor is it sufficient to intended intersectional approach that merely conforms to the politics of mere inclusion. In other words, the academy and its academics cannot believe that the answer is simply to introduce more Women of Color into the conversation (e.g., in syllabi, hiring processes). Rather, they need to critique the very structures that have led to the exclusion of Women of Color in the first place. Such a conversation furthers issues of systemic oppression without depoliticizing intersectional theorizing as Bilge (2013) would describe it.

DIRECTIONS FOR FUTURE RESEARCH

Beyond generating implications for educators, we also want to consider what it would look like to take up intersectionality in research about teaching and learning. To begin, one potential line of research would involve understanding the experiences of classroom instructors who actively center intersectionality in their pedagogy. Such scholarship would reveal the challenges and successes that these educators face in attending to systemic oppression in their courses. Researchers would specifically benefit from taking a concerted look at minoritized faculty who do this work, considering the literature showcasing the ways that minoritized individuals embody the knowledge they are teaching when educating from a power-based lens (e.g., Duran & Okello, 2018; Hill, 2014). Moreover, as highlighted throughout this chapter, it is important to explore the ways that educators engage in these practices across academic disciplines like STEM, higher education, and cultural studies.

Additionally, researchers should also broaden their scope to see how knowledgeable college educators are about issues relating to overlapping systems of inequality. Beyond simply studying those who already integrate intersectional theorizing into their pedagogy, it is imperative to understand the influences and experiences that lead to this understanding in the first place. For example, the work done by scholars like Boveda and Aronson (2019) who validated the Intersectional Competence Measure for special education preservice teachers emerges as an example of what this could look like. Future scholars can consider expanding upon this body of scholarship within collegiate settings and across academic disciplines.

Finally, much of what is known about intersectional erasure in the classroom stemmed from studies that center on minoritized college students. However, it is imperative to acknowledge that this area of research is in no way exhausted at this current moment. Therefore, we would recommend that scholars continue to question the experiences of those with multiple minoritized identities in the college classroom. How do they experience curricula? Pedagogy? Their interactions with peers? All of these questions need to be centered in order to continue to push a focus on intersectional praxis within the classroom.

Conclusion

As the study of teaching and learning continues to evolve to meet the needs of an increasingly diverse college student population (Quaye et al., 2019), it is imperative that educators attend to interlocking systems of power in their curricula and in their pedagogical approaches. Made evident throughout this chapter, the implications of intersectional pedagogy extend beyond the mere introduction of "intersectional" thinkers or the inclusion of Women of Color into syllabi. Although these are important steps, we suggest that the potential of intersectionality in its ability to transform educational environments by expanding ideas of how power, privilege, and oppression operate within the curricular space and in society as a whole. It is only when educators address these systemic issues that higher education institutions can start the process of becoming a place for liberation, especially for those with multiple minoritized identities.

Questions for Further Reflection

To facilitate reflection upon one's ability to integrate intersectionality into one's philosophies of teaching and learning, we offer the following questions for reflection:

- In what ways am I open to incorporating an attention to power and oppression? In what ways am I hesitant to?
- How might the answers to the two questions above themselves be indicative of the ways that I have been socialized to view a discipline in a particular fashion?
- How can I engage in critical reflexivity as it relates to my current teaching practices? What learning do I need to do in order to participate in critical reflexivity more fully?

Appendix A

Artifact—Identity Paper Assignment

Note: This assignment is the collective work of the Department of Interdisciplinary, Gender, & Ethnic Studies at University of Nevada, Las Vegas. It has undergone many revisions with each instructor making it their own. Romeo, for example, added the following question to the assignment to

reflect the ways that identities inform and shape each other: "Based on your understanding, detail the relationship between your social categories (for ex: how does your race inform your relationship to your gender?)"
Assignment: Write 1500–2500 words (12 point, Times New Roman font, 1 inch margins, double spaced) on your identity in relation to the six social categories (class, citizenship, ability, gender, sexual orientation, race/ethnicity/nationality).
Learning outcomes:

- Engage in constructive discussion and demonstrate knowledge of gender and sexualities.
- Apply broad knowledge of the social categories/lived experiences, including but not limited to gender, race, class, sexuality, ability, and nationality.
- Identify the relationship between privilege and oppression on both individual and systemic levels.
- Analyze women, gender, and sexuality from a cultural and institutional perspective.

Task:

- Explain how, and when you come to understand your relationship to social categories (women, citizen, bicultural, etc.) and how those social categories are created through power, privilege, and oppression.
- Based on your understanding, detail the relationship between your social categories (for ex: how does your race inform your relationship to your gender?).
- Answer the questions posted in the below table.
- Your paper should have an introduction, conclusion, thesis, and reference page.
- Cite AT LEAST **Seven (7) course readings/videos/podcasts**.
  - No more than about 20 words from quotes per page.
  - Introduce and analyze quotes to demonstrate the understanding of the readings' key arguments and critical understanding of key concepts.

SOCIAL CATEGORY QUESTIONS

Category	Question
Ability (physical, emotional, mental)	What are/were your physical, emotional, mental abilities? How, if at all, have they changed over time? How have you or others reacted to them?
Citizenship	Where were you born? Where were your parents born? What expectations or social treatment results from where you were born and where you live now?
Race/Ethnicity/Nationality	How would you describe your race? Your ethnicity? Do you perceive a difference between these two terms? What, aside from your name, helps you understand how your ethnicity is treated by your community, your region, your state, the United States? Did you grow up in a community where others shared your racial/ethnic/national background? In answering this question, discuss what it means to be one of a few or one of many based on race/ethnicity/nationality
Gender Identity	What is your gender? How has gender been shaped by your family, community, and/or schooling?
Sexual Orientation	When did you first learn how you preferred romantically? How did you feel about that desire? How did your community respond to the expression of that preference?

Criteria for Success:

1. Follow the directions listed under tasks.
2. Demonstrate awareness and engage in constructive reflection of your own personal, communal personal adversity.
3. Articulate personal knowledge of the intersection of social categories in your life: such as ability, education, family, gender, race, class, and sexuality.
4. Identify and interpret social issues that emerge in your life—moving, family change. Talk about your experiences with family, peers, your larger community.
5. Explain, through lived experiences—relationships to other people, to institutions, to places (geographic), to time—what helps define your sense of self.

6. Use correct spelling; strong organization and grammar conventions.
7. Cite material appropriately; AT LEAST 7 READINGS/VIDEOS/PODCASTS.
8. Show a clear understanding of the readings cited.
9. Provide word count at the bottom of the assignment (after references' section).

REFERENCES

Ahmed, S. (2017). *Living a feminist life*. Duke University Press.

Bailey, M., & Mobley, I. A. (2019). Work in the intersections: A Black feminist disability framework. *Gender & Society, 33*(1), 19–40. https://journals.sag epub.com/doi/full/10.1177/0891243218801523.

Blockett, R. A. (2017). "I think it's very much placed on us": Black queer men laboring to forge community at a predominantly White and (hetero)cisnormative research institution. *International Journal of Qualitative Studies in Education, 30*(8), 800–816.

Bilge, S. (2013). Intersectionality undone: Saving intersectionality from intersectionality studies. *Du Bois Review, 10*(2), 405–424.

Boveda, M., & Aronson, B. A. (2019). Special education preservice teachers, intersectional diversity, and the privileging of emerging professional identities. *Remedial and Special Education, 40*(4), 248–260.

Byrd, W. C., Brunn-Bevel, R. J., & Ovink, S. M. (2019). *Intersectionality and higher education: Identity and inequality on college campuses*. Rutgers University Press.

Carastathis, A. (2008). The invisibility of privilege: A critique of intersectional models of identity. *Les Ateliers de L'Éthique, 3*(2), 23–38.

Carastathis, A. (2013). Basements and intersections. *Hypatia, 28*(4), 698–715.

Case, K. A. (Ed.). (2017). *Intersectional pedagogy: Complicating identity and social justice*. Routledge.

Cho, S., Crenshaw, K. W., & McCall, L. (2013). Toward a field of intersectionality studies: Theory, applications, and praxis. *Signs: Journal of Women in Culture and Society, 38*(4), 785–810.

Collins, P. H. (2015a). Intersectionality's definitional dilemmas. *Annual Review of Sociology, 41*(1), 1–20.

Combahee River Collective. (1993). A Black feminist statement. In G. Hull, P. B. Scott, & B. Smith (Eds.), *All the women are white, all the Blacks are men, but some of us are brave: Black women's studies* (pp. 13–22). New York, NY: Feminist Press at CUNY (Original work published in 1977).

Crenshaw, K. (1989). Demarginalizing the intersection of race and sex: A Black feminist critique of antidiscrimination doctrine, feminist theory, and antiracist politics. *University of Chicago Legal Forum, 8*(1), 139–167.

Crenshaw, K. (1991). Mapping the margins: Intersectionality, identity politics, and violence against women of color. *Stanford Law Review, 43*(6), 1241–1299.

Davis, K. (2008). Intersectionality as buzzword: A sociology of science perspective on what makes a feminist theory successful. *Feminist Theory, 9*(1), 67–85.

Dittmar, L. (1985). Inclusionary practices: The politics of syllabus design. *Journal of Thought, 20*(3), 37–47.

Dill, B. T., & Zambrana, R. E. (2009). *Emerging intersections: Race, class, and gender in theory, policy, and practice.* Rutgers University Press.

Duran, A. (2019). A photovoice phenomenological study exploring campus belonging for queer students of color. *Journal of Student Affairs Research and Practice, 56*(2), 153–167.

Duran, A., Jackson, R., & Lange, A. C. (2019). *The theoretical engagements of scholarship on queer and trans people in higher education: A look at the last ten years.* Paper presented at the Association for the Study of Higher Education Annual Conference in Portland, Oregon.

Duran, A., & Okello, W. (2018). An autoethnographic exploration of radical subjectivity as pedagogy as pedagogy. *Journal of Curriculum and Pedagogy, 15*(2), 158–174.

Ferguson, R. (2004). *Aberrations in Black: Toward a queer of color critique.* University of Minnesota Press.

Ferguson, R. (2012). *The reorder of things: The university and its pedagogies of minority difference.* University of Minnesota Press.

Ferguson, R. (2017). *We demand: The university and student protests.* University of California Press.

Hancock, A.-M. (2016). *Intersectionality: An intellectual history.* Oxford, UK: Oxford University Press.

Hesse-Biber, S. N. (2017). *The practice of qualitative research* (3rd ed.). Sage.

Hill, D. C. (2014). A vulnerable disclosure: Dangerous negotiations of race and identity in the classroom. *Journal of Pedagogy, 5*(3), 161–181.

hooks, b. (1981). *Ain't I a woman: Black women and feminism.* South End Press.

Hudson, J. B. (1995). Scientific racism: The politics of tests, race and genetics. *The Black Scholar, 25*(1), 3–10.

Hull, A., Bell-Scott, P., & Smith, B. (Eds.). (1982). *But some of us are brave: Black women's studies.* Feminist.

Hurtado, S., Alvarez, C. L., Guillermo-Wann, C., Cuellar, M., & Arellano, L. (2012). A model for diverse learning environments. In J. C. Smart & M. B.

Paulsen (Eds.), *Higher education: Handbook of theory and research* (Vol. 27, pp. 41–122). Springer.

Jones, S. R., & Wijeyesinghe, C. L. (2011). The promises and challenges of teaching from an intersectional perspective: Core components and applied strategies. In M. L. Ouellett (Ed.), *An integrative analysis approach to diversity in the college classroom* (New Directions for Teaching & Learning, no. 125, pp. 11–20). Jossey-Bass.

Kelly, B. T., & Bhangal, N. K. (2018). Life narratives as a pedagogy for cultivating critical self-reflection. In J. P. Dugan (Ed.), *Integrating critical perspectives into leadership development* (New Directions for Student Leadership, no. 159, pp. 41–52). Jossey-Bass.

Kumashiro, K. K. (2002). *Troubling education: "Queer" activism and anti-oppressive pedagogy.* Routledge.

Lange, A. C., Duran, A., & Jackson, R. (2019). The state of LGBT and queer research in higher education revisited: Current academic houses and future possibilities. *Journal of College Student Development, 60*(5), 511–526.

Lewis, G. (2013). Unsafe travel: Experiencing intersectionality and feminist displacements. *Signs: Journal of Women in Culture and Society, 38*(4), 869–892.

Martin, E. (1991). The egg and the sperm: How science has constructed a romance based on stereotypical male-female roles. *Signs, 16*(3), 485–501.

May, V. M. (2015). *Pursuing intersectionality, unsettling dominant imaginaries.* New York, NY: Routledge.

McCall, L. (2005). The complexity of intersectionality. *Signs: Journal of Women in Culture and Society, 30*(3), 1771–1800.

McNeely, C. L., & Fealing, K. H. (2019). Moving the needle, raising consciousness: The science and practice of broadening participation. *American Behavioral Scientist, 62*(5), 551–562.

Mitchell, D., Jr. (2019). *Intersectionality & higher education: Research, theory, & praxis* (2nd ed.). Peter Lang.

Mobley, S. D., Jr., & Johnson, J. (2015). The role of HBCUs in addressing the unique needs of LGBT students. In R. T. Palmer, C. R. Shorette II, & M. Gasman (Eds.), *Exploring diversity at historically Black colleges and universities: Implications for policy and practice* (New Directions for Higher Education, no. 170, pp. 79–89). Jossey-Bass.

Moradi, B., & Grzanka, P. R. (2017). Using intersectionality responsibly: Toward critical epistemology, structural analysis, and social justice activism. *Journal of Counseling Psychology, 64*(5), 500–513.

Museus, S. D., Ledesma, M. C., & Parker, T. L. (2015). Racism and racial equity in higher education. *ASHE Higher Education Report, 42*(1), 1–112.

Nash, J. C. (2016). Feminist originalism: Intersectionality and the politics of reading. *Feminist Theory, 17*(1), 3–20.

Nash, J. C. (2019). *Black feminism reimagined: After intersectionality*. Duke University Press.

Pliner, S. M., Iuzzini, J., & Banks, C. A. (2011). Using an intersectional approach to deepen collaborative learning. In M. L. Ouellett (Ed.), *An integrative analysis approach to diversity in the college classroom* (New Directions for Teaching & Learning, no. 125, pp. 43–51). Jossey-Bass.

Quaye, S. J., Harper, S. R., & Pendakur, S. L. (Eds.). (2019). *Student engagement in higher education: Theoretical perspectives and practical approaches for diverse populations*. Routledge.

Roberts, D. (1997). *Killing the Black body: Race, reproduction, and the meaning of liberty*. Pantheon Books.

Saini, A. (2019). *Superior: The return of race science*. Beacon Press.

Steele, C. M. (2010). *Whistling Vivaldi: How stereotypes affect us and what we can do*. W. W. Norton.

Stein, S. (2017). A colonial history of the higher education present: Rethinking land-grant institutions through processes of accumulation and relations of conquest. *Critical Studies in Education*. Advance online publication. https://doi.org/10.1080/17508487.2017.1409646.

Wilder, C. S. (2013). *Ebony & ivy: Race, slavery, and the troubled history of America's universities*. Bloomsbury.

Recommended Readings

Collins, P. H. (2015). Intersectionality's definitional dilemmas. *Annual Review of Sociology, 41*(1), 1–20.

Combahee River Collective. (1993). A Black feminist statement. In G. Hull, P. B. Scott, & B. Smith (Eds.), *All the women are white, all the Blacks are men, but some of us are brave: Black women's studies* (pp. 13–22). New York, NY: Feminist Press at CUNY (Original work published in 1977).

Crenshaw, K. (1989). Demarginalizing the intersection of race and sex: A Black feminist critique of antidiscrimination doctrine, feminist theory, and antiracist politics. *University of Chicago Legal Forum, 8*(1), 139–167.

Crenshaw, K. (1991). Mapping the margins: Intersectionality, identity politics, and violence against women of color. *Stanford Law Review, 43*(6), 1241–1299.

Nash, J. C. (2019). *Black feminism reimagined: After intersectionality*. Duke University Press.

CHAPTER 17

Conclusion

C. Casey Ozaki and Laura Parson

In the Teaching and Learning for Social Justice in Higher Education series, the goal was to utilize the science of learning, effective teaching, and social justice perspective to illustrate and recommend practice, in and out of the classroom, for creating equitable environments for college students that also challenge them to critically exam and consider social justice as part of their academic, professional, and personal worldviews. Volume I of this series presented, examined, and advocated theories of teaching and learning and critical perspectives that can be implemented in the classroom and academic contexts to promote equity and diversity. In this volume, Volume II, the authors turn to an examination and highlighting of approaches, strategies, and application of theory in their content areas. The chapters reflect wide ranging academic areas from

C. C. Ozaki (✉)
Education, Health, & Behavior Studies, University of North Dakota, Grand Forks, ND, USA
e-mail: carolyn.ozaki@UND.edu

L. Parson
North Dakota State University, Fargo, ND, USA
e-mail: laura.parson@ndsu.edu

C. C. Ozaki and L. Parson (eds.), *Teaching and Learning for Social Justice and Equity in Higher Education*,
https://doi.org/10.1007/978-3-030-69947-5_17

professional programs, such as social work, to social sciences, STEM, and humanities. While some of these areas are more likely than others to integrate and utilize social justice approaches and critical theories within their academic study and teaching and learning practices, higher education remains heavily siloed into academic corners. Therefore, cross-pollination of theory and practice has been less common, hindering the ways that they might learn from each other. This isolation across disciplinary and professional areas has meant often starting from scratch despite the unanimous need to address social justice in classroom practices and environments. The goal of this volume is to initiate a crack in the historic academic walls and expose readers to disciplinary and professional practices, perspectives, and pedagogical strategies. Given the context of the United States in 2021, we feel this volume is particularly timely.

At the beginning of this Volume the world was pushing toward change and active action as evidenced by unrest related to the killing and brutality of black bodies by police, swelling Black Lives Matter protests, and greater attention to missing and murdered indigenous and trans people. And yet, since that time there has been a number of significant developments that make the advancement of social justice in the United States more difficult or even serve as barriers, including the securing of a conservative majority on the Supreme Court with the appointment of Amy Coney Barrett and evidence of a deeply divided nation in the 2020 election.

But, possibly the most impactful for the efforts of colleges and universities to address inequities and build more inclusive and socially just campuses was President Trump's Executive Order 13,950—Combating Race and Sex Stereotyping issued in September 2020 (https://www.whitehouse.gov/presidential-actions/executive-order-combating-race-sex-stereotyping/). For federal contractors and agencies, which includes institutions that receive federal grants, this executive order prohibitsed training on "divisive concepts." While "divisive concepts" is a vague and seemingly neutral term, the executive order identifies disallowed concepts that are often considered core to diversity and social just training (although often using different language), such as an "individual should feel discomfort, guilt, anguish, or any other form of psychological distress on account of his or her race or sex"; "an individual, by virtue of his or her race or sex, bears responsibility for actions committed in the past by other members of the same race or sex"; and "an individual, by virtue of his or her race or sex, is inherently racist, sexist, or oppressive, whether consciously or unconsciously" in addition to other topics. This context is both a red flag for higher education educators and an implicit call to examine the pedagogies and strategies employed to promote equitable success and outcomes for students and expand opportunities for learning about injustice and inequities and building antiracist and socially just perspectives. Even as higher education institutions were prevented from providing diversity, equity, and inclusion training for employees during the Trump presidency, now that we've moved into the Biden presidency, campuses should recommit to and advance this work with students, faculty, and staff. We hope that Volume II helps to provide theoretical approaches and practical applications to do this.

While Volume I focused on theory and frameworks and Volume II purposefully explored specific content areas, the presence and use of theory and frameworks as applied to these content areas was explicit and robust throughout this volume. Each chapter draws on a combination of teaching and learning and critical or social justice focused theories, but many advance and demonstrate the application of theories and frameworks in their field. For example, in Chapter 6 the authors presented two social justice frameworks, STEMJ and the transgressive STEM teaching model, that were developed for STEM and engineering specifically. Similarly, in Chapter 16 intersectionality is applied to teaching and learning classroom practice. While intersectionality is not an uncommon theory used within teaching and learning, it is less commonly applied to the practice of teaching and learning. There were also a number of chapters that draw on theories and frameworks rarely seen in these content areas, unlike other chapter examples provided which use frameworks and theories that are commonly used or embedded within their fields. In Chapter 5, the authors examined culturally relevant education (CRE) within Science, Technology, Engineering, and Mathematics (STEM) Education, with an emphasis on gateway courses, drawing on critical pedagogy and culturally responsive teaching, and offering practical and accessible examples. Similarly, in Chapter 8, the author proposed a framework for applying feminist poststructuralism as a pedagogical tool to improve the teaching and learning environment. The use of theory and frameworks throughout the volume reflects the underpinning of this work in critical and equity-minded perspectives and applying them to practice in fields and disciplines. The reader leaves each chapter with both theory and practical strategies for applying these ideas in their own classrooms.

Although a strength of this volume is the variety of theories and frameworks applying to a broad range of discipline and professional areas, another important offering is the emergence and identification of pedagogical approaches and strategies that were found across many of the chapters, suggesting their utility and broad application. First, many authors described and promoted the focus on a social and value orientation toward social justice (Chapter 3), the development of a social consciousness about societal inequities (Chapter 4), and cultural competence (Chapter 10)—all related concepts. Second, multiple chapters advocate for the importance of including the history of a discipline, but doing it in a way that integrates a social justice lens, examining history through that lens. For example, in Chapter 7 the authors describe using a social justice lens within physics education, demonstrating how physics history and concepts can and should be used to identify and address inequities within physics. Similarly, an author explored the application of an antiracist education framework to teach about race and discrimination within an Asian American Studies course (Chapter 14). The author describes using current and historical events and examples to illustrate concepts. Finally, throughout the volume the authors described centering students' experiences as important to a social justice education (Chapters 4, 11, 12), but this was often linked to writing and narrative as a pedagogical strategy. Chapters describing ecocomposition (Chapter 4) and Integrated Reading and Writing Instruction (Chapter 11) center student learning and development about social justice in the writing process and experience. Analogous, autoethnography (Chapter 12), and narrative (Chapter 13), the act and process of "storying," are promoted as critical ways that students can be deeply engaged in this learning.

While the fate of the United States remains unknown, we believe that higher education has a responsibility to advance conversations about social justice, equity, inclusion, and diversity—and do so in ways that are thoughtful and prompt reflection and action. Through the wide variety of content areas addressed in this volume, it is clear that this work is both possible and important across content areas.

Index

A

active learning, 79, 85, 101, 135, 153, 156–158, 164, 166

affective learning, 21, 23, 24, 27, 158–160, 164

antiracism, 301, 303, 306, 307, 309, 311–313

Asian American Studies (AAS), 5, 34, 301, 312, 364

asynchronous discussion, 13, 14, 16, 22, 23, 25, 26

autoethnography, 4, 245, 246, 248, 250, 251, 255–257, 261, 262, 264, 265, 267, 364

B

broadening participation initiatives, 98, 99

bystander effect, 272–275, 279, 285–288

C

cisgender, 213, 349

connected knowing, 246, 248, 250, 251, 254–256, 259, 261, 262, 267

constructivism, 153, 159

courageous conversations, 3, 7–17, 21–24, 27, 28

critical pedagogy, 68, 77, 79, 80, 90, 363

critical race theory, 344

critical thinking, 44, 153, 155, 160, 169, 188, 222, 226, 246, 248–251, 253–256, 259, 261, 264, 267, 304, 307, 313

cultural competence, 4, 80, 81, 83, 179, 181, 185, 186, 188, 191, 200–203, 205, 207, 210, 211, 214, 364

culturally relevant education (CRE), 3, 77, 78, 80–84, 86, 88–90, 96, 363

Printed by Printforce, the Netherlands